East and West Germany: A Comparative Economic Analysis

Martin Schnitzer

The Praeger Special Studies program—utilizing the most modern and efficient book production techniques and a selective worldwide distribution network—makes available to the academic, government, and business communities significant, timely research in U.S. and international economic, social, and political development.

East and West Germany: A Comparative Economic Analysis

HC286.6
.S285

PRAEGER SPECIAL STUDIES IN INTERNATIONAL ECONOMICS AND DEVELOPMENT

Praeger Publishers   New York   Washington   London

PRAEGER PUBLISHERS
111 Fourth Avenue, New York, N.Y. 10003, U.S.A.
5, Cromwell Place, London S.W.7, England

Published in the United States of America in 1972
by Praeger Publishers, Inc.

All rights reserved

© 1972 by Praeger Publishers, Inc.

Library of Congress Catalog Card Number: 72-83008

Printed in the United States of America

PREFACE

Two countries, East and West Germany, were formed from the partition of the Third Reich. Each country since its inception has followed a different set of institutional arrangements imposed to a major degree by the conquering countries under whose jurisdiction they happened to fall. Regardless of this fact, both countries have become major industrial powers. The fact that West Germany is essentially a capitalist country and East Germany is essentially a socialist country, however, affords an interesting comparison. Given the set of circumstances that prevailed in each country at the beginning, which one has performed better over time in terms of economic development and providing for the welfare of its citizens? Even though a different set of priorities have existed in each country, it is still possible to make penetrating judgments.

The approach used in this book is easy to follow. In Chapter 1 the historical development of East and West Germany beginning with the immediate post-World War II period is compared. In Chapters 2 through 7, the existing institutional structure of West Germany is presented. This structure is divided into a general presentation of the political and economic system, followed by chapters on industry and agriculture, the fiscal system, income distribution, money and banking, and labor. Chapters 8 through 13 follow the same approach for East Germany. The position taken is that the economic arrangements in each country can readily be compared—fiscal system vs. fiscal system, banking vs. banking, and so forth. Since East Germany has been hermetically sealed off, so to speak, from the West, most of the materials on banking, taxes, and other areas of the economy are not available in English. An attempt has been made to limit the presentation to postreform materials.

It is apparent that no utopian system exists in either East or West Germany. Although the means of production have been socialized and thus owned by the East German state, representing the entire population, it cannot be said that the state has acted as the compliant agent of the people in the production of goods and services. Moreover, East Germany has failed to overtake West Germany in terms of living standards; in fact the gap between the two countries widened during the last decade. West Germany, however, has not been free of problems. Although its record with respect to full employment and a high rate of economic growth has been good, a recession occurred in 1967, and a situation of "stagflation," which began in 1971, has continued in 1972. Other problems associated with a highly developed industrial economy—e.g., income distribution, pollution—have also developed.

    The author is indebted to the numerous Germans with whom he made contact during his trips to Germany, particularly to Herman Buerger of the Commerzbank in Munich. He is also indebted to Richard Benedick and other members of the U.S. embassy in Bonn for their assistance and to Crista Pirie and Dieter Pelz for their assistance in translation. Invaluable assistance was provided by Jim Buchanan of Virginia Polytechnic Institute and State University who read all of the chapters on public finance and income distribution and by George Garvy of the Federal Reserve Bank of New York who read the banking chapters. Wherever possible, a conscious effort was made to use first-hand data collected in East and West Germany by the author.

CONTENTS

	Page
PREFACE	v
LIST OF TABLES, CHARTS, AND MAPS	xiii
GLOSSARY	xix

Chapter

1	EAST AND WEST GERMANY: A COMPARATIVE ECONOMIC ANALYSIS	3
	Introduction	3
	The Postwar Development of East and West Germany	5
	The Development of the West German Economy	7
	Soziale Marktwirtschaft	8
	Postwar Monetary and Fiscal Policies	11
	The Development of the East German Economy	15
	Summary	20

2	GENERAL CHARACTERISTICS OF THE WEST GERMAN ECONOMIC AND POLITICAL SYSTEM	23
	Introduction	23
	Geography and Population	23
	The Political System	25
	The Federal Government	25
	Political Parties	27
	State and Local Governments	29
	The Status of Berlin	31
	The Economic System	32
	The Private Sector	33
	The Public Sector	35
	Industry	38
	Agriculture	39
	Foreign Trade	42
	Economic Planning	44

Chapter		Page
	The Medium-Term Fiscal Plan	45
	Summary	47
3	ORGANIZATION OF INDUSTRY AND AGRICULTURE IN WEST GERMANY	49
	Introduction	49
	Organization of Industry	50
	Industrial Organization in the Third Reich	52
	Postwar Allied Occupation Policies Toward Industry	53
	Postwar Development of German Industry	54
	Industrial Concentration in Germany	56
	The State and Industry	60
	Organization of Agriculture	70
	Government Support of Agriculture	72
	Summary	75
4	THE FISCAL SYSTEM OF WEST GERMANY	77
	Introduction	77
	The Tax System	78
	The Tax Reforms of 1969	79
	The Value-Added Tax	81
	Income Taxes	84
	The Trade Tax	87
	Excise Taxes	88
	Other Taxes	88
	Revenue Equalization	90
	Government Expenditures	90
	Federal Expenditures	92
	Expenditures of State and Local Governments	97
	Equalization of Burdens	99
	Aid to Berlin	100
	Fiscal Policy	101
	Summary	107
5	INCOME DISTRIBUTION IN WEST GERMANY	109
	Introduction	109
	Social Security and Other Welfare Measures	111
	Old-Age, Disability, and Survivors' Benefits	115

Chapter		Page
	Sickness Insurance	118
	Work-Injury Compensation	119
	Unemployment Compensation	119
	Family Allowances	120
	War Pensions and Related Assistance	121
	Other Social Assistance Measures	122
	Income Redistribution Effects of Social Welfare Programs	122
	Income Redistribution Through Taxes	126
	Direct Taxes	129
	Indirect Taxes	135
	Social Security Contributions	136
	Summary	137
6	MONEY AND BANKING IN WEST GERMANY	140
	Introduction	140
	The Banking System	141
	The Deutsche Bundesbank	142
	Commercial Banks	146
	Savings Banks	148
	Credit Cooperatives	150
	Mortgage Banks	151
	Specialized Credit Institutions	152
	Other Credit Institutions	154
	Recent Trends in West German Banking	154
	The Banks and the Economy	155
	The Capital Market	158
	Savings and Investment	159
	Monetary Policy	161
	Summary	166
7	LABOR UNIONS IN WEST GERMANY	169
	Introduction	169
	The Development of Trade Unions in Germany	170
	Union Membership	172
	The German Trade Union Federation	173
	The German Salaried Employees Union	177
	The Federation of Christian Trade Unions	178
	Employer Organizations	179
	Collective Bargaining	181
	Codetermination	183

Chapter		Page
	The Role of the Federal Government	186
	Labor Courts	188
	Summary	189
8	GENERAL CHARACTERISTICS OF THE EAST GERMAN ECONOMIC AND POLITICAL SYSTEM	191
	Introduction	191
	Geography and Population	191
	The Political System	193
	Organization of the Government	193
	The SED	196
	The East German Economy	199
	Industry	201
	Agriculture	202
	Foreign Trade	203
	Economic Planning	204
	The Mechanics of Plan Preparation	205
	The Annual Operating Plan	209
	The National Economic Plan, 1971-75	214
	Summary	217
9	THE ORGANIZATION OF INDUSTRY, AGRICULTURE, AND TRADE IN EAST GERMANY	219
	Introduction	219
	The New Economic System	221
	Organization of Industry	226
	The VVB	230
	The Combine	232
	The Semistate-Owned Enterprise	233
	Production Cooperatives	234
	The Enterprise	234
	Private Enterprise	238
	Organization of Agriculture	240
	State Farms	244
	Collective Farms	246
	Organization of Domestic Trade	248
	Domestic Trade	248
	Foreign Trade	252
	Summary	253

Chapter		Page
10	THE FISCAL SYSTEM OF EAST GERMANY	255
	Introduction	255
	The State Budget	256
	The Development of the Fiscal System	257
	The Organization of the Fiscal System	258
	The Preparation of the State Budget	261
	The State Budget for 1971	262
	Government Expenditures	264
	Government Budget Receipts	269
	Summary	280
11	INCOME DISTRIBUTION IN EAST GERMANY	282
	Introduction	282
	Wage Systems	283
	The Leistungsprinzip	284
	Industrial Wages	284
	Agricultural Wages	288
	Nonmaterial Incentives	290
	Income Differentials	291
	Income Redistribution Through Taxes and Transfer Payments	295
	The Effect of Taxes on Income Redistribution	296
	Social Insurance	299
	Prices	304
	Summary	304
12	MONEY AND BANKING IN EAST GERMANY	307
	Introduction	307
	The Development of the Banking System	308
	The Monetary Reform of 1948	309
	The Banking Reforms of 1967-68	312
	The Organization of the East German Banking System	315
	The Staatsbank	315
	The Industrial and Commercial Bank	318
	The Agricultural Bank	320
	The Foreign Trade Bank	321
	The Cooperative Bank for Handicrafts and Industry	322

Chapter		Page
	Savings Banks	323
	The Role of Credit in East Germany	324
	Summary	328
13	LABOR UNIONS AND THE EAST GERMAN STATE	330
	Introduction	330
	Labor Unions in East Germany	332
	Major Characteristics of the FDGB	334
	Summary	345
14	COMPARATIVE OPERATING RESULTS OF THE EAST AND WEST GERMAN ECONOMIES	347
	Introduction	347
	A Comparison of Output	350
	Labor Productivity	363
	Agriculture	365
	The West German Economy, 1960-72	373
	Economic Growth, 1968-72	376
	The East German Economy, 1960-72	379
	Economic Growth, 1968-72	380
	The 1972 Plan	384
	The State Budget, 1972	385
	Summary	386
15	A COMPARISON OF INCOME DISTRIBUTION AND LIVING STANDARDS IN EAST AND WEST GERMANY	389
	Introduction	389
	Income Distribution	392
	Comparison of Wage and Salary Differentials	398
	Real Wages	403
	Taxes and Transfer Payments and Their Impact on Income Distribution	413
	Comparison of Taxes and Tax Burdens	414
	Transfer Payments	416
	Summary	426
NOTES		428
ABOUT THE AUTHOR		447

LIST OF TABLES, CHARTS, AND MAPS

Table		Page
2.1	West German Gross Social Product, 1970	35
2.2	General Government Revenues and Expenditures in Relation to West German GNP, 1970	37
2.3	Comparison of Contribution of Industry to GDP, Selected Countries	40
2.4	Industrial Production, by Source, West Germany, 1969	41
3.1	Breakdown of Number of Firms and Workers in West German Industry, 1968	57
3.2	Fifteen Largest West German Firms, Classified by Sales	58
3.3	Sales Turnover in West German Industry, 1967	61
3.4	Number of Farms in West Germany and Percentage Change, 1960-69	72
3.5	West German Federal Budget Support of Agriculture	74
4.1	Tax Revenues of West Germany, 1971	80
4.2	Example of German Turnover Tax	82
4.3	Example of Value-Added Tax	83
4.4	West German Federal Budget Expenditures, 1971	92
5.1	Expenditures in West German Social Budget, 1970	114
5.2	Revenue Sources in West German Social Budget, 1970	115
5.3	Comparison of Income Distribution Before Taxes, by Quintiles, West Germany, 1950-67	124
5.4	Annual Unemployment Rates, West Germany, 1960-70	127

Table		Page
5.5	Gross Wages and Salaries and Income Taxes, by Income Group, West Germany, 1969	132
5.6	Distribution of Personal Savings and Property, West Germany, 1969	133
5.7	Redistributional Effect of West German Income Tax on Wages and Salaries	134
5.8	Marginal Tax Rates for Various Levels of Monthly Income, West Germany, 1965	135
6.1	Major National and Regional West German Commercial Banks in 1970	147
6.2	Volume of Credit Outstanding by Type of West German Banking Institutions, by Maturity Length, July 1971	156
6.3	Sources of Saving and Investment, West Germany, 1969	160
7.1	Membership in West German DGB Unions, 1970	174
8.1	Contributions to East German Net Product, by Economic Unit	200
8.2	Contributions to East German Net Product, by Sector, 1970	200
8.3	Industrial Gross Production, by Industry Group, East Germany	202
8.4	East German Foreign Trade, by Major Source, 1969	204
8.5	East German Plans Since 1949	206
10.1	Changes in Distribution of Tax Income, East Germany, 1946-50	258
10.2	Comparison of State Budget Expenditures to National Income, East Germany, 1960-69	260

Table		Page
10.3	Structure of Expenditures in East German State Budget, 1971	266
10.4	Income Tax Rates, East Germany	275
10.5	Changes in Monthly Income and in Income Taxation, East Germany	277
10.6	Comparison of Marginal and Average Income Tax Rates, East Germany	278
11.1	Average Monthly Income for Industrial Groups, East Germany, 1969	293
11.2	Personal Income and Average Monthly Income, Taxes and Social Security Contributions, East Germany, 1969	298
12.1	The Financing of Investment, by Sources, East Germany	314
12.2	Investments to Increase Fertility of the Soil	327
14.1	Comparison of Real National Income and Real Net Social Product, East and West Germany, 1960-70	351
14.2	Comparison of Yearly Growth in Gross Social Product and Investment, East and West Germany, 1960-70	352
14.3	Gross Industrial Production, East and West Germany, 1960-68	353
14.4	Comparison of Relative Gains in East and West German Industry, 1960-68	355
14.5	Gross Industrial Investment, East and West Germany, 1960-68	357
14.6	Comparison of Capital Productivity, by Industry, East and West Germany, 1968	358

Table		Page
14.7	Comparison of Capital Investment and Labor Force Employment, East and West Germany, 1960 and 1968	360
14.8	Comparison of Capital Intensity, by Industry, East and West Germany, 1968	362
14.9	Output and Productivity in East and West German Industry, 1967 and 1968	364
14.10	Land Use by Type of Agricultural Enterprise, East Germany, 1970	365
14.11	Number of Farms and Land in Farms, West Germany, 1969	366
14.12	Use of Commercial Fertilizer, East and West Germany, Selected Years	368
14.13	Vegetable Production, East and West Germany, Selected Years	369
14.14	Performance Comparisons per Animal Unit, East and West Germany, Selected Years	370
14.15	Comparison of Agricultural Production, East and West Germany, 1957-61 and 1968	371
14.16	Structure of Food Production, East and West Germany, Selected Years	372
14.17	Index of Industrial Production, West Germany, 1962-70	377
15.1	Property Ownership Based on Property Classes, West Germany, 1966	393
15.2	Average Monthly Earnings for Industrial Workers, West Germany, 1970	395
15.3	Net Income for Major Occupational Groups Expressed as Percentage for Income Class, West Germany, 1970	397

Table		Page
15.4	Comparison of Gross Monthly Income, by Industrial Group, East and West Germany, 1969	399
15.5	Average Monthly Income for Blue and White Collar Workers, by Household Size, East and West Germany, 1960 and 1967	401
15.6	Comparison of Distribution of Net Income by Quintiles for White and Blue Collar Workers, East and West Germany, 1960 and 1967	402
15.7	Prices and Purchasing Power of Hourly Wages, East and West Germany, 1969	406
15.8	Structure of Expenditures in Four-Person Household, East and West Germany, 1968	411
15.9	Comparison of Average Family Income, Income Taxes, and Social Security Contributions, East and West Germany, 1960, 1964, and 1967	417
15.10	Comparison of Cash Outlays for Social Welfare Measures, East and West Germany, 1969	423
15.11	Breakdown of Average Monthly Household Income, East Germany, 1968	424
15.12	Comparison of Income, Transfers, and Taxes for Selected Households, West Germany, 1970	425

Chart		
7.1	Schematic Diagram of Organization of Industrial Unions and German Confederation of Free Trade Unions (FDGB)	176
8.1	Model for a Perspective Plan with Special Consideration of the Planning of Structurally-Determined Economic Objectives and Object-Planning, East Germany	210
8.2	Components of East German Plan, 1971-75	212

Chart		Page
9.1	Simplified Survey of Organization of East German Industry	229
9.2	Organizational Structure of a VVB	231
9.3	Administrative and Control Organs of East German Agriculture	241
9.4	Future Structure of Cooperative Management of Hog Production in Jena	243
9.5	Reproduction Process of East German Agricultural Production Cooperatives	249
9.6	Organization Chart of Domestic Trade, East Germany	251
12.1	Structure of Banking System, East Germany	316
13.1	Organizational Scheme of FDGB	339
14.1	Profit Building and Profit Application in Industry and Construction Enterprises, East Germany	387
15.1	Lorenz Curve Comparing East and West German Income Distribution, by Quintiles, 1960 and 1967	404

Map

1	West Germany	xxii
2	East Germany	xxiii

GLOSSARY

East Germany

Betriebe mit Staatlicher Beteiligung	Semistate enterprise, public-private ownership.
Bezirk	District administrative unit.
Deutsche Demokratische Republik (DDR)	German Democratic Republic, or GDR.
Freier Deutscher Gewerkschaftsbund (FDGB)	Confederation of Free Trade Unions.
Gemeinde	Local administrative unit corresponding to a township.
Kombinat	Industrial combine of two or more firms.
Kreis	County administrative unit.
Landwirtschaftliche Produktionsgenossenschaft (LPG)	Collective farm.
Leistungsprinzip	Performance principle on which the wage system is built.
Ostmark	East German domestic currency unit.
Produktionsgenossenschaften des Handels	Production cooperatives.
Sozialistische Einheitspartei Deutschlands (SED)	Socialist Unity Party, the major political party in the GDR.
Staatliche Amt für Arbeit und Löhne	State Office for Work and Wages.
Staatliche Plankommission	State Planning Commission.

Staatsbank	Central bank of the GDR.
Staatsrat	State council.
Technisch Begründete Arbeitsnorm (TAN)	Technically based wage standards.
Umsatzsteuer	Turnover tax.
Valuta Mark	East German currency unit used in foreign trade.
Vereinigung Volkseigener Betriebe (VVB)	Association of state industrial and trade enterprises.
Vereinigung Volkseigener Erfassungs und Aufkaufbetriebe (VVEAB)	Agricultural equivalent of a VVB.
Volkseigene Betrieb (VEB)	Individual state enterprise.
Volkseigene Gut (VEG)	Individual state farm.
Volkskammer	Most important legislative branch in the GDR.

West Germany

Bund	Federal government.
Bundesrat	Upper house of parliament.
Bundesrepublik Deutschland (BRD)	Federal Republic of Germany (FRG).
Bundestag	Lower house of parliament.
Bundesvereininigung der Deutschen Arbeitzeberverbande	Confederation of German Employers' Association.
Christlich-Demokratische Union (CDU)	Christian Democratic Union, a major political party.
Deutsche Bundesbank	Central bank of West Germany.

Deutsche Gewerkschaftsbund (DGB)	German Trade Union Federation.
Deutsche Mark (DM)	West German currency unit.
Gemeinde	Local government or commune.
Grundgesetz	Basic Law.
Konjunkturausgleichsrucklagen	Conjunctural accounts.
Kreditanstalt für Wiederaufbau	Reconstruction Finance Corporation.
Land	State government.
Lastenausgleichsbank	Equalization of Burdens Bank.
Mehrewertsteuer	Value-added tax.
Mittelslandspolitik	Middle estate policy.
Sozialdemokratische Partei Deutschlands (SPD)	Social Democratic Party, a major political party.
Soziale Marktwirtschaft	Social market policy.

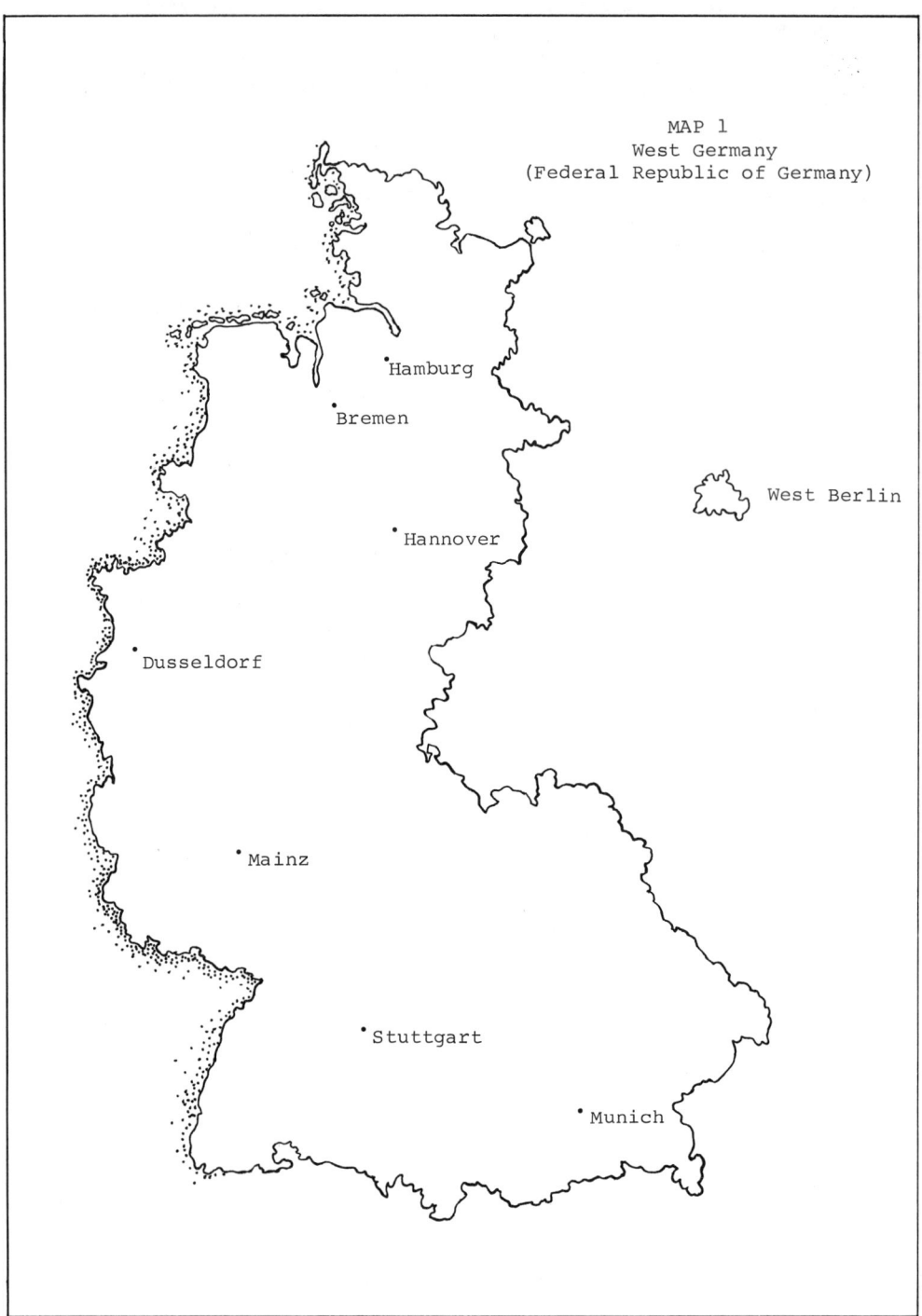

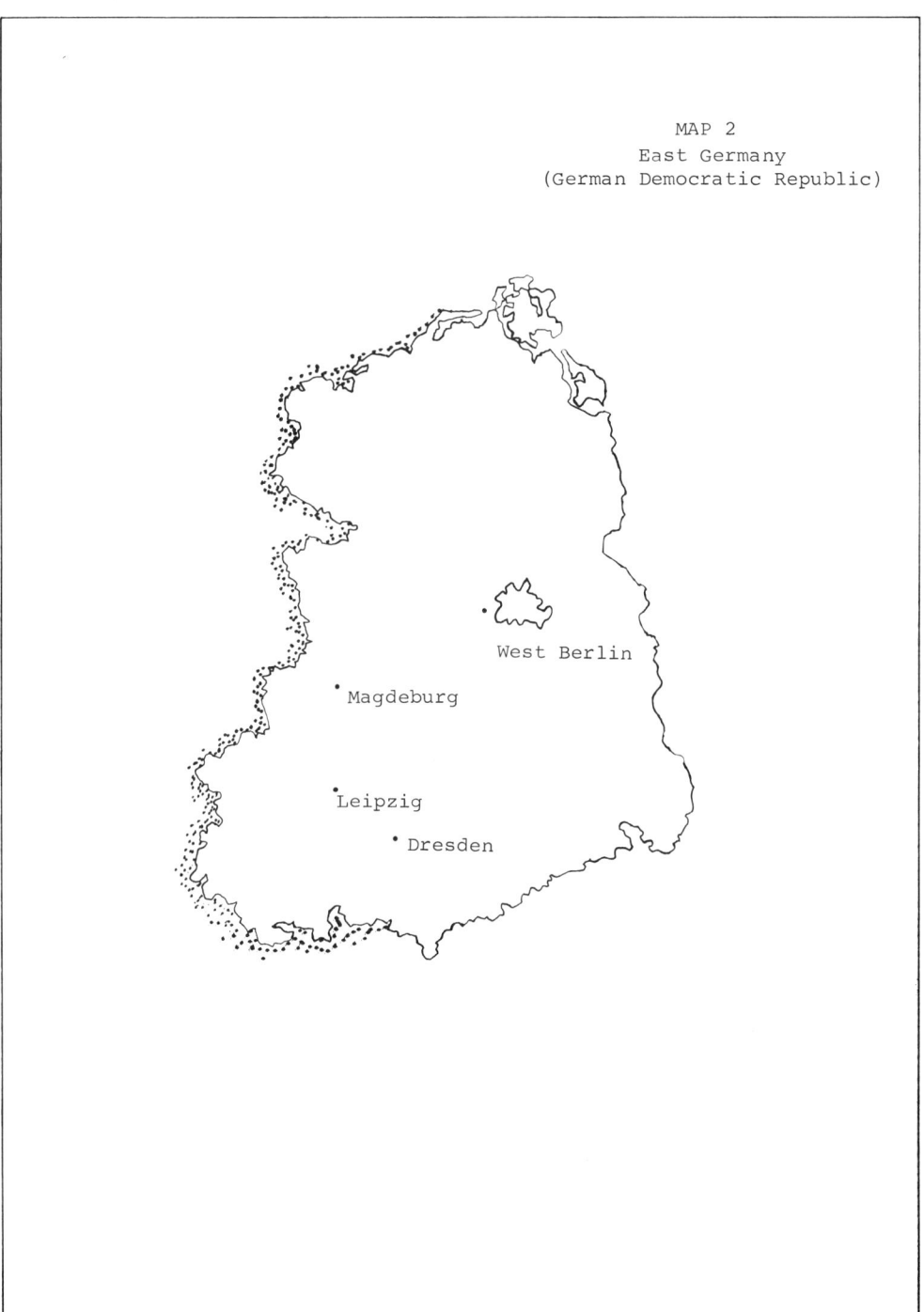

East and West Germany:
A Comparative
Economic Analysis

CHAPTER

1

**EAST AND WEST
GERMANY:
A COMPARATIVE
ECONOMIC ANALYSIS**

INTRODUCTION

The purpose of this book is to compare the economic systems of East and West Germany in terms of their institutional arrangement and economic development. The choice of these two countries affords an interesting and important comparison of an essentially market-directed economy to a socialist-command economy. Each country was formerly a part of the German Third Reich. After the end of World War II, the Reich was partitioned among the victors. In the western part, a particular set of economic and political institutions was imposed by the democratic powers—England, France, and the United States. In the eastern part, an entirely dissimilar set of institutions was imposed by the Soviet Union. Yet both West and East Germany have emerged at the present as established industrial nations with high living standards within their respective spheres of influence.

Before a comparison of West and East Germany can be made, it is important to review briefly the basic elements of two competing economic systems—capitalism and socialism. First of all, it is necessary to point out that the advanced industrial countries of today do not fall neatly into a rigid classification system labeled capitalism or socialism. It is more useful instead to think of a spectrum of systems ranging from those that rely heavily upon market mechanisms to allocate resources to those that rely on central command for resource allocation. The United States lies near the market end of the spectrum, but even it has substantial elements of command. Japan and the countries of Western Europe lie near the center of the spectrum. Although their agents of production are for the most part privately owned, there is some government operation of industry and extensive participation by government in the economy. Even in those countries that have command economies, market arrangements are used to some degree to supplement central command. The degree varies from one country to another.

As a starting point, it is possible to identify a set of institutions for capitalism and socialism that provide a frame of reference. These institutions are based on the organization of an economy. What is done largely and rather automatically by market forces, competition, and the profit motive in the United States and other Western countries is done for the most part through conscious bureaucratic state action in a country such as the Soviet Union. Formally approved plans, buttressed by rules of behavior and various types of incentives, both material and nonmaterial, must guide managerial decisions and operations of firms. In such macroeconomic areas as public finance and banking, considerable differences exist between the capitalist and socialist countries.

In a capitalistic system, the operation of supply and demand in the marketplace allocates resources in production and determines the rewards in distribution. The relationship of supply and demand determines the relative value of individual resources and commodities. In monetary terms, these values are prices, and the pricing system is the unconscious planning mechanism that guides private individuals, in pursuit of maximum individual rewards, to allocate fully the resources of the economic system. A favorable price-cost relationship will induce the production of a given commodity; an unfavorable price-cost relationship will restrict production of a commodity. Thus, profit-making can be considered the lodestar of capitalism. Anyone who produces goods that do not, either directly or indirectly, yield a profit will sooner or later go bankrupt and so cease to be a producer. Profit is in essence the test of whether any given thing should be produced and, if so, how much of it should be produced.

Probably the most important difference between the capitalist and socialist countries is the role that economic planning plays in socialist resource allocation. Fundamental to the operation of planning is the public ownership of the agents of production, which joins industrial, agricultural, and trading enterprises into a single economic unit. Since there is no meaningful competition between rival firms, there is no price competition. In turn, the profit motive is rendered important as an automatic regulator, which is its role in the market price system of a market economy. So in the absence of the market price system, economic planning is necessary to make the complex of state enterprises function. To organize the uninterrupted operations of these enterprises, full and exact account must be kept of the national requirements for their particular products and of the channels through which they must be distributed.

It is necessary to point out, however, that profit as an economic category has always existed in the socialist countries. Before the economic reforms it was treated as an accounting device for the purpose of ensuring that enterprises covered their costs of production and handed any surplus over to the state treasury. After the economic reforms, profit became a measure of enterprise efficiency. Incentives are tied to profits in that the reward system is tied to performance. To promote enterprise performance, a system of bonuses is employed that is based on profit. Special funds have been created in enterprises to provide for an increase in money and material incentives to workers. This bonus system links rewards directly to performance, for as profits increase so does the amount that becomes available for distribution to the workers.

Another aspect of the reforms pertains to pricing. Producer prices have been brought closer in line with production costs to reduce the need for state subsidies and to enable enterprises to be profitable. Similarly, the procurement prices payable to the farms have been raised in relation to industrial prices in order to encourage agricultural production and to improve living standards in rural areas. There have been changes in the retail and wholesale trade network designed to improve service to consumers and to enable effective transmission of consumer preferences to producing enterprises. Profit is now generally calculated on the basis of output sold, not merely produced or handled, so that it is in the interest of both industry and trade to supply customers with what they want.

THE POSTWAR DEVELOPMENT OF
EAST AND WEST GERMANY

In 1945 the dreams of national power, glory, and prestige held by the National Socialists had come to an end. Hitler was dead in his bunker at the Reich Chancellery, and the disintegration of the German economy was complete. When the Germans surrendered in May, the Allied forces were in control of most of the country. The question remained of what to do with the country. There were those who thought that Germany, like Carthage, should be literally razed to the ground. On the other hand, there were those who thought that Germany should be rehabilitated in one form or another. There was no consensus over what form this rehabilitation should take; Germany was occupied by four different Allied powers, each of which was anxious to impose its particular set of institutional arrangements.

Allied agreements concerning Germany were developed in a series of conferences, the most important of which were the conferences at Moscow, Yalta, Tehran, and Potsdam. These agreements provided the basis for the attempt at common Allied rule of Germany. The zonal pattern of occupation, the German surrender terms, and the machinery of Allied control were worked out before the end of the war by the European Advisory Commission, representing the United States, Great Britain, the Soviet Union, and France. The agreements were announced and put into effect on June 5, 1945, when the four Allied commanders-in-chief met in Berlin.

Germany, according to these agreements, was divided into four zones of occupation. The American zone comprised the states of Bavaria, Hesse, Wurttemberg-Baden, and the enclave of Bremen. The British zone took in North Rhine-Westphalia, Lower Saxony, Schleswig-Holstein, and Hamburg. The French zone included the Rhineland Palatinate, South Baden, South Wurttemberg, and the Saar. The Saar was to remain under the jurisdiction of the French government for 15 years, after which time the people were to be given the option of voting for its return to Germany or for its permanent annexation to France. The zone allotted to the Soviet Union comprised the states of Saxony, Thuringia, Mecklenburg, Saxony-Anhalt, and Brandenburg. East Prussia was divided between the Soviet Union and Poland, and Poland was also given the former German territory east of the Oder-Neisse line, which included Silesia, and eastern Pomerania and eastern Brandenburg. A special status was given to Berlin. Even though it was in the heart of the Soviet zone, it was occupied and ruled jointly by all four powers.

The purposes of the Allied occupation policy, as set forth in the Yalta and Potsdam agreements, were to demilitarize Germany, to compensate countries that had suffered Nazi aggression by transfers of German industrial equipment and foreign assets, and to replace Nazism with the free formation of non-Nazi parties. An essential feature of the Potsdam agreement was the proviso that Germany be treated as an economic unit and that central administrative departments be established to take care of such fields as transportation, finance, exports, and imports. The four governments, however, were never able to reach an agreement on measures for dealing with Germany as one economic unit. The Soviet Union and France both embarked on policies of unilateral exploitation of their zones.

By the end of 1946 all attempts by the four occupying powers to form a common economic policy for Germany formed a record of failure and frustration. While the differences among the United States, Great Britain, and France lent themselves to adjustment and compromise and the three Western powers achieved on the whole a unity of purpose as well as action, no such unity with the Soviet Union was effected. Instead, general acrimony existed, culminating in the blockade of Berlin by the Soviets in 1948. As long as it could hope to bring Germany within its sphere of Communist influence, the Soviet Union was not interested in any agreement with the Allies that would allow Germany to develop peacefully as a reunited nation.

The Allies, after several years of separate zonal rule, embarked on a policy that resulted in the creation of a West German Federal Republic. In 1948 the three zones were unified under the name of the Federal Republic of Germany (FRG). A number of organic laws were passed to take the place of the constitution that, it was still hoped, would be written for a reunited Germany. These laws were in fact very similar to the constitution of the Weimar Republic, although the chancellor was given greater power than before. The Allied powers agreed to an Occupation Statute to govern the conditions under which the new state would operate. The new republic was proclaimed on May 23, 1949, and, after the first general elections, held on August 14, 1949, Konrad Adenauer, former mayor of Cologne, became chancellor of the new state.

The Soviet Union countered the move in the west by the creation of a German state in the east. In October 1949 the German Democratic Republic (GDR) was created. Formal sovereignty, however, was not granted by the Soviet Union until 1954. After an initial united front that included elements from all political parties that had opposed the Nazis, East Germany became a one-party state ruled by the Socialist Unity Party, produced by the forced merger of the Social Democratic Party with the Communist Party. Walter Ulbricht, a long-time German Communist, became the leader of the Democratic Republic.

THE DEVELOPMENT OF THE WEST GERMAN ECONOMY

Many problems confronted the peacetime development of West Germany. The war had been lost, damage to industrial capacity was considerable, and the country was split in half. Moreover, West Germany was cut off from its traditional sources of agricultural materials in the eastern part of the Third Reich. But like the legendary bird, the phoenix, West Germany rose from the ashes to become one of the world's leading industrial powers. The factors that explain this renaissance are as follows.

1. The amount and extent of war damage was overrated. The amount of industrial capacity that was destroyed by allied bombing was counterbalanced by that which was constructed during the war. For example, the index of total armaments production was 223 in 1943, 227 in 1944, 227 in January 1945, 175 in February, and 145 in March.[1] Daily freight-car loadings, which averaged 139,000 in 1943, were still 70,000 in January 1945.[2] At the end of the war, Germany found itself with better than prewar industrial capacity. War damages and

dismantling policies pursued by the allies led to replacement of old plants with new and more modern ones.

2. Although split in two by the partition, the western part of Germany retained most of the prewar industrial base. This base was concentrated in the capital-goods industries. These goods were needed not only for German reconstruction but for world markets in general. Moreover, the highly industrialized Ruhr Valley, which was the heart of German steel production, was retained by West Germany. The chief mineral resources were also located in West Germany. In 1938 West Germany produced 98 percent of the hard coal and 95 percent of the iron ore in Germany.[3] Postwar investment flowed largely into those sectors where rapid increases in productivity were possible and the export potential enormous. While other countries concentrated on the production of consumer goods for export, West Germany concentrated on the production of capital goods.

3. West Germany has been similar to Japan in that defeat left the economies of each country unburdened by heavy defense expenditures. The actual cost of defense was assumed by the occupying powers. This meant that both Germany and Japan had additional resources that they could utilize for the development of their economies. In the period immediately following the end of the war, the absence of a defense burden was balanced by the occupation costs each country had to bear. After 1950, however, the gradual expansion of Germany's defense forces was offset by the reduction of the occupation costs.

4. American aid, particularly the Marshall Plan, also played an important role in the revival of West Germany. Some 4.5 billion dollars were spent in helping Germany recover from its war losses. This aid supported the modernization of plants and equipment by supplying foreign exchange and investment funds.

5. Another factor, which was to be of considerable economic assistance in the development of West Germany, was the influx of refugees from the east, the great bulk of whom arrived during the years 1945-50. Although they constituted a burden in that they absorbed a large amount of scarce capital, they provided an enterprising and skilled addition to the labor force. They helped keep wages down during the critical years of reconstruction and stimulated entrepreneurial competition.

Soziale Marktwirtschaft

The German economy relied on market forces instead of controls to accomplish recovery from the devastation brought about by the war. Anti-inflationary and sound currency policies were pursued. To channel profits into investment and saving, income-tax rates were modified in favor of savers and investors. A policy of free markets was adopted, but it was by no means uniformly applied to all sectors of the German economy. The guiding concept that governed this policy was that of the Soziale Marktwirtschaft, or social market economy, which was originally formulated by a group of scholars at the University of Freiburg during the war years. The leader of this group, Walter Eucken, formulated the principles upon which the social market economy is based.[4]

Eucken maintained that political freedom and maximization of welfare can be ensured only by the creation and maintenance of the market form of competition throughout the economy. This competition would be enforced by the government through the banning of restrictive business practices, the establishment of a monopoly office designed to reduce the power of monopolies and cartels, and encouragement of competition, including open markets, by means of various instruments of economic policy. Not only would protective tariffs and state controls over private industry be removed; quasimonopolistic privileges granted by the state would be reduced to a minimum, and one would have maximum freedom in choosing one's trade or profession. Private ownership of the means of production and freedom of contract were essential in the competitive order, but only to the extent that they helped rather than hindered competition.

Eucken also felt that the contradistinction was not between free and planned economic systems, nor between capitalist and socialist economic systems, but between a market economy with free price level adjustments and an authoritarian economy with state control extended over production and distribution. In this market economy, any mistake in judgment in the management of production or distribution produced concomitant repercussions through price changes in the marketplace. In a state-directed economy, the same mistakes would not be reflected in changes in the pricing mechanism; they would be covered up, eventually causing serious misallocation of resources. Market reaction to mistakes would be eliminated and the consumer deprived of all freedom of choice.

Moreover, Eucken believed that the implementation of the social market economy would obviate the need for countercyclical measures, such as the active manipulation of taxes or public expenditures. He felt that if competition were widely established and monetary policy conducted automatically on the principle of price stability then economic fluctuations would automatically disappear. This optimism was based first of all on the belief that the miscalculations of many investors in an exchange economy was a prime reason for booms and slumps and that an efficiently working price mechanism and a constant economic policy would eliminate these. Second, Eucken believed that tight control over the quantity of money in circulation was an effective way of countering cyclical movements.

The principles of the social market economy were transmitted into practice by Ludwig Erhard, who became minister of economics during the Adenauer government and later chancellor of Germany. Erhard, who had the support of the nonsocialist parties, believed that the incentives of a free market economy would stimulate long-dormant productive capacities. He felt that the function of the government was to provide the economy with principles and broad guidelines of economic policy. Government was to see that neither social privileges nor artificial monopolies impeded the natural process by which economic forces reached and maintained a state of equilibrium and that the operation of supply and demand was allowed full play.[5]

In general, the economic policies of the West German government during the immediate postwar years reflected a reaction to the overt public controls practiced in the Third Reich, as well as some adherence to the social market policy. The principles of the social market economy were applied with respect to economic controls that were scrapped as rapidly as Economics Minister Erhard thought feasible. A system of selective decontrols was utilized. Manufactured goods were first freed from controls, while controls were maintained over foodstuffs, agricultural products, and essential raw materials. Except for agricultural prices, the controls were largely abandoned by the end of 1948.

Even though official government policy sought to prevent mergers and concentration of industry, progress was limited to some extent because of the opposition of the government's political backers in industry. Erhard himself expressed disapproval of cartels, which he termed the "enemies of the consumer."[6] The government's formal opposition to cartels was manifested in the Law of Cartels, which became effective in 1958 and was amended in 1965. Despite the avowed intention of the government, however, the cartels tended to revive; some of the former proprietors, like the Krupp family, the great titans of the Essen steel industry, returned to their old positions.

One of the fundamental conditions of the social market economy was the existence of a stable currency unit. In 1948, a reform of the German currency unit took place. The money supply was contracted, and a new currency, the Deutsche Mark (DM), was issued at a rate one-tenth of the old currency. This caused a reduction in liquidity on the part of the public and the commercial banks. The latter were provided with new government obligations and reserves on deposit with the central bank, which were set at 15 percent of demand deposits and 7.5 percent of time deposits. Contractions in cash holdings were accompanied by a scaling down of debts to one-tenth of their market value. Profits arising from the revaluation of mortgage debts were subject to special taxes designed to eliminate this type of windfall. A capital levy was also imposed on net assets. The reason for these

A COMPARATIVE ECONOMIC ANALYSIS

levies was that the currency reform of 1948 effected a drastic scaling-down of cash holdings and monetary claims without corresponding losses in the value of land and business property.

The German currency reform provided monetary stability to the economy.[7] It was considered to be a remarkable success by both friends and foes of the government. It raised incentives to produce. It favored debtors and penalized creditors by reducing, generally to one-tenth, the claims of creditors. It reduced the burden of carrying the unproductive segments of the economy—the aged, pensioners, and owners of savings—and encouraged productivity of the most viable segments—businessmen, entrepreneurs, and debtors. A system of monetary exchange was substituted for wasteful hoarding and bartering.

Although the currency reform provided an indispensable framework for economic recovery, two other factors also played a contributing role. First, the Marshall Plan provided a supply of foreign exchange for essential imports as well as for investment funds during the years immediately following the currency reform. Second, the Organization for European Economic Cooperation (OEEC), of which West Germany became a member soon after the currency reform, facilitated the establishment of the nation's foreign markets.

Postwar Monetary and Fiscal Policies

Postwar German monetary and fiscal policies were oriented toward production. Incentive elements favored the strong and discriminated against the weak. Considerable income inequality was permitted. Although the position of the weak and economically less viable segments of the economy was buttressed through the provision of a comprehensive social welfare program that consumed and distributed a sizable part of the national income, there is no question that the bulk of the economic gains went to business firms and individual entrepreneurs. Monetary and fiscal policies were tight and served to intensify competition among business firms to create markets for their products. General policies aimed at stimulating aggregate demand whereby a sellers' market would be ensured, were avoided. Aggregate demand was held relatively constant and aggregate supply was stimulated through various factors, such as tax incentives. The hallmark of German economic policy was the priority given to production. As Economics Minister Erhard said: "It is a fact that the standard of living can only be raised by expanding national output through increased production."[8]

With priority placed on production, particularly of capital goods, tax policies were designed to encourage incentives to work, save, and invest. In 1946 the Allied occupation authorities had imposed a progressive income tax with steeply graduated rates.* To circumvent these rates, concessions were utilized to promote savings and investment. Although most of these concessions were eventually removed from the tax system, there is no question that they were of singular importance in promoting the rapid growth of the German economy during the postwar period. An acute shortage of capital existed throughout the economy. At a time when any investment promised to be profitable, the propensity to invest was extremely high and most profits were reinvested. Tax concessions provided an extra premium for investment.

Most tax concessions were introduced during the period 1948-51. By 1951, however, the government had come to believe that the first period of reconstruction had ended and that there was no longer any need for tax concessions to stimulate general investment. Instead, it was decided to make tax concessions selective in order to stimulate investment in specific types of industries. In particular, the export industries and those industries that suffered particular handicaps as a result of the war were favored. Exports were exempted from the turnover tax. Another export incentive took the form of a deduction from taxable income equal to from 1 to 10 percent of taxable income.

The demand for capital throughout the early postwar period always exceeded the volume of saving. Therefore, increases in savings were necessary for capital formation. To stimulate savings, tax incentives were also employed. Allowances were given for income tax deductions for regular savings made under contracts with financial institutions and for payments to building and housing associations. Tax exemption privileges were given on the interest from state and local bonds. The proceeds from the sale of these bonds in general went for the purpose of financing low-rent housing facilities. Tax incentives for savings were simply another way of promoting economic growth during the period of reconstruction.

West German budgetary policy during the postwar period was conservative. There was no attempt to utilize the budget to offset short-term fluctuations in economic activity. Under the Basic Law, which was passed in 1949, the German government was not permitted to have an unbalanced budget, preventing the use of the budget as an instrument of fiscal policy. A reason for this provision was to prevent legislative abuse of the budget. Public debt was only to be incurred

---

*High personal income tax rates, which were a holdover from the war years, were raised 25 percent in 1945 and were made steeply progressive the following year. The progressive rates, necessitated by reparations, were to combat inflation.

for productive purposes. Moreover, a conservative budget policy that avoided deficits to stimulate economic activity was consistent with the principles of the social market economy. One tenet of Soziale Marktwirtschaft was that reliance should be placed on monetary policy to control the business cycle.

During the postwar years monetary policy was the main instrument for achieving price stability. Memories of the inflation in the period following World War I were still strong. That inflation had created distress among the workers and destroyed the middle classes. Prices had outdistanced wages, and there had been resulting strikes and unemployment. Economic chaos had occurred, and the Weimar Republic had been undermined by various nationalistic elements. Thus, price stability became a basic economic policy desideratum. In 1948, the Bank Deutscher Länder was set up as an interim central bank, pending the creation of a Federal Republic. It maintained no branches, and the central banks (Landeszentralbanken) of the individual German states carried out its functions, including that of note issue.

Monetary policy in Germany was aimed primarily at the maintenance of price stability and a favorable balance of payments. This policy was maintained during the first phase of reconstruction when, at a time of massive unemployment, the Bank Deutscher Länder continued to preserve price stability. During the Korean crisis, also, the Bank held to a restrictive policy, from October 1950 to May 1952, until prices were seen to be falling. During the first post-Korean boom of 1955-56, the Bank again intervened, using discount rates, open-market operations, and minimum legal reserve requirements to preserve price stability. Emphasis on price stability enhanced West Germany's position in the world markets. From 1952 onward, helped by its comparatively low price level, the country began to build up enormous export surpluses. As a result, by 1957 West Germany's monetary reserves had increased to the point where the increase in its gold stock alone exceeded that of all other Western European countries put together.

The performance of the West German economy, particularly during the period 1948-52, was spectacular. The restoration of free exchange, which was accomplished by the currency reform of 1948, and the subsequent removal of price controls were stimuli that contributed to a rapid increase in the rate of economic growth. Immediately after the currency reform, industrial production rose by 37 percent within a half year. This rate of production was 42 percent in 1949, 26 percent in 1950, and 19 percent in 1951. The index of industrial production, with 1936 set as a base of 100 percent, was 70.1 percent in 1948, 89.8 percent in 1949, 113 percent in 1950, 134.8 percent in 1951, and 144.4 percent in 1952.[9] The gross national product (GNP) of West Germany increased from DM 70.2 billion in

1948 to DM 136.6 billion in 1952.[10] In 1936, 11.2 million persons were employed in West Germany; in 1948, 13.5 million; and in 1951, 14.9 million.[11] The average rate of unemployment in 1949, 1950, and 1951, however, was around 10 percent—a high rate, attributable in part to the influx of refugees and expellees from the eastern territories.

A factor that contributed to the revival of the German economy was that wages, particularly during the early years of reconstruction, increased more slowly than productivity. In part, this phenomenon was attributable to an excess supply of labor. Labor unions, which were reorganized after the end of the war, pursued a policy of moderation in wage demands. This moderation was based in part on the existence of an excess supply of labor, which would normally temper demands for higher wages. A more important reason was the fact that German workers knew it was necessary to work hard in order to rehabilitate the economy. Moreover, real income improved as money wages exceeded increases in the price level. Because wages were in general lower in Germany than in other Western European countries and because of the labor surplus, the Germans were able to make larger investments in capital goods and maintain a high level of exports over imports.

The period 1952-60 marked a return to normality in West Germany. The time of reconstruction was over, and the refugees from other areas were assimilated into the population. Basic institutional arrangements, such as the organization of the government, were set. The economy entered a period of consolidation. Production continued to grow but less rapidly. Unemployment declined to a rate below 3 percent by 1958, and wages began to rise rapidly. Since there was no lack of overall aggregate demand, a shortage of investment funds was the main limiting factor in the economy. Fiscal policy sought to alleviate this shortage, first, by encouraging both private investment and private saving and, second, by providing more capital from public sources.

Gross national product, which amounted to DM 136.6 billion in 1952, increased to DM 279.8 billion by 1960.[12] The index of industrial production, set at 100 percent in 1950, increased to 248 percent by 1960.[13] During the period 1948-57 the annual rate of growth was 8 percent, the highest among the Western European countries. For the years 1958 and 1959 the rate of growth was around 7 percent. General economic policies emphasized price-level stability under conditions of full employment and improvement of employment conditions in recessionary situations.

Beginning in 1959 an ascent into boom conditions occurred. The flow of manpower from the east had declined, and a condition of overfull employment was reached. By 1961 the rate of unemployment was less than 2 percent of the total labor force. Prices rose, and the Deutsche Mark was revalued in March 1961 to reduce the balance-of-trade surpluses that posed a threat to the internal price level. This had the effect of reducing the growth in exports, and by 1963 the rate of economic growth declined to 3.4 percent. West Germany, however, was now one of the world's economic powers.

THE DEVELOPMENT OF THE EAST GERMAN ECONOMY

After the Zusammenbruch of 1945 the eastern part of Germany fell under the control of the Soviet Union. A temporary boundary line was drawn from the border of Czechoslovakia to the Baltic Sea along the rivers Neisse and Oder, extending west of the Oder, near its mouth, to include the city of Stettin on the Polish side of the line. This arrangement was intended to be a temporary one; it was to last only until a peace conference met and a definitive treaty of peace between the Allied powers and Germany was signed. Legally, therefore, the territories east of this boundary are temporarily under Polish and Soviet administration. Nevertheless, the countries of the Communist bloc have recognized these lands as permanently and legally incorporated either into Poland or into the Soviet Union.

East Germany was created out of the provinces of Brandenburg, Mecklenburg, Pomerania, Saxony, Saxony-Anhalt, and Thuringia. In land area it is about one-fourth of the prewar Third Reich. In the zonal division of Germany, the Soviet Union received the leading agricultural area, while the more important industrial areas went to the Western powers. Nevertheless, the area of East Germany was also highly developed industrially. For example, in 1936 industrial production in East Germany amounted to 15.1 billion Reichsmarks out of a total of 61.4 billion for the German Reich.[14] In 1944 industrial production in East Germany had increased to 25.3 billion Reichsmarks out of a total of 95 billion for the entire country.[15] By 1939, as a result of war preparations, per capita industrial output was 16 percent higher in East Germany than in the present area of West Germany. East German industry was particularly well developed in the production of consumer goods, basic chemicals, textile machinery, machine tools, synthetic rubber, and office equipment. In 1944 chemical production amounted to 30 percent of total chemical production in the country.

Conditions following the end of the war were less favorable for the development of the East German economy than for West Germany's. Even though many areas within East Germany were relatively undamaged by the war, the treatment accorded by the Soviets was far more punitive than Allied treatment in the Western zones of occupation. Almost immediately the Soviet Union introduced a new social and economic system and altered the structure of domestic production.

There was also the political objective of imposing a Communist system in the Soviet zone. This system was to follow the Soviet model; no independent German way to Communism was tolerated.

There were several factors that affected adversely the development of the East German economy during the postwar years. First, the Soviet Union pursued a policy of dismantling East German industry as reparation for war damage to its own industry. This policy lasted from 1945 to the mid-1950s. Machinery and equipment were carried away from German plants to the Soviet Union. Livestock, industrial goods, timber, and railroad rolling stock were also commandeered for use in the Soviet Union. Much of the East German rail trackage system was also dismantled.[16] Levies were placed on production, and the Germans also had to pay occupation costs. Unlike West Germany, East Germany received no help in the form of Marshall Plan aid; on the contrary, it had to contribute to the reconstruction of Eastern Europe. It is estimated that up to $20 billion in goods and services were appropriated by the Soviets in one form or another during the period 1945-55.[17]

Second, East German trade, which had been traditionally tied to West Germany and to Western Europe, was cut off. Before the war East Germany received most of its coal and steel from West Germany and sent in return chemical products, precision machinery, and agricultural products. After the war there was a reorientation of trade toward the Soviet Union that first took the form of uncompensated deliveries. Markets in the Soviet Union and other Communist countries were not large enough to compensate East Germany for the loss of its prewar markets. In turn Soviet deliveries were insufficient to satisfy East German industrial needs. There was a lag until the late 1950s before the Soviet Union began to satisfy East German fuel requirements. The Soviets were particularly deficient in supplying petroleum. East Germany also had to readjust to the problem of inadequate steel supplies. It was not until the early 1960s that steel imports from the Soviet Union and other sources came up to the prewar level of imports from West Germany.

A third factor that had an adverse effect on the development of the East German economy was the exodus of many of its better-trained persons to the West. During the period 1950-62 more than 2 million persons left the Soviet zone of occupation to go to West Germany. At first this exodus proved to be a blessing in that it helped to relieve the problem of unemployment in East Germany. It soon became apparent, however, that many skilled workers, physicians, engineers, and scientists were leaving. This talent drain caused a decline in the quality of the labor force. Eventually the exodus led to the creation of the Berlin Wall in 1961, and for all practical purposes contact with the West was cut off.

After the Soviet occupation in 1945 it was necessary to create some sort of political apparatus that would eventually become responsible for running the zone. There were four parties licensed by the Soviet Military Administration to participate in politics: the Kommunistische Partei Deutschlands (KPD), the Sozialdemokratische Partei Deutschlands (SPD), the Christlich-Demokratische Union (CDU), and the Liberal-Demokratische Partei (LDP). Each party had a record of opposition to the Nazis. This united front was maintained for only a short period of time. In 1946 there was a forced merger of the KPD and SPD parties into a new party called the Sozialistischen Einheitspartei Deutschlands (SED) or Socialist Unity Party. When the German Democratic Republic was created in October 1949, for all practical purposes the Socialist Unity Party became the official state party. Eventually the opposition parties, which had done quite well in the postwar elections, were forced to express the policies of the state and its representative, the Socialist Unity Party.* In 1952 the nominal federal structure was replaced by a highly centralized administration with the traditional provincial divisions giving way to purely administrative districts.

The governmental structure of East Germany was laid out in the May 1949 Constitution of the German Democratic Republic. Upon the approval of the Constitution, the German Democratic Republic was formally created. The Soviet Military Administration handed over nominal power to the East German regime but continued to demand reparations until the 1953 uprising. Full sovereignty was not granted until 1957. East Germany, however, has remained more tightly bound to the Soviet Union than any of the other East European Communist regimes, and Soviet troops continue to remain in its territory.

The Soviet contribution to the development of Communism in East Germany was enormous. The leading figures in the postwar imposition of Communism, such as Ulbricht and Pieck, received their training in the Soviet Union. When the war was over, Ulbricht and other German Communists were sent from the Soviet Union to supervise the integration of the Soviet part of the Third Reich into a Communist state system. In cooperation with the Soviet occupation authorities, the German Communists were able eventually to extend their control over East Germany. The proximity of East Germany to the Soviet Union and the presence of Soviet troops and tanks in the country tended to make any overt opposition to the development of Communism unwise. The existence of West Germany, however,

―――――――――

*In 1946 the Socialist Unity Party polled less than 50 percent of the total vote in national elections.

with an entirely different set of institutional arrangements, tended to restrain the immediate imposition of Communist political institutions on the East German people.

The economic development of East Germany followed an almost diametrically opposite direction from the social market economy of West Germany. From the very start, the Soviet Union began to cut up the large Junker estates and initiated a policy of nationalization. Much of East German heavy industry was transferred to the control of a Soviet corporation, Sowjetische Aktiengesellschaften (SAG), which operated until the early 1950s. Profits from this corporation were used to provide reparations to the Soviet Union. In 1947 a central planning agency, the German Economic Commission (Deutsche Wirtschaftskommission), was created. Its purpose was to facilitate the transformation of East Germany to a planned economy. Its efforts were directed toward the preparation of a two-year plan that had as its objective increasing production to 81 percent of the 1936 level. Subsequent plans also stressed the development of industrial capacity.

The private sector of the economy was eliminated by degrees. At first, only the basic industries, such as coal and electric power, were nationalized. Private wholesale and retail trade was left virtually intact, at least during the years immediately following 1945. As the Communist regime came into a position of being able to exploit fully its control over the economy, however, state control was extended over all areas of economic activity. But the extension of control was gradual. For example, in 1955 private firms accounted for around 21 percent of industrial production, 44 percent of construction activity, and 16 percent of retail trade.[18] In 1955 the private sector of the East German economy contributed 26.7 percent of total production.[19]

There were two reasons for this state tolerance of private industry. First, there was a shortage of consumer goods and services, which compelled the state to rely far more than it desired upon private industry. Outright nationalization would have caused a disruption of supply. Second, the existence of West Germany also imposed some restraints upon the Communist regime. As long as there was open access to West Germany, some toleration of private businesses was necessary. This open access put East Germany into direct competition with West Germany in terms of economic development—a competition that it lost. Toleration of private enterprise was a part of the East German approach toward motivating people to produce more. As the West German economy developed, however, it became more and more attractive for skilled workers and management in East Germany. When the exodus was curtailed in 1961 with the erection of the Berlin Wall, state control over the private sector was increased. Actually, increased control over private industry had begun in 1958. Various devices were used to force private businesses to acquire the state as a partner.*

It is a Communist article of faith that private ownership of land hinders development in agriculture and is responsible for the existence and perpetuation of antagonistic social classes in the countryside. In East Germany before the war, large proportions of land were concentrated in the hands of wealthy landowners, while many farmers had very small holdings. One of the first acts of the Soviets in 1945 was the breaking-up of the large estates of the Junker aristocracy. Small farmers were allowed to hold their properties, however, for a considerable period of time. There were several reasons for this. It was necessary for the Communist regime to obtain a food supply for the population, and forced collectivization would have resulted in a probable drop in output and efficiency. Moreover, to a certain extent the freedom of egress to West Germany was an inhibiting factor as far as collectivization was concerned.

The collectivization of agriculture was only a matter of time, however. When the regime felt that its position had been sufficiently consolidated, it moved to eliminate private landholdings. In 1950 state ownership of agricultural land amounted to 5.7 percent.[20] The process of collectivization began in earnest in 1952, and at the end of 1953 26 percent of all agricultural land was in the hands of state agricultural cooperatives.[21] Increased pressures to collectivize were placed on the farmers, and by 1959 almost 50 percent of agricultural land belonged to the state cooperatives.[22] After 1959 the decline in the percentage of land held by private farmers was rapid, and by 1962 93.3 percent of agricultural land was held by the cooperatives.[23] The transition from private to public ownership of agricultural land was not peaceful, for a policy of unrestricted terror was practiced against farmers who refused to enter the state cooperatives.

The goal of altering property relationships was attained during the early 1960s. By 1962 practically no private property was left in agriculture. With very few exceptions, the state was the sole owner of all productive industry. Wholesale trade had been placed under state control. In retail trade small enclaves of private businesses existed, subject to state controls and regulations. Labor unions, for all practical purposes, had been subverted to state control.

---

*Unfavorable tax treatment of private businesses was one device. Private businesses were also discriminated against in that the state controlled the supply of materials and could withhold them.

The institutions of capitalism had been eliminated, but the state itself had become the capitalist. A command economy had been developed in which the state determined what would be produced and how it would be distributed. Economic plans set forth the major guidelines for production and distribution.

Economic planning was formally introduced in 1949 with the creation of a comprehensive two-year plan. In 1950 the State Planning Commission was organized, and a five-year plan was announced in 1951. One objective of this plan was to increase worker productivity. The plan also had as its goal the doubling of 1936 production levels by the end of 1955. There were frequent plan revisions and the goals of the plan were unfulfilled. A second five-year plan was started in 1956. Its purpose was to raise worker productivity and to concentrate on the development of heavy industry. The plan was abandoned in 1958, however, because the Soviet Union had shifted to a seven-year plan. A new plan of the same length was adopted in East Germany for the period 1959-65. Collectivization of agriculture was one purpose of the plan. Competition with West Germany, particularly in the production of agricultural goods, was declared to be a basic objective of the plan. The superiority of the socialist state in terms of production was to be demonstrated, but this superiority failed to materialize.

By 1960 the German Democratic Republic had been firmly established and the rubric of the planned economy created. Agriculture had been largely collectivized, and most industry had either been nationalized or forced to accept the state as a partner. The performance of the economy during the period 1945-60 was less spectacular than the West German economy. Using 1936 as a base of 100 percent for both East and West Germany, East German gross national product was 77 percent of the base compared to 117 percent for West Germany.[24] In 1955 the respective percentages were 108 and 184, and in 1960, 137 and 249.[25] To some extent there were extenuating circumstances that worked against the East German economy. Its recovery had been delayed by Soviet dismantling policies, and its prewar markets were lost. East Germany, however, possessed the advantage of a command economy in that it could force the allocation of resources away from the production of consumer goods into the production of capital goods. Wages were also kept far lower than gains in productivity and the difference appropriated for capital formation.

SUMMARY

After the end of World War II Germany was partitioned among the victors. The western part came under the control of the British, French, and Americans, and the eastern part came under the control of the Soviets. It was natural that each power would attempt to impose its particular set of political and economic institutions upon the territory for which it was responsible. An eventual dichotomy occurred, with the western part of Germany assimilating the institutions of the Western democracies and the eastern part assuming the institutions of the Soviet command economy. By 1949 two separate political entities were created: the Federal Republic of Germany and the German Democratic Republic. Any hope of reunification of the two German economies became a thing of the past.

The postwar reconstruction of the two Germanies evolved under a set of particularly different circumstances. The Soviet Union imposed punitive measures on its zone of occupation. Much of the East German industrial property was expropriated by the Soviets as indemnification for war damages. Demands for reparation were far less punitive in the western zones of occupation. While West Germany received international assistance in the form of Marshall Plan aid, no such help was forthcoming to the East Germans. On the contrary, East Germany was forced to contribute heavily to the reconstruction of territories in Eastern Europe that the Germans had destroyed during World War II. In each of the two Germanies, the victors attempted to impose a new political and economic system. In the Soviet zone, however, the entire structure of production was changed from a capitalist to a Communist system.

The postwar redevelopment of West Germany can be divided into roughly four periods. The first, from 1945 to the currency reform of 1948, was a period during which Allied policies were designed to emasculate the German economy through restrictions of industry and production. The second period was one of reconstruction, which lasted from the currency reform to the end of 1951. Marshall Plan aid, the restoration of free exchange, and the removal of price controls contributed to a rapid rise in the rate of economic growth. A social market policy was followed by the government, which placed priority upon the maintenance of competition in the market place. By the end of 1951 the West German economy had been firmly established. Unemployment remained very high, however. The period 1952-56 was one in which the economy began to stabilize, and by 1957 the rate of unemployment had been reduced to less than 4 percent. After 1957 the West German economy entered into a period of overemployment and prosperity that has lasted with some interruptions until today.

East German economic development followed a different pattern. Aside from the contrasting occupation policies, East Germany was cut off from its prewar markets. The recovery of the economy was delayed until the 1950s, partially as a result of Soviet dismantling policies and partially as a result of the loss of specialized trade with

West Germany. The institutions of a command economy were imposed by degrees. During the period 1945-48 large agricultural holdings were broken up and divided among the peasants, and large-scale industry, trade, and finance was nationalized. In 1948 formal economic planning was introduced in the form of a two-year plan. An independent farm population was tolerated, at least up until the mid-1950s, out of a need to secure an adequate food supply. As their control of the economy became more absolute, however, the Communists instituted a campaign of collectivization that began in 1958 and culminated in 1961 when practically all farmers were in collectives. Private businesses were forced into partnership with the state or were nationalized outright. During the period 1958-59, more than one-half of private enterprise moved into a semistate category.

During the period 1945-60 East German growth lagged behind that of West Germany. It was not until 1959 that East Germany reached the 1939 level of economic development achieved for its area while the West German economy had attained this level in the early 1950s. Per capita GNP in East Germany ran consistently about 75 percent of the West German level during the postwar period. Before the war, per capita GNP was about the same in each area. Output per worker in East Germany, which was practically the same as in West Germany before the war, was two-thirds of the West German level in 1960. Comparisons between the two Germanies purely in terms of economic development can be misleading, however, because in East Germany priority was given to the creation of a new economic and political system.

CHAPTER 2

GENERAL CHARACTERISTICS OF THE WEST GERMAN ECONOMIC AND POLITICAL SYSTEM

INTRODUCTION

To understand a country, it is necessary to know something about its institutional arrangements. The present structure of both West and East Germany represents the latest and perhaps most permanent shift in the territorial development of an area that was unified into one state by Bismarck in 1871.* Since that time, as a political entity Germany participated in two major world wars, gaining and losing territory that extended over much of Europe. Moreover, since 1870 Germany developed into the most powerful industrial nation in Western Europe, a position it regained despite the loss of two major wars. Its strong industrial position can be attributed to a major degree to the energies and organizing abilities of the German people.

GEOGRAPHY AND POPULATION

The Federal Republic of Germany has an area of 248,528 square kilometers (95,927 square miles) and a predominantly urban population of approximately 60.8 million persons.[1] The country ranks sixth in land area among the Western European nations, but is only a little more than half the size of the prewar Third Reich. About one-fifth

---

*The German Reich came into being in the Hall of Mirrors in Versailles on January 18, 1871, as the product of a series of victorious wars, and the constitution as adopted was the handiwork of Bismarck.

of the population lives in 11 large cities, each with more than 500,000 persons, and the population density per square mile is among the highest in Europe. There are three cities with over 1 million inhabitants: Berlin, Hamburg, and Munich.

The Federal Republic consists of 10 states, which are as follows: Schleswig-Holstein, Lower Saxony, Bremen, North Rhine-Westphalia, Hamburg, Hesse, Rhineland-Palatinate, Saarland, Baden-Wurttemberg, and Bavaria. In addition, there is West Berlin, which, although territorially separated, is an appendage of West Germany in terms of economic and political development. The main population concentrations are in the Rhineland-Ruhr areas and in Bavaria. In land area Bavaria is the largest state and Lower Saxony the second largest. The urban sector of the West German population has grown rapidly, and with it the percentage employed in industry. Most of this increase has taken place during the period from 1950 to the present as a result of the industrial prosperity that has pervaded the country during this period.

Although West Germany represents only a little more than half of the territory of the Third Reich, in many respects it is the most varied and valuable part. Most of the prewar industrial base, particularly in the heavy industries, was located in West Germany. It contains the Ruhr coal fields and the vast industrial complex that has developed around them. It also contains the small but important oil fields of northwest Germany, Bremen and Hamburg (the great ports of the North Sea coast), and the locus of German history and culture in the Rhineland and South Germany. It contains a very large share of the mineral resources of the former Reich, and, although its agricultural potential is severely limited in some areas, about 30 percent of its total area is under cultivation.

The partition of Germany worked to the disadvantage of the western part in terms of agricultural production. The eastern provinces, which were on balance a food-surplus region, passed under the control of Polish and Soviet administration. The structure of agriculture in western Germany was less well developed, and for over a century a substantial part of all the foodstuffs consumed had to be imported. To a considerable degree the factor that has worked against the development of agriculture is the relatively limited area of quality soil. Large areas of West Germany are either heavily forested or covered with a sandy soil that is not conducive to the growing of agricultural crops. Intermediate in agricultural quality is the land area of much of South Germany and the less-sandy areas of the northern plains regions. Intensive crop farming is important only in the areas, rather limited in extent, of medium and good quality soils.

In terms of mineral resources, however, West Germany is somewhat better endowed. The coal fields of the Ruhr had formed the basis of the creation of the most heavily industrialized region in Europe. There are also large coal deposits in the Saar. Iron ore is also a mineral of some importance; West Germany has large reserves, but most of these are of low grade and have been exploited only in recent years. The modern German iron industry, however, is based mainly on good quality imported ores, a large part of which have been furnished by Sweden. The development of petroleum has been largely a postwar phenomenon. At the present, the domestic production of oil is sufficient to cover about one-third of domestic requirements. With respect to other basic mineral resources, such as manganese and zinc, Germany is deficient and must import them from other countries.

THE POLITICAL SYSTEM

West Germany is a federal republic with a bicameral parliament, consisting of a lower house (Bundestag) and an upper house (Bundesrat). Members of the Bundestag are elected by direct popular vote, and members of the Bundesrat are appointed by the governments of the ten states. The former serve for terms of four years and may be reelected; the latter serve at the discretion of the state governments. West Berlin is represented in each chamber by nonvoting members.

The political structure of West Germany was created by the Basic Law of the Federal Republic, which was passed in 1949. This constitution reflected the historical fact that Germany was really a federation of states. Bismarck's constitution of 1871 had left the states with considerable autonomy even though they had been formed into a confederation under the control of a monarchy. Under the Weimar Republic, however, and even more so under the Third Reich, political control was subverted by the central government. A monolithic political structure developed during the period 1919-45. The Basic Law, however, did not result in a complete reversion to federalism. The tradition of a unified Germany remained strong, and a loose federation of German states was impractical in view of the fact that the area of the country had been greatly reduced.

The Federal Government

The Federal Republic consists of a bicameral parliament (Bundestag and Bundesrat), the federal chancellor (Bundeskanzler) and his cabinet, and the federal president (Bundespräsident).

The Bundestag

The principal functions of the Bundestag are legislation, the election of the federal chancellor, and the control of the federal government, which can continue in office only as long as it has parliamentary support. In addition, the Bundestag participates in the election of the federal president and in shaping the federal budget, which is passed in the form of a statute. It also has the power to declare war or to proclaim peace. The Bundestag consists of 496 deputies from the 10 states, plus 22 members furnished by West Berlin as a result of its special position under international law. These 22 have a consultative voice only.

The Bundesrat

The Bundesrat consists of 41 members appointed by the 10 state governments, plus 4 representatives from West Berlin who have a consultative voice only. It is constituted as a federative organ of parliament and is designed to facilitate cooperation between parliament and the state governments. All laws proposed by the Bundestag are sent to it, and it has the right of veto over legislation involving state taxes and territory. In cases involving the rights and interests of the states, agreement between the Bundestag and Bundesrat is necessary before legislation can be passed into law.

The Chancellor

The chancellor holds the highest elective office in the Federal Republic. He is elected by the Bundestag on the basis of a majority vote once every four years. Once elected, the chancellor has very strong powers. He determines and assumes responsibility for general economic policy. He does not have to ask the legislature either for a vote of confidence for his government program or for approval of the list of ministers whom he asks the president to appoint. As long as he retains control of his party, the Bundestag is unable to enter a no-confidence vote and thus bring about new elections. On the other hand, the chancellor may, on occasions of his choosing, ask the Bundestag to give him a vote of confidence, but even if he loses he need not resign.

The Federal President

The Basic Law of the Federal Republic contemplated a parliamentary system of government and not a government of divided powers as in the United States. The functions of the president are largely, but not exclusively, formal and representative. As the head of state, he represents the Federal Republic in dealing with other nations. He is obliged to appoint and dismiss the chancellor upon the discretion of the parliament and to appoint and dismiss ministers upon the request of the chancellor. The president is appointed by a special federal assembly that consists of the deputies of the Bundestag and an equal number of electors appointed by the legislative assemblies of the states.

Political Parties

There are two major political parties in West Germany: the Christian Democratic Union (Christlich-Demokratische Union, or CDU) and the Social Democratic Party (Sozialdemokratische Partei Deutschlands). There is also the Free Democratic Party (Freie Demokratische Partei), which represents laissez-faire liberalism and presents a platform that stresses private property rights and free markets. During the postwar period, the Christian Democratic Union has been the dominant political party. To a major degree this dominance can be attributable to the leadership of Konrad Adenauer, who was chancellor of the Federal Republic from 1949 to 1963.

The Christian Democratic Union

The Christian Democratic Union, with its Bavarian affiliate, the Christian Social Union (CSU), has been the dominant political party in Germany during the postwar period. It was created in 1945 as an amalgam of the Catholic Center Party, which functioned during the pre-Hitler period, and various right-of-center Protestant parties. The strong personal leadership furnished by Konrad Adenauer was the catalyst that held the party together during the early years of its formation. It originally desired as a national goal a planned economy with the nationalization of key industries. Under the leadership of Adenauer and his minister of economics, Ludwig Erhard, however, the CDU modified its position considerably. Many voters and groups rallied to support it because of a fear that left-wing parties, particularly those led by Communists, would be dominant in postwar Germany. The social market policy (Soziale Marktwirtschaft) followed by Erhard attracted many businessmen and industrialists to the CDU, and it also became a catch-all for a large number of predominantly middle-class voters.

The Social Democratic Party

The other major political party in Germany is the Social Democratic Party (SPD). The SPD, unlike the CDU, is a party that has been in existence for a long period of time. Originally a socialist working-class party when it was formed during the time that Bismarck was chancellor of Germany, it was pledged to the eradication of private property and the abolition of capitalist society. By 1914, at the outbreak of World War I, it was the largest party in the Reichstag. Despite a split with the Communists, it remained during the postwar period of the Weimar Republic as one of the dominant parties in Germany. During the period of Nazi dominance from 1933 to 1945, the SPD was outlawed and its leaders sent to concentration camps.

After World War II, the partition of Germany having eliminated part of the geographical base from which the SPD drew its traditional support, the party was unable to gain political control over the West German economy. The doctrinaire approach of the SPD to most economic problems alienated most of the middle-class voters who were attracted to the CDU. To shed its image of a working-class party, the SPD abandoned most of its doctrinaire solutions and embraced an economic philosophy that is not too far removed from that of the CDU. It accepts private ownership of the agents of production as a social and economic right as long as it does not stultify the development of a just social order.

The Free Democratic Party

The third party, the Free Democratic Party (FDP), cannot be considered a major political party. To a certain extent, it occupies the same position in West Germany that the Liberal Party does in the United Kingdom. In the 1969 national elections, however, it was able to shift the balance of power to the Social Democratic Party. The FDP is also an old-line political party that existed prior to World War I and stressed economic liberalism. It represented the dominant political force of German free-market, laissez-faire liberalism until the latter part of the Weimar Republic. After World War II, it lost a considerable part of its strength to the CDU and SPD. Today, the FDP draws its support mainly from middle-class Protestants who range from classic liberals to outright nationalists. The party favors a more active Eastern policy, especially in economic matters and in dealing with East Germany.

The 1969 Elections

In October 1969 the Social Democrats replaced the Christian Democrats as the ruling political party in Germany. This was the first time during the postwar period that the SPD achieved the status of the dominant party. Although the Christian Democrats received 46.1 percent of the popular vote compared to 42.7 percent for the Social Democrats, the latter formed a coalition with the Free Democrats who received 5.8 percent of the votes.[2] Willy Brandt, former mayor of Berlin and leader of the Social Democratic Party, became the chancellor of West Germany, thus becoming the first socialist to lead a German government since 1930. His first act was an upward revaluation of the German mark from an unrealistically low price that had allowed Germany to accumulate enormous trade deficits at the expense of the economies and currencies of other countries. The Social Democrats campaigned on a platform to increase social security benefits and effect improvements in the educational system. A radical departure from the domestic economic policies followed by the Christian Democrats during the postwar period is unlikely, however.

The area of foreign relations is a different matter. The Brandt government has effected a détente with the Soviet Union. One objective of the détente is to improve economic relations between West Germany and the Eastern European countries. Improved diplomatic relations have also been achieved with Poland. West Germany has given up its claim to all of the former German territory east of the Oder-Neisse line. In return, Poland has agreed to allow all German residents of the area the opportunity to migrate to West Germany. No appreciable thaw has occurred in the relationship between West and East Germany, however. Neither accords the other formal diplomatic recognition. Although some effort has been made by the West German government to accomplish some sort of rapprochement, as demonstrated by the Brandt-Stolph meeting in Erfurt in 1970, nothing of substance appears to have been accomplished.

State and Local Governments

State (Länder) and local (Gemeinden) governments constitute the remainder of the West German political system. State governments are organized on the principle of parliamentary democracy. They have a popularly elected legislature, which, except in Bavaria, is unicameral. The constitution of 1949 gave the Länder administrative jurisdiction in such areas as the interior, the police, justice, and education. Personal and corporate income taxes are the responsibility of the Länder, with the federal government having the right to lay claim to part of these taxes. There is also concurrent federal-state legislative jurisdiction that covers a variety of fields, including the regulation of commerce, industry, mining, banks, and private insurance; public welfare, war claims and restitution to victims of Nazi persecution; public roads and shipping; and civil and criminal law and the organization of the courts. In the field of concurrent federal and state legislation, the states retain the right to legislate unless and until the federal government preempts the field, which it is authorized to do under certain conditions that demonstrate a need for federal legislation.

It can be said that the Länder do not have the power that state governments do in the United States. The distribution of powers between the national and state governments has been one of the major problems of German federalism. In Germany fundamental economic and social problems tend to become national problems calling for solutions on a nationwide basis. Thus Länder politics have come to center around national issues. Although the Länder have a certain amount of autonomy, particularly in the field of education, the main legislative function of their parliaments is to enact the budget. But even here taxes and revenues are circumscribed to a considerable degree by the needs of the federal government. There is a trend toward the centralization of legislative powers in the Federal Republic.

The basic unit of local government is the Gemeinde, or township. It is responsible for a wide range of activities, including the operations of such municipal enterprises as public utilities, streetcars and buses, slaughterhouses, and hospitals. Gemeinden are also responsible for the construction of public facilities and for social welfare expenditures. The Gemeinden owe their status to the Länder, as embodied in the Basic Law of the Federal Republic. Each township has its own council and its own head, or burgomaster, and other elected officials. To some extent, there is also reliance upon a town director (Gemeindedirektor) who is responsible to the town council. The functions of the Gemeinden have been subverted to some degree to the objectives of the Länder. Fields like social welfare and housing have increasingly come under federal or state jurisdiction. The Gemeinden are compelled to rely upon the percentages of federal and state taxes turned over to them to finance their activities.

Midway between the Länder and the Gemeinden comes the Landkreise, which would roughly correspond to an American county. Larger cities are known as city counties, which often means that county and municipal governments are identical. The administration of the Landkreise is in part autonomous and in part in the hands of the Länder. The typical Landkreise is headed by an official called the Landrat, or county director. There is also an executive council called the Kreistag, which is concerned with such activities as road construction and social welfare. County governments are to a certain extent dependent upon the state governments for financial assistance in the form of grants-in-aid. A state government can also staff the county director's office with state civil servants.

The Status of Berlin

Following the end of World War II Berlin was not included in any of the zones of occupation but was made a separate area under joint quadripartite control. Berlin was the seat of the Allied Control Authority, which was to govern Germany as a whole, and was to be the seat of the eventual central German government. In 1948, however, the Soviet Union repudiated its wartime agreements and refused to participate any longer in the quadripartite administration of Germany. At the same time it refused to cooperate in the joint administration of Berlin, drove the government elected by the people of Berlin out of its seat in the Soviet sector, and installed a puppet regime in its place. After the failure of the Soviets to amalgamate the city by blockading it in 1948, the split of Berlin into East and West Berlin occurred.

West Berlin has formally operated as an independent entity since September 1, 1950, under a constitution similar to that of the Federal Republic. The German attempt to have West Berlin incorporated into the Federal Republic as a full-fledged state was, however, thwarted by a veto of the Western Allies who, while not interested in maintaining occupational rights, insisted on at least formal continuation of Berlin's occupational status. A change in that status would have given the Soviet Union a pretext to abrogate the Western rights of free access to West Berlin through Soviet zone territory. Thus, the tripartite Allied authority is still in control today, although government and administration has shifted into the hands of the Germans.

To the extent compatible with the special status of the city, the Western Allies have turned over control and management of city affairs to the Berlin Senat, a government established by constitutional process and chosen on the basis of free elections. At Bonn itself, the semi-inclusion of West Berlin in the Federal Republic is symbolized by the presence of 22 members from Berlin in the Bundestag and of four members in the Bundesrat. On Allied insistence, these representatives have no voting rights in plenary session, but they do vote in committees; on the other hand, the Bundestag members are not directly elected by the Berlin people but are elected by the Berlin parliament.

West Berlin's economic ties to the Federal Republic are as strong as its political ones. The city could hardly have survived without first American and then West German financial aid. This aid is a significant item in the national budget. West Berlin's financial situation is mainly characterized by items of expenditures for social purposes, since out of its inhabitants an exceptionally large number depend wholly or in part on public assistance. It is granted special subsidies from the Federal Republic to cover its budgetary and social insurance expenditures.

East Berlin has followed a separate route. Politically and economically it has been merged into the East German socialist state and is the seat of government. The Soviet Union has been as anxious as the West to observe the formalities of East Berlin's four-power status. East German statutes, for instance, do not automatically extend to East Berlin; the status of East Berlin's members in the East German Peoples' Chamber is limited; and there is a court system separate from, although similar to East Germany's. In regard to budget, economic planning, and enterprises, it is treated entirely as an integral part of the German Democratic Republic.

THE ECONOMIC SYSTEM

In spite of partition from its eastern part, West Germany has emerged as a world power. This fact can be attributed almost exclusively to the amazing performance of its economy. With one of the higher growth rates among the world's industrial countries, West Germany has achieved a GNP that now places it fourth in the world behind the United States, the Soviet Union, and Japan. Its industrial development is remarkable when one considers the economic base from which it has had to operate. The resource base is modest by some standards in variety and, with a few notable exceptions, in amount, but without it the country could not have achieved its present position. Moreover, West German industrial expansion has been marked in those branches of industry that were located primarily in the eastern section prior to partition, particularly electric power, chemicals, fertilizers, paper, glass, and ceramics.

The postwar reliance on a free market system represented somewhat of a break with traditional German reliance on state intervention in economic affairs, which predated the Hitler era by a considerable time period. The West German economic system, then, is a mixed economic system in which there is both public and private ownership of the agents of production. The bulk of German industry is in private hands, and pricing decisions are determined in the market place. It has been the government's stated policy to denationalize some of its holdings as it did in the case of the Volkswagen company in 1961. Distribution is also primarily a function of private enterprise with the government responsible for seeing that it is shared equitably by all income groups. To this extent, allocation of resources, as determined in a purely competitive market economy, is circumvented.

The term "welfare state" is certainly applicable to the West German economy. The main principles of a welfare state are a commitment to an equitable distribution of income and a minimum living standard for all of its citizens and to full employment as the most important goal to be supported by public policy. The objectives of full employment and social welfare have been accomplished through state intervention in the economy. Aggregate demand has been managed in such a way as to keep it at a high level. Government purchases of goods and services have added directly to the demand for output, while its expenditures for interest, social security benefits, and various other transfer payments have added to private incomes and spending power.

The West German economy can be divided into two sectors, private and public, each of which contributes to the total output of goods and services. The private sector is the most important in terms of consumption, production, and employment. The public or government sector is also important not only from the standpoint that it contributes to consumption and investment but also because it has come to play the paramount role in the maintenance of full employment and the redistribution of income. For a variety of reasons the government sector has entered into certain business activities that it shares to a greater or lesser degree with private enterprise.

The Private Sector

Business and industry in West Germany are primarily in the hands of private enterprises. Most of the GNP is contributed by the private sector of the economy; the basic institutions of capitalism, freedom of enterprise, private ownership of property, and consumer sovereignty prevail, subject to certain modifications. Nevertheless, government control is substantial as a result of fiscal, monetary, and regulatory measures of the kinds familiar in other highly developed industrial countries, and the government has large interests in various sectors of the economy.

It has been the policy of the federal government to denationalize some of its holdings. The stated objective is to promote the diffusion of economic power by achieving a wider distribution of property. A case in point is the Volkswagen company. In 1961, 60 percent of the capital shares of the company, worth DM 360 million, was sold by the government. To spread the ownership of these shares, the government sold them at a special graduated discount to persons whose taxable income did not exceed DM 16,000 a year. Moreover, if these purchasers pledged not to sell the stock within a period of five years, further price concessions were made available. Capital shares could be paid for in installments. Altogether, some 1.5 million persons purchased shares in the company.

There are other examples of the government's denationalization policies. In 1959, the Prussian Mining and Smelting Company (Preussag), was partially denationalized. Preussag shares, amounting to DM 81.5 billion, were offered at a discount to persons whose

taxable income did not exceed DM 16,000 a year. Each purchaser was limited to five shares. In 1965, the state holding company VEBA (Vereinigte Elektrizitäts und Bergwerke, A.G.), which controls subsidiaries producing coal, lignite, and coke, was partially denationalized. This time 3.7 million shares at DM 100 each were offered at a graduated discount to persons whose annual yearly taxable income did not exceed DM 14,000, with a limitation of five shares per person.*
Shares could be paid for in installments.

One measure of the contribution of the private sector to the West German economy can be obtained by comparing the amounts of private consumption and investment expenditures to gross social product. When this approach is used from the standpoint of the national economy, gross social product is equal to the sum of private and public consumption and investment expenditures. The familiar Keynesian equation, Y=C+I, can be used where Y is equal to total output or product, C represents consumption expenditures, and I represents investment expenditures. C+I represents the total outlay on goods and services. Investment can be subdivided into two categories, domestic and foreign. Government expenditures, which also contribute an important component, are divided between public consumption and public investment.

Table 2.1 presents the contributions of the private and public sectors to the West German gross social product for 1969. It can be said that in terms of direct contributions to the total level of aggregate demand or expenditures, the private sector is responsible for around 80 percent of the total, compared to around 20 percent for the public sector. It is necessary to point out, however, that the importance of the public sector is understated in the table. Transfer payments from the public to the private sector would be incorporated into the total for private consumption.

Investment expenditures occupy a highly significant role in the West German economy. There are two reasons why this is so. First, the total demand, both public and private, for investment goods represents a large part of the gross social product. In 1970, for example, total gross domestic investment amounted to DM 180 billion out of a gross social product of DM 679 billion.[3] Second, investment expenditures are significant because of their impact on the economy's productive capacity. Investment expenditures involve the acquisition of capital goods, whose function is to produce other goods and services. This means that investment expenditures not only affect the level of

---

*The general act was the Capital Accumulation Act (Bundesgesetzblatt, Part I, July 1965).

TABLE 2.1

West German Gross Social Product, 1970[a]

Expenditures at Current Prices	Billions of DM[b]
Private consumption	371.5
Government consumption	106.4
Gross domestic investment	180.0
Machinery and equipment	81.8
Construction	98.2
Public gross investment	29.4
Changes in inventories	9.6
Net foreign investment	11.6
Gross social product	679.0

[a]Provisional figures.
[b]The West German currency unit is the Deutsche Mark. In 1969 the DM was revalued and the rate of exchange between it and the U.S. dollar was set at 3.6 to 1. In 1971 the value of the dollar weakened vis à vis the DM, so that the rate is less than 3.6 to 1.

Source: Deutsche Bundesbank, Geschäftsbericht der Deutschen Bundesbank, 1970 (Frankfurt am Main, April 1971), p. 7.

income and employment but are also a vital factor in economic growth, which depends to a great extent upon how rapidly productive capacity is being enlarged. Economic policy in West Germany has focused on the attainment of a high investment level.

The Public Sector

The public sector in West Germany is engaged in two major types of activities, both of which can be measured by the expenditures incurred in carrying them out. One activity involves the government in the provision of a broad array of goods and services to its citizens, including expenditures on roads, police protection, and education. These expenditures represent a transfer of resources from the private sector to the public sector of the German economy and also represent the contribution of the government sector to the total GNP.

The other activity involves the use of transfer payments as an instrument for the redistribution of income, generally with the dual objectives of greater income equality and the provision of some minimum standard of living for everyone. Transfer payments, as distinguished from government expenditures on goods and services, involve only the transfer of income from one group to another through taxation and provide no equivalent value in terms of goods and services in exchange. There is no return flow to the government in goods and services in exchange. Transfer payments include family allowances, old-age pensions, maternity grants, and unemployment compensation. Some services, such as free medical care, are considered to be a direct expenditure on the part of the government in that they absorb resources.

The West German public sector—that is, federal, state, and local governments—absorbs a substantial proportion of the resources of the GNP in the form of goods and services for consumption and investment. A considerable proportion of expenditures in the public sector, particularly by the federal government, consists of income transfers to other sectors of the economy. While these outlays do not in themselves make any demands on real resources, the direct transfers from the federal government to households and to state and local governments do result in an immediate demand for goods and services.

A significant economic dimension of total governmental activity is its outlay not only for the purchase of goods and services but interest on its debt, subsidies, and transfer payments for welfare and similar purposes. The combined expenditures of the federal, state, and local governments eliminating duplications that arise in such a total from grants-in-aid from the federal and state governments to the local governments amounted to DM 244.6 billion in 1969 out of a GNP of DM 679 billion. The breakdown of total government outlays compared to GNP is presented in Table 2.2.

The public sector in West Germany plays a more important role in terms of its contribution to GNP than does the public sector of the United States. In 1968 total public revenue in the United States amounted to 30 percent compared to 37.1 percent for West Germany.[4] Total expenditures of the United States and West Germany in comparison to GNP were 28.8 percent and 32.6 percent, respectively.[5] Direct government expenditures on goods and services, which form one of the components of GNP, amounted to 21 percent in the United States, compared to 15.7 percent in West Germany.[6] Transfer payments amounted to 6.1 percent of GNP in the United States, compared to 14.8 percent for West Germany.[7]

On the other hand, the public sector of West Germany occupies a less prominent position in the economy when compared to the public sectors of France and Sweden.[8] In 1968, for example, total government revenues in France and Sweden amounted to 37.7 percent and 48.1 percent of GNP, respectively, compared to 37.1 percent for West Germany. Government expenditures in France and Sweden amounted

TABLE 2.2

General Government Revenues and Expenditures
in Relation to West German GNP, 1970

	Billion DM	Percent of GNP
GNP at market prices	679.0*	100.0
Total public revenues	256.2	37.6
Social security contributions	78.2	11.5
Direct taxes	72.3	10.5
Indirect taxes	91.0	13.4
Business and property income	10.2	1.5
Other income	4.5	0.7
Total public expenditures	215.2	31.7
Expenditures on goods and services	108.2	16.0
Subsidies	9.5	1.4
Interest on the public debt	6.2	0.9
Transfers to private households	86.1	12.7
Other expenditures	5.2	0.7
Net savings	30.7	4.5
Gross investment	29.4	4.4

*All figures are provisional.

Source: Deutsche Bundesbank, Monatsberichte der Deutschen Bundesbank (Frankfurt am Main, October 1971), p. 17.

to 34.5 percent and 37.4 percent of GNP, respectively, compared to 32.6 percent for West Germany. Direct government purchases of goods and services amounted to 12.7 percent of GNP in France, 21.9 percent in Sweden, and 15.7 percent in West Germany. Transfer payments to households, which reflect the income redistribution effects of a government's tax-transfer policies, amounted to 16.1 percent of GNP in France, 12.8 percent in Sweden, and 14.8 percent in West Germany.

The contribution of the public sector to the West German economy has remained quite stable during the period 1950-68.[9] Government purchases of goods and services amounted to 14.3 percent of GNP in 1950, compared to 15.7 percent in 1968. Total government revenues amounted to 31.5 percent of GNP in 1950, compared to 37.1 percent in 1968, with most of the increase occurring in the 1950s. Government expenditures of all types amounted to 28.3 percent of GNP in 1950, compared to 32.6 percent in 1968. There has been a decrease in the level of consumers' expenditures from 64.7 percent of GNP in 1950 to 56.2 percent in 1968. This decrease was counterbalanced to some extent by an increase in investment expenditures from 18.5 percent of GNP in 1950 to 23.1 percent in 1968.

Certain activities of economic importance are legal monopolies in West Germany. The federal government has a monopoly of the telephone, telegraph, and postal systems. It owns practically all the railways and airlines, although Lufthansa has been partially denationalized. Other economic activities are in the nature of public utilities, i.e., electricity and water, which are typically operated by local government units. The federal government has a monopoly of the manufacture, importation, and sale of certain alcoholic beverages. Many other activities that are carried out in the United States by private enterprise are owned and operated by the government in Germany. According to a recent survey, this ownership includes 40 percent of the coal and iron mining industries, 72 percent of the aluminum industry, 62 percent of the electrical industry, 27 percent of shipbuilding, 13 percent of housing, and properties in the transportation industry producing two-thirds of its income.[10] The federal government owns the central bank (Bundesbank) and about 60 percent of all other credit institutions.

Industry

Industry is the cornerstone of the West German economy. Recovery from the effects of World War II has been achieved, and an industrial base that has made West Germany one of the major industrial countries in the world has been established. To some extent the base was already in existence prior to World War II. Mining and metallurgy were largely concentrated in West Germany—in the Ruhr and Saar valleys. West Germany was well developed also in the investment goods industries, specializing in the production of heavy industrial equipment, motors, pumps, and compressors. Moreover, West Germany contained the resource base necessary to produce iron and steel. It contained virtually all the hard coal mined in prewar Germany. In addition, it produced more than 90 percent of the iron ore produced during the prewar period. Pig iron, crude steel, and rolled steel production was concentrated in West Germany. In addition, the chemical industry had developed, particularly in the production of pharmaceutical products, tires, and synthetic fibers. Given the existing base, postwar industrial expansion occurred in a number of other industrial areas.

THE WEST GERMAN SYSTEM 39

In terms of contribution to the value of the GNP of West Germany, industry is by far the most important contributor. In fact, in comparison to other industrial countries, West German industry contributes the largest share of gross domestic product (GDP) to its economy. In Table 2.3 international comparisons are presented listing the contribution of industry to the GDP of selected countries for 1969.

In 1968 the most important contributor to West German industrial production was the manufacturing industry. Manufacturing can be broken down into the following industrial categories: basic materials and production goods, capital goods, consumer goods, and food and related goods. For 1968 industrial turnover of all manufactured goods amounted to DM 396 billion compared to DM 255 billion for 1960.[11] Turnover of basic materials and producer goods amounted to DM 122 billion in 1968 compared to DM 85 billion for 1960.[12] Investment goods produced amounted to DM 142 billion in 1968 and DM 88 billion in 1960. Turnover of consumer goods and foodstuffs amounted to DM 73 billion and DM 59 billion, respectively, in 1968, compared to DM 48 billion and DM 37 billion for 1960.[13] When mining is added to industrial production, along with manufacturing, total turnover of production for 1968 amounted to DM 406 billion.

Industrial production can also be broken down on the basis of the contributions of individual industries, i.e., the chemical and iron and steel industries, to the value of output.[14] In Table 2.4 West German industry is divided into the categories of basic industries, metal manufacturing industries, light industries, and food industries. Under each category, the contribution of individual industries is listed in value of gross production. The chemical industry is the single most important contributor.

Agriculture

In contrast to industry, agriculture makes a minor contribution to the West German GNP—contributing less than 4 percent. In terms of employment, however, agriculture employs around 10 percent of the total labor force. But despite the employment of a rather large percentage of the labor force, agricultural production is insufficient to support the population. Only in milk and butter production is output generally sufficient to meet consumer demand. In other areas, such as the production of wheat, fruits, and vegetables, production falls far short of consumer requirements. Thus, foreign trade is a necessary adjunct to West German agriculture. In 1969, imports of agricultural products comprised 19 percent of the total value of imports, while farm exports comprised only 3 percent of the value of total exports.[15]

TABLE 2.3

Comparison of Contribution of Industry to GDP,
Selected Countries
(in percent)

Country	Contribution to GDP
Germany	53.9
France	48.1
United Kingdom	45.8
Sweden	45.2
Japan	39.1
Italy	38.9
Canada	38.5
United States	35.8

Source: Organization for Economic Cooperation and Development, "Germany," Economic Surveys (Paris, 1971), pp. 66-67.

Livestock products account for three-fourths of the value of agricultural production. Hog-raising is particularly important in West German agriculture because pork consumption is higher than that of any other meat. In terms of self-sufficiency, West Germany is able to produce about 94 percent of the hogs used for slaughter. Of lesser importance is the production of cattle. Cattle are raised primarily for milk production; however, in recent years, beef production has received more attention. Most cattle are used for dual purposes in that they are also used as draft animals. In the production of beef, veal, and other meat, West Germany is not self-sufficient and must import meat products from other countries. In 1969 imports of meat and meat products amounted to DM 1.7 billion.[16]

The major grains produced in the Federal Republic are wheat, rye, barley, oats, and corn. In terms of physical output, wheat is the most important grain product, with rye second. With respect to the growing of grains, West German farmers practice intensive farming with heavy application of capital and fertilizer. One result is that very high yields are maintained. In comparison with the United States, West German farmers have achieved better results in the production of grains. For example, using 1963-67 as a base period, West Germany averaged 52.4 bushels per acre of wheat harvested compared to 26 bushels for the United States, and 45.6 bushels per acre of rye compared to 20.6 bushels per acre for the United States.[17]

TABLE 2.4

Industrial Production, by Source, West Germany, 1969
(1962 prices)

Industrial Classification	Output (Billion DM)
Basic industries	180
Energy	27
Mining	14
Metallurgy	43
Chemical	83
Construction	13
Metal manufacturing industries	140
Electrotechnical	36
Shipbuilding	3
Other industries	101
Light industries	78
Woodworking	15
Textiles	22
Clothing	12
Leather, shoes, hides	5
Pulp and paper	11
Polygraphic	8
Glass and ceramic	5
Food industries	57
Total	455

Source: Deutscher Bundestag, Materialien zum Bericht zur Lage der Nation 1971, Drucksache VI/1690 (Bonn-Bad Godesberg: Dr. Hans Heger Verlag, 1971), p. 272.

Other agricultural products of importance in the Federal Republic are potatoes, sugar beets, and fruits and vegetables. Potatoes are still one of the major crops grown in West Germany, but their importance has been declining in recent years. The acreage devoted to potatoes has declined to the point that it is about half of what it was in 1955. Higher yields per acre, however, have counterbalanced to some extent the decline in acreage. With respect to fruits and vegetables, production has been increasing in response to consumer demand. But West Germany is far from being self-sufficient in the production of fruit and vegetables in that output accounts for around 57 percent of domestic needs. In 1969 imports of fruits and vegetables accounted for 30 percent of the value of total agricultural imports.[18]

Unlike East German agriculture, with large-scale state and collective farms, the typical West German farm unit is small. In 1969 the bulk of the farms consisted of 10 hectares or less. To a considerable degree through the use of intensive farming methods, the West German farmers have achieved high yields per unit of input. In many cases, the far smaller West German farms have achieved better operating results than the collective and state farms of East Germany. It is necessary to point out, however, that West Germany is one of the world's largest import markets for agricultural commodities. Moreover, there is the problem of surplus workers and inadequate farm incomes. Agriculture contributes less than 4 percent of the GNP but employs around 10 percent of the labor force.[19] More farmers have to leave the land, and farms need to be consolidated in order to achieve better use of economies of scale.

Foreign Trade

Foreign trade is important to the West German economy. In 1969 over one-fifth of the GNP was exported, including those exports that took the form of services of German nationals abroad and income from property held abroad. Imports, including services and income from property held by foreign nationals in West Germany, also amounted to over one-fifth of the GNP. The proportion of exports in the GNP has declined during the 1960s, as has the excess of exports over imports in absolute terms. The external balance-of-payments position has been strong; only in 1965 did the external balance show a deficit, the first since 1950. The balance-of-payments position was strengthened considerably during the late 1960s and early 1970s. While a deficit on current account is accepted to the extent that it reenforces measures adopted to curb domestic inflation, government economic policy has emphasized the importance of bearing in mind the competitive position of the nation's producers on the world markets.

In 1969 the total value of exports, both visible and invisible, amounted to DM 141.5 billion, and the total value of imports, both visible and invisible, amounted to DM 126.3 billion, for a net balance of DM 15.2 billion.[20] The bulk of exports of goods consisted of manufactured products. Exports of machinery and equipment, including automobiles and railway stock, amounted to DM 52.2 billion.[21] Of this total, exports of electrical equipment amounted to DM 24.6 billion, the single most important export. Exports of the chemical industry amounted to DM 14 billion. Other important exports were iron and steel, with a value of DM 8.2 billion; textiles, with a value of DM 4.9 billion; and metal-ware, with a value of DM 4 billion. On the import side, there was more of a concentration on raw materials

THE WEST GERMAN SYSTEM 43

and food products. Imports of food products amounted to DM 15.4 billion compared to exports of DM 2.8 billion. Raw material imports, including petroleum and coal, amounted to DM 22.1 billion compared to exports of DM 6 billion. On the other hand, imports of machinery and equipment amounted to DM 24.7 billion, compared to exports of DM 52.2 billion.

Exports and imports follow similar patterns in that the leading countries in terms of receipts of West German exports are also the leading countries in terms of West German imports. The great bulk of West German exports go to other European countries, particularly those members of the European Economic Community (EEC). Exports to France amounted to DM 15.1 billion while imports amounted to DM 12.7 billion.[22] In terms of trade, German manufactured products were exchanged for French raw materials and foodstuffs. Exports and imports to and from Holland amounted to DM 11.5 billion and DM 11.3 billion, respectively. Again, in terms of trade exports of manufactured goods were exchanged for foodstuffs and raw materials. Exports to the United States amounted to DM 10.6 billion compared to imports of DM 10.3 billion.[23] In terms of trade, there was more of a balanced exchange of manufactured goods. Trade with the Eastern bloc of European countries is of minor importance. Total exports to the Soviet Union, Hungary, and other Eastern European countries amounted to DM 3.6 billion, or less than 3 percent of the total value of exports of goods and services, while total imports from Eastern European countries amounted to DM 3.3 billion.[24]

There is some trade between West and East Germany. Under interzonal agreements between the two countries, East German agricultural products are purchased by West Germany. In particular, pork products have been imported to fill domestic needs. Wheat is another product that is imported through interzonal agreements. Poultry and eggs are also imported from East Germany. East Germany has been able to benefit from trade barriers to countries exporting agricultural products to the EEC, of which West Germany is a member. These countries have exported their products to East Germany, which, in turn, exports its own products to West Germany. According to EEC rules, East Germany is considered a part of West Germany for trade purposes. As a result, products originating in East Germany and shipped to West Germany or other EEC countries are considered to be part of internal trade by the EEC. Although no West German trade figures are available, an East German source shows exports to West Germany of 1.2 billion Valuta Marks and imports of 1.7 Valuta Marks for 1969.[25]

ECONOMIC PLANNING

Virtually all countries have government planning policies of one sort or another to accomplish economic growth through proper resource allocation. An economic plan is supposed to harmonize the economic activities of different sections of society in the interest of optimal economic growth and structural balance. A good plan provides information on two matters. First, it provides a forecast of how an economy should perform in the future. Second, it provides a set of targets that can be obtained through the implementation of necessary measures. Supporters of economic planning contend that it is free from the defects of the unplanned free market economics that existed in the United States and Western Europe prior to World War II.

Economic planning in the Western European countries is primarily of the indicative type. Indicative planning would apply to an economy in which the government indicates a series of economic goals and indirectly stimulates certain economic activities through the budget, taxation, and interest rates to accomplish planning by inducements. It can be viewed as a set of directives or guidelines that help to guide the planning of private industry as well as the public sector of the economy. In France and Japan, planning of the indicative type is an integral part of economic policy and has assumed the character of officially authorized plans, which cover a four- or five-year period. In other countries, notably Sweden, economic planning takes the form of a long-term forecast that is designed to provide information so that relevant economic decisions can be made by public and private enterprises.

Economic planning has not been a fait accompli on postwar German economic policy. Unlike the French economic plans, there have not been any overall growth targets toward which state planners attempt to guide the economy as a whole through the means of specific interventions. There have been certain types of plans, however, which have been applied to various sectors of the economy. For example, in agriculture the so-called Green Plans have been utilized. There also have been annual European Recovery Program (ERP) plans. Funds have been used from this source for economic stabilization purposes. Each year a plan has been prepared for the disposal of ERP funds. The funds have been used as an emergency reserve to finance key sectors in the economy when structural difficulties have arisen.

Recent events have prompted a rethinking in West Germany concerning the role of planning, however. First, a sharp recession in 1967 caused a shift in attitude away from the free market and conservative budgetary and monetary policies, with emphasis on price stability, toward a Keynesian-oriented economic policy that stresses full employment, economic growth, and balanced foreign trade, as well as price stability. One point at which German expenditure policy can be said to have moved in a direction that brings it close to elements of French economic planning is in the adoption of medium-term financial or budgetary planning. This planning, however, is fiscal in nature and is designed to mesh government expenditures more closely with desired economic goals.

A reform of the German budgetary system occurred in 1967. The Bundesrat passed the Law for Promoting Stability and Growth in the Economy (Gesetz zur Förderung der Stabilität und des Wachstums der Wirtschaft). In connection with this law, both houses of parliament gave approval to a required change in the Federal Republic's Basic Law. The provision for independent budgeting processes of the federal government and the states was altered to permit coordination of fiscal and other economic policy actions at different levels of government. The separation of federal and state budgets has heretofore been an important obstacle to an effective countercyclical fiscal policy.

Moreover, the federal budget is supposed to be drawn up within the framework of a five-year financial plan.[26] An investment program with a priority scale has to be included. The plan has to set forth the projected development of expenditures and revenues over the planning period, relating each to the likely development of the economy's resources. The financial plan is prepared by the Federal Ministry of Finance and is adjusted and rolled forward each year. In the event of a weakening in the general level of economic activity, the planning of suitable investment projects is to be accelerated in such a way that their implementation can be started on short notice. Each year a list of investment projects has to be prepared. In addition to the financial plan, the federal government is required to submit to the Bundestag and Bundesrat an annual economic report that includes a declaration of its economic and fiscal policy objectives for the coming year. Thus, a system of medium-term budgetary planning has been introduced in the Federal Republic.

The Medium-Term Fiscal Plan

The medium-term fiscal plan was the offshoot of a study prepared by the Economics Ministry in 1966 as a projection of economic prospects in Germany through 1970 for the EEC. This study was transmitted to all federal ministries and to the states to be used as a common basis for medium-term budget plans. The plan was actually developed for the period 1968-72 and was applied for the first time in the budget estimates for 1969.

The plan consisted of a series of projections or forecasts, as well as a plan of action, for the economy until 1971.[27] The GNP was projected to increase at the rate of 4 percent a year, and private consumption was projected to increase at the same rate. The individual components of investment were expected to increase at a differential rate. Public investment, because of anticipated further heavy demand for infrastructure and social investment, was to increase by 5.5 percent a year, whereas private investment in plant and equipment was to increase by 3.7 percent. For the labor force, an absolute decline was projected, attributable to a decrease in the rate of population growth. Labor productivity was expected to increase by 3.5 percent a year.

The medium-term fiscal plan, however, was more than just a forecast of expected developments. It included an investment program for special social and economic measures involving additional government expenditures of DM 5.3 billion and investment in scientific research amounting to an increase of 16 percent a year.[28] The federal budget formed the basis of the plan in that priorities were marked out for expenditures. Investment programs of public authorities had to be planned on the basis of budgetary projections covering the five-year period of the plan.

The plan gave equal priority to the following economic policy goals: price stability, full employment, stable economic growth, and a balance-of-payments equilibrium. Federal and state budgets were to be drawn up and managed in accordance with these objectives. Expenditures, particularly on investment, were to be adjusted year by year to conform to the economic situation. If aggregate demand was found to be excessive, provision was made in both budgets for allocation of funds to a special cyclical equalization reserve that is held by the Bundesbank. If economic activity showed a decline, additional expenditures would be undertaken from funds available in the cyclical equalization reserve.

In the medium-term fiscal plan for the period 1969-73, GNP was projected to increase at a nominal rate of 6.5 to 7 percent a year.[29] The average yearly growth of total expenditures in the federal budget was expected to be at a rate of 7.5 percent. On the basis of these projections, the following expenditure goals were established for the period of the plan.[30]

1. Social welfare expenditures were projected to increase from DM 23.7 billion in 1969 to DM 31.4 billion in 1973. The average yearly increase was set at 7.3 percent.

2. Expenditures on agriculture were projected to increase from DM 5.9 billion in 1969 to DM 7.9 billion in 1973.

3. Defense expenditures were projected to increase from DM 19 billion in 1969 to DM 23 billion in 1973. The average yearly increase was 4.9 percent.

4. Transportation expenditures were to increase from DM 8.8 billion in 1969 to DM 11.5 billion in 1973.

5. Expenditures on education and scientific research were to increase from DM 2.5 billion in 1969 to DM 5.6 billion in 1973, for an annual increase of 22.1 percent.

6. Funds for housing construction were projected to increase from DM 1.3 billion in 1969 to DM 3 billion in 1973.

In the area of agriculture DM 2.1 billion of additional budget funds were to have been made available in 1970 to compensate farmers for losses attributable to the revaluation of the Deutsche Mark. In addition, an amount of DM 200 million was allocated in 1970 to compensate for inventory losses attributable to the currency revaluation.

It is to be emphasized that the medium-term plan is rolled forward each year. In other words, the base year is moved ahead one year for each plan. Within the framework of the budget plan, the federal government can vary personal and corporate income tax rates by 10 percent. It can also introduce special depreciation allowances for a limited period and similarly restrict allowances if need be. Thus, planning in West Germany is limited to the use of the federal budget as a device to counter undesirable cyclical movements. In particular, the plan is based on medium-term investment programs developed by the various departments of the federal government. Also, any rise in federal expenditures, outside of debt repayment, is supposed to correspond roughly to the rate at which GNP grows during the plan period.

SUMMARY

The Federal Republic of Germany was formed from the postwar division of the German Third Reich. Like the United States, it possesses a federal system of government. The three main levels of government are the Bund (federal government), the Länder (state governments), and the Gemeinden (local governments or communes). Although principles of federalism are supposed to apply to the creation of the Federal Republic, it can be said that most basic powers are concentrated in the hands of the federal government either through exclusive or concurrent legislative jurisdiction. In the field of exclusive federal legislative jurisdiction, state legislation is permitted only insofar as it is expressly authorized by law. The federal government has also made wide use of its concurrent legislative powers, particularly in the area of public welfare.

The mixed economy typifies the economic system that is prevalent in West Germany today. There is both public and private ownership of the agents of production, with the latter type of ownership being dominant. Although the market is the primary allocator of resources, the indivisible character of most social goods makes it manifestly impossible to use this mechanism, which is firmly rooted in the act of individual exchange. As a consequence, economic resources are allocated to public use through the medium of taxation. So when taxation is taken into consideration, more than one-third of the GNP is diverted from the private to the public sector.

Since the postwar division of Germany, the Federal Republic has succeeded in regaining its position as the outstanding industrial country of the Western European mainland and a major world industrial power, ranking fourth behind the United States, the Soviet Union, and Japan in the amount of GNP. Although its resource base is modest by some standards in variety and, with a few notable exceptions, in amount, its industrial development has been exceptional. Its industrial expansion during the postwar period has been especially marked in those branches of industry that were predominantly located in the eastern sections prior to partition, specifically, electric power, heavy chemicals, fertilizers, precision and light instruments, synthetic fibers, paper, glass, and ceramics.

Unlike France, Germany has not utilized economic planning during the postwar period. In part, this may be attributed to the fact that German economic policy reflected the psychology of a people thoroughly disillusioned by the overt public controls imposed by the Nazis and, in part, to the social market policy adopted by the Adenauer and Erhard governments, which involved the belief that maximization of welfare could be achieved by means of a system in which the role of the government is limited to enforcing competition in the private sector of the economy.

The Law Promoting Stability and Growth, however, which was promulgated in 1967, marked a new era in German economic policy. Among other things, the law provides that the federal government must plan its budgets for periods of five years and must prepare an investment program with a priority scale. A series of medium-term fiscal plans have been developed. The objective is to accomplish a balanced rate of economic growth. The first plan went into effect for the period 1968-72. It was applied for the first time in the budget estimates for 1969, however.

CHAPTER 3

ORGANIZATION OF INDUSTRY AND AGRICULTURE IN WEST GERMANY

INTRODUCTION

In the mixed economies that exist in the Western European countries, Japan, and the United States, most of industry is privately owned. In these economies, individual producers are free to produce whatever they wish, for whomever they wish, and however they wish, subject to certain limitations. The key regulator in a mixed system is market price competition in conjunction with the pursuit of profit. There is, however, considerable governmental regulation and control and various other elements that hinder the perfect functioning of objective market forces. A set of rules have been established over time to provide a framework within which private enterprise functions; they modify the operation of the market. Together with government expenditure and taxation, the rules of government supplement the price system in directing the operation of the market economies.

Within the modified market economies that exist today, the role of banking and government tax and expenditure policies exercise an enormous leverage on the operations of individual producers. The activities of the central banks influence the money supply, interest rates, and foreign exchange rates. Such activities are designed to achieve defined national goals, such as the reduction of price inflation, the flow of foreign trade, and the rate of economic growth. Tax policy can be used to channel productive efforts into desirable roles. For example, large depletion allowances available to mineral producers have encouraged such production. The exemption of exports from certain domestic taxes has the effect of stimulating the development of export-oriented industries. Government expenditures contribute to the overall level of aggregate demand. A large part of these expenditures are for goods produced by private enterprise.

Given the above influences in a modified market economy, it is through a free but interdependent enterprise system rather than a comprehensive national plan that the critical production functions are performed, coordinated, and integrated on a national scale. The interaction between the competitive price system and the pursuit of profits tends automatically to keep economic mistakes within reasonable limits. This joint economic regulator rather effectively solves the key economic problems of what and how to produce, how much of each item to produce, and for whom to produce. It tends to ensure that production is carried on in a reasonably efficient manner. Moreover, it tends to encourage innovation in products and processes, since such activity often results in a competitive advantage for the innovating producer.

There are also imperfections in the modified market economies. For example, distribution of income can be so unequal that the wants of many persons are unsatisfied. To a considerable extent, however, this problem has been solved through income redistribution measures, even though there is often interference with objective market forces. The modified market economies have an additional problem in that they are typically democratic states, and the voters inject substantial ethical content into the system, often at the expense of efficiency. Hence, the support of inept small farmers by government subsidies and protection of certain industries from competition may have the effect of putting too many resources into a given industry, causing redundant capacity, higher than necessary prices, and general economic inefficiency. To some extent ethical considerations have hampered the effective operation of market forces.

ORGANIZATION OF INDUSTRY

During the period 1870-1914 Germany was transformed from a basically agrarian to a predominantly industrial society. This development can be attributed to a primary degree to the unification of the German states into one nation and to the Franco-Prussian War of 1870 that gave Germany recognition as a world power. Even before the unification of Germany, a solid base for industrial development had been laid. An extensive railway system had been built; a modern banking system was in existence; and German industry had provided advanced leadership in the chemical industry. But it was under the economic and political leadership of Bismarck that Germany developed into a modern industrial nation. Although in general Bismarck's domestic politics were repressive with respect to liberal political parties, particularly the Social Democrats, he was able to maintain and harness the support of the business and industrial elements in society. Under

Bismarck, a paternalistic and authoritarian government developed to set a pattern that prevailed up through Hitler's Third Reich. Germany became a system of mixed private and public ownership. During the Bismarck era, much of the railroad system was nationalized, and foundations were laid upon which the war economy of a later period could be built.

An interdependent relationship developed between the banking system and industry. The main function of banks before World War I was to serve as institutions for the financing of industry. Loans, usually on a long-term basis, were made by the banks to industrial and commercial enterprises. Banks also served as agents for the placement of issues of stocks and bonds. Over the years prior to the war the banks also acquired substantial holdings of corporate securities. Thus, the banks through their control of corporate stock were in a position to exercise control at stockholders' meetings. Policy decisions were often dictated by bank officials who were active on the board of directors of industrial corporations. Conversely, the industrial concerns were represented on the boards of the banks with which they had business connections. This interlocking pattern existed for the major banks and many large industrial firms up to World War II.

Another development that occurred during the period 1870-1914 was participation on the part of government in business. Public ownership of the railroads, as mentioned above, was expanded during Bismarck's chancellorship. Full unification occurred in 1919. The state also owned and operated iron mines and blast furnaces. The postal, telephone, and telegraph systems were state owned. Mixed public-private ownership and operation of industry existed in a number of fields. This arrangement was used for public utilities and municipal transportation. In banking, a mixed relationship also existed. The Reichsbank, the central bank of Germany, was privately owned in that its stock was owned by private individuals; its management, however, was appointed by the state. There were also individual state banks, including the Prussian State Bank (Preussische Seehandlung). Most savings banks were owned by the municipalities.

Following the defeat of Germany in 1918, the Weimar Republic was created and remained in existence from 1919 to 1933. During this period, the mixture of private and public ownership and management of certain industries was continued. Moreover, there was an increase in the role of the public sector. In housing, the state and municipal governments supported the construction of housing through the use of loans and grants. The central government (Reich) assumed a dominant role in banking. The Reich established a credit bank of its own, the Reichskreditgesellschaft, and the state governments created special banks to provide money for housing construction.

The world depression that began in 1929 was a prime contributor to the eventual dominance of banking by the central government. A banking crisis occurred in 1931, a moratorium was declared, and most major German banks were reorganized with government financial assistance. The Reichsbank provided these banks with new share capital, providing the central government with control over almost all of the banking system.

Industrial Organization in the Third Reich

In 1933 the National Socialism of Adolf Hitler became a fait accompli. One base of Hitler's support came from bankers and industrialists who hoped that there would be a turnabout from the economic policies of the Weimar Republic. They were soon to be disappointed, however. The National Socialists had been in power for about a year when their official organizations for controlling production were set up. Industry was placed under the control of an economics minister, and many restrictions were placed on private enterprise.

Mergers and cartels became a standard form of business development during the Third Reich. There was a strong, government-sponsored concentration movement in industry and business. Thousands of small industrialists and businessmen were eliminated, and many new combinations and cartels were formed. Large firms were assigned the responsibility for founding and operating the new firms and industries made necessary by the national self-sufficiency program. It was felt by the Nazis that cartels would result in greater industrial proficiency, and power over the cartel arrangement was transferred to the minister of economic affairs, who could decide whether the arrangement was desirable. The minister was given the power to make outside firms join cartels, and he could prohibit the establishment of new firms.

When the National Socialists came into power in Germany in 1933, they adopted economic planning to cope with the depression. The first four-year plan was introduced in May 1933 and was designed to deal with the problem of unemployment. Included in the plan were public works, subsidies for the employment of older workers, marriage loans, subsidies to stimulate building construction, restrictions on dismissals, and the reintroduction of compulsory military service. Expenditures on a national program of rearmament were also included in the plan.

In the fall of 1936, the second four-year plan was introduced. It, too, dealt with a specific problem, namely the need to make Germany self-sufficient so that it could wage war. The aims of the plan were to increase the production of raw materials, to increase agricultural production in general and especially in those lines that produced raw materials for industry, to distribute labor with special regard for the needs of military and armaments industries, and to control and distribute foreign exchange. To facilitate these objectives, many phases of German economic life were brought under rigid economic control. The government organized controls over prices and wages, international trade, and credit and investment operations.

Almost from the beginning of their regime, the Nazis attempted to control prices. In 1936 fear of a possible rapid price rise led the government to freeze all prices, and thereafter, until the end of the regime, no price changes were allowed without official sanction. Thus, the function of prices in a market system was subverted to the requirements of the state. German factory owners were told what to produce, how much to produce, and how to produce it. Industry had to function within the framework of economic planning, in which the objective was to make the Reich as nearly self-sufficient as possible. The operation of industry was directed toward this end.

Postwar Allied Occupation Policies Toward Industry

Postwar Allied occupation policies were aimed at breaking the strength of monopolies and cartels. Deconcentration measures were taken in the coal and steel industry, the chemical industry, and banking.[1] This action was taken to reduce the degree of monopoly that existed under the Nazis. In particular, the German chemical industry occupied a key position in the development of the Reich's war potential. Here were developed and produced the substitutes for the war materials that were lacking in Germany. The chemical industry was not only an important contributor in the technological aspects of making war but also led a prominent and successful front in the economic warfare that was waged by Germany through cartel agreements and other means long before armed hostilities started. The chemical industry represented one element in the economy that was second to none in terms of developing the German war-making ability.

Decartelization policies were also followed by the Allies. The development of cartels predated the Nazi period, however. Cartels epitomized the development of monopoly capitalism in Germany, particularly in the basic heavy goods branches of industry. The trend toward concentration of economic power was almost completely unopposed in Germany. The legislation of the Weimar Republic for cartel regulation did not have the desired effect of curtailing cartel power. Economic and legal developments during and after World War I stimulated the growth of vertical and horizontal combines.

When the Nazis assumed power in 1933, they inherited an economy in which both basic and supplementary industries were dominated by cartels and syndicates as well as by combines. This concentration of economic power, however, formed the foundation for the economic structure created by the Nazis. From the very beginning, this structure was planned with a view to mobilization for war.

More extreme forms of cartels, such as sales syndicates and market quotas, were eliminated by the Allies. Firms, like Krupp, that had been ordered to divest themselves of parts of their industrial empires, however, were able to avoid the implementation of these orders. A shift away from punitive measures occurred among the Allies. For one thing, it was felt that the policies of the military governments were paralyzing the German economy. Political considerations were also a factor in that relations between the Western Allies and the Soviet Union had worsened by 1947. There was the feeling that it was necessary to have an economically strong Germany to serve as a buffer against the expansion of Communism. The Korean War was also a contributing factor, particularly with respect to the revival of the Krupp firm, because it became necessary for the United States to purchase armaments from Germany.

In banking, the Allies broke up the three major banks that had dominated the prewar German banking system. These banks were the Deutsche Bank, the Dresdner Bank, and the Commerzbank. Each bank had been a part of the concentration of economic power that existed before the war. The banks exercised a considerable degree of control over industrial firms through the ownership of stock. They had also played an important role in the financing of the war. It was felt by the Allies that the banks had exerted an influence on trade and industry that rendered any attack on restrictive business practices nugatory. Thus, the banks were dismembered within each Western zone of occupation. The three banks were eventually restored to their initial position, however, and continue to function today under the same names.

Postwar Development of German Industry

Postwar German business development has been marked by a return to earlier patterns under which large sectors of the economy rest in the hands of a small number of business firms and bankers. To some extent, ambivalence has existed in the domestic policy of the German government toward business. A policy of free markets was adopted under the leadership of Ludwig Erhard, who felt that Germany should rely on market forces instead of controls to accomplish recovery from the war. Competition was to be the order of the day. Even though official government policy sought to prevent mergers and consolidation, however, progress was limited to some extent because of the opposition of the Christian Democrats' political supporters in industry. So the free market policy was not uniformly applied to all sectors of German industry.

The Law Against Restraints of Competition

The opposition of the government to cartels was manifested in the Law Against Restraints of Competition (Gesetz gegen Wettbewerbsbeschränkungen), which was passed in 1957 and subsequently amended in 1965. The Law Against Restraints of Competition did several things with respect to cartels. It prohibited horizontal and vertical restrictive agreements between groups, with certain exceptions. For example, certain types of horizontal agreements, such as agreements necessitated by a structural crisis in a particular sector of the economy and agreements that were deemed good for the economy as a whole and the public welfare, were exempted. There were exceptions to vertical agreements, particularly with respect to the resale price maintenance of branded goods as long as the products concerned were open to price competition. The law also denied cartel agreement the aid of the courts.

The law also created a Federal Cartel Authority (Bundeskartellamt). Again, the ambivalence on the part of the government toward economic concentration showed through in that the authority was given little enforcement power. One function of the authority was the supervision of cartels. All cartels had to register with it. The authority, however, was given little power to act on mergers, where the enterprises concerned were in a position to take over a share of 20 percent or more of the market for a specific product. With respect to individual enterprises that had no competition or were not exposed to any substantial competition with regard to a particular category of goods, the authority could take court action if they abused their position.

In 1965 the Law Against Restraints of Competition was amended. New powers were given to the Federal Cartel Authority. Details of horizontal and vertical agreements on the part of business groups had to be filed with the authority. It was made easier for the authority to take action against sole-agency agreements that unduly restrict entry to the market. In addition, all mergers in which the participating firms together employed 10,000 persons or more at any time during the previous year, or had a turnover of DM 500 million and over, or had a balance of DM 2 billion or over in the last completed business year, have to register with the authority.

In general, the federal government has been permissive with respect to antimonopoly legislation. This may be attributed in large part to German entry into the EEC. The position is that monopoly of a product in Germany does not need to be regarded seriously provided, within the limits of the EEC, several producers are going to remain in competition. It would be disadvantageous unilaterally to control mergers and concentrations as well as restrictive practices if elsewhere in the same economic area other governments are actively encouraging them. Indeed, to prevent concentration in certain areas may be to preclude the economies of scale that are one of the chief advantages of the formation of the EEC.

One example of this point is the policy of the French government with respect to large-scale enterprises. During the last few years mergers have melded the country's leading steel, glass, and electronics industries. In January 1972 the largest French industrial combine of all, with $2.7 billion in annual sales, was formed when a new stock issue united two companies, Pechiney and Ugine Kuhlmann, that dominate Europe in the production of aluminum, stainless steel, specialty steels, and nonferrous metals such as titanium, zirconium, and tantalum. The combine plans to take advantage of a worldwide marketing and manufacturing network set up by Pechiney. In the United States, Pechiney controls Howmet Corporation, an aluminum maker and fabricator that had sales of $250 million in 1970. The Pechiney-Ugine Kuhlmann combine is negotiating with the Soviet Union to help design and build a $500-million aluminum complex in Siberia that will have an output equal to nearly half of Pechiney's worldwide capacity.

Industrial Concentration in Germany

The point has been made that in general there has been a reversion to the concentration of market power in the hands of a few large firms in major industries, despite the efforts of German neoliberals to promote a social market economy. It cannot be said that this in itself is good or bad. There is a trend toward large-scale industrial enterprises that is prevalent in both the capitalist and socialist countries of the world. Certainly, there is nothing in the economies of the Soviet Union and East Germany to indicate a policy of encouraging competition between small firms. In comparing the German and French economies since the end of World War II, the French government has encouraged bigness on the part of enterprises, whether they are privately or publicly owned. In part this policy may be considered as a reaction to the American industrial challenge, and in part the policy is grounded on the belief that large-scale enterprise operations bring about economies of scale.

The purpose of Table 3.1 is to present a breakdown of West German industry on the basis of the total number of enterprises and

TABLE 3.1

Breakdown of Number of Firms and Workers
in West German Industry, 1968

Firm Size by Number of Workers	Number of Firms	Number of Workers
1-9	43,298	162,826
10-49	32,183	771,753
50-99	10,050	704,966
100-199	6,567	921,184
200-499	4,672	1,438,376
500-999	1,561	1,073,453
1,000 and over	1,152	3,137,499
Total	99,483	8,210,057

Source: Statistisches Bundesamt, Statistisches Jahrbuch für die Bundesrepublik Deutschland, 1970 (Wiesbaden: W. Kohlhammer Verlag, 1970), pp. 190-91.

the number of workers. The extent of industrial concentration is considerable. In 1968 approximately 1 percent of all industrial enterprises employed close to 40 percent of the total industrial labor force.[2] This concentration of employment was heaviest in the capital-goods industry. In the electrotechnical industry, more than one-half of the workers were employed by firms with 1,000 or more workers.[3] In industries manufacturing transportation equipment more than 80 percent of the workers were employed by firms with 1,000 or more employees. In the manufacture of machinery, including machine tools, 185 firms out of 7,073 firms employed 50 percent of the labor force. In the chemical industry, 94 firms out of a total of 4,859 firms employed 60 percent of the labor force. The four industries—chemical, machinery, transportation, and electrotechnical—contained more than one-half of all firms with 1,000 or more workers.

The importance of the large enterprise of 1,000 or more workers is reflected in data involving contributions to gross domestic investment. In 1966, these enterprises contributed around 60 percent of total investment.[4] The most important concentration of investment by large firms was in the chemical industry, with transportation and machinery ranking second and third.

Table 3.2 presents the 15 largest business enterprises in terms of volume of sales in 1970. These enterprises are concentrated into four groups—chemicals, cars and trucks, electrical equipment, and iron

TABLE 3.2

Fifteen Largest West German Firms, Classified by Sales

Firm	Product	Volume of Sales (million U.S. dollars)
Volkswagenwerk	Cars, trucks	4,314
Siemens	Electrical equipment	3,214
Farbwerke Hoechst	Chemicals	3,167
Farben Bayer	Chemicals	3,041
Daimler-Benz	Cars, trucks	3,020
Thyssen-Huette	Iron, steel	2,973
Badische-Anilin	Chemicals	2,874
AEG-Telefunken	Electrical equipment	2,334
Kloechner	Machinery	2,268
VEBA	Holding company	2,202
Ruhrkokle AG	Coal	2,077
Mannesmann	Mining, iron, steel	2,012
Gutehoffnungshuette	Iron, steel	1,733
Krupp	Steel machinery	1,588
Metallgesellschaft	Mining, chemicals	1,530

Source: Data provided by German-American Chamber of Commerce.

and steel. It is necessary to point out that some of these enterprises form a part of a group. For example, the enterprise Thyssen-Huette forms a part of the Thyssen Gruppe, which is West Germany's major steel producer. The true concentration of enterprises into business combines is not reflected in the table. Neither is the extent of government ownership or participation through stockholding reflected in the table, even though government holdings of stocks in various enterprises is extensive. The holding company, VEBA, is owned in part by the federal government, although some of its shares were made available to the public.

In 1967, 13 of the 50 largest industrial firms operating outside of the United States were located in West Germany. As measured in terms of sales volume, two companies, Volkswagenwerk, with total sales of $2.3 billion, and Siemens, with total sales of $2 billion, ranked seventh and ninth, respectively.[5] German law, however, requires stock companies to consolidate only domestic enterprises in which the parent holds over one-half of the capital. Thus, a number of German companies exclude foreign subsidiaries from their consolidated sales. Hence, to some extent the total sales picture for many large German companies is distorted.

Other West German companies listed in the top 20 largest firms were Farbwerke Hoechst, a producer of chemicals and pharmaceuticals, which ranked fourteenth; Thyssen-Huette, an iron and steel producer, which ranked fifteenth; Daimler-Benz, an automobile manufacturer, which ranked seventeenth; and Farben Bayer, a producer of chemicals, which ranked eighteenth. As stated, most of the large German firms are concentrated in four groups—chemicals, cars and trucks, electrical equipment, and iron and steel. In chemicals, three of the five largest chemical producers in terms of sales volume were West German firms. In sales volume of automobiles, Volkswagenwerk was the leading producer, while Daimler-Benz ranked third. The largest iron and steel producer was a West German firm.

In comparison to other countries, 25 of the 200 largest companies were West German firms, whereas 53 were British firms, 43 Japanese, and 23 French. In a ranking of 1 to 100, 25 of the firms were British, 18 German, 17 Japanese, and 14 French. Among the top 25 firms, however, the picture changes somewhat in that 7 of the firms were British, or have joint British-Dutch ownership as is the case of Royal Dutch-Shell, 6 were German, 5 were Japanese, and 2 were French. The concentration of German firms in terms of sales volume indicates to some extent the importance of the large producer in the chemical and heavy goods industries to the West German economy. The combined sales of the four largest German companies, however, were less than those of Royal Dutch-Shell.

In 1970 Volkswagenwerk climbed to third among the 200 largest industrial firms outside of the United States, with total sales of $4.3 billion, while Siemens, with total sales of $3.2 billion ranked tenth.[6] Four German companies—Farbwerke Hoechst, Farben Bayer, Daimler-Benz, and Thyssen-Huette—were also among the top 20 firms. One significant shift that occurred during the period 1967-70, however, was the change in the position of the Japanese firms relative to other firms. In 1970 two Japanese firms, Nippon Steel and Hitachi, were among the 10 largest firms, while 51 Japanese firms were listed in the 200 largest companies, compared to 26 for West Germany. Also, for the first time since records have been kept Japan supplanted the United Kingdom as the most heavily represented country in the list of 200 largest firms.

The position of West German firms relative to industrial firms in other Western European countries was enhanced over the period 1967-70, both in terms of sales volume and in ranking of firms. In comparing 1970 to 1969 sales, the 25 German firms listed for both years had a sales gain of 27.3 percent, compared to an 11.9 percent gain for British firms listed for both years. The percentage sales gains for 1969 over 1968 using the same number of German and British firms were 19.6 percent and 7.2 percent, respectively. German comparisons with French firms were also favorable. French firms' sales gains for 1970 over 1969 were 12.2 percent, compared to the 27.3 percent for the German firms. The French position was affected by the fact that one of its largest firms, Citroen, was a money loser over the period.

In terms of ranking based on sales volume, eight West German firms were listed among the top 25 in 1970, compared to six in 1970. Six British firms, two Italian firms, and one firm each from the Netherlands, France, and Switzerland were also in the top 25. In general, there was a movement upward in rank for the German firms in 1970 over 1967 and a movement downward for firms of other European countries. For example, Volkswagenwerk went from seventh place in 1967 to third place in 1970, while Daimler-Benz went from seventeenth to twelfth place.

Of the various branches of West German industry, it is the chemical industry, the electrotechnical industry, and the automobile and truck industry that have made the most progress over the last decade. Whereas the industrial production index has increased from 1962 to 1969 by an average of 53 percent, the production index of the chemical industry rose by 127 percent, that of the electrotechnical industry by 81 percent, and that of the motor vehicle industry by 75 percent.[7] In contrast, the increase in the machine-building industry, which has the largest share of exports, increased by only 31 percent over the period. The textile industry increased its production by 32 percent during the period. With an increase in production of 55 percent, the iron and steel industry was just above the average increase.

Table 3.3 presents the sales volume of major German industries for 1968. This turnover is presented under the basic categories of basic materials and production-goods industries, capital-goods industries, consumer-goods industries, and food and fine fare industries.

The State and Industry

Business is affected in many ways by the activities of government. Government provides the institutional foundation upon which business rests, the legal framework within which it functions, and many of the instruments through which its activities are carried on. The economic system within which business functions is shaped by the government; the character of its performance depends on decisions that are made by government. The demand for the products of business and the nature of its costs are influenced by public regulations,

TABLE 3.3

Sales Turnover in West German Industry, 1967
(million DM)

Industry Group	Sales
Mining	12,104
Basic materials and production-goods industries	124,297
Building materials	11,685
Iron and steel	21,317
Chemicals	42,081
Nonferrous metals	20,425
Other	28,789
Capital-goods industries	146,819
Machinery	46,846
Transportation vehicles	27,209
Electrotechnical	35,404
Iron, tin, and metalware	15,495
Other	21,865
Consumer-goods industries	71,342
Wood processing	5,510
Printing	7,799
Textile	20,148
Clothing	11,589
Other	26,296
Food and fine fares	63,041
Food	54,232
Tobacco	8,809
Total sales	416,637

Source: Statistisches Bundesamt, Statistisches Jahrbuch für die Bundesrepublik Deutschland, 1970 (Wiesbaden: W. Kohlhammer Verlag, 1970), p. 183.

by the character of public expenditures, and by the types of taxes that are used in raising revenues to finance expenditures. Its expectations of profit or loss depend to some extent on the policies adopted by central banking authorities in controlling the volume of credit and on those pursued by government in balancing its budget, accumulating a surplus, or running a deficit.

    The federal government exercises a degree of control over industry in several ways: through the national budget, which absorbs and disburses a large part of the national income; through tax incentives, which have been designed to stimulate savings and investment; through functions that are carried out by private enterprise in some countries but are performed by publicly owned enterprises in Germany; and through a high degree of administrative authority wielded by government agencies. Intervention in economic affairs, however, is a tradition that predates the present government by a considerable time period. Bismarck used state intervention to make Germany a world power. During the Hitler period, state intervention was carried to its ultimate extreme in order to prepare the economy for war. Actually, the postwar attempt to create a more liberal free market economy represents a break with past traditions and a reaction to extreme state controls.

Expenditure Policies

In terms of fiscal leverage, the public sector of the West German economy contributes significantly to aggregate expenditures and the growth of output. In 1970 total expenditures of the federal, state, and local governments amounted to DM 244.6 billion.[8] The impact of these outlays on the level of aggregate demand cannot be minimized for the reason that purchasing power, employment, inflation potential, and the rate of economic growth are affected. Government expenditures are a part of total outlays on goods and services provided by industry. Purchases by the public sector provide a large and, in some cases, dominant component of the demand for products of industries, such as mining and construction.

A case in point is housing, for it is a major area of government support. An acute need after World War II was the repair and construction of residential housing. Housing for the refugees from East Germany and other areas was also needed. To encourage the construction of housing, tax incentives and direct subsidies were offered by all levels of government. For example, newly built homes were exempted from the local real estate tax. Generous depreciation allowances were provided for the construction of houses and apartments, and rents for many dwellings were subsidized. Loans at subsidized interest rates as low as 1 percent per annum were also made to encourage housing construction.

All levels of government continue to be active in financing and subsidizing houses. Public support on the part of the federal government alone has averaged around DM 4 billion a year.[9] Housing construction continues to be supported out of subsidies financed out of general tax revenues, interest subsidies, and accelerated depreciation allowances. Government-subsidized housing has contributed to a higher level of demand than would otherwise exist in the housing industry. Tax revenues have been channeled into housing investment, reflecting the postwar priorities of German fiscal policy. This means that the average German is subsidizing, to some extent, the cost of his housing through the taxes he pays to the various levels of government.

Mention must also be made of the fiscal and monetary policies of the federal government that are used for demand management purposes. Increases or decreases in expenditure, revenue, and the money supply have either an expansion or a contraction effect on the level of economic activity. In particular, the Stabilization Law of 1967 is a hallmark of fiscal policy in that it established a policy that is designed to smooth out the fluctuations in the level of economic activity. Four goals—price level stability, full employment, equilibrium in the balance of payments, and a steady rate of economic growth— were established with equal priorities, and fiscal and monetary policies are subverted to achieve these ends. Budget and monetary policies from the period 1967-71 reflect this fact. Increases in investment budgetary expenditures in 1967 and 1968 stimulated the level of aggregate demand, and industry was one of the beneficiaries. Later, as the economy recovered from the recession and boom conditions prevailed, more restrictive fiscal and monetary policies were utilized. The rediscount rate was raised to its highest level ever, and the money supply was reduced through changes in reserve requirements. Higher interest rates and a reduction in the increase of government expenditures had a contractionary impact on the level of aggregate demand. This, of course, had an effect on industry in terms of the cost of borrowing and the volume of demand.

Tax Policies

It is generally recognized that economic growth can stem from a number of sources: a general advance in technology, mass education, or improvement in the quality of the labor force. One of the main sources of economic growth, however, is investments, which is required not only to increase the total stock of equipment and buildings but also to allow labor to be employed on increasingly productive jobs as old plants and machinery are replaced by new. Thus, to stimulate investment, tax devices have been used as an instrument of economic policy in the Western market economies and Japan. All sorts of liberalized depreciation schemes, investment allowances, and tax exemptions have been tried. Tax incentives have been used as a macroeconomic device, available to all industries, or as a microeconomic device, available to some industries but not to others.

The effect of tax policies on industry is obvious. Incentives in the form of accelerated depreciation or investment credits have the result of decreasing the base of taxable income. A reward is gained if a specific function is performed. Tax incentives can be used to influence the location of industry. Normally, in a laissez-faire economy, industry would locate in those areas in which it could make the greatest return on its investment. Market factors rather than the conscious efforts of the government would determine the location of industry. Moreover, governmental intervention to influence industrial location would be opposed on the grounds that efficient allocation of resources would be hindered.

Tax incentives have been widely used in West Germany, particularly during the period following the end of World War II.[10] Export incentives were provided to make the German economy competitive in the international markets. Incentives were also provided to assist the rehabilitation of certain industries, such as the shipbuilding industry, that were damaged during the war. The German government continued to intervene intensively in favor of investment and exports during the period after the currency reform, until the basis for growth and stability had been achieved. In the following period, lasting until about 1962, many incentives were removed. Since 1962 those incentives that exist are designed to achieve specific objectives, such as the location of industry in West Berlin and the development of certain problem regions within the boundaries of the Federal Republic.

Accelerated depreciation is one type of incentive. The main advantage of accelerated depreciation is that it reduces the tax burden on a firm, at least on a short-term basis. It is also true that a firm will be able to pay off an investment project in a shorter period of time. This means a significant reduction in risk and uncertainty, both of which increase with the life of an asset. This factor serves to stimulate investment by raising cash flow and present value and by lowering the discount for uncertainty. Accelerated depreciation is also equivalent to an interest-free loan. That is, since the firm is not required to pay the tax during the immediate period, it has the use of a greater supply of funds, interest free, which it would not have had without the depreciation allowance.

In general, accelerated depreciation has been granted by the federal government to accomplish various microeconomic objectives. One example is the aid given to industries that locate in West Berlin. A desired objective is to create employment opportunities for residents of the city. A special depreciation allowance can be claimed for fixed assets that form part of a business enterprise located in West Berlin. In addition to the Berlin inducement, accelerated depreciation can be used for the following purposes:[11]

1. Investment in facilities designed to prevent water or air pollution—an initial allowance of 50 percent in addition to normal linear depreciation is permitted.

2. Investment in research and development facilities, including buildings used for these purposes—an initial allowance of 50 percent for movable assets and 30 percent for buildings, which may be spread over a period of five years, is permitted.

3. Investments of enterprises that are located near the border of the Iron Curtain—allowances of 50 percent of the cost of movable assets and 30 percent of the cost of fixed assets are permitted within a period of two years.

4. Investments in coal and iron ore mining industries—in addition to normal linear depreciation, amounts equal to 30 percent of the cost of buildings and 50 percent of the cost of plant and machinery may be deducted.

In addition there are tax-free reserves designed to encourage investment in developing countries.[12] An initial allowance of 15 percent of the investment is granted in the year it is made. Tax-free reserves may be created up to 50 percent of the remainder of the investment. The investment may include either the provision of capital or the supply of machinery or other depreciable assets, and the enterprise must be one considered suitable for the development of the economy in question. The reserve remains tax free for six years; after this period it must be brought into charge for tax in six equal annual installments.

Accelerated depreciation may also be used as an antirecessionary measure. It was used for the first time during the recession of 1967. The purpose was to stimulate an increase in investment with a concomitant effect upon the level of employment. Additional depreciation to the extent of 10 percent of cost for movable property and 5 percent for buildings was allowed for. The use of accelerated depreciation as a countercyclical instrument was limited, however, for it was replaced in 1969 by an investment credit.

Government Ownership and Regulation of Business

Reference has already been made to the contribution of the public sector to the West German economy. Government ownership of industry is extensive. This does not follow from a conscious policy of nationalization, however, for government ownership of industry predates Bismarck. In Prussia, state ownership of mines existed until 1865 when a mining law did away with state operations. Also in Prussia, ownership of the railroads was taken over in 1876, and the other German states followed suit. Government expansion into industry had nothing to do with socialist doctrine. In fact, one paramount reason for state ownership of industry was the desire to develop a strong and viable economy that could compete with success against other Western powers. The desire to make Germany militarily strong was another reason, particularly with respect to state control of the railway system.

Government ownership of industry is partially concentrated in areas where state ownership is traditional. For example, telephone and postal communications and railway transportation are supplied by public enterprises. In addition, various public utilities, and to some extent bank services, are also owned and supplied by the public sector. Government ownership, however, also extends to areas that are the domain of private enterprise in the United States. Although the federal government has divested itself of a part of some industries, its ownership of others remains substantial. It is estimated that the federal government owns over two-thirds of aluminum production, one-third of iron ore mining, one-fourth of coal production, and one-fifth of shipbuilding.[13] Its ownership is also significant in the oil, natural gas, and petroleum industries. It is also estimated that the federal government owns commercial assets valued at more than DM 4 billion, including stock in more than 3,000 enterprises.[14] Almost all of these properties, government owned before World War II, were inherited by the present government.

Participation on the part of the federal government in business is channeled primarily through several holding companies. One of them, Vereinigte Elektrizitäts und Bergwerke, A.G. (VEBA) controls subsidiaries that produce coal, lignite, and coke. Another holding company, Vereinigte Industrienunternehmen, A.G. (VIAG) holds interests in firms producing steel, aluminum, and chemicals. A third holding company, A.G. für Berg und Hüttenbetriebe, has control over coal mining, transportation, and engineering firms. The federal government also controls titles to real estate properties through another holding company, Industrie Verwaltungs-Gesellschaft.

The federal government receives income from its holdings in these companies. In 1970 dividends from VEBA amounted to DM 48.4 million, and dividends from VIAG amounted to DM 30.4 million.[15] Total dividends accruing to the federal government from the holding companies amounted to DM 88.6 million. In addition, the federal government receives interest from companies in which it owns either more than 50 percent of the capital or less than 50 percent. Dividends and interest for 1970 amounted to DM 98.9 million; financial support for investment amounted to DM 82.5 million.[16] For the period 1968-71 the federal government contributed DM 96.1 million to finance investment in the Saarbergwerke, A.G. in Saarbrucken.[17]

In 1969 the federal government owned one-fourth or more of the capital stock of 650 companies, some of which were foreign. This ownership usually took one of two forms: indirect ownership and participation through holding companies, such as VEBA and VIAG, and direct ownership of a particular company, such as Lufthansa. Examples of each type of arrangement are presented below.

VEBA is one of the 10 largest companies in West Germany. In 1970, total sales amounted to DM 8.1 billion and total profits amounted to DM 52.3 million.[18] VEBA is a holding company based in Düsseldorf, in which the federal government has a 40 percent interest. It has a controlling interest in the following subsidiaries: Hibernia, in which it controls 100 percent of the capital; Preussische Elektrizitäts, in which it has 86 percent capital ownership; and Hugo Stinnes, in which it controls 98 percent of the capital.[19] A wide variety of industrial and commercial activities are provided by the various companies under the control of VEBA and its subsidiaries. In 1969 the following areas of activity contributed to VEBA's total sales: coal, chemicals, electricity, fertilizers, glass, petroleum, natural gas, trade, and commerce.

The spread of VEBA's activities is considerable. For example, 27.5 percent of the capital of Aral, a major distributor of gasoline, is owned by VEBA-Chemie A.G., which is under the control of Hibernia.[20] Hibernia also owns one-fourth of the capital of Chemische Werke Hüls, an important chemical manufacturer, and one-fourth of the capital stock of Phenol-Chemie, a producer of synthetic fibers. It owns all of the capital of Ruhrglas Glaswerk and 13.3 percent of Ruhrkohle, the eleventh-largest industrial firm in West Germany, based on 1970 sales. VEBA-Chemie and Chemische Werke Hüls together own all of the capital stock of Schoeller, a glass manufacturing company. Preussische Elektrizitäts also has a wide variety of holdings, particularly in utilities. It owns 58 percent of the capital of Thüringer Gasgessellschaft of Cologne, 68 percent of the capital stock of Nordwestdeutsche Kraftwerke of Hamburg, and 77 percent of the capital stock of Hannoversche Verkehrsbetriebe of Hannover. In addition to German firms, VEBA and its subsidiaries also own stock in a number of foreign companies, including several U.S. firms.

VIAG ranked forty-sixth among West German industrial firms in terms of sales in 1970, with a turnover of DM 1.8 billion.[21] It holds interests in firms producing steel, aluminum, and chemicals. The capital stock of VIAG is owned by the federal government and the Reconstruction Loan Corporation (Kreditanstalt für Wiederaufbau), a government financial institution, in a ratio of 84 percent to 16 percent.[22] Through its subsidiary, Vereinigte Aluminium Werke, VIAG holds ownership in most of West Germany's aluminum industry. It controls half of the shares of Aluminium Norf, all of the capital of Aluminium Verwaltung, all of the capital of Ritter Aluminium, and 97 percent of the capital of Nemag Metallhandel.[23] In addition, VIAG owns 70 percent of the capital of Süddeutsche Kalkstickstoff Werke, an electrotechnical company, and 25 percent of Ilseder Hütte, a producer of steel.

Salzgitter, a mining company, ranked thirty-second in terms of sales volume among West German companies in 1970, with sales of DM 2.8 billion.[24] The parent company, Salzgitter Aktiengesellschaft of Salzgitter, possesses an original capital of DM 300 million, all of which is owned by the federal government.[25] Under the parent company are a number of subsidiaries that function both domestically and abroad. Although primarily engaged in the mining and production of coal, iron, and steel, Salzgitter is also engaged in other activities. Through ownership of the Salzgitter Ferngas it is into the production of natural gas, and through ownership of the Salzgitter Maschinen it produces machines and earth-moving equipment. Through other subsidiaries Salzgitter produces equipment for restaurants, kitchens, and canteens. The Salzgitter Verkehrsbetriebe produces rails for the German railway system and equipment for ports and harbors.

There are other German companies in which the German government has capital ownership. Sixteen percent of the capital stock of Volkswagenwerk, the largest industrial firm in Germany, is owned by the government.[26] In 1970 dividends of Volkswagenwerk accruing to the federal government amounted to DM 26.4 million.[27] These dividends, unlike the dividends from VEBA and VIAG, are not listed as revenues in the federal budget. (The dividends are placed in a separate account.) The federal government also owns 74 percent of the capital stock of Saarbergwerke, a mining, chemical, and petroleum-producing concern.[28] In 1970 Saarbergwerke, with gross sales of DM 1.6 billion, ranked fifty-second in size among all German industrial firms.[29] The bulk of Saarbergwerke's revenues comes from the production of coal. It controls a number of subsidiaries, including the Saarland-Raffinerie, a producer of petrochemicals and the Saar-Gummiwerk, a producer of dyes for the automobile industry.

The federal government owns 74.3 percent of the capital of Lufthansa.[30] The Deutsche Bundespost owns 1.8 percent of the capital, and the Deutsche Bundesbahn owns 0.8 percent. Lufthansa, in turn, controls a number of domestic and foreign subsidiaries. Through Lufthansa, the federal government has interests in the Intercontinental Hotel chain in Germany. In 1970 Lufthansa's total sales volume amounted to DM 1.9 billion.[31] The federal government has ownership in the capital of housing construction firms. It owns 64 percent of the capital of Frankfurter Siedlungsgesellschaft and 60 percent of the capital of Deutsche Wohnungsbaugesellschaft of Stuttgart.[32]

In the field of antimonopoly legislation, West Germany has adopted legislation providing for the registration and control of cartels. The purpose of such legislation was to improve the functioning of a competitive market system. As has already been mentioned, however, there is a degree of ambivalence in the end result of the legislation. Cartels are permitted, provided they serve the interest of the economy or the general welfare. On the other hand, cartels are deprived of legal protection, and the Federal Cartel Authority seeks to prevent abuse by market-dominating enterprises. In the main, large-scale enterprises with considerable economic power have emerged.

In addition, there is in Germany what is called "middle estate policy" (Mittelslandspolitik), whose purpose is encouraging the development of small- and medium-sized business firms to serve as a sort of buffer to the large enterprises. The federal and state governments support the middle estate policy through the use of financial support. Grants and guarantees are provided to support research and development. Credits are provided to create new business enterprises. The European Recovery Program Special Fund has been used to provide financial support for small business firms, particularly those locating in regionally depressed areas. Moreover, apart from direct financial assistance, there is an attempt on the part of the federal and state governments to give preference in the placing of public contracts with small- and medium-sized firms. Defense and building contracts, where feasible, are placed with medium and small business units.

Another aspect of the middle estate policy is the use of taxation designed to help small business firms. The value-added tax is a case in point. Business firms with a previous tax-year turnover of less than DM 60,000 are taxed at a rate of 4 percent.[33] This rate is based on the old form of the turnover tax. Business firms may also claim a tax-free exemption of DM 12,000 that is gradually reduced when their annual turnover, including the tax, exceeds DM 40,000.[34] The 4 percent rate is computed on the price including the turnover tax, so that the effective tax rate on the net price is 4.167 percent.

It has been mentioned that West Germany has sold off or reduced to less than 50 percent its interest in many of hundreds of companies, such as Volkswagenwerk, that had come into government hands by the end of the Third Reich. The West German government's remaining majority-owned industrial holdings are mostly unsalable; the largest is Salzgitter, a producer of coal, steel, and machinery that lost $36 million on sales of $819 million in the fiscal year that ended in September 1967.[35] For the fiscal year ending in September 1970 Salzgitter lost $41 million on total sales volume of $784 million.[36] Salzgitter is subsidized to some extent from funds of the federal budget. At the end of 1968 federal government ownership in the capital structure of the company was valued at DM 166 million.[37] In 1970 and 1971 interest payments for Salzgitter paid from the federal budget amounted to DM 5.2 million, whereas investments to improve the infrastructure of the firm amounted to DM 62.4 million of budget funds in 1970 and DM 75 million in 1971.[38]

Subsidies to Business

On several occasions in this chapter reference has been made pertaining to government subsidies in some form that benefit business enterprises. Business has benefited directly from the support given by the government sector to housing. The German transportation system is supported by the payment of operating subsidies, designed to make up the difference between their expenditures and their revenues. The construction as well as the operation of ships is subsidized. Also, as mentioned above, support to various state-controlled enterprises such as Salzgitter comes in the form of subsidies from the federal budget. Support has been given from general government revenues to various types of government-owned or -controlled credit institutions that exist for the purpose of providing capital at favorable interest rates to certain types of business enterprises. Subsidies are also paid in one form or another to the coal industry.

These types of subsidies have generally been made in the form of payments from the budgets of the federal and state budgets. In 1971, for example, subsidies listed as such amounted to DM 6.1 billion out of federal budget expenditures of DM 100.1 billion.[39] More often, however, the federal and state governments have given aid in less overt ways: by selling goods and services for less than they are worth in the marketplace, by buying goods and services for more than they are worth in the marketplace, and by exempting some enterprises from taxes that others must pay. Acting directly, the federal government has subsidized enterprises by sheltering them from the full force of competition and by granting them to some extent the privilege of monopoly.

ORGANIZATION OF AGRICULTURE

As has been mentioned, West German agriculture accounts for less than 4 percent of the GNP but employs around 10 percent of the labor force.[40] Livestock production is the major source of revenue for farmers, accounting for nearly 80 percent of total farm income. In terms of overall farm output, West Germany is only 75 percent self-sufficient in the production of foodstuffs and is on balance one of the world's largest import markets for agricultural products. To an increasing extent there is a reliance on other countries in the EEC to supply foodstuffs and other farm products.

West Germany's most serious agricultural problems are the small size of farms and the fragmentation of landholdings. Although the latter is largely a thing of the past, its effects are still being felt in the farm sector. In the southern and southwestern regions of the country the situation is the worst; not only the land but also the houses and barns have been divided. This is not a recent occurrence; it began 150 years ago when Napoleonic law became the basis of inheritance. According to this law, all children had equal rights to the family property when the household head died. Thus, a farm was divided into enough pieces to give each surviving member of the family an equal share. Since the land on a farm might vary in quality, each inheritor would demand a portion of each share of land. To end this destructive tradition, a Field Consolidation Law was passed in 1953. Later, in 1962, the dividing of a farm at the death of its owner, without the special permission of the Ministry of Agriculture, was declared illegal.

Small-sized farms typify the structure of agriculture in West Germany. Even though the merging of farms into larger land units has been a cardinal point of agricultural policy, more restructuring is necessary. In 1969 there were 1.3 million farms with a total area of 12.9 million hectares and an average farm size of 9.6 hectares.[41] In terms of land concentration, farms of 20 to 30 hectares had the most land—2.4 million hectares. Basically, as farms are being consolidated and people migrate to the urban areas the number of farms with less than 15 hectares is declining while the number of farms with more than 20 hectares is increasing. The average farm size has increased from 8.1 hectares in 1960 to 9.6 hectares in 1969.[42] With the reduction in the number of farms there has been a concomitant reduction in the size of the labor force in agriculture from 3.1 million in 1960 to 2.5 million in 1969.[43]

Table 3.4 presents the number of farms based on farm size for the period 1960-69. As the table indicates, there has been a trend over the period toward a reduction in the number of farms, particularly those of 15 hectares or less. On the other hand, there has been a moderate increase in the number of farms of 50 hectares or more.

Land fragmentation has proved to be a difficult problem from the standpoint of government agricultural policy. The federal government has strongly supported the consolidation of farmland into economically viable farm units. A main purpose is to reduce time-consuming movements from plot to plot, thus improving farm productivity. Consolidation enables farms to make use of machinery where formerly it did not pay. Consolidation has been accompanied by aid for other purposes, such as drainage, fencing, and mechanization. It has also encouraged those farmers who benefit by it to devote additional attention to improved practices, including greater use of fertilizers.

TABLE 3.4

Number of Farms in West Germany
and Percentage Change,
1960-69

Farm Size Category (hectares)	Number of Farms (thousands) 1960	1969	Percentage Change
0.5-1	232.5	185.3	-20
1-2	230.4	177.6	-23
2-5	387.1	279.2	-28
5-10	343.0	252.3	-26
10-15	188.2	169.1	-10
15-20	98.3	111.6	+13
20-30	79.2	99.7	+26
30-50	42.8	49.5	+16
50-100	13.7	15.2	+11
100+	2.6	2.8	+1
Total	1,617.7	1,342.1	-17

Source: Economic Research Service, The Agricultural Economy and Trade of the Federal Republic of Germany (Washington, D.C.: U.S. Department of Agriculture, November 1971), p. 20.

Government Support of Agriculture

West German agricultural policy has been directed toward the protection of the farmer through price supports and subsidy measures. The Agricultural Act, passed in 1955, contains the principal objectives of German agricultural policy. One major goal has been to reduce the disparity between agricultural and nonagricultural incomes. Another is a steady increase in agricultural productivity sufficient to generate an adequate food supply at reasonable prices. Because of adverse natural and economic conditions, German policymakers have recognized the need to provide for government assistance measures if the objectives of the act were to be met.

The bulk of financial support for agriculture comes from the federal budget. Each year the Ministry of Agriculture is required to submit to parliament the Green Plan, which contains the measures to be carried out and the budget allocations needed. It is also required to submit the Green Report, which contains an annual report on the conditions of agriculture. Together, the plan and report provide the framework for West German agricultural policy.

The amount of support for agriculture emanating from the federal budget is considerable when compared to the contribution of agriculture to GNP. This support takes several forms, as follows: direct subsidies on prices and inputs; support designed to improve the structure of agriculture, including technical improvement and market promotion plans; special assistance and support for promotion measures; and social measures, including pensions to encourage farmers to retire at an earlier age and funds to encourage out-migration from the farms.

Table 3.5 presents the amount and types of financial support made available to agriculture in the federal budget for 1971. This aid is divided into several categories, one of which is improvement of the agricultural structure. Included are various measures designed to improve the rationalization of agriculture. Another category provides subsidies for fuel. A third category provides subsidies to improve the marketing of agricultural products. It is necessary to point out, however, that not all support for agriculture is listed in the table. When all support for agriculture is taken into consideration, total federal budget expenditure in 1971 was in excess of DM 5 billion. This amount excludes additional assistance that is provided by state governments.[44]

Traditionally, West German agricultural policy has been directed toward the protection of the farmer. To some extent, this policy is a result of political pressures exerted by the farm sector of the population. West German farmers are highly organized to promote their common interests. The most important organization is the German Farmer's Association (Deutsche Bauernverband), whose activities center on improving the social and economic welfare of the farm population. Although farmers and farm workers constitute around 10 percent of the labor force, they are in a position to apply to produce sufficient food to feed its entire population.

When West Germany became a member of the EEC in 1958, national agricultural policy goals were gradually meshed with those of the EEC during a transitional period. The Rome Treaty, agreed to by EEC members, took into consideration the special agricultural problems of community members and set up a series of objectives that were to be achieved over time.* These objectives were to increase productivity of the agricultural sector of the EEC, to maintain an adequate standard of living for the rural population, to stabilize markets

---

*The Rome Treaty establishing the EEC was signed on March 25, 1957, by member-state representatives for France, West Germany, Italy, Belgium, Luxembourg, and the Netherlands, and came into force on January 1, 1958.

TABLE 3.5

West German Federal Budget Support of Agriculture
(in millions of DM)

Type of Support	Amount of Support
Improvement of the agricultural structure	
Interest subsidies for buildings	412
Road building	119
Land clearing	245
Other	383
Subtotal	1,159
Social policies	
Old-age pensions to farmers	675
Measures to encourage persons to leave farming	298
Subtotal	973
Fuel subsidies	
Gasoline	430
Kerosene	923
Subtotal	1,353
Marketing support	218
Investment	65
Total	3,768

Source: Bundesministerium der Finanzen, Bundeshaushaltsplan für das Haushaltsjahr 1971 (Bonn: Bundesdruckerei, March 1971), p. 1,176.

for farm products, and to maintain reasonable consumer prices. To some extent these goals coincided with West German goals as expressed in the Agricultural Act of 1955.

Eventually a Common Agricultural Policy had been developed that prescribed basic regulations applied to the marketing of agricultural commodities or groups of them. The most pervasive element is the reliance on a minimum import price and on some form of variable levy to protect and insulate the domestic price from lower world prices. Because the EEC is an exporter as well as an importer of many commodities, the regulations provide for export subsidies to permit sales at competitive prices on world markets. The result is a separation of the internal market, where trade is relatively unrestricted, from the world market. A linkage is provided by variable import levies and export subsidies. The magnitude of EEC trade in many commodities relative to total quantities traded in world markets is large enough to have significant price effects.

A key element in the operation of the Common Agricultural Policy is the European Agricultural Guidance and Guarantee Fund (Fonds Europeen d'Orientation et de Garantie Agricole). This fund was set up to provide for common financing of programs supporting EEC agriculture. Member countries contribute to the fund, which consists of two sections: a guarantee section responsible for the cost of price supports and subsidies, and a guidance section that finances expenditures on structural reform in farming. Contributions are based partly on import levy receipts, paid directly into the fund; the remainder is derived from direct payments out of the national budgets of the member countries. Eventually, a portion of the value-added tax, the common denominator sales tax of the EEC countries, will go into the fund. The financing of the fund has resulted in the major agricultural importing countries making substantial contributions. Fund disbursements tend to accrue to countries producing the largest volume of agricultural products, particularly those in surplus and thus exportable. Therefore, substantial inter-country financial transfers occur. Although an obvious consequence of the provisions of the Guarantee Fund, these transfers have been a continuous source of irritation for countries such as Germany and Belgium, which find their contributions considerably exceeding their receipts.

SUMMARY

West Germany is one of the most heavily industrialized countries in the world. In terms of importance to the German economy as measured by the value of output and sales turnover, the chemical, electrotechnical, machinery, and automotive industries are the leading contributors. These and other industries are for the most part privately owned. In comparison to other major industrial countries, many West German firms are among the 25 largest firms in existence, with a concentration in the above-mentioned industries.

There is a substantial degree of state intervention in the industrial and agricultural sectors of the West German economy. This is partly attributable to the size of the public sector and to the extent of the public ownership of industry, which gives the state a ready opportunity to exercise control over investment, pricing, and other decisions in the public sector. But it is control rather than ownership that is relevant, and public ownership does not always increase state control over all industries. Rather, state intervention in the West German economy consists of measures designed to ensure that the market mechanism works as effectively as possible. Emphasis has been placed on preventing excessive concentration of economic power through anticartel action and by the encouragement of small- and medium-sized firms. The development of these types of firms has been furthered through the use of various types of state support.

Postwar German business development has been marked by a return to earlier patterns under which control over large sectors of the economy rests in the hands of a small number of business firms and banks. Even though official government policy has sought to prevent continued mergers and business concentrations, progress has been somewhat limited. The government's opposition to cartels was manifested in the Law of Cartels that became effective in 1958 and was amended in 1965. Such business practices as price-fixing and market-sharing have also been curtailed to a degree. The concentration of German industry has, to a certain degree, been inimical to the free market policy pursued by the postwar Adenauer and Erhard governments. In a modern industrial society, however, concentration of industry is apparently inevitable, and it is to be doubted that the pattern of industrial control is much different in Germany than in the United States.

While predominantly a manufacturing nation, West Germany has maintained its agriculture to the extent of providing about three-fourths of the nation's food requirements. This degree of self-sufficiency is the result of protection through tariffs, subsidies, and price supports, for only a small proportion of the land is well suited for cultivation. The federal government has embarked upon an extensive program for the structural reorganization of German agriculture as well as modernization of plant and equipment. Under the program, it grants long-term loans to consolidate uneconomically small units, to finance investments, and to improve housing for farm workers in areas lacking adequate farm labor. Government assistance on a large scale is anticipated for a number of years in view of the basic structural changes involved.

CHAPTER 4

THE FISCAL SYSTEM OF WEST GERMANY

INTRODUCTION

In recent decades public expenditures in all the capitalist countries have increased greatly, both in total amount and as a percentage of GNP. This growth in the direct power of the state as a purchaser and as an employer of note is a vital development. The state has come to exercise a decisive role in the capitalist economies not only through the sheer weight of its spending power but also on account of the vital quality of much of its expenditure, especially on investment in research, education, and training. Moreover, the state, by its expenditures on goods and services, contributes substantially to aggregate demand. The question of the management of aggregate demand and its possible manipulation in an attempt to influence economic growth has therefore come to be given great prominence in any discussion of economic policy. In one sense the division between liberal and collectivist thinking is much narrower in this area of public policy than in other areas; for in respect to public expenditures the state may be regarded much as a single vast enterprise, and the necessity of planning within the enterprise is accepted even by those who are opposed to the superimposition of planning on a sector or industry.

The overall amount of state participation in the West German economy is considerable. The contribution of the public sector, as measured by combined federal, state, and local budgetary outlays, has averaged around 35 percent of the GNP. Certainly, the existence of this large public sector has had an impact on resource allocation, for it is inevitable that some modification would occur in the structure of aggregate demand. It is hardly likely, in other words, that individuals, in the absence of the public sector, would prefer exactly the same collection of goods and services that are purchased when some such collective entity as the government sector exists. The question can be raised as to how far state participation in the economy is consistent with the market principles on which German economic policy has been based since 1948.

Before starting a detailed analysis of the fiscal system of the Federal Republic, it is necessary to have a frame of reference with respect to the place of budgetary measures in relation to the economy. Taxes, which accomplish the allocation of both real and financial resources to the public sector, will be classified into two broad groups. The first comprises taxes that are levied directly on individuals and enterprises. An example is the personal income tax. The second comprises taxes levied on a particular kind of expenditure. The appropriate nomenclature would be direct and indirect taxation. Expenditures can also be divided into two groups: those that involve direct purchases of goods and services and those that are transfer payments. The latter augment the level of aggregate demand in that they give the recipients the power to spend.

THE TAX SYSTEM

The present tax structure of West Germany is primarily the inheritance of history and political processes. There is somewhat of a similarity between the German and the United States tax systems in that there is a tripartite structure (legislative authority over tax matters is divided between federal, state, and local governments), and certain taxes are regarded as the prerogative of each. Under the Basic Law of the Republic, the more affluent German states transfer certain portions of their revenue to those states whose collections are not sufficient to defray their expenditures.

There are three distinct levels of public expenditures. At the top is the budget of the federal government (Bund), together with the two special funds, the Equalization of Burdens Fund and the European Recovery Program Fund. The Equalization of Burdens Fund is designed to compensate war victims; the European Recovery Program Fund is designed to repay Marshall Plan aid. Below the budget of the federal government are the state (Länder) budgets. Finally, there are the budgets of the local government units (Gemeinden), of which there are some 25,000. The control of the federal government over the size of public expenditures has been weakened by the fact that there are three levels of public budgeting.

In West Germany, the budgets of the state and local governments constitute an important expenditure source in the economy. In this way, there is also similarity between the fiscal systems of West

Germany and the United States. In comparison with the public finance of France, which is highly centralized, the German system allows the states to have large separate budgets that, when combined with local government budgets, provide a greater volume of expenditures than the national government. Public enterprise investment expenditure is done primarily by the local governments. The social security system is similar to that of the French in that the tax-transfer arrangement is largely independent of the federal government. The overall pension system is administered by various federal agencies, while private health organizations (Ersatzpassen) subject to public regulation work in the field of health insurance.

The Tax Reforms of 1969

The purpose of the tax reforms of 1969 is to improve the financial resources of local governments.[1] Starting in 1970 the local governments received a part of income taxes from both federal and state budgets. The federal government has also committed itself to contributing to the localities income from the gasoline tax to the amount of three pfennigs per liter. In 1972 income from the local land tax is to increase through a reassessment of land and property values. The reforms are supposed to add an additional DM 2 billion to the revenue of the localities. The trade tax, which is a revenue mainstay for the localities, is to be downgraded in use, however. The trade tax is tied too closely to the business cycle, thus causing wide fluctuations in local revenues. The tax also creates wide differences between localities from the standpoint of revenue receipts, for the reason that both the rate and the base of the tax vary considerably.

The most important elements of the tax reform concerned the value-added tax and the personal and corporate income taxes. The value-added tax, like the turnover tax before it, was exclusively a federal tax. Effective in 1970, the federal share of the value-added tax was reduced from 100 percent to 70 percent, with the states receiving the remaining 30 percent. Income taxes have been shared between the federal and state governments, with the states serving as the collection agencies. The federal share of personal and corporate income taxes was 39 percent in 1966, 37 percent in 1967 and 1968, and 35 percent in 1969. As of 1970, the federal share of the personal income tax was increased to 43 percent, and its share of the corporate income tax was increased to 50 percent. One reason for the increase was to give the federal government more leverage in the use of fiscal policy. The federal government is also now entitled to certain other revenues, including 20 percent of local trade taxes and the insurance tax.

Each level of government in the Federal Republic has its own sources of revenue. The federal government receives all revenues from customs duties and excise taxes excluding the beer tax. It also shares the revenues of the value-added, personal, and corporate income taxes with the states. Besides their share of these taxes, the states receive revenues from the automobile, property, inheritance, and beer taxes. The local governments receive revenues from the taxation of property, entertainment, trade, and beverages. The revenue from these taxes has been insufficient for many localities to carry out their tasks, and they have had to receive considerable support from the budgets of the state governments. The local governments depend almost exclusively on indirect taxes, while more than two-thirds of the states' revenue comes from personal and corporate income taxation. The federal government derives most of its revenue from indirect taxation.

The tax revenues of the federal government for 1971 are presented in Table 4.1. In terms of federal, state, and local governmental

TABLE 4.1

Tax Revenues of West Germany, 1971
(billion DM)

Taxes and Tax-Related Income	Revenue
Shared taxes	
Personal income tax	25.3
Corporate income tax	4.6
Value-added tax	20.1
Trade tax	8.6
Other taxes	3.7
Subtotal	62.3
Federal taxes	
Customs duties	3.0
Tobacco tax	6.8
Alcohol monopoly	2.3
Coffee tax	1.1
Gasoline tax	12.2
Miscellaneous	3.6
Subtotal	29.0
Total	91.3

Source: Bundesministerium der Finanzen, Bundeshaushaltsplan für das Haushaltsjahr 1971 (Bonn: Bundesdruckerei, March 1971), pp. 3,208-10.

relationships, the division of total tax resources results in a distribution of tax revenues in an approximate ratio of 5:3:1. In 1970, for example, total tax collections at the federal level of government amounted to DM 86 billion, total tax collections at the state level amounted to DM 53 billion, and total tax collections at the local level amounted to DM 19 billion.[2]

The West German fiscal system is characterized by a multiplicity of taxes. Altogether some 50 different types of taxes, most of which are excises, are used in West Germany. The bulk of tax revenues, however, are derived from a half-dozen major taxes. In the subsequent sections, the characteristics of the most important taxes will be discussed. In recent years indirect taxes have increased in importance relative to direct taxes as sources of government income.

The Value-Added Tax

The value-added tax (Mehrwertsteuer) was introduced in January 1968. It was developed in accordance with an EEC harmonization directive that called for a value-added tax in all EEC countries by January 1, 1970. The tax is levied primarily on sales at the production and wholesale levels. The tax is collected in a series of fractional payments; each taxpayer making a taxable sale is liable for the tax not on the full sales price he receives but only on the portion of the price that represents the value added by him in the course of the manufacturing and distribution process. Each taxpayer in the production and distribution process chain contributes only a fraction of the total tax due—a fraction based on his contribution to the final value of the product.

The value-added tax replaced the turnover tax (Umsatzsteuer), which for many years was an extremely important tax in the fiscal system of Germany. It was a cascade tax in that it was collected from nearly all types of transactions at all levels of production at a basic rate of 4 percent. There were lower rates on foodstuffs and transactions involving wholesaling. The tax was introduced during World War I as the simplest and most inexpensive method of raising revenue and was collected at all stages of production, leaving to business firms decisions as to what amounts of the tax would be passed on to the consumer. At each stage, the turnover tax became an inseparable and unidentifiable part of the price, and at each succeeding stage the rate was applied to the total price, including all turnover taxes paid in previous stages.

The turnover tax was a cumulative tax. Table 4.2 presents an example of how it was used in Germany. The tax is reflected at each stage in the production and distribution process and is levied on

TABLE 4.2

Example of German Turnover Tax
(in DM)

Stage	Sales	Tax Rate (percent)	Amount of Tax	Total Amount of Tax	Effective Rate (percent)
Raw materials	150	4	6	6	4.0
Production 1	300	4	12	18	6.0
Production 2	750	4	30	48	6.4
Wholesale	800	1	8	56	7.0
Retail	1,100	4	44	100	9.1

Source: Compiled by the author.

the gross monetary value at each stage. Two rates are used, the basic, or most commonly used rate of 4 percent, and a 1-percent rate on wholesaling. The summation of the turnover tax paid at every stage indicates that a total tax payment of $100 was made on a final price of $1,100. This illustrates that the effective rate of 9.1 percent is much higher than the stated rate of 4 percent.

The turnover tax was criticized on several grounds, as follows:

1. It favored large, integrated companies that processed goods mainly within their own organization over smaller companies that were unable to do this.[3]

2. It was hard to apply to imports, for it was difficult to impose an equalization tax equal to the same commodities if produced domestically.

3. It amounted to cumulative taxation, resulting in a considerable burden on consumption items and increasing the regressiveness of the German tax system. The combined effect of cumulation was quite heavy. Depending on the number of taxable transactions preceding the sale of a product to the ultimate consumer, the turnover portion of the retail price was often two to three times the nominal rate of the tax.

A more important reason for the demise of the turnover tax, however, was that it impaired Germany's export position in the world market.[4] Other countries, France in particular, were subject to more generous tax laws that guaranteed them a slight edge in export price competition over Germany. Although German exports were exempted from the turnover tax, prior tax applications at different production and distribution stages left the price relationship of German to foreign goods extremely distorted.

The value-added tax, as now utilized by West Germany, is levied at a general rate of 11 percent of value added in each stage of the production process. There are, however, numerous items to which a lower rate is applied. For example, many food and agricultural products are taxed at a rate of 5.5 percent,[5] and exports and certain items and services are exempt from the tax. In the case of imports, the importer pays an import equalization tax equal to the value-added tax.

In essence, the tax is computed on the value added by any company, as represented by the difference between the values of the company's total sales and total purchases. For a manufacturer, the latter would include all components, either as raw materials or semiprocessed goods, capital goods such as plant machinery and equipment, goods used up in manufacture, business furniture, and so forth. The company would apply the 11-percent rate to find the total tax due. From this the company subtracts the 11-percent tax it has paid on its purchases. The manufacturer would pay only the difference between the tax calculated on the turnover and the tax already paid on the goods and services bought.

The value-added tax is invoiced separately on all sales and is thus not hidden in the sales price.[6] The tax is collected at the end of each month. For example, a manufacturer would add the 11-percent tax as a separate item onto all bills he writes for the goods he sells. At the end of the month, he adds up the taxes that have been billed to him for the goods and services he has bought. If he billed his customers DM 50,000 for taxes on the goods he sold but paid DM 30,000 for taxes on the things he bought he owes the federal government only DM 20,000 for his total value added for the month. An example of the value-added tax is presented in Table 4.3. The calculation of the tax is void of any cumulative effect and the possibility of acceleration by paying a tax on taxes is excluded.

TABLE 4.3

Example of Value-Added Tax
(in DM)

Value of Product at Each Stage	Value Added	11-Percent Tax (percent)
Stage 1: 100	100	11.0
Stage 2: 180	80	8.8
Stage 3: 240	60	6.6
Stage 4: 330	90	9.9
Stage 5: 400	70	7.7
Total	400	44.0

Source: Compiled by the author.

As under the former turnover tax system, the value-added tax is payable on each sale made or service rendered in the Federal Republic, unless a specific exemption applies. The basic difference between the two taxes is that under the system of the value-added tax the seller receives credit against the tax billed to his customer for the tax paid to his supplier. Unlike the rule that the tax must be treated as a "hidden charge" (which was one of the characteristic features of the turnover tax), the taxpayer subject to the value-added tax is required to show the tax as a separate item on every bill for goods or services. Since the value-added tax is fully passed on to and borne by the ultimate customer, it is not an element of cost or expense to the manufacturer or trader and does not appear as such on his financial statements.

Income Taxes

Income taxes were originally the domain of the German states. The personal income tax is derived from the Prussian income tax of 1820 that based liabilities for tax payments on the basis of social classes, with burdens increasing with the descent of the social order. Income taxes remained state taxes until the end of World War I. The loss of the war resulted in a shift of power from the states to the central government, so between 1920 and 1945 income taxes were federal taxes. After the end of World War II they became state taxes again.

Income taxes, then, are levied by the states partly as a matter of historical right and partly under powers delegated by the federal government, and the proceeds are divided between the government and the states in a ratio that changes from time to time. At present both the federal and the state portion of the proceeds from personal and corporate income taxes amount to 43 percent. The state portion is allocated on the basis of the share of total income taxes collected by each state. Although this arrangement would tend to weight the portions heavily in favor of the more densely populated and heavily industrialized states, there is a federal statute that provides for an equitable distribution of revenue among the various states, accomplished through equalization payments made by the affluent to the needy states. All states are required to grant a part of their share of income taxes to the municipalities located within their territories.

Personal Income Tax

The German personal income tax (Einkommensteuer) is progressive. The rates vary from 19 percent on taxable income of

THE FISCAL SYSTEM OF WEST GERMANY

DM 8,009 or less to 53 percent on taxable income in excess of DM 110,039 for single persons.[7] Married persons are entitled to income splitting and pay the same rates on taxable incomes of DM 16,018 or less to DM 220,079 or more. In addition, there is a special 3-percent surcharge on taxable incomes in excess of DM 16,020 for single persons to DM 32,040 for married persons. This surcharge, however, is gradually being phased out. The rates of the personal income tax are reduced for taxpayers who are residents of West Berlin; reduced rates also apply to income of other taxpayers from sources in West Berlin.

Exemptions and deductions under the personal income tax are somewhat similar to those permitted in the United States.[8] There are general exemptions of DM 1,680 for the taxpayer and his wife. There are additional exemptions of DM 1,200 for the first child, DM 1,680 for the second child, and DM 1,800 for the third and subsequent children. Single persons over 50 years of age with no children receive a further exemption of DM 840. Single persons and couples over 65 years of age receive additional exemptions of DM 720 and DM 1,440, respectively. Wage and salary earners are entitled to a special DM 240 exemption; this amount is to be doubled in the future.

There are a number of deductions that are permissible under the German tax system. First, depreciation is deductible, as in the United States. Expenditures designed to acquire and maintain income are deductible. These include certain types of interest payments, real estate taxes, transportation to and from work, and expenses for tools and clothes required for work. Specified insurance premiums, deposits with building and loan associations, property and church taxes, and contributions for charitable, religious, or political purposes are also deductible. There is an automatic lump-sum deduction of such outlays up to a maximum of DM 936 for every employed person. Then there are special allowances for extraordinary expenses incurred through unusual circumstances. The typical example results from an accident or a prolonged illness of the taxpayer or a member of his immediate family. The taxpayer can reduce his taxable income by the amount the extraordinary expenditure exceeds the amount he could be reasonably expected to bear himself.

Income from dividends, with some exceptions, is subject to a 25-percent withholding tax that can be applied to the taxpayer's total income tax. Income from interest, also with some exceptions, is subject to the regular income tax. Capital gains, as a general rule, are not taxed; however, capital losses cannot be deducted. As an exception to this rule, gains from speculation are subject to taxation at regular tax rates. There is, however, a holding period of two years for real property, and six months for personal property. If these periods are exceeded, the capital gain is not taxed. Losses from speculative transactions can be offset against gains from the same source realized within the same taxable year.

Corporate Income Tax

The corporate income tax (Körperschaftssteuer) applies to corporations, limited liability companies, mutual insurance companies, associations, societies, foundations, institutions, and enterprises owned by public corporations operated for profit. If the corporation operates within the confines of the Federal Republic, its entire income is subject to the tax, regardless of where it is earned. For corporations not located in the Federal Republic, only income derived from German sources is subject to the tax. In computing the corporate income tax, contributions for charitable, religious, and political purposes are deductible up to 5 percent of total income, or 0.2 percent of total turnover plus wages and salaries paid during the calendar year. Contributions for scientific purposes are deductible up to 10 percent of total income. Dividends from corporate subsidiaries are not taxable when received by a parent corporation subject to unlimited tax liability if it owns at least one-fourth of the stock of the subsidiaries. Property and income taxes are not deductible, but tax deferments may be granted for investments in developing countries.

The rate of the corporate income tax is 51 percent of undistributed profits for corporations with unlimited tax liability and 49 percent for corporations with limited tax liability.[9] Distributed profits of corporations with unlimited tax liability are taxed at a rate of 15 percent. Graduated tax rates apply to the undistributed profits of small commercial entities owned primarily by individuals, including certain credit institutions. The 3-percent surcharge mentioned in the discussion of personal income taxes is also applicable to the corporate tax. Corporations located in West Berlin are entitled to a reduction of their income tax under the provisions of the Berlin Aid Law. Consequently, the regular corporate income tax rates are reduced from 15 percent to 8.8 percent for distributed profits and from 51 percent to 37.6 percent for retained earnings.[10]

Over the years West German enterprises have been favored with a wide variety of tax incentives. This was particularly true during the immediate postwar period. For example, in shipping tax incentives were used to help rebuild the German merchant marine. Investment credits to the extent of 40 percent of the construction and repair costs of vessels were permitted during the period following the war but were withdrawn in 1959. The use of depreciation allowances has also been of major importance. A depreciation base in excess of original cost was allowed along with various forms of accelerated depreciation. Enterprises in the coal, iron, steel, and energy-producing industries were allowed to write off 50 percent of the cost of new equipment and 30 percent of the cost of new plant construction in the first year. Less accelerated write-offs were permitted in other industries. As the German economy developed, these incentives were gradually withdrawn. Most tax incentives are currently applicable to investments in developing countries.

The Trade Tax

The trade tax (Gewerbesteuer) is an important source of revenue to local governments. It is levied on all business enterprises and is a combined tax on business income and capital and payrolls. The tax is regulated by federal law but is collected by the municipalities. Federal law defines the taxpayers and the basic rates of the tax. The trade tax on business profits is based on the taxable income as computed for the purpose of the income tax. Taxable business capital is the assessed value of the business as most recently determined prior to the end of the taxable year.[11] Although the trade tax must always be computed on the bases of business profits and capital, the use of the payroll base is optional with the localities. The payroll tax is based on monthly salaries and wages paid by an enterprise to its employees. While rates differ from locality to locality, the average trade tax comes to about 14 percent of income and payrolls subject to the tax.

As one result of the 1969 tax reforms, local governments now receive 14 percent of the yield of the personal income tax. This share is deducted from total personal income tax receipts before the remainder is divided equally between the federal and state governments. In return, however, the federal and state governments now receive 40 percent of the trade tax revenues of the localities, which are also equally divided between them. One consequence of the trade-off between the personal income and trade taxes is an improvement in the stability of local government finance. The trade tax had been the main source of local government income but was subject to cyclical fluctuations in business activity. Income tax revenues now provide a more solid financial base.

The importance of the trade tax as a local government revenue source is reflected by the fact that in 1969 DM 15.4 billion out of a total of DM 18.8 billion in local tax revenues was accounted for by the tax.[12] The basic purpose of the trade tax is to compensate the localities for such financial burdens as schools, roads, police, and public welfare, which necessarily result from the existence of business enterprises in their areas. As a result of certain deductions, however, the actual burden of the trade tax on business enterprises is much less that the nominal rate, since the trade tax is deductible from the undistributed income of all business enterprises subject to the corporate income tax, which is taxed at the rate of 51 percent.

Excise Taxes

One characteristic of the West German tax system is the reliance on a wide variety of excise taxes (Verbrauchsteuern) as a source of revenue. These taxes, with the exception of the beer tax, which is a state tax, are levied by the federal government on a wide variety of articles including tobacco, salt, tea, coffee, matches, electric bulbs, alcohol, petroleum, and playing cards. The producer, manufacturer, or importer is expected to shift the tax to the buyer by including the amount in the purchase price of the article. The impact of excise taxes on the individual taxpayer is very heavy, as may be gathered from the fact that the revenue from the two principal excise taxes, tobacco and gasoline taxes, has been almost as much as the federal share of income taxes. In 1969, for example, the federal share of personal and corporate income taxes amounted to DM 18.4 billion compared to a take of DM 16.4 billion for the tobacco and gasoline taxes.[13] In 1971, however, the respective amounts were DM 29.9 billion and DM 19 billion.[14] The bases of the various excise taxes vary with the taxable products. In some cases, the measure of the tax is the weight or liquid volume of the product; in others, it is the sales price of the product.

Other Taxes

Among the other taxes in the Federal Republic that provide additional sources of revenue are the property tax, capital transactions taxes, customs duties, and the inheritance tax.[15]

Property Taxes

Property taxes are of two types: the general property tax (Vermögenssteuer) and the real estate purchase tax (Grunderwerbsteuer). The general property tax is a revenue source for local government units. Real property, with certain exemptions, is subject to an annual tax rate of 1 percent on its assessed value. This basic rate is fixed by federal law. It may, however, be reduced to 0.75 percent if the value of real property does not exceed an amount stipulated in the Equalization of Burdens Law. The real estate purchase tax is imposed on the transfer of property. The rate of the tax is usually 7 percent, based on the sales price of the property or, in some cases, on the assessed value of the property. The purchase tax is a joint tax because both state and local governments use it.

Inheritance Taxes

The inheritance tax is a state tax. It has special rates based on the consanguinity of the inheritors to the person who is deceased. There are five rates, which are levied upon inheritances and also gifts. The lowest rate is paid by those inheritors who were closest to the deceased, including the children and surviving spouse. The rates range from 2 percent on taxable property of DM 10,000 or less to 15 percent on taxable property of DM 10 million and over. Exemptions are quite generous. For example, the surviving spouse is not taxed on the first DM 250,000 in value of taxable property if children are living at the time the liability for the tax originates. Other exemptions also serve to reduce the effective rate of the tax. The highest tax rate for inheritances, as well as gifts, ranges from 14 percent on taxable property of DM 10,000 or less to 60 percent on taxable property of DM 10 million and over. This rate applies to cousins and friends of the deceased or donor.

Capital Transactions Taxes

There are two types of capital transactions taxes. The first type is the company tax (Gesellschaftssteuer), which is levied on the initial sale of newly issued domestic shares of equity capital. The rate of the tax, 2.5 percent of the value of the transaction, may be reduced to 1 percent if, for example, the sale was made to reduce excessive indebtedness. The second type is the stock exchange turnover tax (Börsenumsatzsteuer). The rate of the tax is 0.25 percent of the transaction but can be reduced for certain types of securities. The yield of both types of capital transfer taxes is low in relation to their cost of collection, and their repeal has been considered from time to time.

Customs Duties

Customs duties (Zolltarifs) account for around 4 percent of federal tax revenues. Rates vary depending on whether the dutiable article is imported from a country that enjoys most-favored-nation privileges under a treaty with the Federal Republic or is a member of GATT, or from a country that is not a party to these agreements. No duties are imposed on goods imported from one of the member states of the EEC. The applicable tariff rate is computed on the customs value of imported merchandise. In the great majority of cases, the rates of the tariff are ad valorem rates. The rates are expressed in percentages of the customs value of the commodity.

Revenue Equalization

Since the ratio of tax receipts both to population and to revenue requirements varies from one state to another, the Basic Law of the Federal Republic (Grundgesetz) provides that an equitable equalization of revenue between financially strong and financially weak states must be ensured by federal legislation. Financially weak states receive grants from financially strong states. The equalization procedure takes account of the differences among the states. Financial strengths or weaknesses of the states are measured as follows:

1. Adjusted tax collection figures are computed for each state. Included among the tax collections are receipts from the property and trade taxes for each commune (Gemeinde) located in the states.

2. A per capita collection figure is computed for the entire area of the Federal Republic on the basis of the combined adjusted collection figures for all states.

3. This per capita figure, multiplied by the number of persons in each state, results in the equalization figure for each state.

As a result of this equalization of revenue among the states, the resources of those with less-than-average tax receipts are increased to 95 percent of the average tax receipts of all states.

The 1969 tax reforms further provide that the proceeds of the personal and corporate income taxes are apportioned in such a manner that they are received in the same proportion in which they were collected.[16] Value-added tax receipts, of which 30 percent are now apportioned to the states, are distributed to the states on the basis of their population. Moreover, financially weak states may receive special equalization grants from the federal government. In turn, local government units also may receive grants under state equalization legislation. The purpose of equalization of revenues among the localities is the mitigation of the differences in their financial resources.

GOVERNMENT EXPENDITURES

Government expenditure policy, particularly at the federal level, has emphasized a comprehensive social security system with constantly expanding individual benefits, public investment in the form of low-cost housing, transportation facilities and other civil construction, and economic assistance to private enterprise. In fact, a substantial part of public investment has been effected through the financing of private enterprise.

Besides providing a comprehensive array of social services, the federal government has an impact on the economy through public investment expenditures in the nationalized industries, as well as in various private sectors of the economy, such as housing.[17] Public investment from all sources has accounted for approximately one-fourth of total investment during the past ten years. The bulk of support has come from savings on the part of the federal government that have been derived from budgetary surpluses, funds secured from accumulations in the social security system, moderate amounts of government borrowing both through bond issues and through direct credits from financial institutions, and surpluses in the budgets of the various German states.

Housing is a major area of government support. An acute need after World War II was the repair and construction of residential housing. There was also the need to provide housing for the refugees from East Germany. To encourage the construction of housing, tax incentives and direct subsidies were offered by all levels of government. For example, newly built homes were exempted from the local real estate tax. Generous depreciation allowances were provided for the construction of houses and apartments, and rents for many dwellings were subsidized. Loans at subsidized interest rates as low as 1 percent per annum were also made to encourage housing construction.

A high proportion of savings emanate from the public sector of the economy and are channeled into government-approved areas. Housing construction continues to be supported out of subsidies financed by general revenues, interest subsidies, and accelerated depreciation. Agricultural enterprises are also entitled to special depreciation provisions that are over and above the normal rate. Structural subsidies are paid to stimulate an increase in the size of the farming unit, and interest subsidies are paid to stimulate capital investment. Government savings have also been directed into such areas as coal mining and shipping. In coal mining the federal government has used a number of subsidies. In the period following World War II, when price controls were in effect, the federal government paid a part of operating losses.

It should be clear that combined federal, state, and local budgets absorb a very large percentage of the German GNP, and many economic functions are influenced by government tax and expenditure policies. Thus, a high degree of control over the economy can be exercised by governmental units through manipulation of taxes and expenditures. A wide variety of tax incentives has been used to stimulate economic growth, and many economic sectors have been favored by government use of tax incentives. Tax policy has sought to create incentives to work, save, and invest in business enterprises, but in turn heavy reliance has been placed on indirect taxation such as excise taxes and the value-added tax, which discriminate against consumption. Expenditure policy has sought to stimulate economic growth and to buttress the position of the average German by providing comprehensive social security measures.

Federal Expenditures

Total federal budgetary expenditures, excluding those social security expenditures that are listed separately in the social budget, were set at DM 100.1 billion for 1971. The major expenditure components are presented in Table 4.4.

Expenditures of the federal budget can be broken down into purchases of goods and services and various types of income transfers. The latter is of particular importance. For example, the federal government finances a part of the general social security program. There are also various capital transfers to public enterprises in the budget, and grants and subsidies are available for specific purposes. Subsidies are given to the city of Berlin to support its economy.
The grant arrangement exists between the federal and state governments for such areas as highway construction, education, and housing.

TABLE 4.4

West German Federal Budget Expenditures, 1971
(billion DM)

Service	Expenditure
General services, including national defense	30.8
Education and scientific research	4.6
Social welfare expenditures, including war pensions	30.0
Health and sports	0.2
Housing construction	1.4
Agriculture and forestry	5.8
Energy and water economics	2.3
Transportation and communication	7.8
General capital expenditures	5.0
General finance services, including interest on the national debt	12.2
Total	100.1

Source: Bundesministerium der Finanzen, Bundeshaushaltplan für das Haushaltsjahr 1971 (Bonn: Bundesdruckerei, March 1971), pp. 31-37.

THE FISCAL SYSTEM OF WEST GERMANY 93

Agriculture receives a wide variety of subsidies, including seed subsidies, compensation for crop failure, subsidies to aid payment of interest on debts, and subsidies for fertilizer purchases. In addition, there are subsidies for storage space construction, rural housing, marketing of various products, and for the purchase of farm machinery. Subsidies go to other industries also, particularly to the coal mining industry. For example, grants supplement the funds in the social security system for coal miners.

National Defense

The main item in the federal budget that contributes directly to the purchases of goods and services is defense-spending, which in the 1971 budget was set at DM 22.4 billion.[18] Of this amount, support of the armed forces, which takes the form of wages and salaries and purchases of equipment, amounted to DM 16.2 billion. Civil defense expenditures were set at DM 500 million. Contributions to scientific research for 1971 were set at DM 1.4 billion. Contributions to the maintenance of foreign troops in Germany amounted to DM 676 million. General administrative expenses came to DM 3.3 billion.

Social Welfare

Social welfare expenditures, including war pensions, relief measures, and partial contributions to various social security funds that are kept separately from the federal budget, comprise the largest single expenditure component in the federal budget. The great bulk of these expenditures take the form of transfer payments in one form or another. The single most important expenditure is in support of the general social security program, which includes old age, disability and survivors' insurance, health and maternity insurance, unemployment insurance, and family allowances. Financing takes place mainly through payroll taxes shared equally by employers and employees. Through transfers from the budget, the federal government finances a part of old-age and survivors' pensions, allowances for the second and additional children under the family allowance system, and part of the cost of maternity benefits. In the 1971 budget, federal government contributions to old-age and survivors' pensions amounted to DM 7.7 billion, and contributions to the family allowance system amounted to DM 3.3 billion.[19]

Expenditures for various war-related illnesses and damages also constitute an important component of social welfare expenditures. Total war-related (Kriegsfolgenhilfe) expenditures were set at DM 9.1 billion in the 1971 budget. The most important single expenditure, amounting to DM 7 billion, was for war pensions (Kriegsopferversorgung). The main provisions for war pensions were contained in the

Federal Pensions Law of 1950. The expenditures under this law were increased by the rise in basic pension rates authorized under the law of June 1960. This new law authorized improvements in pension rates; it also introduced new kinds of pensions, in particular one for compensation for loss of occupation and also a supplementary payment to severly disabled persons. The total cost of war pensions has risen considerably as a result of the continued adjustment of pensions to keep up with increases in the cost of living. In 1971, for example, the total amount paid out for war pensions amounted to DM 7 billion, compared to DM 4.2 billion in 1962.

Education, Science, and Research

Expenditures on education, science, research, and related matters in the 1971 budget amounted to DM 4.6 billion.[20] Of this total amount, research support came to DM 1.1 billion; most of it went to the universities and research institutes. Construction funds for educational facilities amounted to DM 744 million. The overall cost of education is a shared responsibility between the federal and state governments. Expenditures on various types of scientific equipment, including computers and data processing machines, amounted to DM 1.1 billion. Also under the major category of education and science comes support to related areas. For example, support for culture in the form of subsidies to theaters, museums, and other activities amounted to DM 53 million. A greater part of the expenditures on cultural matters is incurred by the states, however.

Transportation and Communication

Transportation expenditures are one of the more important components in the budget. In 1971 total expenditures amounted to DM 7.8 billion.[21] This amount can be broken down into direct outlays for goods and services and subsidies to state and local governments. The single most important type of expenditure was for the construction and maintenance of the federal highway system. A total of DM 4.9 billion was allocated for this purpose. Subsidies to state and local governments amounted to DM 720 million. Funds for road construction are earmarked from the revenue of the petroleum tax. Another expenditure was for federal aid to air transportation, which, including subsidies for mail services, amounted to DM 326 million. A total of DM 652 million was allocated for the improvement of waterways and harbor facilities, and a total of DM 534 million was allocated for the construction and maintenance of railway tracks.

Agriculture and Forestry

Expenditures in the federal budget on agriculture, forestry, and related areas amounted to DM 5.8 billion in 1971.[22] The great bulk of this amount is listed under the category of income support measures (Einkommensstabilisierende Massnahmen). These measures include various subsidies previously mentioned. Included are direct income payments to farmers and price subsidies. Other measures of financial importance are those for reducing fuel prices and for reducing the price of artificial manure. The Green Plan also provides funds for the improvement of the farming structure, such as the improvement of farm roads. Excluded from this budget category are indirect aids to agriculture. For example, the federal government owns and operates enterprises that serve either for pioneering purposes in agriculture or as direct auxiliaries to farming, such as experimental farms.

Development Assistance and Contributions to International Organizations

Included under this category of expenditures would be contributions to various European economic organizations and aid to developing countries. For example, the Federal Republic contributes to the EEC and the Organization for Economic Cooperation and Development (OECD) and their special funds. In addition there are payments to multilateral agencies such as the International Bank for Reconstruction and Development (IBRD). A series of development loans have been made to developing countries in Africa and Asia. In addition to this direct assistance, the tax laws of the Federal Republic contain provisions for special concessions designed to facilitate and encourage private investment in the developing countries. Total budget expenditures for the category of development assistance and contributions to other countries amounted to DM 5.1 billion.[23] Of this amount, DM 2.4 billion went for development assistance and DM 1.1 billion for contributions to international organizations.

Energy, Water Economics, Industry, and Services

Expenditures under this category constitute a minor item in the federal budget. In 1971 DM 2.3 billion were allocated for this purpose.[24] One type of expenditure is compensation to coal miners who have been displaced by the rationalization efforts of the European Coal and Steel Community (ECSC). Allocations for the development of nuclear energy amounted to DM 600 million. Improvement of the energy infrastructure of the economy received an allocation of DM 300 billion. Other expenditures were for coal and energy research.

Measures to Stimulate the Economy

Although not listed under this category in the federal budget, certain expenditures are designed to stimulate or contribute to the development of the economy. One measure that has played a prominent role since its inception is the European Recovery Program, which was created out of Marshall Plan funds provided by the United States. By the London Debt Agreement of 1953, only a part of the Marshall Plan assistance had to be repaid, leaving the remainder of the aid in a special fund. This special fund was originally used for giving general financial assistance, but since the recovery of the German economy it has been applied more to give special financial assistance to projects of importance to the national economy where problems of structure are involved. It has been utilized when it has not been possible to raise required investment funds in the capital market.

The European Recovery Program Special Fund has been an important instrument for guiding the flow of private investment. The assistance given from the fund, which is separate from the federal budget, has in recent years been concentrated in certain special fields in order to make it more effective; for example, to help the domestic economy it has been used to provide support for the owners of small trades and businesses and for capital expenditures on water-supply facilities. Aid to Berlin measures have been financed in part by the fund. The fund has also been used to finance certain measures for the solution of special economic problems. For example, funds provided for small firms have been increasingly directed at fulfilling regional and social objectives—firms locating in regionally depressed areas have been given greater financial assistance, as have those established by refugees and expellees from East Germany. Currently, funds are used to grant aid to developing countries and to prevent air and water pollution.

The use of the special fund takes the form of credits or grants. Loans from the fund are administered by the minister for federal property through the Kreditanstalt für Wiederaufbau, the Lastenausgleichsbank, and, in Berlin, the Berliner Industriebank; grants are provided either directly by the fund or by the ministries to which money has been allocated. Each year a plan is drawn up to decide how funds are to be distributed. The funds are used as sort of an emergency reserve that can be used to inject money rapidly and flexibly into certain key points in the economy where structural difficulties have arisen or where social problems have emerged. Since the inception of the special fund in 1967 more than DM 20 billion have been injected into the economy in the form of loans and grants, of which approximately DM 7 billion have gone to Berlin, particularly after the building of the Berlin Wall in 1961.

In addition to the European Recovery Program support, there are other measures for promoting the development and growth of the economy. In regional development the objective is to improve the productivity of areas that are economically weak. In the promotion of regional development, the federal and state governments share a mutual financial responsibility. In recent years special assistance has been given not only to areas adjacent to the East German border but to other regions on the periphery of the EEC area in order to enable these regions to adjust themselves to the European market.

Expenditures of State and Local Governments

In the case of the federal government, expenditures are concentrated primarily under the two categories of defense and social services; these two classes of expenditures together account for around 60 percent of the budget total. The budgets of the states and the communes show no corresponding concentration; with them, expenditures are distributed under a number of main headings, and these determine the structure of their respective budgets. Because of the tasks for which they are responsible under the Basic Law, the main headings of their expenditures are education, public law and order including the administration of justice, transportation, public health, and public facilities. State and local budgets also differ from the federal budget in another way. The federal budget is affected to a much greater degree by current expenditures, that is, such as do not affect assets, than the state budgets or, even more, than local budgets. Around 10 percent of total federal expenditures is of a capital nature, compared to around 33 percent for the combined expenditures of the states and communes.

State Governments

State governments receive their revenues from two sources—taxation and grants from the federal government. The chief functions of the state governments are the provision of justice, education, social welfare, and road construction. The cost of these functions is usually borne jointly by the states and communes or by the states and the federal government. The 1969 financial reform of the Basic Law has enlarged the number of services that are provided jointly by the federal and state governments. In 1970 estimated expenditures of the state governments were DM 60.9 billion. This amount can be broken down into the following categories.[25]

1. Outlays for education, science, research, and cultural activities amounted to DM 17.7 billion. This represents the share of state costs in performance of services that are financed jointly with the communes.

2. Payments for indemnification and compensation amounted to DM 5.6 billion. Under the Federal Indemnification Law, the cost of compensation to victims of National Socialist persecution, restitution of property, and reparations to Israel are borne by the federal and state governments. Most of these payments were made to claimants living outside of the Federal Republic.

3. Outlays on social services form another component of the state budgets. This includes outlays on social assistance in cash and kind, which are borne by the states and communes. It also covers the cost of social institutions, including those used in connection with the war (Kriegsfolgenhilfe). In 1970 expenditures amounted to an estimated DM 5.4 billion.

4. Road construction and maintenance expenditures amounted to an estimated DM 4.5 billion.

5. Housing assistance, including direct loans, amounted to an estimated DM 3.4 billion.

One difference between the budgets of the federal and state governments is that a higher percentage of expenditures in the state budgets is allocated for capital expenditures. When state expenditures are divided between current and investment outlays, the ratio is approximately 70:30. Expenditures on investments, including investment subsidies and transfers to reserves, amounted in 1970 to an estimated DM 17 billion. The largest item in this total, consisting of loans and subsidies for investment purposes, amounted in 1970 to 65 percent of the whole. This item is made up chiefly of loans and premiums paid to encourage home building; such expenditure is shared between the federal government and the states. Another important factor in this total consists of investment subsidies and loans to the communes. These are used especially for the improvement of traffic facilities, the support of agriculture (insofar as this is within the competence of the communes), school construction, water works, and the construction of hospitals and other public facilities.

Local Governments (Communes)

Revenues for the communes come from three sources: taxation, grants, and income from fees, administrative charges, and commercial undertaking. Most of the grants are paid by the state governments and merely pass through the local budgets. The bulk of public investment in West Germany is done by the local governments and is to a large extent financed by subsidies and loans from the states. In general, the state governments have considerable control over the activities of the local governments. For example, the states have a formal control over the debt policies of the communes. In the Basic Law, the federal structure of the Federal Republic is defined solely in terms of the federal and state level. The communes are treated as part of the states, and the distribution of tasks and of revenues is largely left to state legislation.

In 1970 tentative expenditures for local governments were DM 31.7 billion.[26] In terms of current and capital expenditures, the approximate figures were DM 22 billion and DM 9 billion, respectively. The bulk of local expenditures can be divided into four categories: education, social welfare, health and sports, and communal services. Current expenditures are primarily for wages and salaries, for the purchase of materials, and for interest. Interest charges normally amount to around 5 percent of current expenditures because the communes generally finance their capital expenditures by means of long-term borrowing. Capital expenditures are primarily for roads, public institutions, and educational facilities, which together represent two-thirds of the whole of local investment expenditures.

There are revenue equalization measures designed to assist local government units. Apart from the yield of taxes assigned to them, communes in some states receive equalization grants under state legislation. The purpose of these grants is to reduce differences in resources among the various communes and to provide them with the necessary resources to perform various functions. The equalization of revenue among the communes varies from one state to another. In general, a formula is used to bring communes up to some sort of a state average.

Equalization of Burdens

In 1952 the Equalization of Burdens Law (Lastenausgleichsgesetz, or LAG) was passed. The purpose of the law was to attempt to achieve some form of an equitable compensation for war losses sustained by the population. In particular, the exodus of many Germans from the eastern part of the country had placed a heavy burden on the economy. The currency reform of 1948 had scaled down the value of cash holdings and monetary claims rather drastically also, without corresponding losses in the value of land and such real estate and business property as had been preserved, so that some compensation for lost savings and other monetary claims had to be devised. Thus, the Equalization of Burdens Law provided for annual contributions in the form of relief that were set to run for a period of 30 years. Funds provided through contributions of the federal and state governments go into an Equalization Fund and come from the following three sources.[27]

1. A capital levy (Vermögensabgabe), amounting to 50 percent of the net worth of all individuals and entities subject to the levy, is applicable to all property owned as of June 21, 1948. The first DM 10,000 of bank and savings accounts and life insurance is exempt. There are also other allowances that reduce the taxable base, including individual exemptions of DM 10,000. The rate of the levy is 1 percent but is reduced to 0.75 percent when the value of property does not exceed the liability under the Equalization of Burdens property contribution.

2. A levy on profits from the redemption of mortgage loans (Hypothekengewinnabgabe) is designed to capture chance gains of persons whose obligations under the mortgage were reduced to one-tenth of their face value by the currency reform of 1949 while the value of the mortgaged property remained intact.

3. There is a levy on book profits (Kreditgewinnabgabe) that claims the book profits arising from the conversion of the balance sheets of commercial and industrial enterprises from the conversion of the pre-1948 currency unit (Reichsmark) to the present currency unit (Deutsche Mark).

The Equalization of Burdens expenditures provide benefits to individuals, as designated under the provisions of the law. Compensation paid for war damages includes allowances for the replacement of household effects, pensions to old persons, loans for new businesses, and the construction of houses. The Equalization of Burdens Fund is administered separately from the budget of the federal government. From 1952, when the law went into effect, to the end of 1969 total expenditures from the fund amounted to DM 63.6 billion.[28] Of this amount, war pensions accounted for DM 22.1 billion and allowances for the replacement of household goods amounted to DM 13.1 billion. These expenditures were covered by revenues from the equalization of burdens levies, accounting for about 75 percent of total revenues, and by grants from the budgets of the federal and state governments, accounting for the remaining 25 percent. Contributions from levies to the Equalization of Burdens Fund amounted to DM 1.7 billion in 1969.[29]

Aid to Berlin

West Berlin, a part of the former capital of Germany, is isolated from the Federal Republic and depends on it for financial support. It has had a special status from the time of the joint occupation of the city of Berlin by the four powers in 1945. Since federal legislative jurisdiction does not extend to West Berlin, the legislature of that city promulgates federal laws as its own statutes. But, in order to support the economy of West Berlin, it has become necessary to provide funds from the federal budget. As West Berlin is included in the federal financial system, it is granted special subsidies to cover the budgetary and social insurance funds deficit. During the period 1951-64 payments made from the federal government to West Berlin, amounting to DM 14.8 billion, accounted for around 40 percent of the total revenue of the city. Additional subsidies were received from the funds of the European Recovery Program. In 1971 help from the federal budget for West Berlin was set at DM 3.1 billion.[30]

Tax benefits also accrue to persons who live in West Berlin. For example, under the provisions of the Berlin Aid Law of 1968 (Berlinhilfegesetz) residents are granted a 30-percent reduction of their assessed income tax to the extent that the tax falls on income from sources in West Berlin. Special depreciation allowances are also available for firms located in Berlin. In addition to tax benefits, individuals with employment income from sources in West Berlin are entitled to premiums, in the form of cash, that are measured by the amount of their wages. These premiums are tax-exempt and are not considered employment income for purposes of the social security laws. Individuals or business entities are also entitled to credits against their personal income tax or corporate income tax if they make certain loans to further the economy of West Berlin. Cash subsidies are also made available for certain types of investments in West Berlin.

FISCAL POLICY

Fiscal policy plays an important role in the operation of the modern welfare state. It involves deliberate changes in government expenditures and taxes as a means of controlling economic activity. The budget of the national government is the key instrument through which fiscal policy is effected. Government expenditures for goods and services directly affect the level of economic activity because they are a component part of the demand function. Transfer payments and taxes, on the other hand, affect disposable income and also the two major components of aggregate demand—consumption and investment. Fiscal policy controls the provision of public goods and services through expenditures and income redistribution through taxes and transfer payments.

Through the intervention of the Allies, West Germany became a federation, a factor of importance in terms of the operation of fiscal policy. Under the provisions of the Basic Law, the budgets of the federal and state governments are supposed to be autonomous and independent of each other. To some extent this independence has circumvented the effective use of fiscal policy, even though the Basic Law also provides that the fiscal management of federal and state budgets must take into consideration the requirements of overall economic stabilization. General government expenditures on goods and services are about evenly divided between the federal, state, and local governments, thus complicating the problem of central management of expenditures. Moreover, public investment expenditures are also divided among the three levels of government, with investments on the part of the local governments constituting the most important share. On the tax side, taxes on consumer spending are fragmented. In fact, they are split up into more than a dozen separate taxes on commodities and services and are collected primarily at the level of production.

The importance of the federal government cannot be minimized, however. Control over the social security system is vested in the federal government as well as the tax revenues of the states and communes. In order to maintain uniform economic conditions and to permit fiscal, monetary, and social policy on a national scale, the Basic Law permits federal legislation even in the area of those taxes whose proceeds are assigned to the states or to the communes. Within the field of concurrent tax jurisdiction, the exercise of legislative power by the federal government displaces the exercise of this power by the states. Expressed differently, the power of the states to regulate a certain tax by state comes to an end once the federal government has preempted the field.

West German budget policy during most of the postwar period sought to avoid deficits, partly because of the difficulty of financing a deficit and partly as a result of legal restrictions confining public debts to those incurred for productive purposes. Under the Basic Law, the German government is not permitted to have an unbalanced budget. This provision prevented use of the budget as an effective instrument of fiscal policy. The reason for this provision was to prevent legislative abuse of the budget. Until recent years, there was no attempt to utilize the budget to offset short-term fluctuations in economic activity.

The economic problems that brought down the Erhard government in 1966 forced a reappraisal of this standard conservative budget policy. Overexpenditure in the public sector of the economy was a factor that was responsible for rising prices, and wage increases had outstripped gains in productivity. A recession occurred in 1966, and by the middle of February 1967 the number of unemployed workers in West Germany amounted to 3.1 percent of the labor force—a high rate for the economy. A provisional contingency budget was introduced, and countercyclical fiscal measures were used to stimulate demand. This contingency budget took the form of a Special Investment Budget, and in the spring of 1967 additional expenditures of DM 2.5 billion ($625 million) were provided for investments in the national railway system, postal services, and road building. Investment orders were also placed with the private sector of the economy. In spite of those additional investments, the countercyclical impact of the contingency budget was diluted and more than counterbalanced by contractions in budgetary spending on the part of state and local governments.

In June 1967 the Bundesrat passed the Law for Promoting Stability and Growth in the Economy.[31] In connection with the new law, both houses of parliament gave approval to a required change in the Federal Republic's Basic Law. The provision for independent budgeting processes of the federal government and the states was altered to permit coordination of fiscal and economic policy actions at all levels of government. The separation of federal and state budgets had been an important obstacle to an effective countercyclical fiscal policy. The new law marked a new era in West German economic policy, for it provided the federal government with a number of Keynesian policy instruments.

The new law represents a delegation of fiscal powers by the German parliament to the federal government. These fiscal powers are as follows.[32]

1. To stimulate the economy in a recession, the Ministry of Finance is authorized to finance supplementary public expenditures by borrowing up to DM 5 billion.

2. The federal government must plan its budgets for periods of five years and must prepare an investment program with a priority scale. State and local governments are also required to prepare long-range budgets, particularly for investment projects, and to discuss them with federal authorities.

3. The federal government can suspend or restrict special depreciation allowances and the application of accelerated depreciation in a boom period.

4. The federal government, and the states, as well, are required during boom periods to make business cycle reserve deposits (Konjunkturausgleichsrücklage) with the Bundesbank.

5. The federal government is authorized to increase or decrease income and corporate taxes by up to 10 percent, according to business cycle requirements.

6. The federal government, with prior approval of the Bundesrat, can restrict new borrowing by federal, state, and local governments for up to one year.

7. The federal government is required to submit to the Bundestag and Bundesrat an annual economic report that includes a declaration of its economic and fiscal policy objectives for the coming year.

The federal government made extensive use of the powers granted by the Stabilization Law during the 1967-68 period. The impact of fiscal policy measures on the economy was considerable. It is estimated that the DM 2.5 billion increase in budget expenditures in April 1967 caused the GNP to increase by DM 5.3 billion.[33] Subsequent measures taken by the federal government involved pumping more than DM 2 billion into the economy during late 1967 and early 1968. Part of the funds were funneled into the construction industry to alleviate the chronic housing shortage.

The increased budgetary expenditures of DM 2.5 billion were distributed based on the following time table: DM 1.46 billion was distributed in the second quarter of 1967, DM 558 million in the third quarter, DM 309 million in the fourth quarter, and DM 171 million during all of 1968.[34] The funds were allocated for federal projects. The states of North Rhine-Westphalia, Bavaria, and Baden-Württemberg received around 60 percent of the total distributed funds. Federal projects were directed to the areas in which the rate of unemployment was the highest. In particular, the construction industry and basic industries were favored with the granting of federal orders for goods. Projects thought to have the quickest effect upon stimulating aggregate demand received the highest priority.

The main problem of the investment program was the hesitancy of private enterprises to invest, despite the efforts of the government. It was apparent that a new boom could be achieved only when the level of private investment increased concomitantly with federal government investment expenditures. To achieve a higher level of private investment, the federal government reduced the rate of the investment tax. The government also initiated a second investment program in 1968, which amounted to around DM 2.1 billion. This program, however, was by no means limited to participation by the federal government; state governments also played a contributory role. The program was divided into several phases, as follows.[35]

1. To stimulate the construction industry and to eliminate the chronic shortage of housing, the federal government granted DM 300 million, of which DM 100 million were given through interest support payments and DM 200 million were used for direct loans. State governments also participated to the extent of DM 360 million. In addition, loans of DM 2.1 billion were made to private home owners.

2. An agreement was reached between federal and state governments to allocate DM 500 million for the improvement of the infrastructures of the localities. The funds were provided under favorable credit terms in order to provide programs designed to improve water

and sewage disposal systems. The localities were obliged to raise
DM 1.5 billion to support these programs, so that the ultimate impact
in terms of expenditures was DM 2 billion.

3. The federal government granted another DM 300 million to
aid depressed areas. These areas are primarily concentrated along
the East German and Czech borders and are dominated by agriculture.

4. Federal and state government direct expenditures on investments were increased by DM 822 million and DM 226 million, respectively.

5. Federal assistance of DM 850 million was made available
in the form of grants-in-aid to the states and localities. State support
amounted to DM 430 million.

The greatest effect of the second expenditure program was felt
primarily in the construction industry, where the highest degree of
government intervention occurred. The structural aims contained
in the program also affected to some extent the redistribution of
economic activities in the country. With respect to the distribution
of support, the two states of North Rhine-Westphalia and Bavaria
received 47.9 percent of the total while the Saarland received only
1.7 percent.[36] The multiplier-accelerator effect of the second program
was estimated to be DM 21 billion. In other words, total government
expenditures of DM 7.4 billion during the second program increased
the value of total output by DM 21 billion.[37]

In 1969 and 1970 fiscal policy became more restrictive as
economic recovery was rapid and boom conditions with corresponding
pressure on prices developed. The 1969 expenditure plans of the
federal government were reduced by about DM 1.8 billion while corporate and individual income taxes were speeded up by an increase
in the size of prepayments.[38] It was recommended by the Business
Cycle Council (Konjunkturrat) that the federal and state governments
set up a contracyclical reserve in accordance with the Law for Promoting Stability and Growth of 1967. This law requires the federal
and state governments to keep interest-free "conjunctural accounts"
(Konjunkturausgleichsrücklagen) with the Bundesbank. The federal
government, with the approval of the Bundesrat, can instruct federal
and state authorities to place up to 3 percent of their tax revenues
of the previous year into the fund.[39] Apart from this, increased
revenue caused by a contracyclical raising of income taxes is supposed
to be automatically paid into the fund. The amounts paid into the
cyclical reserve fund may only be withdrawn for contracyclical expenditures, with the ordinance of the federal government and the
approval of the Bundesrat.

To some extent, the cyclical reserve is like the Swedish investment reserve. In Sweden the government has attempted to influence
the timing of private investment projects through special tax concessions

to firms that are willing to postpone their particular investment projects so as to fit them into a more stable pattern.[40] The device used is the investment reserve. Its purpose is to encourage private corporate savings in periods of prosperity and private capital expenditures in periods of unemployment. Companies are encouraged to set aside part of their pretax profits in a reserve that is deposited in the Bank of Sweden (Sveriges Riksbank), and if these funds are used for investments in buildings, machinery, and inventories during a period in which investment is needed for employment purposes, substantial tax privileges are attainable. Of course, the German cyclical reserve is a tax reserve of the federal and state governments, but the objectives of the two types of reserves are basically the same. In each country, the release of the reserves is permissible only for the purpose of avoiding a weakening of overall economic activity that endangers the goal of a high level of employment.

During 1969, the Bundesrat approved the creation of a contracyclical reserve of DM 3.6 billion, which had a restrictive impact on bank liquidity in that the monetary base of the economy was reduced by the amount of the reserve. In addition, debt management policy was pursued by the Treasury and other public authorities. Short-term debt, primarily in the form of Treasury bills, was reduced by around DM 6 billion, and the amount of long-term debt was increased by almost DM 4.5 billion.[41] A surplus was run in the budgets for all levels of government for 1969, compared to a deficit for 1968. Moreover, for the public sector as a whole, direct taxes, exercising an automatic stabilizer effect, increased by 11 percent over 1968, and total receipts increased 16 percent.[42] Total public sector expenditures increased only 9 percent, and public sector surplus or savings amounted to DM 9.1 billion, compared to a deficit of DM 4.1 billion for 1968.

Despite the moderately restrictive fiscal and debt-management policies, the boom continued into 1970. In 1969, real GNP rose by some 8 percent, while money GNP rose by 11.5 percent.[43] In spite of growing demand pressures, price increases remained moderate until mid-1969. After this period, prices began to rise and the expansion of demand continued at a high rate into 1970. Fiscal policy measures called for restriction in expenditure increases in the federal budget to around 8.5 percent. The Business Cycle Council put into effect a further increase in the contracyclical reserve fund of DM 2.5 billion. A tax reduction for wage and salary earners, originally set for the beginning of 1970, was temporarily postponed. For the public sector as a whole, total receipts were in excess of expenditures by some DM 14 billion, creating a surplus in the budgetary accounts.

SUMMARY

The fiscal system of West Germany is based on the provisions of the Basic Law of 1949. In accordance with the federal structure of West Germany, the exercise of governmental powers and the discharge of governmental functions is incumbent on the states insofar as the Basic Law does not otherwise prescribe. The distribution of governmental tasks between the federal government and state governments determines the distribution of the financial burdens that the fulfillment of these task involves. Local governments, or communes, are treated basically as parts of the states, and their tasks and distribution of revenues is largely left to state legislation. Thus, the fiscal system of the Federal Republic is a tripartite system in which all three levels of government are entitled to certain sources of revenues and have specific functions to perform.

The federal government bears the cost of defense, foreign relations, federal highways, and waterways, as well as the subsidies to the German railway system and the expenses of the federal revenue authorities. Moreover, the burdens caused as a consequence of two world wars and the bulk of the cost of social security are also borne by the federal government.

In principle, the states bear the cost of the administration of justice and, together with the communes, they bear the cost of police, education, welfare, health, and road services, to the extent that these are not federal responsibilities. As between the states and their communes, the distribution of the financial burdens of these services is determined by state legislation. The states also share common tasks with the federal government, such as the improvement of the agricultural infrastructure and the construction of new universities. The 1969 reform of the financial provisions of the Basic Law has enlarged the number of services that are performed jointly by the federal and state governments.

The federal government derives its revenue from fiscal monopolies, shared taxes, and taxes over which it has exclusive jurisdiction. In keeping with the newly defined area of common tasks, the 1969 financial reforms increased the extent of tax sharing between the federal and state levels. Formerly, they shared only the receipts of the individual and corporate income taxes; now value-added tax receipts are also shared. The yield of individual and corporate income taxes is shared equally, while the distribution of the value-added tax is 70 percent for the federal government and 30 percent for the states. This relationship, however, is subject to alteration on a year-by-year basis.

Local governments receive a 14-percent share of the yield of the individual income tax. This share is deducted from total individual income tax receipts before the rest is divided equally between the federal and state levels. In compensation, the latter two receive a share of 40 percent of the trade tax revenues of the communes, which is also divided equally between them. Other local sources of revenue are the taxes on real property, amusements, beverages, and other taxes on consumption. In most cases, state legislation determines whether and to what extent receipts from shared taxes and state taxes accrue to the localities.

The active use of fiscal policy as an anticyclical weapon was very rudimentary in Germany up until 1967, when a reform of the budgetary system occurred. The federal government, as an antirecessionary measure, implemented two special public investment programs. The Stabilization Law provided the federal government with a number of Keynesian fiscal policy instruments to attain an overall economic equilibrium with stable prices, bull employment, a positive trade balance, and moderate economic growth. The investment budgets of 1967 and 1968, designed to pump money into the economy, were successful. The federal government was also given the power to increase the level of taxation during a boom period in order to reduce the level of aggregate demand and to lower the level of taxation during a downturn to increase purchasing power.

CHAPTER

5

**INCOME
DISTRIBUTION
IN WEST GERMANY**

INTRODUCTION

Income distribution in a market economy is based on certain institutional arrangements, such as the pricing process, that are associated with this type of system. High prices are set on scarce agents of production and low prices on plentiful agents. In terms of rewards to labor, those persons whose skills are scarce relative to demand enjoy a high level of income, while those persons whose skills are not scarce do not. In a market economy, people are supposedly rewarded on the basis of their contribution to marketable output that, in turn, reflects consumer preferences and incomes. The implication is that persons whose productivity in value terms is low will earn little, regardless of whether the low productivity is attributable to lack of effort, lack of skill, or low demand for the skill.

Income in a market economy emanates from two sources: income from wages or salaries and self-employment and property income. Property may be regarded as a stock of claims or rights to the value of wealth, whether it be natural resources or man-made capital and consumer durable goods. The structure of property claims in a capitalist economy is generally a complex one; individuals' claims on wealth owned by corporations, for example, may be represented by common or preferred stock, by corporate bonds, and by notes and mortgages held by persons. Ultimately, property rights or claims can be traced to the objects of wealth underlying them or to claims on income to which the wealth gives rise.

One of the most important economic and social developments of this century has been the creation of the welfare state. In general, this creation stems from a dissatisfaction with the distribution of income. One result of market capitalism has been an extreme inequality in the distribution of income. This inequality can be attributed primarily to the receipt of income from claims on property, such as interest, rent, and dividends. Thus, efforts have been made to effect a more equitable distribution of income. The progressive income tax has been introduced in the capitalist countries. It accomplishes a redistribution of income in the direction of greater equality because the proportionate share of the upper-income groups in the total income is reduced and the proportionate share of the lower-income groups is raised. The progressiveness of the income tax structure brings about this result because the effective rate of taxation—the ratio of total taxes paid to income received—increases with the size of the income. The effect of the personal income tax as a redistributive device is rather modest, however.

Another manifestation of the welfare state has been the use of transfer payments to effect a redistribution of income. The reason for this is clear because transfer payments, as well as taxes, are the chief means by which a government can provide for a greater degree of equality in the distribution of income, which is the hallmark of the welfare state. The existence of a tax-financed system of transfer payments will alter a market-determined pattern of income distribution in that most transfers of money income go to people. Transfer payments, such as family allowances, old-age retirement benefits, and unemployment compensation, have a direct effect on the distribution of income in a society. Taxes, of course, provide the state with control over economic resources.

The most important aspect of the welfare state, however, has been a commitment to the goal of full employment. Unemployment, the bête noire of capitalism, was a paramount economic problem in the Western industrial countries, particularly during the decade prior to World War II. During this period the average annual umemployment rate in the United Kingdom and Sweden was well over 10 percent. In Germany, adverse economic conditions contributed to the rise in political strength of both the Communist and National Socialist parties. In 1932, for example, there were 6 million unemployed workers. In the United States conditions were no better. It seemed apparent, at least during this time, that the Marxist prediction of the collapse of capitalism was correct. But the war intervened and solved the problem of unemployment.

After the end of the war, there was a general commitment on the part of the Western countries to the goal of full employment. In France, formal economic planning occurred with the creation of the Commissariat General au Plan in 1946. The responsibility of the government was extended more deeply than ever before into the economy. The influence of Beveridge and Keynes on the United Kingdom is well known. In addition to the implementation of the basic elements of the Beveridge Plan, the British adopted the economic policies of Keynes. The British budget became a powerful weapon for influencing the level of economic activity in the economy. In Sweden, full employment received top priority as a policy goal, and fiscal, monetary, and manpower policies were subverted to this end. Thus, during the postwar period the unemployment rate in the United Kingdom and Sweden has rarely been in excess of 3 percent.

Full employment policy has an impact on the distribution of income in that it creates a shift in favor of labor incomes and against property incomes. This shift has been occasioned in part by a tight labor market, which has prevailed in most of the Western countries during much of the postwar period. There has also been a movement away from agriculture in response to the growth of better-paying jobs in the urban industrial sector. The tight labor market, which has prevailed in such countries as Germany and Sweden, has been responsible not only for an increase in labor's share of national income but for a narrowing of occupational differentials as well. Labor market policies, which have had as their objective full employment and the transfer of labor to more productive branches of industry that offer better pay, certainly have had some effect on income distribution. Included under labor market policies are all measures designed to affect both the demand for and the supply of labor, including vocational guidance and job training.

The major purpose of the remainder of this chapter is to describe in detail the workings of the West German social security system and the extent to which it has become an instrument for the redistribution of income in the economy. It will also analyze in a general way the manner in which income distribution is altered as a result of welfare expenditures by the government and will stress a number of important structural characteristics of the German economy, showing how these have influenced the functioning of the social security system.

SOCIAL SECURITY AND OTHER WELFARE MEASURES

Social security programs in Germany date back to Bismarck's opposition to socialism and his jealousy of the trade union movement, which led him to sponsor the health insurance law of 1883. This first national insurance law in the world covered most industrial workers. Workers contributed two-thirds and employers one-third of the cost. The coverage of the law was constantly widened. By 1911 when the Insurance Consolidation Act brought all German insurance systems under one statute, the majority of workers were insured against sickness and invalidity. Benefits include medicine, hospitalization, maternity benefits, and payment of 50 percent of the wages lost by illness.

Bismarck was a political pragmatist of the first order who realized that concessions to the working classes had to be made to check the rise of socialism. He sponsored social legislation in order to remove the causes upon which socialism was developing. Thus, the health insurance program was followed in 1884 by legislation that sponsored employment-injury insurance, or workmen's compensation as it is called in the United States. The workmen's compensation law was also the first of its kind in the world and provided benefits regardless of the circumstances of the injury. The cost of compensation was placed entirely on the employer. In 1889 the Old Age and Invalidity Law was passed, providing an old-age pension payable to wage earners who had been regularly employed and who had reached the age of seventy. It was financed by a tax on both the employer and employee, each paying half; the government granted additional subsidies. The law was extended to cover salaried workers in 1911.

Between World Wars I and II a pension system was established for miners in 1923; unemployment insurance, which had originated in the United Kingdom in 1911, was introduced in 1927. Social assistance of various types for those who were not covered by insurance or who had exhausted their benefits was established in 1924. World War II gave rise to special programs for assisting victims of both world wars, including widows and orphans or war veterans, and for equalization of burdens measures that are designed to distribute among the population war and postwar losses.

In the Federal Republic, the bulk of social security expenditures are kept in the social budget (Sozialbudget), which is administered separately from the federal budget. The social budget, however, is under the jurisdiction of the federal government. Basically, the bulk of the German social security system is financed by payroll taxes and other contributions, which are reflected in the social budget, and from the general revenues of the federal budget. The family allowance, as is typical of most European social security systems, is financed primarily from general government revenues. The social budget is broken down into two categories: expenditures according to institutions and expenditures according to categories. The budget is required to make projections concerning social security requirements over a four-year period.

A basic characteristic of the West German social security system is its fragmentation into a number of funds or special systems. One example is the special insurance scheme for miners, which was first introduced in 1923. Under this scheme, special pensions and benefits are paid to miners for premature reduction of earnings capacity and for old age. In addition, pensions and benefits are paid to survivors of miners killed in employment. There is also a pension scheme for independent farmers that provides certain benefits. Public employees, self-employed artisans, and building and clockworks also have their own social security schemes. Contributions and benefits vary according to the system.

In looking at the financing of the West German social security system, it is necessary to make the following observations. The bulk of the cost is financed by social security taxes proper—i.e., taxes levied directly on the beneficiaries of the system. The revenues are not adequate to cover all outlays of funds by the system, however. A part of the cost must be covered by the general revenue of the government, which comes from direct and indirect taxes. Thus, some portion of all taxes paid by individual income recipients are used to finance the welfare expenditures of the social security system. With respect to direct taxes, it is difficult to determine what proportion of taxes on individuals are allocated to social security expenditure. There is also the parallel problem of the incidence of these taxes. These problems would not be especially difficult to solve if all government expenditures were financed by direct taxation and if the federal government did not run a deficit.

The federal government depends upon indirect taxation for the bulk of its revenue. The three main indirect taxes—the value-added tax, the tobacco tax, and the petroleum tax—all of which are taxes on consumption, accounted for almost half of federal tax revenues in 1971. It is difficult to measure the redistributional effect of the social security system when part of the revenue is derived from indirect taxation. This is so because of the price effects that are associated with indirect taxation. The existence of indirect taxation as a major source of revenue requires both that the incidence of these taxes be determined and that the proportion of total revenue raised by these taxes, to be allocated to social security expenditures, be determined. The former requires a precise knowledge not only of income but, more importantly, of consumption patterns for all income and social groups. Moreover, any allocation of tax revenue from different tax sources to social security expenditure will be arbitrary, for there is no way to determine in the federal budget the exact use of revenue from a particular source.

In 1970 total expenditures on all forms of social welfare assistance in the social budget amounted to DM 123.6 billion, and total revenues from all sources amounted to DM 127.2 billion.[1] Included under the category of social welfare assistance are the basic social security system, family allowances, war pensions and related assistance, equalization of burdens funds, and other forms of social help. The basic social security system includes old-age, invalidity, and survivors' benefits and pensions, work-injury compensation, sickness and maternity benefits, and unemployment compensation. The social security system can be broken down further into various types of pensions for different categories of workers. Family allowances are

TABLE 5.1

Expenditures in West German Social
Budget, 1970
(billion DM)

Type of Expenditures	Amount of Expenditures*
Old-age and survivors' pensions and benefits	54.4
Old-age help for farmers	0.9
Sickness and maternity benefits	23.6
Workmen's compensation for injury	3.8
Unemployment compensation	3.0
Social security proper	85.7
Family allowances	3.0
Social help	3.7
Rent subsidies	1.2
Youth help	1.1
Other	0.9
Social services	9.9
Pensions and other assistance to public employees	18.0
War pensions and related assistance	7.6
Equalization of burdens	1.7
Other expenses	0.7
Total for all social welfare	123.6

*All figures are preliminary.

Source: Bundesminister für Arbeit und Sozialordnung, Sozialbericht 1970 (Bonn, 1970), pp. 172-73.

excluded, for, technically, the financial arrangement is outside of the social security system proper.

The bulk of German transfer payments are contained in the German social assistance program. In Table 5.1 expenditures for all forms of social assistance are presented. Included are the standard social security expenditures, family allowances, war pensions, equalization of burdens, rent subsidies, and other types of assistance. The total amount of DM 123.6 billion, which includes administrative costs, can be compared to a GNP for 1970 of DM 679 billion. Of this total of DM 123.6 billion, around 70 percent, or DM 85.6 billion, was allocated for social security measures, and the remainder was allocated for other forms of social assistance.[2] The DM 123.6 billion can also be broken down into the following costs: cash payments, or direct transfers, to individuals, DM 83.8 billion; payments for services performed, such as medical costs and payments in kind, DM 25.7 billion; other payments, DM 4.9 billion; and administrative expenses, DM 4.9 billion.[3]

In Table 5.2 revenue sources to finance social assistance measures are presented. These sources can be broken down into five categories: revenues from levies on employers, revenues from levies on employees, government contributions out of general budget revenues, earnings from social security and other types of funds, and surpluses. Virtually all of the revenues derived from levies on employers and employees go for social security expenditures, while the bulk of government support is for family allowances, war pensions and war-related assistance, and for various forms of subsidies.

TABLE 5.2

Revenue Sources in West German
Social Budget, 1970
(billion DM)

Revenue Source	Amount of Revenue
Levies on employees	33.6
Levies on employers	34.4
Government revenues	47.1
Property and other income	4.7
Surplus on account	7.7
Total	127.5

Source: Bundesminister für Arbeit und Sozialordnung, Sozialbericht 1970 (Bonn, 1970), p. 172.

Old-Age, Disability, and Survivors' Benefits

Old-age, disability, and survivors' benefits constitute the largest expenditure in the West German social security program. Preliminary expenditures as listed in the 1970 social budget amounted to DM 54.4 billion, of which DM 20.6 billion came from contributions of employees, DM 21 billion came from employer contributions, DM 11 billion came from government revenues, and the remainder from other sources.* These expenditures can also be divided on the basis of monetary transfers that go directly to persons and on the basis of expenditures for services provided to the group. In 1970 direct cash transfers to individuals amounted to DM 44.5 billion. This is the kind of transfer that has the most direct effect upon the distribution of money income in a society.

Old-age and survivors' benefits, including disability pensions, are provided by an insurance scheme that is compulsory and covers all wage earners and salaried employees. Special systems are provided for miners, civil servants, self-employed persons, artisans, and farmers. There is also the option of private insurance, which is optimal to persons provided their premiums equal the contributions under the public programs. In either case, employers and employees generally each pay half the cost of the premiums. In 1971 the general public old-age and survivors' insurance scheme was financed by a tax of 8 percent of payrolls levied on the employer, a tax of 8 percent of earnings levied on the employee, and an annual subsidy provided by the federal government out of general revenues, which usually amounts to around one-third of the cost of the program.[4] To some extent the employer also subsidizes the program in that he is required to pay the entire amount of the contribution when employee earnings are 10 percent or less of the assessment limit.

The monthly earnings ceiling for the assessment of contributions to the pension scheme as well as the rate of the contribution are constantly subject to change. The ceiling is adjusted each year for wage changes. The monthly earnings ceiling for the assessment of contributions in 1968 was DM 1,600; by 1971, the ceiling had increased to DM 1,900. The rate of the tax increased from 7.5 percent to 8 percent. Therefore, the maximum monthly contribution in 1971 was DM 304, which is equally shared by the employer and employee. It is to be emphasized, however, that the rate and ceiling apply to the bulk of wage and salary earners but not to all groups. Miners, for example, have an earnings ceiling of DM 2,300 a month, with special support coming from revenues of the federal budget. Different ceilings apply to self-employed workers, including farmers, who have to carry the full cost of the insurance.

Cash benefits are geared to the relative position of an insured person's earnings rather than to the absolute amount and to a policy of continually adjusting existing benefits to the current general level

---

*All contributions and expenditures for old-age, disability, and survivors' benefits are listed on pages 105 and 106.

of money income. Maximum contributions are measured by earnings as compared with the national average during the last three calendar years prior to the assessment. The old-age pension amounts to 1.5 percent of a worker's assessed wage multiplied by the years the worker was insured. A worker credited with 45 years of coverage whose compensation during the period of insurance equalled the national average is entitled to a pension of 67.5 percent (1.5 percent multiplied by 45) of the national average earnings of employees during the three calendar years prior to the date of his retirement. In addition to the old-age pension there is an invalidity pension computed in the same manner; a widow's pension, which is 60 percent of the old-age or invalidity pension; children's supplements, which when added to the widow's pension amount to 100 percent of the regular pension; and funeral grants of a lump sum of 20 to 40 days' earnings or three months' pension, if a pensioner.

There are old-age pensions for special groups, such as farmers and miners. One purpose of pensions for farmers is to further agricultural policy. It is contended that payment of an old-age pension accelerates the transfer or sale of farms, thus contributing to the rationalization of agriculture. Funds to support the financing of old-age pensions come from the farmers and general funds of the federal budget. Funds are administered by the General Association of Agricultural Old Age Insurance Institutions. In 1970 old-age assistance (Altershilfe für Landwirte) amounted to DM 888 million, of which DM 838 million represented direct cash payments to farmers.[5]

Pensions for miners represent an interesting case in point with respect to the fragmentation of the West German social security fund. As early as the fourteenth century, because of the special dangers to life and health associated with work in the mines, miners formed mutual aid societies for the purpose of providing financial assistance to those persons who were disabled by accidents to their dependents. These associations, called "Knappschaften," have largely been maintained up to the present. Included under assistance to miners are pensions related to age or incapacity for work, pensions for dependents of miners, medical care and other health measures, and vocational training for miners who are being shifted into other occupations.

In 1970 total preliminary expenditures for old-age, disability, and survivors' benefits for miners amounted to DM 6.2 billion. Of this total, DM 5.4 billion represented direct cash transfers. Insofar as expenditures of the miners' special pension funds are not covered by contributions from miners and employers and other income from investments, the federal government is required by law to make up any yearly deficiency. In 1970 federal subsidies were projected to amount to DM 3.7 billion out of total income of DM 6.2 billion.[6]

Sickness Insurance

Sickness insurance is a second component of the West German social security system. In terms of its relationship to other social welfare measures, it is the second-most-important expenditure component in the social budget. In 1970 preliminary expenditures were DM 23.3 billion, most of which took the form of subsidies designed to provide medical goods and services at costs not reflected in the marketplace.[7] Revenues to finance sickness insurance came primarily from social security contributions from employees and employers; federal budget support was negligible.

Sickness insurance benefits involve the payment of medical expenses, and the payment of an allowance to compensate for the loss of earnings during the period of sickness. Persons covered by sickness insurance are reimbursed for the cost of hospitalization, drugs, and the fees of physicians and dentists in an amount usually equal to 100 percent of the cost or fee. Physicians and dentists are not, as in the case of England, employees of the state. A scale of fees is established by consultation between the appropriate social security administration and the organization representing doctors or dentists. Doctors are not legally obligated to observe the scale of fees, so the actual extent to which a patient is compensated for the cost outlay in a particular illness may vary. Patients are required to pay a maximum of DM 2.5 for medicine.

Cash benefits paid to persons who are sick include an amount equal to 65 percent of weekly earnings during the first six weeks of confinement and 75 percent of weekly earnings thereafter up to a period of 78 weeks. During the first six weeks, employers must pay the difference between the cash benefit and the regular wage. In addition to the regular sickness benefit there is a supplementary benefit of 4 percent of weekly wages for the first dependent and 3 percent for the second and third dependent. Maternity benefits include a payment of 100 percent of earnings for six weeks before and eight weeks after childbirth; and a maternity grant of DM 100 per birth. Nonworking wives of insured persons are also eligible for maternity grants.

Sickness and maternity benefits are financed by contributions from employees, employers, and government revenues. This system is fragmented into a number of insurance funds. As of January 1, 1970, there were 1,838 independent sickness insurance funds in the Federal Republic. All are under the general supervision of the Federal Ministry of Labor and Social Affairs (Bundesministerium für Arbeit und Sozialordnung). Employee and employer contributions range from 4 to 5.5 percent of earnings and payrolls, depending upon the sickness fund. The federal government contributes the cost of the maternity grants.

Work-Injury Compensation

Benefits are paid to any person who is prevented for physical reasons from earning a living. All insured workers are entitled to compensation for all medical expenses arising out of the work-injury that is the cause of disablement. The disabled person also is eligible for a pension, the amount of which is generally equal to 65 percent of weekly earnings. This amount is paid for the first 18 days of disablement from the insured worker's sickness fund; thereafter, it is paid out of special industrial and agricultural accident funds. If the disablement is permanent, the pension is increased to 66 2/3 percent of the weekly wage or salary and may be further augmented if the disabled person requires the attention of other persons. Minimum and maximum pensions are DM 100 and DM 2,100 a month. In addition, there is a supplement of 10 percent of the pension for each child under 18.

In 1970 total preliminary expenditures on work-injury benefits amounted to DM 3.8 billion. Of this amount DM 2.7 billion went for cash payments to disabled persons. In terms of financing work-injury benefits are financed by a payroll levy on employers' payrolls that averages 1.5 percent. The federal government subsidizes the agricultural accident funds. In 1970 about 90 percent of the cost of workmen's accident insurance was borne by employers.

Unemployment Compensation

Unemployment compensation is almost an anomaly in West Germany for the reason that the rate of unemployment has been very low during the last dozen or so years. In 1970, for example, the average unemployment rate for the year was 0.7 percent.[8] In the event that unemployment does occur, benefits ranging from 40 percent to 90 percent of earnings are paid for a period of from 13 to 52 weeks depending on the extent of insured employment. In addition, there are cash supplements for dependents, which amount to DM 9 a week for the wife and for the first child and DM 3 a week for the second child. Unemployment compensation, subject to a means test, is also payable after the exhaustion of benefits.

Benefits are financed by a tax on insured persons of 0.65 percent of earnings up to DM 1,300 a month and by a tax of 0.65 percent of the payrolls of employers. Responsibility for the disbursement of benefits rests with regional and local employment offices. In 1969 outlays for unemployment compensation amounted to DM 2.9 billion, of which virtually the entire amount was in the form of direct cash benefits to the unemployed.

Unemployment compensation is the last component of what can

be called social security proper. Social security includes various insurance schemes designed to protect German workers from the vicissitudes of life. These schemes are financed primarily by two taxes, one on the employer and the other on the employee, and by general revenues from the federal budget and other sources.

Family Allowances

The family allowance, or children's allowance as it is commonly called, is a regular cash payment to families with children. It is paid in all major industrial countries with the exception of the United States and Japan and is generally carried as a social security benefit. The family allowance is a method of improving the welfare of children by attempting to correct, at least in some measure, the imbalance between family income and family need. In essence, it constitutes a device for redistributing income in such a way as to benefit the child-rearing portion of a nation's population. The family allowance, however, differs from the social insurance aspect of social security in that the benefits do not depend upon the actual wage or salary of the worker but instead on the number of children in the family. It is usually financed by a tax on employers or out of general government revenues. The amount of the allowance is either the same for all children or it increases progressively with the number of children in the family.

In West Germany the children's allowance (Kindergeld) is financed out of the revenues of the federal budget. In 1971 DM 3.3 billion were allocated for this purpose.[9] There is a children's allowance fund (Kindergeldfonds), which has been constituted an independent fund under public law and is administered by the Federal Institution for Labor Exchange and Unemployment Insurance. The West German family allowance system is fairly unique in comparison to systems in other countries in that the first child is excluded from the allowance. A monthly allowance of DM 25 is paid for the second child provided that the annual family income is less than DM 13,200 or when a family has three or more children. The allowance for the third and fourth child is DM 60 for each, and for the fifth and subsequent children DM 70 for each. The allowance is paid for all children under the age of 18. In addition, education allowances are paid to families with two or more children.

It can be said that the income redistribution effect of the West German family allowance is small. In comparison to the French family allowance system, which accounts for around 15 percent of total social welfare expenditures in France, the German family allowance system accounts for less than 3 percent.[10] Most of the income redistribution effect of the family allowance is among units in the same income class.

Individuals and families with no children subsidize families with children. The redistributional effect is horizontal rather than vertical. The transfer payments of the family allowance are progressive within classes in that they are tied to the size of the family. A family without children with a given income would pay a higher income tax than a family with children receiving the same income but would receive the children's allowance.

In addition to the family allowance, there are other general social welfare measures. There is social assistance (Sozialhilfe), which includes welfare and charitable expenditures for such things as aid to the aged and infirm, medical care for the insane, and grants to tubercular persons. In general, such assistance is directed to persons who, for one reason or another, are not eligible for benefits or assistance under the regular social security programs. A second form of assistance is aid to youths (Jugendhilfe). This assistance primarily takes the form of educational grants to enable students to attend school. Rent subsidies are also included under general social measures. In Germany rental allowances are paid to low-income families that spend a certain proportion of their income for rent and live in residences that meet certain minimum conditions of health and sanitation. Rent subsidies are typically provided for persons with low fixed incomes.

War Pensions and Related Assistance

War and war-related pensions and financial assistance comprise an important component of total German welfare expenditures. In the years immediately following the end of World War II, expenditures were grouped under two categories: war assistance (Kriegsfolgenhilfe) and war pensions (Kriegsopferversorgung). The former consisted of special welfare measures relating to expellees, refugees from the Soviet Zone, former political prisoners, and dependents of prisoners of war and missing persons. In addition to these, there were also various measures for the creation and maintenance of transit and reception camps for the assistance of those persons in need. This assistance was primarily the responsibility of the states and communes; in later years, the federal government assumed more financial responsibility. As conditions became more stable within the Federal Republic, the amount of money allocated to war relief measures declined. In 1971 expenditures as listed in the federal budget were around DM 400 million.[11]

The most important expenditures are pensions to veterans and other war-related assistance measures. There are a variety of forms of assistance to war veterans and their dependents, including not only pensions but such things as medical care, homes for the aged and disabled, financial aid for vocational training, scholarships, and the care of war orphans. The main provisions were contained in the Federal Pensions Law of 1950; since that time a number of amendments have been added. Covered under war pensions are all veterans of World Wars I and II and widows and orphans of veterans. Veterans and related persons suffering from war injuries and damages are also covered. In 1970 expenditures on war-related measures amounted to DM 7.6 billion. Of this amount, DM 7.5 billion came from federal budget revenues.[12]

Other Social Assistance Measures

Listed separately under the social budget are pensions and other welfare measures for public employees. As is true in other countries, government employees have their own retirement system. There are old-age pensions, health insurance provisions, allowances for children, and other social welfare measures. In 1970 total funds for these purposes amounted to DM 18 billion, virtually all of which was financed out of general budget revenues.[13] A second category of expenditures includes the Equalization of Burdens Fund and various other reparation measures. The Equalization of Burdens Fund, as mentioned previously, is designed to redistribute equitably among the population of West Germany war and postwar losses, which have affected the citizens to an uneven degree. Other reparation measures, including reparations to Israel, are a minor expenditure component.

Apart from protecting the income and health of the West German population, there are also social measures that embrace other areas. The cost of these measures is not reflected in any inflow and outflow of revenues. One such measure concerns regulations governing working conditions and the labor market. Under this category come various laws designed to protect the welfare of the workers. Labor offices exist to provide vocational advisory services and vocational guidance and also to attend to unemployment insurance. There are management and labor relations codes that govern employer-employee relations. Minimum-wage legislation and other standards also affect the general conditions of employment.

INCOME REDISTRIBUTION EFFECTS OF SOCIAL WELFARE PROGRAMS

In 1970 total expenditures for social security and other social welfare measures, excluding clearing accounts, amounted to DM 115.8 billion. This expenditure can be divided into four categories: direct cash payments of DM 83.8 billion, payments in kind of DM 25.7 billion, administrative costs of DM 4.8 billion, and other costs of DM 1.5 billion. Total net expenditures of DM 115.8 billion amounted to around 16 percent of the GNP of DM 679 billion, or 21.8 percent of the national income of DM 522.9 billion. The concept of national income is of fundamental importance, for it represents to an economy as a whole the major source of money income or purchasing power for the purchase of the bulk of the GNP. National income is defined as the cost of producing the GNP or, more specifically, the aggregate earnings of labor and property that arise from the production of goods and services by a nation's economy. The degree to which a government has become an instrument for the redistribution of income can be measured by computing transfer payments as a percentage of national income. The percentage relationship indicates the proportion of earned income that has been redistributed by action of the public sector.

Data on personal income also illustrates the impact of welfare expenditures on the origins of income. Personal income refers to money income actually received rather than to income earned in the process of production. In 1970 transfer payments in the form of pensions and other types of cash assistance amounted to DM 85.5 billion out of total personal income of DM 457.9 billion.[14] Net wages and salaries for employees amounted to DM 241.2 billion, and rent, dividends, interest, and entrepreneurial income amounted to DM 131.2 billion.[15] Transfer payments amounted to 18.6 percent of personal income in 1970. It can be said that in 1970 81.4 percent of personal income in West Germany was derived directly from participation in the production process, whereas 18.6 percent originated from cash transfer payments.

The trend in social welfare expenditures has been upward over time. In 1938 net expenditures on all forms of social assistance amounted to DM 7.3 billion, or 8.9 percent of GNP.[16] By 1950 net expenditures had increased to DM 15.7 billion, or 14.9 percent of GNP. In 1970 net expenditures had increased to DM 115.8 billion, or 18.6 percent of the GNP. Net outlays for social security proper increased from DM 8.9 billion in 1950 to DM 78.1 billion in 1970. There has also been a shift in the character of total social assistance expenditures during the period 1950-70 in that on a relative basis expenditures on social security proper have increased from 50 to 65 percent of total expenditures, whereas expenditures on other forms of assistance have declined to 35 percent of the total.[17]

A general impression of income distribution in the Federal Republic before the imposition of income taxes, excluding transfer payments, can be obtained from Table 5.3. Included in the distribution of income are wages, salaries, and incomes from other sources, such as dividends, interest, and income of unincorporated enterprises. In the table, income distribution by quintiles for two time periods, 1950

TABLE 5.3

Comparison of Income Distribution Before
Taxes, by Quintiles, West Germany, 1950-67
(percent)

Quintiles	1950	1967
First quintile	4.0	8.7
Second quintile	8.5	13.0
Third quintile	16.5	17.1
Fourth quintile	23.0	23.0
Fifth quintile	48.0	38.2
Total	100.0	100.0

Source: Data for 1950 are from United Nations, Economic Survey of Europe (Geneva, 1957), p. 6; data for 1967 are from Deutscher Bundestag, Materialien zum Bericht zur Lage der Nation 1971, Drucksache VI/1690 (Bonn, 1971), p. 98.

and 1967, is presented. As is evident in the table, there has been a shift during the two periods toward an increase in the distribution of income in the lowest two quintiles and a decrease in income in the highest quintile. On an a priori basis the explanation for the shift in income distribution can be attributed to various economic and social factors, not the least of which has been a high level of employment and a tight labor market over most of this time period.

The meaning of income distribution becomes more apparent in the analysis of national income data. National income, as mentioned previously, pertains to factoral income distribution or the claims of the national output that arise out of the ownership of economic resources. The productive process requires the services of economic resources, and payment must be made to the owners of the resources in order to secure their services. This requirement gives rise to a claim by resource owners to a share of the national output. The broadest allocation of the national income is a two-fold division, with wage and salary income on one side and the various forms of property income on the other. Property income consists of income derived from the ownership of economic resources in the form either of capital equipment or of national resources. In national income accounting, property income takes the form of rents, interest, and profits. Beyond this fundamental division between labor and nonlabor income, the factoral distribution concept has to do with the relative shares of the income total that accrues to the different types of nonhuman economic resources, that is, the relative share in the income total of different types of property income.

In Table 5.3 the shift in the period of time from 1950 to 1967 is readily apparent when comparisons are made of income received from wages and salaries and income received from property and entrepreneurship. In 1950 compensation of employes in the form of wages and salaries and employers' contributions to social security amounted to DM 44.1 billion, whereas income from property and enterpreneurial income amounted to DM 31.1 billion. In 1967 total compensation of employees amounted to DM 247.9 billion, whereas income from property and entrepreneurship amounted to DM 127.2 billion.[18] On a percentage basis the breakdown between compensation of employees and property and entrepreneurial income was 59 to 41 percent in 1950, compared to a breakdown of 66.1 and 33.9 percent for 1967. Most of the change that has taken place occurred during the period 1958-67, when a high level of economic activity coupled with a very low unemployment rate prevailed in Germany. For example, during this period, compensation of employees increased from DM 109 billion to DM 247.9 billion, while income from property and entrepreneurship increased from DM 71.1 billion to DM 127.2 billion.[19]

Thus, there has been a gradual shift in favor of labor income and, as a result, a change in the distribution of income by quintiles. Interest, rent, and dividends, all of which would typically accrue to upper-income groups, have shown a relative decline in relation to labor income for the period 1950-67. Wages and salaries increased from DM 44.1 billion to DM 247.9 billion during the period, whereas property income increased from DM 26.1 billion to DM 100.4 billion. Wages and salaries have increased by approximately 600 percent, whereas property income has increased by approximately 380 percent.

It is suggested that one source of the trend toward more equalization in the distribution of income is full employment, which has been maintained with only minor interruptions over the past 15 years. West German economic policies have focused upon the maintenance of a high level of employment. Unemployment of labor resources obviously detracts from productivity and thus creates a loss of real income for society as a whole. In Germany, jobs have been available for those who want them, and general labor shortages have driven real wages upward. Workers have been brought in from Yugoslavia, Italy, and other Mediterranean countries, and they have comprised on occasion as much as one-tenth of the labor force.* When

---

*The number of foreigners employed in West Germany as of July 1, 1971, amounted to 2.2 million, or around 10 percent of the labor

unemployment of any magnitude occurs, as during the 1967 recession, these workers are the first to be laid off, so unemployment for the most part has been exported to the Mediterranean countries, compounding their own problems with unemployment.

The annual rate of unemployment for the period 1960-70 is presented in Table 5.4. By any unemployment standard, American or European, the rate has been phenomenally low.* One contributing factor to this low unemployment rate is the fact that the German labor force itself has been relatively constant over time. Economic policy has not had to contend with providing jobs for an ever-increasing labor force.

Coupled with the low rate of unemployment has been a shift in the occupational composition of the labor force.[20] There has been a gain in relative numbers for the professional and clerical workers, largely at the expense of the skilled and unskilled manual laborers and occupations connected with sales and agriculture. In particular, the movement out of agriculture is pretty clearly a response to the growth of better-paid job opportunities in the urban-industrial sector. The end result of occupational shifts is net upgrading of income over time and a decline in inequality in the distribution of income. So it can be concluded that there has been in recent years a shift in favor of labor incomes and against incomes from property; at the same time the distribution of people among occupations has changed in such a way as to promote a more even distribution of income.

INCOME REDISTRIBUTION THROUGH TAXES

Table 5.3 presents only the distribution of income before taxes and transfer payments. Income redistribution, or income after taxes and transfer payments are taken into consideration, is more difficult to measure. The impact of both taxation and transfer payments on the German economy is considerable. But it is necessary to examine

---

force. Of the 1.6 million men and 600,000 women employed, 21.6 percent came from Yugoslavia, 19.6 percent from Turkey, 18.6 percent from Italy, 12.6 percent from Greece, and the remainder from other countries.

*German unemployment statistics are based on a count of unemployed registrants at employment offices. Registrants include persons who seek unemployment benefits and those who wish to use the services of the offices. In terms of the American system, the German unemployment rate is understated by about 0.8 percent.

TABLE 5.4

Annual Unemployment Rates, West Germany,
1960-70
(percent)

Year	Unemployment Rate
1960	1.3
1961	0.8
1962	0.7
1963	0.8
1964	0.8
1965	0.7
1966	0.7
1967	2.1
1968	1.5
1969	0.9
1970	0.7

Source: Deutsche Bundesbank, Monatsberichte der Deutschen Bundesbank (Frankfurt am Main, October 1971), p. 63.

the nature of the tax-transfer mechanism before some observations can be made with any degree of accuracy. Is there much of an income redistribution effect downward in favor of the lower-income groups, or is the redistribution lateral within groups?

The major problem in any attempt to determine the extent to which a given tax structure brings about a redistribution of income is that of determining the incidence of taxation. Tax incidence is the point where the ultimate or final burden of the tax rests. Since most modern governments employ many different types of taxes to obtain this revenue, this is a problem of considerable complexity. The problem, moreover, has a dual aspect, for it is necessary, on the one hand, to identify the persons or groups upon whom a tax is normally levied and, on the other, to identify the income recipients who actually pay the tax. The latter is the problem of the ultimate incidence of taxation.

In examining the basic features of the West German tax system, it is convenient to group the taxes according to the conventional categories of direct taxes, indirect taxes, and social security taxes; then these taxes can be classified on the basis of their presumed incidence. That is, they are grouped according to whether they are borne directly by individuals, indirectly by individuals through higher prices for consumer goods and services, or by business firms. In 1970 direct taxes amounted to DM 77.2 billion, of which DM 62.2 billion came from taxes on individuals and DM 15 billion came from taxes on businesses.21 Indirect taxes, most of which are broad-based taxes on consumption, amounted to DM 91.3 billion, and social security contributions amounted to DM 75.7 billion. These contributions came from three sources: levies on employers, on employees, and on self-employed persons.

Generally speaking, the more direct the tax, the more difficult it is to shift it to someone else; the more indirect the tax, the greater the possibility of transferring its burden from the point of impact to another point of incidence. This is explained by the fact that a direct tax usually is applied to a tax base close to the individual, such as income or wealth. Direct taxes, in most instances, are further removed from subsequent market transactions after the taxes are imposed than are bases of indirect taxes. Thus, direct taxes, such as the personal income tax, are not especially conducive to the further market transactions that are necessary for the shifting of a tax. On the other hand, indirect taxes, such as retail sales and excise taxes, are more closely associated with further market transactions and, hence, are more conducive to tax shifting than direct taxes.

Tax shifting must occur through the market mechanism of supply and demand. This means that shifting will usually occur through a change in the market price of an economic good or productive resource. Taxes may be either shifted forward or backward. The former occurs when the price of a good is increased as a result of a tax allowing a part or all of the tax to be transferred onto someone else. On the other hand, if the result of the tax is a decrease in the price of a factor of production, and if this permits transference of all or a part of the tax burden, the tax has been shifted backward. Forward shifting ordinarily results in the rise in the price of an economic good in the product market, and backward shifting results from a reduction in the price of a productive resource in a factor market. In the first instance the burden of the tax has been shifted onto the consumer, while in the latter case the burden has been passed backward to the factor of production.

There are a number of factors that affect the extent to which a tax can be shifted. Probably the most important are the elasticities of supply and demand for a product in the marketplace. In general the more inelastic the demand for a product, the more nearly price will rise by the full amount of the tax and the more complete the shifting. The more inelastic the conditions of supply, the less the market price will rise and the less the extent of shifting. A second factor is the degree of monopoly in a particular market. In general the greater the control of prices in a market, the easier it is for a firm to shift taxes. Finally, the more broad-based a tax is, the easier it is to shift the tax. With a broad-based tax, consumers have no alternative to spend in areas where there is no tax, and sellers are in a position to raise prices in order to shift the tax. In particular the West German value-added tax is an example of a broad-based tax that is levied on consumption.

It is possible that a system of social welfare expenditures might function in such a way as to bring about a redistribution of income from upper-income to the lower-income groups. This is rarely the case in actuality, however. This particular pattern of income redistribution would come about if practically all of the beneficiaries of social welfare expenditures were found in the lower-income brackets and the system were financed wholly by a progressive income tax. This, of course, is not the case, for most existing systems adhere to a greater or lesser degree to the principle that the beneficiaries should at least contribute in part to the cost of the system. This is particularly true with respect to the social security system, but less true for more general government expenditures of a welfare nature.

Direct Taxes

Direct taxes in West Germany include the personal and corporate income taxes; the trade tax (Gewerbesteuer), which is levied on business income, capital, or payrolls; and inheritance, gift, net-wealth, and other minor taxes. In 1970 personal income taxes amounted to DM 51.1 billion out of total direct taxes of DM 77.2 billion.[22] The total of DM 51.1 billion is divided into DM 35.1 billion from wages and salaries of workers, and DM 16 billion from other sources of income, including income of unincorporated enterprises. When personal income taxes are compared to West German personal income, a very general idea of their burden is obtained. The comparison for 1970 is DM 51.1 billion to DM 457.2 billion.[23] In other words, around 14 percent of personal income flows out to the government sector in the form of personal income taxes. The effective tax rate, computed by dividing total income tax payments by personal income, was 14 percent in 1970—a low rate in comparison to a marginal rate structure of the personal income tax of 19 to 53 percent.

It is through the progressiveness of the income tax rates that some amount of income redistribution is achieved. The extent of income redistribution can be overrated, however. For example, in Sweden, which has the highest rate of progressive income taxation of any country in the world, it is estimated that only 1 percent of taxable income is actually redistributed by the personal income tax.[24] In West Germany itself, the potential progressiveness of the personal income tax is actually reduced by several factors, as follows.

1. The use of income splitting provides an important rate modification under the West German personal income tax rate structure. Married couples filing a joint return compute their joint liability by applying the statutory tax rates on one-half of their combined taxable income and multiplying the result by two. The German income tax rates are in actuality applied to two sets of taxable income. The lowest marginal tax rate of 19 percent is applied to incomes exceeding DM 8,009, or DM 16,018 for taxpayers entitled to income splitting, while the maximum marginal rate of 53 percent is applied to any income in excess of DM 110,039, or DM 220,078 in the case of income splitting. This means that the maximum marginal income tax rate is reached for taxpayers entitled to income splitting of around $60,000. In Sweden and the United States, two countries which much higher maximum marginal rates, the maximum rates are reached at incomes of $29,000 and $100,000, respectively.* Moreover, per capita and average family incomes are much lower in West Germany than in the United States and Sweden.

2. To some extent, unearned income, including income from capital gains, is taxed more lightly than earned income in West Germany.[25] Capital gains, with the exception of gains from speculative transactions involving property not held for a specific period of time, are exempt from taxation. Dividends are taxable at the source, and the tax is credited against an individual's total tax liability for the tax year. Interest from certain government bonds and other securities is tax exempt. Other forms of interest are treated as income from capital and are subject to a tax rate of 25 percent, which may be credited against the regular income tax liability. Rent income is also taxed separately from regular income from wages and salaries.

3. Regular income tax rates are reduced for so-called extraordinary income. This income is taxed at one-half of the average tax rate applied to the entire taxable income. Extraordinary income includes gain from the sale of an unincorporated enterprise or partnership; gain from the sale of corporate shares or membership rights in certain commercial entities other than corporations; damages for the loss of past, present, or future income, or for the discontinuance of an income-producing activity; and income from scientific, artistic, or literary work that an employee or independent professional person performs outside of his regular activities.

4. The family size of the West German taxpaying unit also carries an important impact upon the effective rate of tax progression

---

*The maximum marginal rate in Sweden is 80 percent and in the United States 70 percent.

under the personal income tax. The right of married couples to file a joint return along with the ability to add additional exemptions for each child in a family greatly reduces the marginal tax rate bracket of taxable income for the family as opposed to that of the single unmarried individual. It can be said that there is an element of regressiveness in the income tax structure through the use of exemptions for children. These exemptions work in reverse in that they benefit least those families that need them the most and benefit most those families that need them the least. For example, a family with two children earning a gross income of DM 5,000 a month receives a monthly allowance of DM 96, compared to a monthly allowance of DM 33 for a similar family with earnings of DM 600 a month.

Income for purposes of the German income tax consists of net income minus personal exemptions. Net income is arrived at by deducting certain types of losses and expenses from gross income. When taxable income is compared to personal income, there is a sharp divergence. In 1969 taxable income constituted less than one-half of personal income. This means that the true progressiveness of the income tax has been reduced through the use of various deductions, exemptions, and other forms of preferential treatment that lower the base of the tax. In 1969 income tax payments of DM 45.7 billion can be compared to personal income of DM 457.9 billion and taxable income of DM 206.1 billion.[26] The effective average tax rate on the taxable income of individuals, partnerships, and unincorporated enterprises is around 20 percent.

In 1969 personal income (Volkseinkommen) amounted to DM 457.9 billion, excluding transfer payments. This income can be broken down into two categories: income from wages and salaries and income from other sources, including property income and entrepreneurial income. Income from wages and salaries amounted to DM 299.5 billion, and income from other sources amounted to DM 158.4 billion. Income taxes on wages and salaries amounted to DM 27 billion, for an effective average tax of 9.5 percent. Income taxes on property and entrepreneurial income amounted to DM 18.7 billion, for an effective tax rate of 11.8 percent.[27] This data, however, does not indicate income distribution and tax burdens by taxpayer groups.

In Table 5.5 a general and incomplete idea can be gained about income distribution in West Germany before taxes. Income from wages and salaries is included in the table, but income from other sources is excluded. The income tax on wages (Lohnsteuer) is presented but represents only a part of the total income tax. The tax represents that part of income taxes actually withheld. With the exclusion of property income and entrepreneurial income, the table loses some of its potential significance. It is possible, however, to draw some conclusions about income distribution and tax burdens.

TABLE 5.5

Gross Wages and Salaries and Income Taxes, by
Income Group, West Germany, 1969

Income Group (DM)	Taxpayers (thousand)	Total Income (million DM)	Income Tax (million DM)
Under 2,400	2,213	2,604.9	9.1
2,400- 4,800	1,412	5,100.6	68.1
4,800- 7,200	1,698	10,269.8	455.9
7,200- 9,600	2,321	19,589.9	1,244.4
9,600- 12,000	2,790	30,143.8	2,079.9
12,000- 16,000	3,781	52,322.6	4,021.9
16,000- 20,000	2,097	37,340.6	3,296.4
20,000- 25,000	1,272	28,065.8	3,048.6
25,000- 36,000	632	18,157.4	2,695.8
36,000- 50,000	115	4,743.3	765.6
50,000- 75,000	34	1,995.3	408.4
75,000-100,000	7	610.2	186.2
100,000 and above	6	1,005.3	334.8

Source: Statistiches Bundesamt, "Bruttolohn und Lohnsteuer," Wirtschaft und Statistik, 1971/73 (Wiesbaden, 1972).

As can be seen in the table, the bulk of wage and salary earners had gross incomes of between DM 9,600 and DM 20,000 and an average gross income of DM 13,300 for all wage and salary earners. Approximately 4 percent of all earners received 11 percent of gross income, while approximately 20 percent of all earners received 4 percent of income. Actually, the 47,000 persons in the three highest wage categories received more gross income than the more than 2 million persons in the lowest income category. The loss in income taxes, however, was more than DM 800 million for the highest groups, compared to DM 9.1 million for the lowest group. The effective average tax rate on the group earning DM 100,000 or more is 33 percent.

This table does not include income from other sources in addition to wages and salaries. Nor does it indicate in any effective way after-tax income distribution. Obviously, property and entrepreneurial income will change the complexion of the table considerably. In Table 5.6 the average value of property owned by different income groups is presented. Although the data does not shed any light on the redistributional effect of the West German tax system, it is possible to

TABLE 5.6

Distribution of Personal Savings and Property,
West Germany, 1969
(DM)

Monthly Net Income	Average Savings	Average Value of Savings and Property
Under 600	2,210	n.a.
600- 1,000	3,500	10,730
1,000- 1,500	4,660	15,020
1,500- 2,500	6,680	27,260
2,500-10,000	9,760	62,050

Source: Data provided by the Ifo Institut für Wirtschaftsforschung of Munich, at the request of the author.

gain a general idea of the distribution of wealth. Included are personal savings and personal property.

More detailed information is available on the redistributional effects of the personal income tax for the year 1965. The redistributional effects, however, fail to include the impact of income taxes on property and entrepreneurial income. As Table 5.7 indicates, the effect of the income tax is limited solely to the after-tax distribution of wages and salaries. The overall effect of the tax shows a modest shift in favor of the lower-income groups. On the other end of the income scale, there is no drastic shift in the after-tax position of the higher-income groups. In this connection, it is necessary to remember that progression is accomplished by the "bracket" method, whereby each successive higher rate applies only to income in excess of the previous bracket maximum. Furthermore, continuing exemptions reduce somewhat the overall burden of the scheduled rates. Actually, therefore, the overall effective rates on total incomes are much less than the maximum bracket rates applied to these incomes.

It is apparent, however, that a shift in income redistribution has occurred over time toward more rather than less equality. Using the Lorenz curve to measure income distribution after taxes on income from wages and salaries, property, and other incomes, Josef Korner has found that over the period 1950-65 the Lorenz curve has become less convex relative to the line of equal income distribution.[28] One factor contributing to this trend toward a more equal income distribution was an increase in the ownership of property on the part of

TABLE 5.7

Redistributional Effect of West German Income
Tax on Wages and Salaries

Income Groups (DM)	Percentage of Gross Income	Percentage of Net Income	Gain or Loss
Under 2,400	2.0	2.1	+ 0.1
2,400- 3,600	2.0	2.2	+ 0.2
3,600- 4,800	3.1	3.3	+ 0.2
4,800- 6,000	4.7	4.9	+ 0.2
6,000- 7,200	6.6	6.7	+ 0.1
7,200- 8,400	8.7	8.9	+ 0.2
8,400- 9,600	11.1	11.2	+ 0.1
9,600-10,800	12.2	12.3	+ 0.1
10,800-12,000	11.0	11.0	0.0
12,000-16,000	20.8	20.7	− 0.1
16,000-20,000	7.9	7.6	− 0.3
20,000-25,000	4.4	4.2	− 0.2
25,000-36,000	3.1	3.0	− 0.1
36,000-50,000	1.1	0.9	− 0.2
50,000 and over	1.3	1.0	− 0.3

Source: Josef Korner, Struktur und personelle Verteilung von Lohn und Lohnsteuer in der Bundesrepublik Deutschland seit 1950 (Munich: Ifo Institut für Wirtschaftsforschung, 1970), p. 21.

many Germans. It has been pointed out in a previous chapter that one objective of postwar government economic policies has been to favor the development of small and medium-sized enterprises. Government policy has also favored property ownership, particularly in the area of housing. Stock ownership in certain industries, such as Volkswagenwerk, has been encouraged through the denationalization policies of the early 1960s.

The personal income tax is on the average less burdensome to the German wage earner than the social security contribution. For example, in 1969 social security contributions amounted to 10.5 percent of the average wage earner's monthly income, compared to 10.3 percent for the personal income tax.[29] The average German worker also received back in the form of tangible transfer payments far less than he paid out in the form of taxes. In 1969 the average direct tax, personal income and social security contribution, for a German wage earner was DM 209 a month, compared to average transfer payments of DM 95 a month.30

It has been mentioned previously that the West German income tax is proportional rather than progressive through a wide range of taxable income. This point is illustrated in Table 5.8. Relevant to the table, but excluded from it, is the point that in 1968 the average German family had a tax-free amount in deductions and exemptions of DM 4,780.

Indirect Taxes

The point has been made that a part of total expenditures on social welfare measures listed in the social budget is financed from general revenues of the federal budget. These revenues come from income taxes shared by the state and communal governments and from a wide variety of taxes whose incidence ultimately rests on the consumer. Included among these taxes are the value-added tax, the tobacco tax, the coffee tax, the gasoline tax, and customs duties. In 1971 the value-added tax, the gasoline tax, and the tobacco tax accounted for one-half of total tax revenues in the federal budget.

These taxes introduce an element of regression into the German tax system. The value-added tax, which replaced the turnover tax in

TABLE 5.8

Marginal Tax Rates for Various Levels of Monthly Income, West Germany, 1965
(percent)

Monthly Income (DM)	Wage Earner with No Children	Wage Earner With One Child	Wage Earner with two Children
500- 600	19.0	19.0	—
600- 700	19.0	19.0	6.5
700- 800	19.0	19.0	19.0
800- 900	19.0	19.0	19.0
900-1,000	19.0	19.0	19.0
1,000-1,260	19.0	19.0	19.0
1,260-1,500	19.0	19.0	19.0
1,500-2,000	19.5	19.0	19.0

Source: Deutscher Bundestag, Materialien zum Bericht zur Lage der Nation 1971, Drucksache VI/1690 (Bonn, January 1971), Tables 96 and 97.

1968, is the single most important indirect tax in Germany, accounting for 30 percent of federal tax revenues and 15 percent of total tax revenues for all levels of government. The economic impact of the value-added tax is essentially the same as the general retail sales tax in that the consumer is the one who ultimately pays it. Although the tax is a consumption-based tax amounting to a larger part of the income of the lower-income groups than of higher-income groups, the extent of its regressiveness is difficult to measure. There are many food and agricultural products that are taxed at one-half of the general rate of 11 percent, whereas services connected with medicine, education, and welfare are exempt from the tax.

The tobacco tax is an example of a so-called sumptuary tax. This type of tax is designed to penalize the consumption of certain products that are generally considered to be harmful. Its use has often been rationalized on the grounds that the consumption of tobacco, alcohol, and other similar types of products is socially undesirable. In fact, however, the very high rates of these taxes reflect a desire to take advantage of an inelastic demand for tobacco and alcohol to increase revenues. Rates must be high before demand is noticeably affected, and short of this point a burden is placed upon the lower-income groups, which, in the aggregate, pay the bulk of the tax.

On an a priori basis, the statement can be made that the indirect taxes are bound to offset to some degree the progressiveness of the German income tax. It is difficult, however, to estimate the extent to which full employment, tax, and social welfare policies individually have affected the redistribution of income. Labor market policies, which have had as their objective full employment and the transfer of labor to more productive branches of industry that offer better pay, certainly have had some effect on income redistribution. The considerable direct redistribution of income through expenditure policy also has had an income-leveling affect. The gain to the majority of the taxpayers may be more than counterbalanced by the loss in taxation, given the extent of indirect taxes. A part of income taxes are proportional, and the progressive income tax achieves its redistributional effectiveness only at the high-income levels.

Social Security Contributions

Several points can be made with respect to the income-redistribution effects of social security contributions in the German economy. First, social security taxes account for around one-third of government revenues from all tax sources—a high ratio in comparison to other countries. For example, in 1969 German social security contributions amounted to 30 percent of total tax revenue in that year, compared to 17 percent for the United States and 16 percent for Japan. This means that social welfare expenditures in Germany are comprehensive, although the cost of financing these expenditures is also comprehensive.

Second, it is possible to advance ideas about the incidence of the social security levies. Unlike France, where the cost of social security is borne almost exclusively by the employer, German employees and employers share the cost about equally. That part of social security payroll taxes that is levied on the employee is very much like an income tax. The major difference is that personal exemptions and exemptions for dependents are lacking. The tax normally is not shifted forward either to the employer or to the consumer. The effect is that of an addition to withholding under the personal income tax. Given, however, a shortage of labor and a high level of aggregate demand, both of which have characterized the German economy, and given the high rate of 8 percent on a ceiling of DM 1,900 a month, which is well above average monthly earnings, it is possible that labor is in a position to try to force a rise in wage rates. The tax would then be pushed forward to the employer, who would try to shift as much as possible to the consumer. That part of the payroll tax levied on the employer would be shifted in all likelihood to the consumer. Given the high level of demand that has prevailed in Germany, most or all of the tax will be shifted forward to the consumer.

The redistribution effects of social security are complicated by the fact that if benefits are not subject to income taxation they are worth more to a man with a high taxable income than they are to a poorer man. Given the broad coverage of the German social security system, it is obvious that the major part must be paid by those who benefit. It is also probable that the social security system has involved some income redistribution downward, particularly from younger, able-bodied, and employed workers to the aged, the ill, and the unemployed. For the most part, this productive group receives less in benefits than it pays in taxes. It is also necessary to point out that a part of this whole redistributive process is covered by taxes on beer, tobacco, food, gasoline, and other indirect taxes.

SUMMARY

The West German government has become an instrument for effecting changes in the distribution of income. Taxes and transfer payments are the main means for accomplishing this objective, with taxes reducing the incomes of some persons and transfer payments adding to the income of others. With respect to transfers, however, it should be noted that some of the services provided by the government are, in effect, nonmonetary transfers. This would be true for such expenditures as free medical care, since the recipients of this service benefit by obtaining it at a cost below its real cost, as measured by the government expenditures for the resources necessary to provide the service.

Income redistribution is accomplished through the provision of government assistance to individuals and families. For the family with children, family allowances and general social welfare measures are provided, irrespective of need; for the aged, an old-age pension is provided, as well as supplementary benefits to family members; for the infirm, there are sickness benefits; for all persons, there are general medical and health benefits. For special classes of persons, such as war veterans and expellees form East Germany, there are special types of benefits. Thus, when transfer payments are expressed as a percentage of national income and personal income, the ratio is higher for West Germany than for all major Western European countries, with the exception of France, and much higher than for the United States and Japan.

The tax effect on the redistribution of income is difficult to measure. The West German income tax is progressive and some income redistribution is effected for the reason that the effective rate of taxation—the ratio of total taxes paid to income received—increases with the size of income. The maximum marginal rate of the personal income tax is 53 percent, however, a rather moderate rate in comparison to 65 percent for Sweden and 70 percent for the United States. The West German income tax system also redistributes income toward those persons with more dependents, so that, generally speaking, a married man is more lightly taxed than a bachelor. Also, as the general level of personal income rises, the progressiveness of the personal income tax creates a continuous redistributionary effect.

The bulk of transfer payments and other expenditures under the social security system are financed from three sources, which are fairly evenly distributed—levies on employees, levies on employers, and general revenues of the federal and state budgets. The first two categories can be considered as direct taxes. Direct taxes on workers cannot be shifted, although in general direct taxes on employers can. General revenues from the federal budget and state budgets are obtained from income and consumption taxes. There is reliance at the federal level, particularly on such indirect taxes as the value-added tax, the gasoline tax, and the tobacco tax. The multiplicity of indirect taxes and their importance as a source of government revenue leads to the conclusion that indirect taxes counterbalance to a certain extent the progressiveness of the personal income tax.

It can be concluded that there is in the aggregate little relationship between what the German citizen pays directly in taxes to support the social security system and what he receives from the system in terms of cash benefits that augment his personal income. The system is financed by direct contributions of employees and employers and from general government revenues. The pattern of financing is one of dependence to some extent on indirect taxation, with a consequent diffusion of the real costs of the system throughout the economy via the price mechanism. Under such circumstances, there may be a considerable unplanned transfer of real income among social groups within the economy, although the magnitude of the latter is not easily measured. If the above is true, it also follows that there is no assurance that the system is necessarily progressive with respect to both the incidence of its costs and benefits.

CHAPTER 6

MONEY AND BANKING IN WEST GERMANY

INTRODUCTION

In the market economies of Western Europe government control over the institutions of money and credit is considerable. In pursuit of specific economic policy objectives, governments have deliberately intervened in economic affairs to further their aims. Money and credit are particularly important areas, for they provide the nexus through which transactions are carried on. The instruments of money and credit provide, in a number of ways, a contrast to those of public finance. The budget in most countries is a single, once-a-year operation, and the measures governments take are clear. The picture of money and credit policy is much more confused, however. The institutional arrangements vary from country to country, as do the monetary systems. Control is normally divided between central banks and central governments. The latter can divert the flow of credit from areas it would normally seek on the basis of prospective gain into areas it considers to be socially necessary or useful. This is often done through the creation of special-purpose lending institutions that are supported by funds from the national budget or from social security contributions. Governments have also attempted to sublimate monetary policy to national economic and social objectives.

Control over conditions governing the quantity of money is inevitable in a modern industrial society. This control has been vested in central banks. These central banks are government operated and controlled. Autonomy in matters of monetary policy varies considerably from country to country, however. There are a number of instances in which the central bank, once created and given its frame of reference, is left to go its own way. This is also true of other government financial institutions. For example, in France the public authorities exercise a tighter control over private credit banks than over the state-owned institutions engaged in medium- and long-term credit.

Monetary policy refers to central bank actions to lessen fluctuations in consumer and investment spending through the regulation and use of the supply of money. It produces its effect on the performance of an economy indirectly, by influencing the level and composition of effective demand for goods and services and the interest rate charged in the financial markets. Its influence on aggregate demand and the interest rate is indirect, as it is primarily upon the stock of money held by households, business firms, and nonfinancial institutions. Changes in the degree of restraint or ease in monetary policy have an effect on the total flow of expenditures and, in turn, on output, employment, and prices.

Although monetary policy instruments differ from country to country, in general they are of three basic types: open-market operations, changes in reserve requirements, and rediscounting. Open-market operations involve central-bank purchases and sales of primarily government securities from commerical banks and other financial institutions. Reserve requirements refer to the percentage of deposits that banks must have on reserve in the central bank. Rediscounting refers to the rate that a central bank charges commercial banks for borrowing on various types of credit instruments. In addition, central banks also rely upon moral suasion to encourage commercial banks to be more or less lenient in the granting of loans.

The most important point that can be made with respect to the banking and credit systems in the modified market economies of Western Europe is that governments participate to a considerable degree. Normal market forces are not allowed to operate freely. Funds are diverted from the national budget, or from social security funds, into capital markets to be used for special purposes. Government lending to households and enterprises includes loans financed by its own funds, as well as loans made by public institutions that it controls. In addition, government authorities mobilize loan funds outside of the budget by subsidizing interest payments.

THE BANKING SYSTEM

The West German banking system has a mixed public-private relationship. The central bank, the Deutsche Bundesbank, is publicly owned, but the commercial banks are privately owned. Two government financial institutions, the Reconstruction Finance Corporation (Kreditanstalt für Wiederaufbau) and the Industry Credit Bank (Industrie Kreditbank), provide funds for business firms. There is direct government intervention in the flow of credit from the financial institutions to the various sectors of the economy through the provision of savings out of budgetary surpluses that are made available for capital formation.

West German banks can be differentiated with respect to their scope of operations.[1] The Deutsche Bundesbank performs functions similar to central banks in other countries. There are commercial banks of three types: nationwide banks; state, regional, and local banks; and private banks. Savings banks and central giro institutions represent a third category of banks. The central giro institutions are regional clearing banks and reserve depositories for the savings banks. There are banks that act as pure financial intermediaries without power to create money. The mortgage bank is the prime example. It issues bonds to finance mortgage loans or loans to local authorities. Other banking groups include the agricultural and industrial credit cooperatives. These institutions provide credit for farmers and small business; they do this primarily through direct credits. Finally, there are the specialized credit institutions and the postal savings banks. The former includes the Reconstruction Finance Corporation, which extends long-term credits to developing countries in the framework of the German foreign-aid program; the Equalization of Burdens Bank; the European Recovery Program Special Fund; various industrial credit banks; and other institutions. Postal savings banks are supervised by the federal government and make long-term loans primarily to public authorities.

The Deutsche Bundesbank

The historical and deep-rooted conflict between federalism and centralism is reflected in the development of central banking in Germany. The Reichsbank, Germany's first central bank, was formed in 1876; but to placate the supporters of federalism banks in the various German states were given the right to issue bank notes. In 1924 the Reichsbank was reorganized under the auspices of the Dawes Commission to make it more independent of the German government. In 1935 it was given the sole right to issue bank notes but lost its autonomy during the Nazi period, when it became a monetary instrument subservient to the economic objectives of the government.

Following World War II the Reichsbank was reorganized as the Bank Deutscher Länder, an interim central bank that existed pending the creation of the Federal Republic. It, however, lost the function of note issuance to the central banks (Landeszentralbanken) of the German states. In 1957 it was reorganized into the Deutsche Bundesbank and given the exclusive right to issue bank notes. The capital stock of the Bundesbank was given to the federal government, and increased authority was also given to the government through the use of appointive powers granted to it. Members of the directorate of the Bundesbank are appointed by the president of the Federal Republic.

The current central-banking system consists of the Deutsche Bundesbank and ten central banks of the states (Landeszentralbanken). The Bundesbank, unlike the central banks in other countries, operates with a considerable degree of autonomy with respect to open market operations and credit policy. It is, however, obliged to advise the government on all matters of importance in the area of monetary policy and to support general economic policies of the government, particularly in the area of currency stability.

The Bundesbank exercises control over monetary policy through various instruments that it can use to regulate the availability of credit and the liquidity of the banking system.[2]

1. It has control over the rediscount rate and the rate it charges for advances on commercial paper. Commercial banks are also allowed to borrow on the basis of bonds as security, for a period of three months. They receive liquid funds at a rate of interest that is usually set at 1 percent above the prevailing rediscount rate. The quantity of commercial paper the Bundesbank stands ready to discount is subject to limits, which are normally three times the liable capital plus the reserves of any given institution.

The extent of recourse to rediscounting by banks is limited through the use of rediscount quotas. The Bundesbank uses standard quotas based on the banks' capital structure and reserves and differentiated according to categories of financial institutions. The rediscount quotas are fixed by the boards of management of the Landeszentralbanken for the banks located in their area. The quota arrangement also applies to the rediscounting of bills aborad. The use of the rediscount quota is a common instrument of West German monetary policy. During the 1969-70 period the quotas for banks were lowered several times as an anti-inflationary measure.

2. Through open market operations the Bundesbank can expand or contract the supply of liquid funds in the banking system. The Bundesbank purchases and sells in the open market for its own account and at the rates fixed by it the Treasury bills and discountable Treasury bonds issued through it and the medium-term notes of the federal and state governments. Also included in the open market arrangement are medium-term notes of the federal railways, the federal Post Office, prime bankers' acceptances, and bonds admitted to the official stock exchange.

3. It can encourage or discourage the placement of banking funds abroad by making it less or more expensive for commercial banks to make covered investments in the foreign-exchange market, thereby

increasing or decreasing the supply of funds available in the domestic market.

4. It has control over minimum legal reserve requirements for commercial banks and other credit institutions. This control is considered a very effective tool in that it directly affects banks' ability to extend credit because they are expected to maintain a certain amount of deposits in legal reserves at the Bundesbank. Legal reserve requirements depend on the size of the bank and the type of deposit. The maximum reserve limits are 30 percent for sight deposits and call money, 20 percent for time deposits, and 10 percent for savings accounts. Any credit institution that fails to meet reserve requirements is subject to a penalty surcharge that is usually set at 3 percent of the rate charged by the Bundesbank on advances.

5. After more than 40 years of regulation, interest rates were freed from official government control on April 1, 1967. The freeing of interest rates had a mixed reception from bankers, who argued that it would severely complicate monetary policy. Under the old system, there was a largely automatic link between interest rates and the Bundesbank's discount rate. After 1967, however, the Bundesbank has had to rely to a greater degree on other instruments of monetary policy, such as reserve requirements, discount quotas for individual banks, and open market operations. It has also had to use what is called a "swap" policy as a means of influencing bank liquidity. This policy has increased in importance during the 1968-71 period. It is suited for West Germany as a country that imports and exports large amounts of capital in highly liquid form.

Since the German mark is fully convertible into foreign currencies, the government has no means at its disposal to control the impact of foreign currencies on the German money market. In other words, freely entering foreign currencies have served to inflate the money supply in Germany, which in turn, has resulted in higher prices as availability of money induces consumers to buy and industries to invest. Both factors combined generate an inflationary effect that is difficult to control. The flow of foreign funds will accelerate because the booming German economy offers high returns. The end result is that the equilibrium of the national economy is disturbed by an inflow of funds that are not based on any trade flow. In the absence of regulatory tools, such as no interest rates on foreign investments or limited currency convertibility, the Bundesbank uses a "swap" policy.

Basically, a swap is a means of insurance against exchange risks. The cost of this type of hedging is expressed as an interest rate per annum and is generally offered in swap points in relation to the respective exchange rate. Hence, swapping may produce a discount or a premium on an exchange rate. By manipulating the swap points, the Bundesbank attempts to induce banks to export or import funds.

Raising the costs of such operations tends to diminish capital outflows, of course, while lowering the costs encourages inflows; thus, bank liquidity is reduced. A swap policy, however, cannot significantly influence the flow of foreign currencies, as events during the 1968-71 period have indicated.

6. Another monetary policy instrument involves the use of the Lombard rate, a unique means of refinancing for banks that allows them to attain liquid funds from the Bundesbank by assignment of bonds. On this basis, funds are made available up to a maximum period of three months at a cost usually 1 percent above the discount rate. Lombard is usually the last resort for a bank in obtaining liquid funds to bridge a temporary shortage of cash. Banks refrain from using this device if possible, as the high cost of refinancing absorbs their profits.

The primary input of the Bundesbank's instruments of monetary policy is on the liquidity position of the banks and on the costs they incur when obtaining central-bank funds, but their ultimate aim is to influence overall conditions on domestic credit markets. Looking beyond the Bundesbank and commercial bank relationships, it is easy to recognize the actual workings of the system. Credits extended by banks are usually taken up, to a very great degree at least, by various industries, primarily for investment purposes. It is common knowledge that investment spending, in contrast to consumer spending, stimulates an economy by an amount far greater than the amount originally injected by the individual investment. Hence, Bundesbank policies that affect the liquidity of the banking system also affect investment spending on the part of industry. Changes in bank liquidity also cause changes in the overall level of interest rates, which forms an important control lever in the transmission system of monetary policy.

The Deutsche Bundesbank, responsible for issuing currency, also holds the country's main gold and foreign-exchange reserves and is responsible for the fixing of official exchange rates. It conducts lending operations on a limited scale—such lending being concerned primarily with loans to state-owned corporations and with certain small loans that are made out of special funds appropriated for social purposes. It makes no direct loans to private households or business enterprises and accepts no deposits, except from a few large businesses. It is permitted to extend credits to the national and state governments to cover temporary budget deficits and national commitments to certain international organizations.

Although the Deutsche Bundesbank is required to support the economic policies of the federal government, to the extent that the latter are consistent with its functions, it is independent of the national government with respect to its statutory powers. The Board of Managers of the Bundesbank is indeed nominated by the national government, but each manager's term of office is fixed at eight years, as a general rule, giving him considerable independence. Furthermore, on the highest organ of the Bundesbank, the Central Bank Council, sit not only the managers but the presidents of the central banks of the states, who are nominated either by the Bundesbank or by the state authorities. Members of the national government can attend meetings of the Council and propose nominations, but they have no vote and are empowered only to defer the making of a decision for a maximum of two weeks.

Commercial Banks

German commercial banks are privately owned and are of three types: nationwide banks; state, regional, and local banks; and private banks. The last type of bank is distinguished by the fact that it is closely held and does not issue shares that can be purchased on the stock exchanges. Commercial banks account for over 50 percent of total short-term deposits and short-term credits but less than 10 percent of total long-term lending. The commercial banks, remembering the banking crisis of 1931, when withdrawals of foreign short-term deposits brought down the superstructure of long-term credits, have pursued a highly liquid position with respect to loans. At the end of 1970 short-term loans, consisting primarily of self-liquidating money market paper, accounted for more than 60 percent of total commercial bank loans.[3] Commercial banks also invest in securities and are the underwriters for the distribution of most nonmortgage issues. The security investments consist chiefly of bank bonds, marketable equities and investment fund certificates, and governmental issues.

In recent years commercial banks have expanded their branch networks, especially in the suburban areas in which attractive opportunities have been created for them by the increasing tendency of business concerns to shift some of their operations there. Also, as a result of their expanding branch network, the commercial banks have attracted some savings deposits that would have otherwise gone to the savings banks. This expansion and the general increase of bank savings deposits as part of total monetary capital formation have enabled the commercial banks to move further into medium and, more especially, long-term credits traditionally made by the savings banks. In their drive to diversify their lending they have also been active in mortgage financing since the end of 1968. Recently, the commercial banks, particularly the Deutsche Bank, the Dresdner Bank, and the Commerzbank, have expanded both the volume of installment credit and small personal loans. There is the attempt to create the image of a bank that is interested in dealing with everybody.

Table 6.1 presents the reserves and the total balance sheet assets of the so-called Big Three commercial banks that operate on a national level and the most important regional commercial banks. One significant aspect of the table is the size of the Big Three in comparison to the regional banks. The biggest German regional bank, Bayerische Hypotheken und Wechselbank of Munich, whose capital is in the hands of 30,000 shareholders, had total assets of DM 12.6 billion, compared to assets of DM 17.4 billion for the Commerzbank, the smallest of the Big Three.

Most of the private mortgage banks in the Federal Republic are under the control of two or more of the big commercial banks. The Commerzbank was the first major bank to acquire a holding of over 50 percent in one of these banks—the Rheinische Hypothekenbank of Mannheim.[4] This development is viewed as a logical concomitant of the practice of offering longer-term loans on the basis of the continuous

TABLE 6.1

Major National and Regional West German
Commercial Banks in 1970
(in millions of DM)

Bank	Balance Sheet
National banks	
Deutsche Bank	31,432
Dresdner Bank	24,833
Commerzbank	19,696
Regional banks	
Bayerische Hypotheken und Wechsel Bank	15,581
Bank für Gemeinwirtschaft	11,791
Bayerische Staatsbank	10,656
Berliner Handels-Gesellschaft* Frankfurter Bank*	4,301
Investitions und Handelsbank	3,982
Berliner Bank	2,540
Westfalenbank	2,128
Vereinsbank in Hamburg	2,063

*Merged in September 1970.

Source: Data provided by the Deutsche Bundesbank, at the request of the author.

inflow from savings deposits, begun by the big German commercial banks in the last decade. But it was thought wise to restrict the term of these loans to 10 years at the maximum, so that in practice their average life was around six years. The commercial banks are able to participate to a greater extent in longer-term loans through control over the mortgage banks.

German commercial banks can be compared with banks in other countries in terms of asset size.[5] Two German banks, the Deutsche Bank and the Westdeutsche Landesbank Girozentrale, were among the 10 largest banks in 1970, ranking sixth and eighth, respectively. The Dresdner Bank ranked twentieth in size, while the Commerzbank ranked twenty-ninth. Other German banks listed among the 50 largest banks were the Bank für Gemeinwirtschaft, the Hessische Landesbank Girozentrale, and the Norddeutsche Landesbank Girozentrale. The last two and the Westdeutsche Landesbank are central savings banks that perform commercial bank functions. The merger of four banks resulted in the appearance of the Norddeutsche Landesbank on the list; acquisition of a mortgage bank partly accounted for a rise in Deutsche Bank's position from eleventh place in 1969 to sixth place.

One important development is the expansion of German commercial banks into the international banking field. A prevalent form of combination is the multinational bank, its shares held by several banks of various nationalities. In 1970 an unusual combination of public, semipublic, and private banking enterprises occurred with the formation of an alliance between the state-owned French bank, Credit Lyonnais, the 91 percent state-owned Italian bank, Banco di Roma, and the privately owned German bank, Commerzbank.[6] Through this arrangement West Germany is becoming more and more closely linked with neighboring economies. The countries of the EEC aim to integrate their monetary policies by 1980, involving the creation of a unified currency for the Federal Republic and other EEC member countries.

Also in 1970 the Deutsche Bank entered into an arrangement with the Dutch Amsterdam-Rotterdam Bank, the Midland Bank of the United Kingdom, and the Belgian Société Générale de Banque. This arrangement, formalized into an organization called European Banks' International Company (EBIG) that was set up in Brussels to coordinate and promote common banking activities. The group added two more partners in 1971, the French Société Générale and the Kreditanstalt Bankverein of Vienna.

Savings Banks

Savings banks can be divided into two categories—the 850 municipally owned banks and the 12 Girozentralen, which are the central banks of the savings banks. The savings banks are oriented more toward local needs—housing, small business loans, and municipal projects. Some of the savings banks rank among the largest credit institutions in Germany, but most are rather small, having assets of less than DM 50 million. The savings banks provide the largest source of capital for the bond market and derive their funds from personal savings. As a rule they engage in both savings and short-term deposit transactions. Savings banks have benefited from savings premium laws, which have encouraged savings from lower- and middle-income groups.

The savings banks, for the most part, have been moving increasingly into short-term lending to small- and medium-sized companies and have also been dealing more and more with industrial borrowers, which generally are customers of the large commercial banks. Whereas their securities business has heretofore been limited almost exclusively to the underwriting of state and federal bonds, the savings banks are beginning to move into the corporate securities market.

It is not so much the individual savings banks, however, that are emerging as competitors of the commercial banks but rather the 12 central savings banks that operate as regional bankers' banks for the savings institutions in their areas by acting as clearinghouses and holders of the individual banks' reserves. They are shifting more and more in the direction of providing the full range of commercial bank services, including foreign-exchange dealings. Their growing importance is pointed up by the merger of Rheinische Girozentralen and Provinzialbank Düsseldorf with the Landesbank für Westfalen at the beginning of 1969. The new bank, called the Westdeutsche Landesbank Girozentrale, with total assets of DM 29 billion in 1970, is larger than any German commercial bank, with the exception of the Deutsche Bank and ranked eighth in size of assets among the 50 largest banks outside of the United States.[7] Another important central savings bank is the Hessische Girozentrale, which had total assets of DM 17 billion in 1970 and ranked fifth among German commercial and savings banks in asset size and 43 out of the 50 largest banks outside of the United States.[8]

The Girozentralen have become a major force in the international banking business. In 1969 the Westdeutsche Landesbank was involved in the management, underwriting, or placing of some 100 international loans. Other foreign activities of the Girozentralen include holdings in industrial companies and banks abroad and in international investment trusts. They have established their own representative offices outside of the Federal Republic and are playing a growing part in the arrangement of cross-frontier mergers, takeovers, and acquisition of holdings. Through the facilities of the Girozentralen, every one of the 850 savings banks in the Federal Republic is in a position to offer its clients a full service of banking facilities, from foreign exchange to letters of credit and from exchange rate guarantees to export credit arrangements. With the growth of West German foreign trade, however, a number of the larger savings banks have established their own international contacts.

The Westdeutsche Landesbank and three foreign banks—the British National Westminster Bank, the Royal Bank of Canada, and the Chase Manhattan Bank of New York—formed an international banking enclave in 1970.[9] Several joint ventures were developed. The first was a new international bank, called Orion Bank, created to advise customers on financing matters and to conduct international loan-issuing operations. A second venture was the creation of a medium-term bank, the Orion Termbank, specializing in large eurocurrency loans with terms of up to 10 years to multinational concerns. The third venture is a management service corporation, known as Orion Multinational Services. The main purpose of this banking entity is to advise customers faced with technical problems of international finance. It also carries responsibility for coordinating the activities of the first two joint ventures and, in its role of a central planning group, for examining new business openings. Both the Orion Bank and the Orion Termbank were given an initial capital of DM 100 million.

As mentioned previously, the central giro institutions act as reserve repositories and clearinghouses and carry out various banking functions, such as foreign-exchange transactions and the issue of securities. Most are also provincial banks making long-term loans to communities and associations after raising funds by issuing bonds in the capital market. The Girozentralen hold a relatively large proportion of their security investment in medium-term notes. In 1970 around 35 percent of all of medium-term notes in circulation were held by the giro institutions.[10] The preference of the giro institutions for shorter maturities results from the fact that they function as reserve depositories for the savings banks.

Credit Cooperatives

Another banking group includes the agricultural and industrial credit cooperatives. The function of these institutions is to provide credit for farmers and small business, done primarily through direct credits. Both groups of cooperatives have regional associations with their central institutions that keep the liquid reserves of the individual cooperatives and through which payments transactions are cleared. The industrial credit cooperatives' central institutions are either cooperatives or joint stock companies, grouped together in the Deutscher

Genossenschaftsverband, while the agricultural cooperatives' central institutions, all cooperatives, are grouped in the Deutscher Raiffeisen-Verband. At the center of these groups of central institutions is the Deutsche Genossenschaftskasse, which is owned by the federal government. Its purposes are lending to and borrowing from the various credit cooperatives.

In 1970 there were 6,363 agricultural credit cooperatives, 696 industrial credit cooperatives, and 13 central cooperatives, including the Deutsche Genossenschaftskasse.[11] These central cooperatives are classified as specialized credit institutions. The agricultural and industrial cooperatives provide various types of short-, medium-, and long-term credit to farmers, small- and medium-sized commercial and industrial enterprises, and the liberal professions. In terms of credit outstanding as of July 1971, all cooperative banks had around 9 percent of the total value of credit among all financial institutions. About 35 percent of their loans were short-term, 15 percent medium-term, and 50 percent long-term. Their security investments, chiefly public issues and bank bonds, mortgage bonds, communal bonds, and bonds of specialized credit institutions, equaled DM 4.1 billion.

Mortgage Banks

Mortgage banks are an important and unique type of West German banking institution. In 1971 of the 46 mortgage banks, 29 were privately owned and 18 publicly owned.[12] Their purpose is to finance house building and municipal development. The privately owned banks are not restricted to any particular area and lend money on old and new properties, in both urban and rural areas. The publicly owned banks, however, are charged with special duties—some to finance the building of small housing units and others to provide finance in particular rural areas. For all of them, the main method of raising funds is by the placement of long-term mortgage bonds in the capital market. The proceeds are invested in mortgage loans and to some extent in communal loans and agricultural real estate loans.

The significance of the mortgage banks to the German banking system lies in the fact that they provide the major source of long-term credit. In July 1971 around 30 percent of all long-term credit outstanding was in the hands of the mortgage banks.[13] This percentage can be compared to 13 percent for the commercial banks. As has been mentioned previously, commercial banks, in order to participate more fully in the long-term credit market, have been acquiring control in the mortgage banks. It also can be said that of all the banks that act as intermediaries without power to create money, the mortgage banks are the most important in that their financial resources are derived from bond issues, which are a major component of the demand side of the German capital market.

Specialized Credit Institutions

There are a number of specialized credit institutions that are also of importance in the German banking system. The most important is the Reconstruction Loan Corporation (Kreditanstalt für Wiederaufbau), set up in November 1948 with capital in equal amounts from the federal government and the state governments. Its purpose was to provide medium- and long-term loans, and in its first few years of operation the coal and steel industries were almost entirely dependent upon it for their capital funds. It was empowered to borrow abroad, to issue its own securities, and in special cases to borrow from the central banking system. It financed projects that would further the reconstruction of the German economy. It particularly took on projects for which other credit institutions were unwilling to provide medium- or long-term loans. This function has been maintained.

Currently, the Reconstruction Loan Corporation is responsible for providing long-term credits for financing exports. It grants loans to domestic suppliers and large customers. In some cases financial credits are granted to foreign borrowers even though they do not trade directly with the German economy. Particular priority is given to developing countries. In addition to granting credit it is also the job of the Reconstruction Loan Corporation to take over surety for investment and export credits. It is responsible for the banking transactions of all loans granted to developing countries within the framework of development aid.

The Reconstruction Loan Corporation receives its financial support from several sources. First, it may issue debenture bonds that other financial institutions can purchase. Second, it receives financial support in the form of loans from the federal government. A third and important source of funds is the European Recovery Program Counterpart funds. It also may receive financial support from the Deutsche Bundesbank and from other private and public institutions at home and abroad. As of December 1, 1969, the total capital of the Reconstruction Loan Corporation amounted to DM 6.7 billion, of which the largest single amount came from the Counterpart funds.[14]

In 1969 the total volume of credit of the Reconstruction Loan Corporation was DM 3.6 billion.[15] Included is the long-term financing of domestic investment and exports, as well as the granting of foreign credits of various kinds. Included among domestic investments were loans of DM 681 million to the processing industry, DM 444 million to the mining industry, and DM 140 million to the communications industry. Also included under areas of support is aid to the Berlin economy. In 1969 total credits to aid domestic investment and export financing in the Berlin economy amounted to DM 146 million. The greatest volume of credit during 1969, however, went to foreign countries. Out of a total of DM 2.1 billion in foreign credits, DM 1.2 billion went under the category of capital aid to developing countries. A part of this amount included the financing of foreign orders from West German shipyards.

The balance sheet of the Reconstruction Loan Corporation showed assets as of December 31, 1969, of DM 20.9 billion, making it one of the five largest credit institutions in West Germany. During 1969 total assets increased by DM 1.5 billion over the preceding year. The net profit for the year amounted to DM 36.9 billion. This amount is set aside in a special reserve fund created under provisions of the 1948 law. In 1970 projected profits of the Reconstruction Loan Corporation are an estimated DM 37.2 billion.

In addition to the Reconstruction Loan Corporation, there are other specialized credit institutions. There is the Industry Credit Bank (Industriekreditbank), which provides short- and medium-term loans to industrial and trading enterprises.[16] The borrowers are primarily medium-sized firms unable to issue their own securities. It receives its funds from its own bond issues and from institutional investors. There is also the Equalization of Burdens Bank (Lastenausgleichsbank), which is responsible for providing loans from funds made available from the European Recovery Program Fund. It is one of the larger German financial institutions, with assets of around DM 9 billion. It currently provides loans primarily to finance the development of industry in certain problem areas. The Berlin Industry Bank (Berliner Industriebank) exists to finance the development of the Berlin economy. Its share capital is mainly in the hands of the federal government. An additional source of capital, private funds, enjoy special tax privileges under the Berlin Aid Law. Also in Berlin is the German Industrial Bank (Deutsche Industriebank), which provides medium- and long-term loans to business firms.

Several private commercial banks have set up the Prime Acceptance Company (Privatdiskont). This company deals in prime acceptances for the financing of foreign trade. The prime acceptance discount rates are usually lower than the Deutsche Bundesbank's official discount rate. The Prime Acceptance Company is particularly important as a source of funds in times when the money market is strained because the private commercial banks admitted to dealings on the prime acceptance market can, within certain limits, pass first-class bills through this institution to the Deutsche Bundesbank for rediscount, without such transactions being reckoned against their individual rediscount quota.

Other Credit Institutions

In West Germany banks in the postal credit system and installment credit institutions are also a part of the banking system. In 1971 there were 15 postal credit banks. They take sight and savings deposits and make loans consisting primarily of long-term credits to public authorities. In July 1971 long-term credits accounted for DM 7.5 billion out of total loans of DM 9.1 billion.[17] Their security investments consist chiefly of bank bonds and to some extent government securities. The installment credit institutions, of which there were 185 in July 1971, are a postwar innovation. Their primary importance is in the area of consumer credit. They also finance the purchase of motor vehicles and machinery for commercial purposes on the basis of bills of exchange. The installment credit institutions derive most of their funds from other credit institutions. The bulk of their business is short-term personal loans and personal purchase loans.

Although not classified as banks, building and loan associations finance residential construction. In 1970 there were 29 private and public building and loan associations. Their rate of growth has far exceeded that of other savings institutions and has persisted, despite the 1959 reduction of concessions for such savings under the income tax and the extension of premiums to rival methods of savings. Although the building and loan associations receive the bulk of their loanable funds from deposits of contracting members, to an increasing extent they have been obtaining funds from other sources. As of 1970 the 29 building and loan associations had savings deposits of DM 32 billion and loans of DM 25.6 billion.

Recent Trends in West German Banking

Important changes are taking place in West Germany's banking structure. As mentioned, interest rates were freed from official control in 1967. The 1936 provisions regulating the competition among banks were removed in 1968. Moreover, with the introduction of the value-added tax on January 1, 1968, the tax privileges that savings banks and credit cooperatives had enjoyed since their establishment in the last century as self-help institutions were abolished. The savings banks, however, still retain a competitive advantage as public institutions, since their capital is secured by the local public authorities. These steps have accelerated a trend, already evident for some time, toward the full-service bank. In the past commercial banks primarily had this characteristic. Regional banks, savings banks, credit cooperatives, and numerous other types of specialized credit institutions, however, are increasingly offering a fairly similar spread of services regardless of their specialized historical origins.

Following the decontrol of interest rates, deposit rates offered by all financial institutions, especially for time deposits, have increased somewhat because of sharpened competition. At the same time liquidity in the economy has remained high, mainly because of balance-of-payments surpluses. The federal government's two large investment budgets of 1967, as well as a subsequent easy-money policy, created a situation in which lending rates tended to decline. One direct result was a squeeze on bank profits from deposit and loan operations. More important, however, has been the fact that the banks have entered into each other's fields in an effort to gain more business and thus offset decreasing yields. This continuous drive marks a significant change in West German banking, in which conservatism has been a prominent feature.

Table 6.2 presents the total volume of credit outstanding for West German banking institutions as of July 1971. It is significant to note the importance of the savings banks and mortgage banks, particularly with respect to the volume of long-term credit. The savings banks and mortgage banks also accounted for more than one-half of the total volume of credit outstanding of approximately DM 572 billion. The commercial banks still remain the most important source of short-term credit, while their holdings of long-term credit remain small in comparison to the holdings of the savings banks and mortgage banks.

The Banks and the Economy

As has been mentioned, there has been a return to prewar patterns, in which a large part of the German economy rests in the hands of a small number of business firms and bankers. In 1964 a study was made of the relationship between banks and industry and trade. The approach was to look into the actual ownership of industrial and commercial firms by the banks, in particular the Big Three. The study indicated that in 1960 the share ownership of all credit institutions amounted to 3.2 percent of the nominal capital of all joint stock companies. In 138 companies the banks had a minority holding capable of blocking decisions—i.e., a holding above 25 percent—and a majority holding in another 58 companies.[18] Two-thirds of the total value of the shares owned by banks was held by the Big Three. Ownership by the credit institutions was spread over all sectors of the economy but was particularly pronounced in the wholesale and retail trades, where it amounted to 27 percent of the nominal capital of all joint stock companies.

In 1966 the German Companies Act was passed. The act forced all joint stock companies to disclose a 25 percent or greater holding

TABLE 6.2

Volume of Credit Outstanding by Type of West German
Banking Institutions, by Maturity Length, July 1971
(million DM)

Bank Group	Short-term	Medium-term	Long-term
Commercial banks			
Big Three	26,275	9,989	20,614
Regional banks	30,255	8,400	25,931
Private banks	9,118	1,314	2,784
Savings banks			
Girozentralen	9,695	9,554	64,984
Savings banks	24,680	10,965	95,544
Credit cooperatives			
Central credit cooperatives	3,000	1,824	2,677
Industrial	11,012	3,241	12,116
Agricultural	6,818	2,392	11,572
Mortgage institutions			
Private	800	1,889	49,274
Public	99	1,052	53,978
Installment credit institutions	1,536	6,440	540
Specialized credit institutions	1,891	4,786	35,713
Postal savings	1,589	68	7,476
Total	126,768	61,914	383,203

Source: Deutsche Bundesbank, Monatsberichte der Deutschen Bundesbank (Frankfurt am Main, October 1971), Table 10, p. 28.

in another company. It was revealed that the Deutsche Bank and more than a 25-percent holding in Daimler-Benz, which in 1970 was the fifth-largest industrial firm in West Germany, and in Julius-Berger and Grun and Bilfinger, both of which are major building contractors.[19] The Big Three banks also had holdings in excess of 25 percent in two major department store concerns, Karstadt of Hamburg and Kaufhof of

Cologne, which ranked fourth and sixth in 1970 in terms of the sales volume of all retail and wholesale establishments in West Germany. In addition the Deutsche Bank had a 25-percent or larger ownership in the capital of four machinery manufacturers, four textile companies, one brewery, one chocolate factory, two public utilities, one construction company, and one shipping company. The Dresdner Bank had a 25-percent or larger ownership in the capital of one shipping company (Norddeutsche-Lloyd); one metal company (Metallgesellschaft), which in 1970 was the fifteenth-largest industrial firm in Germany; three breweries; two textile companies; and one coal and oil concern (Gelsenberg), which ranked twenty-seventh in 1970. The Commerzbank had a 25 percent or larger interest in the capital of one coal company, one machinery company, two building firms, two shipping firms, and one hotel chain.

Ownership of capital was by no means concentrated in the hands of the three largest commercial banks. The Bayerische Vereinsbank had ownership in 11 industrial and commercial companies and the Bayerische Hypotheken und Wechselbank in 25. Included among the holdings of the Bayerische Hypotheken und Wechselbank were a 25-percent ownership of the capital of three paper companies, ten breweries, one champagne company, one shoe company, and five textile companies. The bank owned over 25 percent of the capital of one graphite company, one metal company, one building firm, one railway, and one ceramics company. It is necessary to point out also that the German Companies Act only required banks to disclose a 25-percent or larger holding in other companies. It is probable that bank holdings of less than 25 percent are at least as large in terms of value as the larger holdings.

This also means that German banks possess, through ownership of capital, voting rights that they can use to influence business decisions. The banks can also use proxy votes given to them by their customers. Through the combination of direct ownership and proxy votes, banks can control over 50 percent of the capital of a company. Bankers also hold positions on the boards of directors of many firms. So banks, through various interlocking relationships, wield considerable influence in the German economy. The banks have tended to favor larger, well-established firms with a broad spread of activities, rather than new, small, and highly specialized firms. Moreover, the banks have tended to promote mergers, which are good business for banks since they provide many services in the process of amalgamation.

It is doubtful, however, that the German banks exercise more economic control than the state banks in France. The control of business financing through government ownership of the major credit institutions has been of importance to the postwar development of the French economy. Ownership has provided the state with direct leverage

for the implementation of credit policies that are consonant with the
objectives of the French economic plans. Favoritism is shown by
the commercial banks to borrowers who intend to follow the objectives
of the plan. In general, French credit policies have favored large-
scale enterprises to produce desired economic results. The French
government actively encourages bigness in business. As was mentioned, mergers have occurred in recent years in the aluminum, electronics, glass, and steel industries.

THE CAPITAL MARKET

During the period following World War II, the capital market was
in a state of disequilibrium, with the demand for capital exceeding the
supply of funds. To offset the lack of supply, many fiscal privileges
were introduced to spur capital formation by individuals and firms.
Self-financing was favored; accelerated depreciation allowances were
introduced; individual savings with savings and credit banks, insurance
companies, and building societies were encouraged; and loans to housing
and shipbuilding were given special advantages. Savings by the federal
government were a further substitute for an effective capital market;
the savings thus generated were used primarily to further the housing
program. The Kreditanstalt für Wiederaufbau was set up in 1949 to
promote medium- and long-term credit for those areas of the economy
that were in particular need and could not raise funds elsewhere. It
was financed with Marshall Plan funds and also through budgetary
surpluses.

A series of direct controls over capital were used during the
immediate postwar period. One such control limited the rate of
interest on mortgage bonds to 5 percent and on industrial bonds to
6.5 percent. These controls were eventually replaced by a scale of
tax advantages for different types of securities. These tax advantages
particularly favored government fixed-interest securities. Eventually
they were withdrawn and the capital market became free of direct
government controls. But the public authorities continue to exercise
considerable indirect influence on the capital market through the
regulation of banking and insurance, as well as through the allocation
of government savings to business enterprises, the stimulation of
construction, and the system of premium and tax privileged savings.

One facet of the German capital market can be found in the
pattern of savings and investment that has emerged since the war.
On balance the government sector, including the social insurance
funds, has generated a large proportion of total national savings
through current account budget surpluses, while the bulk of physical
investment takes place in the business sector. In 1968, for example,

savings in the government sector amounted to DM 20.6 billion compared to DM 11.3 billion for business enterprises and DM 57.4 billion for private households. Since savings by the government sector have been larger than its physical investment, the government sector is a large net supplier of investment funds to other sectors of the economy. These funds are made available to business firms in the form of direct credits or through loans from the banks.

The bulk of external financing by business enterprises is done through direct credits from financial institutions. A part of this financing finds its counterpart in bonds issued by credit institutions, but most of it is based upon the liquid savings of consumers. Personal savings have increased rapidly in recent years. For example, in 1964 personal savings amounted to DM 41.2 billion compared to savings of DM 57.4 billion in 1968. The government has encouraged savings through the use of premiums and tax exemptions. Much of personal savings has been placed in savings accounts, particularly with the extensive network of municipally owned savings banks. Although a part of the savings collected locally are redistributed by the Girozentralen, most of the funds are lent locally.

Among the other institutional characteristics of the West German capital market, the two methods of issuing bonds deserve mention in this summary. The first method is continuous sales by mortgage banks and certain banks making local authority or communal loans. The second is the so-called one-time issues of all other borrowers. The latter type is underwritten by banking syndicates whose members undertake to subscribe to fixed amounts at fixed prices. The composition of the underwriting syndicates as well as the subscription quotas change very little from issue to issue.

Savings and Investment

The German economy over time has been characterized by a high proportion of government savings relative to total savings, whereas the bulk of physical investment has been done by business enterprises. The sources of government savings have been budget surpluses on current account and funds accumulated by the social security system. These savings are supplemented by a moderate amount of government borrowing, both through security issues and through direct credits from financial institutions. Altogether the government sector has contributed around one-fifth of the total savings resources available for investment in recent years. Around half of these savings are loaned to business enterprises, partly through specialized credit institutions such as the Reconstruction Finance Corporation, the Equalization of Burdens Bank, and certain agricultural banks, and lesser amounts are placed on deposit with banks or used to purchase securities.

In Table 6.3 sources and uses of savings and investment are presented for the German economy in 1970. Savings by enterprises are made through retained earnings and depreciation. A differentiation is made between depreciation and savings in the table. There are two major sources of gross savings: depreciation and savings. Depreciation is broken down into public and private savings; savings is divided into personal or household savings, government saving, and retained earning emanating from business firms. Investment represents the counterpart to the flow of savings.

Business firms rely primarily on internal financing, although the proportion of total resources derived from this source has tended to remain relatively constant over the last decade. Retained earnings in particular have shown considerable fluctuations over time. In 1960 retained earnings amounted to DM 19.1 billion but declined to DM 15.3 billion in 1962. In 1966 retained earnings had increased to

TABLE 6.3

Sources of Saving and Investment,
West Germany, 1969
(billion DM)

Source	Amount
Depreciation	
General government	3.0
Private enterprises	60.8
Saving	
General government	27.4
Private enterprises	14.2
Private households	47.7
Other sources	
Foreign transfers	2.9
Total	156.0
Internal and foreign investment	
Private enterprises	133.0
Public enterprises	23.0
Total	156.0

Source: Deutsche Bundesbank, Monatsberichte der Deutschen Bundesbank (Frankfurt am Main, October 1971), pp. 13, 15, 17, and 22.

DM 17.8 billion. In 1969 the decrease was to DM 14.2 billion. In 1970, however, retained earnings increased to DM 16.6 billion.[20] To some extent the high level of internal financing has been made possible by a high level of profits, particularly during the mid-1960s and by liberal tax rules pertaining to depreciation. Even though special depreciation incentives have been reduced over the years, the rapid growth of new investments has kept the level of depreciation in excess of 40 percent of total gross investment.

The primary source of external financing is in the form of direct bank credits, including short- and medium-term credits. Bank credits normally account for more than one-half of external financing. Another source, which has increased in importance over the years, is financing through security issues. Stock is sold on the various German stock exchanges. In general, private savers have had a disinclination to invest in stocks. This reluctance can be attributed to the aftermath of the war and the subsequent currency reforms. Insurance companies and other institutional investors are the prime purchasers of stock. Bonds are another type of security issue. Typically, industrial bonds are underwritten by banking syndicates, whose members undertake to subscribe to fixed amounts at fixed prices. For all practical purposes, there is one major underwriting syndicate that is composed of representatives of the Big Three banks, other commercial banks, and the central giro institutions. A final source of external financing is direct borrowing from the government sector.

MONETARY POLICY

The Bundesbank has recourse to the standard instruments of monetary policy—control over the rediscount rate, control over minimum reserve requirements, and open-market operations—to accomplish stabilization objectives. Its influence on credit, however, has been obviated considerably during most of the postwar period through the existence of several factors that have been present in the German economy. For one thing, the interest elasticity of investment has been low, reflecting a strong investment demand, and interest rate changes via the rediscount rate have had little effect. Furthermore, German banks have also possessed considerable excess liquidity during the postwar period and have not had to resort to rediscounting commercial paper to any significant extent. The existence of an export surplus has provided the foreign exchange to enhance the liquidity of the banking system. High interest rates have attracted foreign accounts that in turn have increased bank liquidity, thereby circumventing attempts at effective discount policy.

The problem of imported inflation has become a major issue in West Germany. Increased liquidity in the economy, caused by surpluses of foreign exchange, has been transformed into inflationary demand. Orthodox monetary policy is placed at a disadvantage. In the first place, the increased liquidity from abroad gives private credit institutions greater independence from the Bundesbank and thus makes it more difficult for the latter to use restrictive measures effectively. Second, if the Bundesbank attempts to use higher bank rates to combat imported inflation, it only aggravates the problem by attracting more capital from abroad. It has been difficult to counter imported inflation through standard monetary policy measures without creating disequilibrium in the balance of payments. The standard response to an increase in reserves is to let internal prices rise until the net inflow of foreign exchange is checked. The addition of internal price stability as an equal or superior objective therefore makes it impossible to maintain balance-of-payments stability by orthodox measures.

The effectiveness of monetary policy has also been subverted in that savings of households are channeled into savings deposits at savings banks, building and loan shares, and insurance companies. Most personal savings flow through these investment channels, but only a part of them flow into capital investments. This has meant that central-bank monetary policy has had little influence over the flow of savings, for the reason that the institutions receiving them do not channel them into the capital market.

During the 1960s prosperity within Germany has been accompanied by an inflow of capital from abroad. When the Bundesbank gave first priority to restraining the boom at home by using a tight money policy, the balance-of-payments problem was exacerbated through the attraction of more liquid funds from abroad. In March 1961 West Germany revalued the mark by 4.7 percent. This caused a large movement of capital out of the country, and an overall deficit of DM 1.9 billion appeared in the balance of payments. The rediscount rate during this period was set at 3 percent. Trade with inflationary foreign countries, however, led to rising prices at home and caused payment surpluses to accumulate. In 1964 the Bundesbank introduced a variety of measures to discourage the inflow of foreign capital and to stimulate the outflow of German capital and later that year used minimum reserves and rediscount quotas to restrict internal liquidity.

From 1965 to early 1966 the balance-of-payments surplus disappeared. Internal prices increased, and the Bundesbank raised the rediscount rate from 3 to 5 percent.[21] Then the growth rate began to drop as the momentum that had propelled the economy forward began to decline, and a recession occurred during the latter part of 1966.

The Erhard government was replaced by a coalition of the two major political parties. This coalition brought into office men, such as Economics Minister Karl Schiller, who were disposed toward dropping the free market economic doctrine of former Chancellor Erhard and adopting a more Keynesian policy of deficit spending and other fiscal measures. The Law Promoting Stability and Growth of the Economy, passed in 1967, provided the federal government with a number of Keynesian fiscal policy instruments.

In 1967 the Bundesbank pursued a policy of monetary ease that brought the rediscount rate down from 4.5 percent to 3 percent and released a total of DM 1.6 billion through reductions in the minimum reserve requirements of commercial banks.[22] After a considerable amount of the resultant increased bank liquidity was diverted into increased exports of capital, the Bundesbank entered the foreign-exchange markets with measures designed to inhibit the outflow of funds and preserve sufficient liquidity in the domestic money market. An interplay of fiscal and monetary policies measures also developed with the creation of special investment budgets and other fiscal measures.

In 1968 the rediscount rate remained at 3 percent for the entire year, and minimum reserve requirements were lowered. Despite a greatly increased supply of capital the interest rate level did not drop as much as expected because of tendencies to rising interest rates on international capital markets. The interest rate differential made the West German capital market very attractive to foreign borrowers. Long-term capital exports did not suffice to offset the foreign-exchange inflow originating in transactions and short-term capital movements. Short-term capital imports resulted primarily from the reduction of banks' foreign assets and from the deposit of foreign money in German banks as a result of the speculation about a revaluation of the Deutsche Mark. The Bundesbank counteracted this inflow by offering foreign-exchange guarantees at costs far below the market rates.

During 1969 the Bundesbank pursued a generally restrictive monetary policy.[23] The discount rate was raised three times. In April the rate was raised from 3 to 4 percent, and the advance rate was raised from 4 to 5 percent. In June the Bundesbank's discount rate was raised from 4 to 5 percent, and the advance rate from 5 to 6 percent. In August special advance rates of 7 and 8 percent were introduced to counteract increased resort to advances. In September the Bundesbank's discount rate was raised from 5 to 6 percent and the advance rate from 6 to 7.5 percent. Special advance rates were abolished. In December the advance rate was raised from 7.5 to 9 percent. In addition, rediscount quotas based on bank's liabilities and differentiated according to the type of lending institution were used. In April 1969 rediscount quotas were reduced by 20 percent for most banks.

Reserve requirements were also altered several times during 1969. In May the minimum reserve ratios for domestic liabilities were raised by 15 percent, and those for external liabilities by 50 percent. This had the effect of decreasing the free liquid reserves of the banks by roughly DM 2.5 billion. In July the minimum reserve ratio was increased by 10 percent, with a resulting decrease in banks' liquid reserves of DM 1.6 billion. Moreover, a 100-percent reserve was placed on all additions to external liabilities. In November the 100-percent reserve requirement was abolished, and reserve ratios for foreign liabilities were brought into line with those for domestic liabilities. During the year minimum reserve requirements were increased by DM 4 billion.

Over the whole of 1969 bank liquidity was reduced by DM 17.9 billion. The free liquid reserves of banks were reduced from DM 37.7 billion at the end of 1968 to DM 19.8 billion at the end of 1969. The greatest reduction was in the banks' rediscount margin at the Bundesbank; unused rediscount quotas decreased by DM 7.9 billion. The financial transactions of the federal and state governments resulted in a contraction of bank liquidity by DM 5 billion. To some extent this was attributable to federal government expenditure cuts decided on for reasons of anticyclical policy. Bank liquidity was reduced through the use of measures designed to reduce the amount of short-term debt. Liquidity was also reduced by the cyclical rise in the circulation of notes and coins, which was mainly due to the growth in personal income.

The most important monetary development of 1969, however, was the revaluation of the Deutsche Mark. In October the federal government fixed the new gold parity of the Deutsche Mark at a level corresponding to a dollar parity of DM 3.66 instead of the former DM 4.00. The domestic result of revaluation was that bank liquidity was reduced. The loss of funds immediately after revaluation was due primarily to the return of speculative money—i.e., to the outflow of short-term funds that had been sent from other countries to banks and other institutions in Germany before revaluation. So that German banks would not be exposed to the full force of the externally induced liquidity outflow, the Bundesbank lowered their minimum legal reserve requirements by 10 percent in November.

In 1970 the Bundesbank took further measures to dampen down the level of economic activity in the West German economy.[24] It became apparent in early 1970 that the revaluation of the Deutsche Mark was not strong enough to contain inflationary pressures that had developed. In the fourth quarter of 1969, the cost of living index increased by 3.1 percent, compared to 2.7 percent for the full year.

In the first quarter of 1970, the cost of living index increased by 3.5 percent. In March 1970 the Bundesbank raised its discount rate from 6 percent to a postwar record of 7.5 percent and introduced additional minimum reserve requirements on banks' foreign liabilities. The purpose was to decrease excess demand by exerting a restrictive impact on private fixed investment and to deter the banks from borrowing abroad, thereby keeping bank liquidity tight.

In addition, the Bundesbank attempted to counteract the inflows of bank liquidity by means of open-market operations. This reduced free liquid reserves only to the extent that long-term debt in the form of public authority bonds from the Bundesbanks' portfolio was sold, and short-term debt was passed on to nonbank institutions. Altogether, just under DM 2.5 billion of liquid reserves was withdrawn from the banks in 1970 by open-market transactions in long-term debt securities, and by selling short-term commercial paper to nonbank institutions.

Between July 1970 and March 1971 the discount rate was lowered four times.[25] With interest rates declining in other countries, it became increasingly difficult to maintain a high level of domestic rates. The Bundesbank felt that differences in interest rates would cause an inflow of funds into Germany and would be detrimental to the pursuit of restrictive domestic monetary policy. In July the discount rate was reduced from 7.5 to 7 percent, and the advance rate from 9.5 to 9 percent. In November the discount rate was lowered to 6.5 percent. There was no internal relation of monetary policy measures, however. Minimum legal reserve requirements were increased in August and November. In December the discount rate was lowered from 6.5 to 6 percent, and the advance rate from 8 to 7.5 percent. In March 1971 the discount rate was reduced to 5 percent and the advance rate to 6.5 percent. There was also a 10-percent reduction in minimum reserve requirements. During the latter part of 1971 there was an increase in the total volume of bank credit. Consumer expenditures on goods and services increased, whereas investment expenditures showed a decline over the first half of 1971.[26] Monetary policy had to contend with a less-than-buoyant economy in which inflation existed along with a general downturn in the level of economic activity. The index of industrial production in the investment-goods industries increased 2.2 percent in July, decreased 7 percent in August, and decreased 0.6 percent in September.[27] Preliminary estimates indicated a decrease for October.

Bundesbank monetary policy, however, ran into external pressures. Although German interest rates declined, they lagged behind the fall in international rates, so that differentials actually tended to increase. This led to an inflow of short-term capital imports, as the business sector took advantage of lower external interest rates. Foreign exchange entered Germany in 1970 to the extent of DM 20.2

billion, the largest amount ever recorded in a single year. This was attributable to two factors: money imports of the banking system and external borrowing of nonbank institutions. As a result, the free liquid reserves of the German banking system increased from DM 19.8 billion at the end of 1969 to DM 25.4 billion by the end of 1970.[28] The great bulk of the increase took place during the fourth quarter of 1970.

In 1971 the pattern was continued. From January to May, internal bank liquidity declined by DM 8 billion.[29] This decline, however, was more than counterbalanced by an inflow of foreign funds to the extent of DM 22 billion. Liquidity was increased overall by DM 14 billion and was transferred into rising internal prices. In using discount rates to combat inflation, the Bundesbank had succeeded in attracting additional capital from abroad. In the period June-December 1971 domestic liquidity declined by DM 7 billion, and there was also a turnabout in the flow of foreign capital.[30] On balance there was an outflow of DM 12 billion during the last seven months of 1971. Overall for 1971 there was a net gain in bank liquidity of DM 2 billion.

The point has been made that German monetary policy has been faced with the problem of countering inflation imported through market forces. High domestic interest rates resulting from a tight monetary policy have made Germany attractive to foreign capital. In 1970 the cost of living index in West Germany increased by 3.8 percent, compared to 6 percent for the United States, 5.3 percent for France, 5.1 percent for Italy, and 6.4 percent for the United Kingdom.[31] This favorable index comparison was instrumental in attracting foreign capital into Germany because the gain differential in terms of real interest rates was quite favorable. A 10-percent return on an investment in a short-term German security, given an increase in the price index of 3.8 percent, is to be preferred to the same return on a British security, given the increase of 6 percent in the price level.

SUMMARY

In a mixed economic system the role of the government in the provision of money and credit is more important than in the United States. The central bank is usually nationally owned and subject to governmental control. In some countries, monetary policies are subverted to the general economic policies of the government. A less direct, but perhaps even more pervasive, influence arises from the policies of some governments to direct a large proportion of the available financial resources to selected areas of the economy, sometimes bypassing the normal market mechanism entirely in the process, but in any event sharply reducing the volume of funds free for investment in other areas of the market.

West German monetary policy is carried out by the Deutsche Bundesbank. The basic instruments of monetary policy are discounting (including the use of rediscount quotas), open-market operations, and minimum reserve requirements. These requirements are differentiated by bank size. In addition, the Bundesbank serves as a repository for special federal and state funds. These funds cannot be invested or deposited elsewhere without the consent of the Bundesbank. The Bundesbank is also responsible for holding the contracyclical reserve funds that were created under the provisions of the Law for Promoting Stability and Growth.

In West Germany, the law of 1957 that created the Deutsche Bundesbank provides that the central bank should keep in line with government economic policy, although the law adds that it should do this insofar as it is consistent with its proper duty, that is, to safeguard the currency. The law also provides the Deutsche Bundesbank with considerable independence—an independence that it has in fact used. The law also requires consultation between the Bundesbank and the government, however; there is no provision for government directives to the Bundesbank.

There are a number of various financial institutions in West Germany, some privately and others publicly owned. The German commercial banks are privately owned. Savings banks, however, are owned by the German municipalities and are used to provide a source of capital for local needs. Specific purpose banks are important in West Germany; they have served to channel funds from the social security system and budgetary surpluses into areas of the economy that are in need of development.

One trend that has developed in the German banking system is the formation of internal and external financial arrangements that have increased the size or sphere of operations of German banks. One such arrangement was the merger of two central savings banks in 1969 into the Westdeutsche Landesbank, which became one of the largest banks in the world. Working arrangements have also been developed between West German banks and banks in other countries. For some years now, the share of international business in total bank activity has been increasing, especially the heavy involvement of the West German banks in the eurocurrency and eurobond markets as underwriters.

West German monetary policy over the years has been the most important stabilization device in terms of use. The Bundesbank relies on the basic instruments of monetary policy, such as reserve requirements, discount quotas, and open-market operations. In recent years, Bundesbank monetary policy has turned full circle. In 1967 and 1968 the Bundesbank pursued a policy of keeping money and capital cheap, as the continuation of domestic expansion appeared desirable. In

1969, however, a combination of using internal demand and external imbalance prompted the Bundesbank to use restrictive measures. Despite these measures, bank liquidity and especially money holdings outside the banking system were abundant, primarily as a result of large inflows of liquid funds from abroad. Much of this influx went to business firms, thus avoiding the 100-percent reserve requirement set for new bank accounts held by foreigners.

CHAPTER 7

LABOR UNIONS IN WEST GERMANY

INTRODUCTION

The role of unions is fundamentally different in a capitalist system than in a socialist system. The chief function of unions in West Germany and the United States is to bargain collectively with the employers to secure better terms of employment for the workers and to secure union recognition. To achieve the objectives of higher wages, fringe benefits, and better working conditions, unions can use such weapons as the strike and the boycott on employers. Unions also participate in politics by supporting political parties and candidates that are sympathetic to their objectives. Many unions also carry on a wide variety of educational, recreational, social, and cultural activities for their members, and some of them provide certain forms of social insurance. On frequent occasions labor unions have been able to participate to some extent in the management of particular enterprises through union-management cooperation and other devices.

In a socialist country, such as East Germany, unions are organized on an industrial rather than on a craft basis. Although union membership is very large, comprising more than 95 percent of the labor force, the reason is tied primarily to the reward structure. Unions carry on several functions that benefit their members; however, the vital collective bargaining function does not exist, because wages and hours are determined by the state. Moreover, the right of unions to strike is prohibited. In terms of political influence, the unions have far less leverage in the "workers and peasants republics" than they do in the capitalist countries.

THE DEVELOPMENT OF TRADE UNIONS IN GERMANY

Trade unions in Germany were a product of the Industrial Revolution. The first attempts to form unions occurred before the revolution of 1848-49. These unions were local in nature in that they attempted to include workers in a given plant. Their efforts resulted in failure. After the revolution, the development of trade unions really began in the 1860s with the relaxation of the previous strict coalition bans that were directed against political groups.[1] In 1865 the General German Cigar Workers Association was formed, and in 1866 the German Book Printers Association followed. Early attempts were made toward the formation of workers into political parties, such as the German General Workers' Association and the Social Democratic Workers' Party. Parallel to these, liberal trade unions closely connected with the German Progressive Party were formed.

In 1878 the Anti-Socialist Law was passed. Its purpose was to destroy the trade union movement. All of the Social Democratic trade unions were disbanded and many leaders were put in prison. One result of the Anti-Socialist Law, however, was that the Social Democratic workers formed themselves into loose craft associations and set up a loose form of centralization.[2] Following the repeal of the law in 1890, unions increased their membership. In 1898 the Christian Trade Unions were formed. A Central Trade Union Committee was formed in 1891. In 1919 it was to become the General Federation of German Trade Unions.

During the early part of the Weimar Republic trade unions increased in importance in terms of membership. In 1918 2.5 million workers were members of trade unions; by 1922, membership had increased to 7.8 million. Declining economic conditions and internal political problems within the General Federation of German Trade Unions, however, caused membership to decline to 3.9 million in 1926. Confronted by the growing antagonism between workers and employers that became manifest after 1923, and with the internal political problems of the republic, union leaders failed to come up with any viable programs that appealed to the mass of union workers.[3] It was assumed by many that, with the collapse of Imperial Germany in 1918, an economic democracy would be brought about through labor action. The unions, however, could never unite around the means to achieve this goal.

In 1933 the system of parliamentary democracy established by the Weimar Republic was replaced by the dictatorship of Hitler's Third Reich. Unions, as well as all other institutions, were affected. In Germany a new single organization, the Labor Front, was set up almost as soon as Hitler came to power. Precise relations between employer, employee, and the state were defined in the Law for the Order of National Labor, which was passed in January 1934. In essence the Labor Front amounted to a company union in which the interests of the workers and employers were made subordinate to those of the state. The regular trade unions were absorbed into the Labor Front and the formal apparatus was eliminated. During the Third Reich many trade union officials were imprisoned or sent to concentration camps.

Immediately after the end of World War II, those trade union leaders who had survived the Third Reich set about to establish committees for the purpose of reviving the union movement. They were determined to avoid any splintering of the new trade union movement into ideological factions, which had worked to their disadvantage during the Weimar Republic. It was agreed that a single organization should be formed, representing all workers regardless of ideology.[4] It was also decided that trade unions, as far as possible, be set up on an industrial basis. It was felt that a communality of interest among the workers would prevent a recurrence of the ideological problems that caused union frictions during the period of the 1920s.

The immediate postwar development of unions depended to a considerable extent upon the various zones of occupation. In the Soviet zone of occupation the German Confederation of Free Trade Unions (Freier Deutscher Gewerkschaftsbund) was established. In the French and American zones a central trade union organization, divided into trade sections, was initially set up in each state. In the British sector, the German Confederation of Trade Unions (Deutscher Gewerkschaftsbund) was established in 1946. In 1949 the trade unions in the American, British, and French zones of occupations combined to form the German Trade Union Federation (Deutsche Gewerkschaftsbund, or DGB). With its 16 constituent industrial unions, the DGB formed the cornerstone of unionism in West Germany. All efforts to create a central confederation of trade unions for the whole of Germany failed as East and West Germany grew further apart.

Other unions also developed during the postwar period. In 1945 white collar workers formed the German Salaried Employees Union (Deutsche Angestellten Gewerkschaft, or DAG). Its purpose was to promote the interests of staff workers in offices. Another union organization that was created in 1948 was the Confederation of German Civil Servants (Deutscher Beamtenbund, or DBB), with the objective of advancing the economic and professional interests of workers in the German civil service. Other unions also developed during the period of the 1950s. In 1959, at Mainz, 15 professional associations of a trade union nature with leanings going back to the Catholic trade unions of pre-Third Reich days merged to form one national union organization—the Christian Trade Union Federation of Germany (Christlicher Gewerkschaftsbund, or CGB).

Union Membership

A minority of German workers belong to trade unions. Moreover, over time the ratio of union workers to all wage and salaried workers has at best remained constant. In 1951 the percentage of wage and salaried workers in unions was 39 percent, compared to 36.6 percent in 1970. In 1970 membership in West German trade unions amounted to 8,223,478 workers.[5] During the period 1966-69 the number of workers in unions actually showed a decline, particularly during the recession. In 1965 union membership amounted to 7.6 million persons, but by 1967 membership dropped to a low of 7.4 million workers. After 1967, union membership showed an increase. Some observers attribute this increase to an intensive recruitment of foreign workers on the part of the trade unions.

The lack of union growth can be attributed to several factors. Although the number of white collar workers and women in unions have increased since 1951, both groups have shown a resistance to union organization. Women typically consider their occupations as temporary, white collar workers in general consider themselves above blue collar workers who are in unions. Turnover in union membership has also been high. As many workers usually leave unions as join during a year. They give up union membership when they move from one area to another or become delinquent in their dues. An expanding economy, with a high level of employment, has also tended to lessen the desire of workers to join unions.

There are currently five trade union federations in West Germany. By far the largest and most important is the DGB, which in 1970 had 6,712,547 members. This membership has tended to remain fairly constant over the last decade, although the DGB registered a total gain of 230,157 members over 1969. Over four-fifths of this gain came from workers who joined the Metal Workers Union and the Chemical Workers Union. A second union is the Confederation of German Civil Servants, which in 1970 had a membership of 723,000. German salaried workers are organized into the German Salaried Employees Union, which had a 1970 membership of 471,000. A fourth German trade union federation is one that has historical roots going back to the last century, the Federation of Christian Trade Unions. It is a small federation with 196,000 members. German police officials belong to a fifth union group, the German Police Union, with 120,931 members.

There is much that is common in the organizational form of these associations and their affiliates. All are federations of trade unions and individual unions are attached to each. In this way, there is a close resemblance between the German federations and the American Federation of Labor. On the other hand, there are sharp contrasts in their political philosophies. The DGB maintains a close political relationship with the Social Democratic Party, while the other federations are more apolitical. The federations are alike in their individual structures, their financial independence, and their obligation to improve the economic and social welfare of union members. Individual trade unions concern themselves with efforts to alter the distribution of the national product. They try to protect union workers from the consequences of automation in industry.

The German Trade Union Federation

The trade union movement in West Germany is dominated by one labor federation, the DGB, which was formed in 1949 as a federation of 16 basic industrial unions comprising every segment of the German economy. For example, office and production employees in the textile industry are organized into a textile union. The DGB represents about one-fourth of the workers in the West German labor force and is the successor to the separate, politically oriented trade union federations that existed before the Hitler era. It has approximately 6.7 million members, nearly half of whom belong to the Metal Workers and the Public Service and Transport Workers Union. Membership in the 16 unions is presented in Table 7.1.

The individual unions and the DGB are very similar in their organizational structure.[6] Each of the 16 member unions of the DGB includes all of the organized workers of a certain industrial field. Each individual union resembles a pyramid, with local plant unions forming the base. The local unions are organized into districts on a state-by-state basis. For example, there are 67 districts in the state of Bavaria and 14 districts in the state of Hesse. District chairmen are elected by the delegates of the local unions during district conferences. The highest organ of the single union is the union council (Gewerkschaftstag), which meets every two or three years. Delegates to the union council are elected by the local unions. The union council makes all decisions for the subgroups under its jurisdiction. It consists of a president and a council of delegates representing each union district. There is also a committee consisting of honorary members. The president and executive council are responsible for policy decisions.

TABLE 7.1

Membership in West German DGB
Unions, 1970

Union	Total Membership
German Metal Workers Union	2,223,467
Public Service and Transport Workers Union	977,031
Chemical, Paper, and Ceramic Workers Union	598,831
Construction Workers Union	504,230
Railroad Workers Union	413,087
Union for Mining and Energy	387,301
Postal Workers Union	360,961
Textile and Clothing Workers Union	302,545
Food Processing Workers Union	247,163
Commerce, Banking, and Insurance Workers Union	157,671
Printing and Paper Workers Union	148,325
Wood and Plastic Workers Union	129,721
Education and Science Union	119,738
Leather Workers Union	62,253
Horticulture, Agriculture, and Forestry Workers Union	46,085
Artists and Musicians	34,138

Source: Data supplied by the Deutsche Gewerkschaftsbund, at the request of the author.

The structure of the DGB conforms to the following pattern.[7] First, there is the Federal Congress (Bundeskongress), which meets every three years and to which all affiliated trade unions send their delegates, who have been elected at national meetings and whose numbers correspond with the total number of each union. The Federal Congress is responsible for the business and financial reports of the DGB, lays down the guidelines for trade union policy, and elects the Federal Executive Committee (Bundesvorstand). The Federal Executive Committee meets every three months as a rule between the Federal Congresses. It consists of a chairman, representatives of the 16 individual trade unions, and the chairmen of the regional organizations of the DGB. The Federal Executive Committee deals with all important questions involving trade union policy, confirms the elections of members of regional committees elected at regional conferences, decides on the amount of the DGB budget, and sets directives for DGB business. Finally, there is also an Advisory Committee (Bundesausschuss), which is responsible for advising the Federal Executive Committee in its policy decisions. This committee consists of a chairman, two deputy chairmen, and six other members.

The DGB organization can be divided still further into regions and districts. The regional committees represent the DGB for the areas they serve. In agreement with the Advisory Committee, the regional committees form the district branches. The regional committees are also made up of representatives from each of the individual trade unions. As in the regional committees, a representative of each of the individual trade unions is a member of the district committees. Within its sphere of activity, the district committee has to represent the DGB, implement its directives and those of the regional committees, deal with trade union affairs, and support individual trade unions in completing their duties. Chart 7.1 shows the connection of the 16 individual trade unions to the DGB. On one side of the chart is the organization of the individual unions and on the other side is the organization of the DGB. The dotted lines show the links at various levels of the unions to the DGB.

Social Action Programs

At its 1949 founding congress the DGB defined its goals as follows: full employment, participation by the workers in the management of the economy, public ownership of key industries, and an equitable distribution of wealth.[8] In 1955 its goals were somewhat modified. Public ownership of basic industries, long advocated by German trade unions, was downgraded in importance. Specific objectives included in the union program were shorter working hours, higher wages and salaries, more social security benefits, comanagement of firms as a guaranteed right, and higher occupational standards.

In 1965 the DGB developed a social action program that became binding upon all member unions. The immediate goal of the program was to ensure labor participation in a rising GNP. Specific economic, social, and political goals were listed in the action program.[9] One goal was a more equitable distribution of wealth. Another goal was an improvement in social security benefits. A third goal, still considered by the unions as the most important goal, was union participation in the operation of business firms. Other goals included improvements in working conditions, shorter working hours, higher wages and salaries, longer vacations with full pay, more opportunities for vocational training, and greater job security. These goals were to be secured over a period of time.

CHART 7.1

Schematic Diagram of Organization of Industrial Unions
and German Confederation of Free Trade Unions (FDGB)

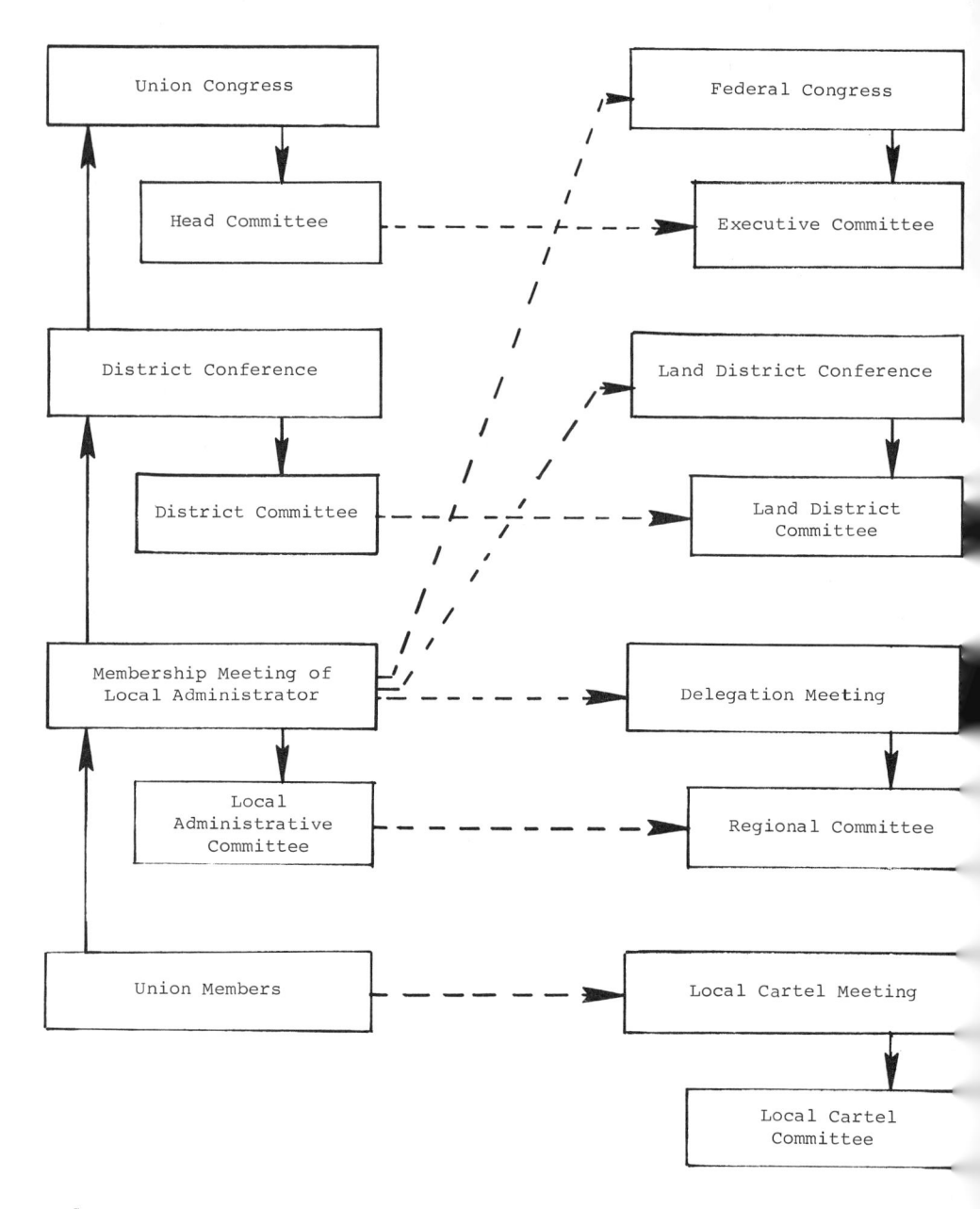

Industrial Unions	FDGB
Union Congress	Federal Congress
Head Committee	Executive Committee
District Conference	Land District Conference
District Committee	Land District Committee
Membership Meeting of Local Administrator	Delegation Meeting
Local Administrative Committee	Regional Committee
Union Members	Local Cartel Meeting
	Local Cartel Committee

Source: Data provided by Deutsche Gewerkschaftsbund.

Work Councils

At the plant level, functions normally performed in the United States by shop committees of union representatives are performed in West Germany by work councils. Although legally independent from the trade unions, work councils usually consist entirely or mainly of union members and work closely with the unions. Furthermore, in many large enterprises the unions have also succeeded in setting up a shop steward system. Work councils carry out day-to-day employee representation and deal with the details of the collective agreement. A council must be established in any private firm with five or more employees; all employees may vote for members of the council and may hold a council office. In contrast with the unions, which are virtually self-regulated, the rights and duties of work councils and the obligations of the employer toward the council are defined by law.

The German Salaried Employees Union

The German Salaried Employees Union (DAG) is a small union of 471,000 members. The DAG was formed in Hamburg in July 1945 and extended its jurisdiction to include the entire areas of the British zone. An eventual conflict developed with the DGB over the craft vs. the industrial union principle. The DAG wished to restrict its membership solely to white collar workers, while the DGB wanted to include all workers in an industry, white collar as well as blue collar. The DAG felt that the principle of industrial unionism disturbed the link of professional solidarity. White collar workers would thus be scattered into various industrial unions and remain a minority with the manual workers in the majority. The splintering of the white collar groups and their annexation to the various industrial unions would raise the question of whether the industrial trade unions would conclude uniform wage agreements for white collar employees and manual workers or whether there would be a special contract on working conditions for members with white collar status.

The DAG and DGB were unable to reconcile their differences and went their separate ways. To some extent the differences reflected views over the status of the white collar worker as opposed to the blue collar worker, with class consciousness being a factor. White collar workers, however, do belong to the DGB and actually are more numerous than those who are affiliated with the DAG. Moreover, the basic goals of the DAG and DGB are somewhat similar. Both favor codetermination in industry and the creation of a participatory democracy. Both are in accord on basic economic policy issues of more wages and greater social security benefits. There is more identification with the point of view of the employers on the part of the DAG, however. It takes a position in opposition to all actions of the industrial unions that propose the leveling of the white collar employees into the social group of manual workers.

The organs of the DAG are the Federal Congress, the Trade Union Council, the Federal Board of Chairmen, and the Advisory Board. The Federal Congress meets every four years. The right to vote is held by delegates elected at various individual congresses. They accept the reports, lay down the principles of trade union policy, and elect the Federal Board of Chairmen as well as the members of the Trade Union Council. This latter group is the highest legislative body between federal congresses. It is made up of representatives of all trade union groups. It is responsible for the supervision of the activities of the Federal Board of Chairmen and decides on the budget. The Federal Board of Chairmen carries out normal business activities within the framework of the statutes and the congress resolutions.

All union organizations affiliated with the DAG are divided further into regional associations, local groups, and factory groups. At the federal level as well as the regional and local levels, there are professional groups with their own conferences and elected committees.

The Federation of Christian Trade Unions

The Federation of Christian Trade Unions was originally formed in 1950 as the German Association of Clerks, although its antecedents go back to 1893. It is a Catholic trade union in terms of origin and orientation, with a history of opposition to the socialism prevalent in the other trade unions. There was the concern on the part of the union leaders after World War II that the DGB and DAG were too closely identified with Marxist ideology. The Christliche Gewerksehaftsbewegun (CGB) set out to pursue an economic and political program that would make a social partnership between labor and management as the central factor in the creation of a new economic system. The CGB rejected a socialist economic order that was to be achieved through the collectivization of property or transfer of key industries into common property. Planned direction of production and distribution was also rejected.

The CGB is a white collar union federation. It has separate unions for commercial and industrial white collar workers, female white collar workers, technicians, and white collar workers in agriculture and forest enterprises. Its objective is to obtain better pay and improved working conditions for its members. Its organizational structure is similar to that of the DAG in that there is a Federal Congress, a Trade Union Council, and an Advisory Board. Unions affiliated with the CGB possess more regional autonomy, however. District units can take care of the business and interests of the national federation. In terms of union membership the CGB has remained small since its inception. To some extent this can be attributed to the fact that it is not a haven for the political, ideological, religious, or professional ambitions of many workers.

Despite the fact that the DGB, DAG, and CGB all attempt to organize white collar workers, the fact remains that this group, as opposed to blue collar workers, is far less interested in the work of trade unions. Around 40 percent of all manual workers belong to trade unions, compared to 23 percent for white collar workers. Many white collar workers, as pointed out previously, view a trade union as an organization for manual workers only. They view the union as an organization fighting against the employer. To them the employer represents such a high authority that they would not think of rebelling against it as manual workers do when they join a trade union. Moreover, for many white collar workers an impersonal labor market does not exist. The function of decision-making is so specialized within many companies that it is tied to the person of the individual employee. Such employees are not so easily replaceable, and the result is that the position in the company and the work performances of these employees are subject to an individual appraisal by the employer that is beyond the influence of the trade union and outside its evaluation.

EMPLOYER ORGANIZATIONS

German employer associations were created during the latter part of the last century as a countermeasure to the development of trade unions. Their development was particularly pronounced during the period immediately prior to World War I. The associations continued to expand and function during the Weimar Republic but were formally dissolved along with the trade unions in December 1933. Employers as well as the trade unions were formed into various economic units under Nazi control. After the end of World War II, the employer associations were allowed to form on a limited basis. General Allied policy was opposed to their formation beyond the single branches of industry. In 1948, however, the trade unions had formed a single federation, and the employers eventually followed suit with the creation of the Central Office of the United Economic Area. By 1949 employer associations as they exist today were established.

Business enterprises belong to various types of trade associations. The most important organization is the Confederation of German Employers' Associations (Bundesvereinigung der Deutschen Arbeitgeberverbände). It consists of 14 regional employers' associations, 43 trade associations, and 750 individual employer associations.[10] It and other employer organizations are concerned not only with business policy and social activities but also function as the representative of individual employers in collective bargaining arrangements with unions. In this respect, the Confederation is similar to other employers' associations in Western Europe. In labor negotiations industrywide or nationwide collective bargining is customary; and employers are represented by one or more employer associations. In fact business enterprises are classified as federated or nonfederated, depending on whether or not they have joined the employer associations qualified to function as their bargaining agents. As terms of collective agreements may be extended by administrative act to nonfederated firms that have not participated in the proceedings, it appears generally advisable for an enterprise to join an employer association.

The principal governing the whole organization of employer associations, however, is that each association is largely independent and thus responsible for its own affairs. Consequently, the Confederation of German Employers' Associations has no authority to give instructions, nor does it have collective bargaining power, which means that it may not conclude direct wage contracts with trade unions. This lies solely within the jurisdiction of the individual employer associations. The Confederation may, however, establish the principles for employer policy in the Federal Republic, make recommendations and suggestions for the realization of them, and strive for agreements with the German Trade Union Federation, which can be adopted as model agreements by member associations.

The basic administrative units of the Confederation are the General Assembly, the Executive Board, the Presidential Board, and the Executive Office.[11] The General Assembly (Mitgliederversammlung) consists of representatives of each of the constituent employer associations. It approves the budget, appropriates membership fees, and decides upon matters referred to it by the Executive Board. The Executive Board (Der Vorstand) consists of all presidents of member associations. It is responsible for the making of policy decisions. The Presidential Board (Das Praesidium) prepares decisions of the Executive Board and is responsible for their implementation. The Executive Office (Die Geschäftsrichtung) attends to the current business of the Confederation. It is divided into nine departments, one of which is responsible for developing a uniform wage policy for the employer associations.

In addition to the Confederation of German Employers' Associations, there are other associations organized by economic sectors, such as the Federal Association of German Industry (Bundesverband der Deutschen Industrie), the General Association of Wholesale and Foreign Trade (Gesamtverband des Gross- und Aussenhandels), the Chief Association of German Retail Trades (Hauptgemeinschaft des Deutschen Einzelhandels), and the Central Association of German Handicrafts (Zentralverband des Deutschen Handwerks). There are also Chambers of Industry and Trade, established on a regional basis. They are united in the German Industrial and Trade Convention (Deutscher Industrie- und Handelstag), which likewise represents German and international chambers of commerce in their promotion of foreign trade.

COLLECTIVE BARGAINING

Although only one-third of all wage and salary earners in West Germany belong to trade unions, collective bargaining agreements cover the bulk of the labor force. By union estimate, about 17 million workers out of a total of 22 million in 1969 were covered by collective agreements.[12] To some extent this fact has lessened the need of many workers to belong to unions. Under traditional collective bargaining procedures the regional office of a union and the corresponding regional employer association for the industry agree upon wages, fringe benefits and other welfare measures, and conditions of employment. The resulting contracts cover all member employers and employees in a given industry. The Ministry of Labor may, under certain conditions, extend the agreements to all nonunion workers in an area. Wage and employment conditions more favorable than those established by the union contract are common, especially in larger firms.

Collective agreements may be signed between one or more employer associations on the one hand and one or more trade unions on the other. There are no provisions for government participation in the negotiations. In particular, a collective agreement does not require official approval, nor has the government any authority to amend it. Disputes over the interpretation of collective agreements as well as other conflicts between employees and employers, however, are usually settled by having representatives of both parties appear in labor courts. There is no compulsory arbitration, but collective agreements may contain provisions for arbitration prior to any hostile action by unions or employers.

A collective agreement is made up of two parts—a normative part and a collective part. The normative part sets up legal standards that govern the relationship between employees and employers who are bound by the agreement; moreover, it determines the details of work conditions by fixing rates of pay and holiday periods. In addition to determining the details of work conditions, the provisions of the normative part may also deal with questions relating to management and work councils. The contractual part of the collective agreement deals with the rights that the contracting parties are entitled to exercise and the duties for which they are responsible. These provisions are intended to facilitate the working of the agreement and to show in detail what general obligations the contracting parties have undertaken by entering into the agreement.

Labor-management relations have been comparatively free from industrial conflicts since the end of World War II. This may be attributed in part to historical factors. As a rule, Germans have always tended to place order and discipline above self-seeking individualism. They are also used to being well protected by social legislation, which came very early and is even today far more embracing than in most other countries. Also for a long period following the end of World War II, there was the necessity on the part of both labor and management to pull together to rehabilitate the economy. Although postwar economic policies favored management, unions cooperated in the interest of the country.

The first major conflicts between labor and management occurred during 1951, when major strikes resulted in the loss of more than one million man-days. Major strikes also occurred in 1953, 1954, and 1957. During 1957 a postwar record of 2.4 million man-days lost was registered. During the decade of the 1960s, 1964 showed a high of 878,000 man-days lost, mainly due to a strike and lockout in the Baden-Wurttemberg metal manufacturing industry.[13] Strike activity during the rest of the decade was insignificant, particularly in comparison to the United States. A loss of 249,000 man-days was recorded in 1969, mostly due to a series of wildcat work stoppages in the late summer. These strikes led to advanced contract renegotiations for iron and steel workers and miners providing pay increases of between 10 and 12 percent.[14]

In 1970 and 1971 there was more aggressive activity on the part of the trade unions. This is attributable in part to growing alienation between trade union leaders and trade union members, which developed during the last decade. In general union members felt that they had not shared equitably in the distribution of income. With a high level of prosperity extending through 1970 and into the first half of 1971, union demands for higher wages increased, although man-days lost through strikes remained at a low level.[15] The government's commitment to maintain high levels of employment and activity has also had some effect on both labor and management by removing the brake that a fear of a recession may have placed on wage and price increases. Wage policies pursued in major neighboring countries to some extent have produced a "demonstration effect" on the rank-and-file members of the German trade unions in that there is pressure on the leaders to emulate gains made elsewhere. Employer attitudes may also have changed in the last two years, since they seem to have avoided strikes at any cost.

CODETERMINATION

A unique feature of labor-management relations in certain German industries is codetermination of business policies on the part of both labor and management. Under the Law of Codetermination of 1951 and succeeding amendments, supervisory boards consisting of labor and management were created in the iron, steel, and coal mining industries. These boards were to have equal representation from labor and management, plus one representative who was supposed to be neutral. This neutral representative, who is selected by both groups, is supposed to function as a tie breaker. The Works Constitution Act also provided that each company in the iron, steel, and coal industries must have one labor representative on its board of directors. This person is supposed to oversee all aspects of company personnel practices.

Codetermination as a principle dates back to the development of German trade unionism in the nineteenth century.[16] It was tied into the idea of creating a just social order that permeated the socialist trade unions. The first relevant legislative provision did not come until 1916; until that time such factory committees as existed depended on voluntary concessions made by employers. In 1916 the Law on Auxiliary Services for the Fatherland (Gesetz über den Vaterlandischen Hilfsdienst) was passed. The creation of workers' committees was made generally obligatory in all enterprises employing more than 50 workers engaged on important war contracts; the trade unions thus gained, for the first time, official recognition as the representatives of their workers. These committees, however, had little say in respect to actual management decisions.

During the Weimar Republic, unions took differing views with respect to codetermination. The Christian Trade Unions held to the notion of creating a just social order in which there would be cooperation between labor and management. Each would sublimate its own personal interests for the good of society. The Free Trade Unions pressed for the gradual elimination of capital ownership with a concomitant democratization of the agents of production. There was the belief on the part of some trade union leaders that codetermination would lead to cooperation between unions and employers to serve the interests of the enterprise against the interest of society. At best participatory democracy in the form of work councils was viewed as a stage along the road to socialism.

In the period of National Socialism all trade unions were prohibited and replaced by the Labor Front.[17] The Works Council Law, dating back to 1916, was repealed, and the interests of labor and management were subverted to the interest of the state. Codetermination, however, was already a firm constituent of the concepts of a new order of society held by the opponents of National Socialism. At the end of the war it was immediately included in the catalogue of the trade union concept of a new and better order of society. This goal was eventually achieved with the passage of the Works Constitution Act of 1952 and the Law of Codetermination of 1951.

The purpose of codetermination is easy to understand. Its objective was and still is to give workers a voice in determining public policy. There have been problems of unemployment, particularly in the coal mining industry, and the unions felt that labor representation was necessary in order to protect the workers from arbitrary layoffs and reduction in salaries. The unions also felt that labor representation would also ensure a more adequate distribution of company profits in terms of labor shares. Codetermination is in essence a social policy that emphasizes the role of the workers as potential decision-makers. Through codetermination an economic democracy was to be created.

To some extent there is a similarity between codetermination in Germany, with the work councils and representation on management boards, and worker participation in the management of Yugoslav enterprises.[18] In Yugoslavia a law on economic organizations was promulgated which stated that the management of all enterprises would be given to their workers. That is, all factories, mines, and other enterprises, which had been under state ownership since the coming to power of the Communist party in Yugoslavia were turned over to the workers of these enterprises to manage. The ownership passed from the state to society in general. Enterprises were defined, not as state property, but as social property, and workers were given the right to manage them, but not to own them. The key instrument through which this management would be accomplished was the workers' council, which in essence became the trustee of social wealth and the provider of self-management for an enterprise. Thus, there has gradually developed in Yugoslavia a system of enterprise management under which managerial functions are shared by the workers' councils and an enterprise director.* The workers' council directs and guides an enterprise; the director manages it.

Participation of labor in the operation of a German enterprise, however, is by no means as extensive as is the case in Yugoslavia. A limited form of codetermination has been achieved in many German industries through the use of worker's councils, which had first originated during World War I.[19] These groups of employee representatives are entitled to some voice in determining the social, personnel, and economic policies in all private firms with more than 20 employees. Their authority is strictly defined and relates to participation in management decisions that may be harmful to the employee, such as a reduction in output, plant closure, transfer, merger, or drastic changes in equipment, production systems, or methods of work. Plants with more than 100 employees must establish an economic committee, consisting of an equal number of employee and management representatives, to be kept informed on business activities and plant conditions. If the employer violates an agreement made with the plant council, the matter is submitted to mediation and the employer may be required to compensate discharged employees.

A much more advanced degree of employee participation in management, however, was achieved through legislation in the mining industry in 1951 under pressure of a strike threat at a time when extreme shortages in coal and steel were delaying reconstruction. The Law of Codetermination of Employees on Supervisory Boards and Management Boards of Mining and Iron and Steel Producing Industries (Gestez über Mitbestimmung der Unternehmen des Bergbaus und der eisen und stahlerzeugenden Industrien) was passed.[20] The law provided for the creation of a supervisory board (Aufsichtsrat), which must have equal representation from labor and management with one neutral member. The law applied, however, only to such enterprises in the coal, iron, and steel industries that took the form of a joint stock company, a limited liability company, or a mining company and that normally employed more than 1,000 workers.

In practice, although union leaders were mesmerized with its potential, codetermination has not had too much impact upon the creation of worker capitalism in the Federal Republic. For one thing, the significance of business decisions in mining has been curtailed by the authority of the European Coal and Steel Community (ECSC). Moreover, it is to be questioned whether workers have found

---

*The director of an enterprise is appointed by a committee consisting of members of the workers' council and representatives of the commune in which the enterprise is located.

themselves better off in that they have been burdened with management responsibilities. Contrary to the expectations of those who opposed codetermination legislation, it is apparent that the end result has been more to obtain the cooperation of employees than in promoting employee control over the enterprises. German workers have been more concerned with wages and other material benefits than with codetermining business policies.

Subsequent efforts since the 1950s to achieve codetermination in other German industries have only been partially successful. After an election setback in 1953, union campaigns for codetermination were temporarily abandoned. Codetermination still remains a basic objective of the DGB, however. At the national trade union congress held in Düsseldorf in 1963, it was accorded top priority by the DGB. The demand for codetermination was held to be necessary for the creation of a new and just social order.[21] At the next congress held in Berlin in 1966 the delegates adopted a resolution on codetermination that indicated beyond all doubt the importance attached to it by the trade unions.[22] In the resolution the trade unions stated that a democratic order of society is possible only if workers are able to exercise a direct and decisive influence on the economy. The unions proposed that membership on the supervisory boards of large companies be equally divided between representatives of employees and management and that one or more additional members represent the public.

At the present, codetermination is limited to certain segments of the West German economy. In stock companies, delegates representing the workers make up one-third of the supervisory board (Aufsichtsrat), which appoints and supervises the managing board (Vorstand). In personal and family-owned companies that have no supervisory board or less than 500 employees, codetermination is limited to the works council. In enterprises with more than 100 employees, industrial committees consisting of an equal number of employee and management representatives are formed. Employee members have to be instructed in the manufacturing and operational methods, production programs, the financial situation of the enterprise, the state of production and sales, and other processes affecting them.

THE ROLE OF THE FEDERAL GOVERNMENT

Labor legislation in the Federal Republic is limited to the barest minimum, with the government complying with the wishes of labor and management that they should be free to regulate the terms of employment and their mutual relations by negotiations. There is no closed or union shop. Legislation on hours and vacations is flexible, enabling labor and management to adjust the application of the statutory provisions involved in collective bargaining to conditions in different industries. A standard five-day work week of 40 hours has been negotiated under collective agreement in all major industries, except public utilities. In general manual and office workers are subject to national minimum standards for paid vacations that have been established by federal law. Direct participation on the part of the federal government involves the provision of mediation services, and tripartite labor courts, with representatives of the government, labor, and management.[23] They are responsible for the interpretation and application of collective agreements as well as labor disputes.

As a general rule labor and social security legislation is enacted on a national basis. Employment regulations are basically covered by the Civil Code, which regulates all service contracts, and is supplemented by the Industrial Code, the Commercial Code, the Crafts Code, the Agricultural Labor Code, and a number of other federal and state laws. Various aspects of individual labor relations, such as paid leave and protection against discharge, are governed by collective agreements and plant agreements, as well as by a considerable number of special rulings or principles established by the Federal Labor Court. For example, dismissal notices for white collar workers must not be less than one month from the payday at the end of the month to the end of the following month. The law governing dismissals provides that employers show a justifiable cause. Provisions concerning collective contracts are contained in the Collective Agreement Act of 1949, as amended.

The basic laws concerning employee representation on various German enterprises are the 1951 Law on Codetermination and the 1952 Law Governing Industrial Relations in the Private Economy. The 1951 Law on Codetermination, as mentioned previously, granted labor a 50-percent representation on the managing boards and supervisory boards of enterprises in the mining, iron, and steel industries. It also required the creation of the position of executive labor director and awarded labor the right to veto a nominee to this position. In 1956 the law was amended to regulate the right to codetermination in holding companies in the coal, iron, and steel industries. The 1952 Law Governing Industrial Relations in the Private Economy covers all work councils at the enterprise level and codetermination in enterprises not falling under the special provisions of the mining, iron, and steel industries. Under this law work councils are entitled to a voice in determining the social, personnel, and economic policies in all private firms with more than 20 employees. The councils may codetermine in decisions that affect basic employment security, such as relocating a plant, mergers, and basic production changes.

The major social legislation of the Federal Republic with respect to labor includes the 1961 Law to Promote the Accumulation of Capital by Employees, as amended, which provides tax incentives for certain benefits paid by employers to employees in addition to their regular compensation, provided the benefits are earmarked for use in building up the employees personal capital. Also included is the Children's Allowance Act of 1964, which was amended in 1965 to add educational allowances, and social insurance laws providing health, accident, unemployment, and old-age and survivors' insurance. In addition, there are provisions for public assistance and social aid.

Labor Courts

Labor courts were given formal status by the Law on Labor Courts (Arbeitsgerichtsgesetz) of 1953. These courts are divided into three categories—Federal Labor Courts, State Labor Courts, and Local Labor Courts—and exist for the purpose of resolving disputes between labor and management.[24] The court of highest authority is the Federal Labor Court. As a federal court it is under the jurisdiction of the Ministry of Labor. All controversies involving questions of labor law are decided in the first instance by the Local Labor Courts (Arbeitsgerichte) and, on appeal, by the state appellate labor courts (Landesarbeitsgerichte).[25] In certain cases a further appeal from a decision of a state appellate labor court may be taken to the Federal Labor Court. This further appeal usually requires the permission of the appellate labor court. Without this permission the appeal is permissible if the opinion of the appellate court conflicts in a question of law with that of the Federal Labor Court or, where the federal court has not passed on the issue involved, if the appellate court's decision conflicts with that of another appellate labor court, or if the amount in controversy exceeds DM 6,000.[26]

Each labor court has a chairman who is appointed after consultation with a committee consisting of equal numbers of representatives of the trade unions, the employer associations, and the labor judiciary. Individual local and state labor court judges are selected from a list of nominations drawn up by trade unions and other associations of workers and by employer associations and are appointed for a term of four years. The Federal Labor Court possesses two chambers, each consisting of three federal judges, including a chairman and two lay members representing the workers and the employers, respectively. For decisions on matters of special importance, a special senate of the Federal Labor Court is convened, consisting of the President of the Court, the chairmen of the Senate, four federal judges, and four lay members, two of whom represent the workers and two the employers.

SUMMARY

West German trade unions are similar in respect to trade unions in other Western democracies. The right to organize and join trade unions is guaranteed by both federal and state constitutions. Under the Basic Law of the Federal Republic agreements restricting or hindering this right are null and void and measures directed to this end are illegal. The right to strike, although not mentioned in the Basic Law, is authorized by most state constitutions. As measured by the number of days lost, however, the incidence of strikes is low in comparison with the United States. Legislation provides for conciliation and arbitration of industrial disputes, and special labor courts hear disputes over the interpretation of individual and collective labor agreements and the application of the various laws of codetermination.

Despite deep historical roots, West German trade unions have not exactly flourished. In 1970 less than one-third of all blue collar and white collar workers in the Federal Republic belonged to unions. In this respect there is a similarity with the United States, France, and the United Kingdom in that a minority of workers also belong to unions in these countries. General factors inhibiting the rate of growth of unions in West Germany include a very high level of prosperity, which lessens the need for workers to join unions, and a reluctance on the part of many white collar workers to identify with blue collar workers in the industrial unions. The unions also had to regroup and reformalize their ideologies after the end of World War II.

West German trade unions are formed on an industrial union basis. One trade union federation, the German Trade Union Federation (DGB), dominates the whole trade union movement. It consists of 16 individual industrial unions comprising about 80 percent of all workers in German unions. The remaining 20 percent are organized into unions affiliated with federations representing white collar workers, civil servants, and police officials. Employers are also organized into associations, the most important of which is the Confederation of German Employers' Associations. Collective bargaining takes place between individual unions belonging to a union federation and individual employers belonging to an employer federation.

The trade unions regard their main task as being to secure the economic and social improvement of their members. They have also concerned themselves with the right of workers to have some say in the operation of an enterprise. Thus, they have pushed the principle of codetermination, which has been codified into law and which allows workers to participate with management in running a firm. In general relations have been good. Growing union demands in the 1960s, however, particularly with respect to higher wages and more fringe benefits, have encountered opposition from management and some serious strikes have occurred.

CHAPTER

8

GENERAL CHARACTERISTICS OF THE EAST GERMAN ECONOMIC AND POLITICAL SYSTEM

INTRODUCTION

The present German Democratic Republic (GDR) was incorporated into the Soviet sphere of political and ideological influence after the end of World War II. Its economic development during the postwar period was guided by the Soviet occupation forces, and it became one of the six so-called satellite states that have emerged outside of the boundaries of the Soviet Union. Ostensibly and formally an independent republic, its status has largely been subordinated to the economic and political desires of the Soviet Union. Its economy, which before the war was largely oriented toward Western Europe, has been remolded and redirected toward Eastern Europe. But within the group of Eastern European countries, including the Soviet Union, it has achieved the highest living standards and per capita income. East Germany has developed into the world's ninth largest industrial power, with a GNP of $29.5 billion.

GEOGRAPHY AND POPULATION

The German Democratic Republic has an area of 108,174 square kilometers (41,648 square miles) and a population as of December 31, 1969, of 17,076,500.[1] The present territory of the GDR represents about 23 percent of the area of the Third Reich of 1937 and includes the former provinces of Mecklenburg, West Pomerania, Mark Brandenburg, Thuringia, and Saxony. The population is similar to West Germany's in that it is highly urbanized and densely crowded into a land area about the size of the state of Ohio. The major cities are East Berlin, Leipzig, and Dresden. But, unlike West Germany, the population of East Germany has at best remained stationary over the years.

In 1946 approximately 18.5 million people lived in the present territory of the GDR; at the end of 1969 the population was approximately 17.1 million.[2] In the four-year period from the end of 1965 to the end of 1969 the net population gain was 29,000. The composition of the population is significant. Females outnumber males by a ratio of about 1.2 to 1.[3] There is also a heavy concentration of population in the older age groups.

The GDR consists of 15 administrative districts (Bezirke), which were created in 1952. These districts are as follows: East Berlin, Rostock, Schwerin, Neubrandenburg, Potsdam, Frankfurt, Cottbus, Magdeburg, Halle, Erfurt, Gera, Suhl, Dresden, Leipzig, and Karl-Marx-Stadt. The three largest districts in population are Halle, Dresden, and Karl-Marx-Stadt. The districts are subdivided into 27 urban districts (Stadtkreise) and 191 rural districts (Landkreise).[4] These districts, which would roughly correspond to a county unit in the United States, are further subdivided into 8,975 local communes (Gemeinden).[5] The local communes would correspond to local government units in the United States.

In the zonal division of occupied Germany, the Soviet Union received the great agricultural food basket of Germany, while the more important industrial areas went to the Western powers, notably the Ruhr in the British zone. When the two German republics were formed, the Federal Republic of Germany could claim much of the prewar industrial base and the German Democratic Republic a strong agricultural base. Before the war the area of the present GDR was agriculturally self-sufficient. The farms in the area were larger than those in West Germany. Only one-fifth of the labor force was engaged in agriculture, yet the area typically produced a grain surplus and was a major exporter of sugar beets and potatoes. After the war, however, the area became a perennial grain importer and a major food-deficit region.

Before the war the East German economy was highly industrialized. It pioneered in the production of synthetic gasoline and rubber. It was the locus of much of Germany's chemical industry and produced office, textile, and precision machinery and a wide line of automobiles. All of Germany's production of electrical goods was centered in East Germany. World leadership in the production of optical goods was held by the Zeiss firm of Jena, which is located in the territory of the GDR. In terms of living standards and levels of income, there was little difference between East and West Germany before World War II. In fact, many of the high-wage, specialized industries were located in the eastern part of Germany.

East Germany is not well endowed with mineral resources. Before the war East German industry depended on West Germany to supply it with coal and steel. After the war this supply source was

THE EAST GERMAN SYSTEM

cut off. The most important mineral resource is lignite, or brown coal, which provides much of the fuel and power base of the economy. The East Germans also use much of their lignite to produce briquets but are also able to produce gasoline and metallurgical quality coke from it as well. There have been problems attendant with the use of lignite, however. Production costs have increased, because deposits are below the surface area. The use of lignite as a source of liquid fuel has also involved high operating costs.

There are also low-grade iron ore deposits, which have been utilized after the former sources of supply from West Germany were cut off. The supply is inadequate in meeting industrial demands. Copper and uranium are also natural resources of some importance. Although the output of copper ore has almost doubled since 1950, the quality of the ore has declined. There are also small quantities of other metallic ores, such as lead, zinc, tin, antimony, nickel, and tungsten. These ores, however, do not begin to meet industrial needs. East Germany produces potash, which is used for fertilizers and commercial purposes. There are also minor petroleum deposits on the shores of the Baltic.

THE POLITICAL SYSTEM

Perhaps the most important point that can be made with respect to the political system of the GDR is the interlocking relationship between the Socialist Unity Party of Germany (Sozialistische Einheitspartei Deutschlands, or SED) and the administrative units of the government. It is difficult to obtain an understanding of the actual operations of the government of the GDR by merely studying the functions of various governmental organizations. Regardless of such functions and organizations, political and governmental power in East Germany is completely in the hands of the SED. In other words the SED dominates the governmental administrative structure of the country and has its members in practically all important offices and positions. Its policies are carried out by all governmental agencies and organizations.

Organization of the Government

The governmental administrative apparatus of the GDR is divided into a multitiered arrangement with control extended from East Berlin downward to the local administrative units. The basic administrative reorganization occurred in 1952, and the current arrangement is essentially as follows.

Territorial Administration

From a territorial administrative standpoint East Germany can be divided into several categories, which have been previously mentioned. First, there is the German Democratic Republic itself, with the capital in East Berlin. Then there are the 15 administrative districts (Bezirke), which are much smaller in size than the typical American state. Each district has its own governmental units and party hierarchy and is responsible for the provision and maintenance of roads and other public facilities. The districts are also responsible for the levying and collection of certain taxes. Below the districts come the county (Kreis) territorial units, which are subdivided into urban (Stadtkreise) and rural (Landkreise) units. Each unit is responsible for such activities as education and road construction. The lowest territorial unit is the town, village, or rural area (Gemeinde). The local unit has certain responsibilities, such as the operation of municipal enterprises and the construction of public facilities. The line of territorial subordination runs from East Berlin to the districts to the counties to the local governmental units.

National Policy Administration

The governmental structure of the GDR is divided into legislative, executive, and judicial branches. Each branch has certain functions as follows.[6]

Legislative Branch. The legislature of the GDR is a unicameral Volkskammer (People's Chamber) consisting of 500 members, including 66 delegates from East Berlin, who are elected from a single joint list on a proportional basis. Although several political parties are represented in the Volkskammer, effective power is concentrated in the hands of the permanent majority party, the SED. The SED cannot and does not recognize any power in the state but itself. Nominations to the Volkskammer are supposed to reflect a cross-section of society, with a certain number of candidates representing the SED and quotas from the other political parties, trade unions, youth and women's organizations, farmers, and cultural and intellectual workers. The SED, however, can exercise the final right of veto power over any one of the nominees. All candidates are then placed on the single list that is submitted to all of the voters in a general election.

The formal functions of the Volkskammer are defined in the East German constitution, which was promulgated in 1949.[7] The Volkskammer is responsible for the approval of state treaties and other international agreements. It can decide to hold elections. It is responsible for the pro forma selection of its own executive bodies

THE EAST GERMAN SYSTEM

and of the national executive committees. It is responsible for the defense of the GDR and for the drafting and enacting of laws. These functions, however, are stronger in theory than in practice. Most bills originate with the executive and are rarely introduced by the Volkskammer. In terms of real decision-making it has little power and passes the bills that are submitted to it. Its power is more symbolic in that, as the name People's Chamber implies, it is supposed to be a microcosm of East German society. Each member of the chamber is supposed to see that the programs and policies of the SED gain the popular support of the group he represents. So the most important function of the Volkskammer is representing the state to the people.

There are also legislative equivalents of the Volkskammer at the district (Bezirke), county (Kreis), and local (Gemeinde) levels. These legislative organs have little formal power, but they do help to coordinate national policy at the district, regional, and local levels. They, too, form an instrument of participation on the part of the masses in that they are supposed to be a microcosm of the areas they represent. Thus, another link is formed between the state and the people. District, county, and local legislative bodies play a rather prominent role with respect to the implementation of economic planning, particularly as efforts have been made to decentralize plan operations. The legislative bodies maintain commissions that are responsible for integrating regional and local problems into the objectives.

Executive Branch. There are two major executive organs in the GDR—the State Council (Staatsrat) and the Council of Ministers (Ministerrat). The State Council, created in 1960, is a 26-member body appointed by the Volkskammer for a period of four years. It functions as the nominal head of state and can be considered as primarily a political body with the power to issue legally binding decrees and to represent the Volkskammer when it is not in session.[8] The Council of Ministers, which consists of 38 members, is the executive decision-making body. It is responsible for the development of economic policy and the enforcement of laws passed by the Volkskammer.[9] It is also responsible for exercising general guidance in the sphere of relations with other countries, and for directing the general organization of the country's armed forces. Within the Council of Ministers and chosen by its members is the Presidium, which consists of 13 members. The Presidium can be considered the real governing body in the GDR and is responsible for making the important policy decisions.

Below the Council of Ministers are groups of ministries that directly exercise control over the East German economy. These ministries function at the national level and can be divided on the basis of industrial and nonindustrial ministries. In 1969 there were seven industrial ministries for the following industry classifications: basic materials, ore mining and metallurgy, chemicals, electrotechnical and electronics, heavy machinery and equipment, processing machinery and vehicles, and light industry. An eighth industrial ministry, which is responsible for food production, has also been created. Nonindustrial ministries include ministries of culture, health, education, material economics, and agriculture. The system of ministries extends downward to the district, regional, and local levels. In other words, counterpart departments with the function of control exist at the district level. In addition, there are departments for economic management at the district level. At the city, county, and local levels are the subdepartments. They are subordinate to the executive organs that exist at these levels and to the administrative agencies directly above them.

East German attempts to find an administrative structure that would allow the ministries to exercise central coordination while avoiding excessive bureaucratic duplication has caused this area of administration to be subject to frequent reorganization. At some periods the individual ministries have been allowed to work fairly independently, exercising strong control over local enterprises and subject only to the overall control of the Council of Ministers. At other times, including the current period, there have been efforts to give regional and local administrative units and individual enterprises greater autonomy.

The SED

For all practical purposes the only political party of any consequence in East Germany is the SED, which was created in April 1946. Other parties exist but provide no political competition to the SED. To some extent their function is to represent the opinions of certain groups such as small businessmen and farmers. In essence these parties are a part of a "popular front," in which the SED is the dominant mass group. Representatives of the minor political parties sit in the Volkshammer but do so with the approval of the SED. When elections are held, a whole slate of candidates represented by all political parties but endorsed by the SED is entered. So elections become a matter of approving the candidates chosen by the SED. Political competition exists within the SED but not between the SED and the other political parties.

Control over government machinery in East Germany is in the hands of the SED. It maintains firm control over every aspect of life through well-organized and disciplined organization. Members are assigned to key positions in all institutions and enterprises in East German society. Control extends down to the local level, where primary party units operate in factories, offices, schools, and villages. These units are responsible for the recruitment of members and for serving to transmit party policy at the local level. Local units are also responsible for the selection of delegates to the local party conference, which in turn selects delegates to conferences covering a somewhat wider geographic area, and this process continues until finally, in district and regional congresses, delegates are selected to the National Party Congress.

The organizational structure of the SED resembles a pyramid. At the apex of the pyramid are the Politburo, the Central Committee, and the Secretariat. The structure continues downward through regional, district, and local levels.[10]

The Politburo

At the Eighth Congress of the SED, held in Berlin in June 1971, the Politburo was increased to 16 members and the number of candidate members, previously 6, was increased to 7.[11] The Politburo is in effect the supreme instrument of political power in East Germany. When the Central Committee is not in session, it is responsible for all phases of national life—foreign policy, domestic economic policy, and military policy. The 16 members exercise the prerogatives and responsibilities of national policy-making. Most also have collateral duties, meaning that they serve in other capacities in addition to their positions as party administrators and policy-makers.

The Central Committee

The Central Committee of the SED consists of 135 full members and 54 elected candidates. It is elected by the National Party Congress, which meets every four years. The Central Committee meets at least once every six months, and on the average four times a year. It is composed of the Politburo, Secretariat, Party Control Commission, and a number of individual sections. It has no effective role as a decision-maker; that function is performed by the Politburo. It does, however, provide a forum or sounding board for the elaboration of the major policies of the SED and its top leaders. It is also responsible for the dissemination of the aims and objectives of the leaders to officials in various departments in the central apparatus and also downward to the various party committees at the regional, district, and local levels.

The Secretariat

The Secretariat consists of 10 members. The first secretary is Erich Honecker who took over the position from Walter Ulbricht in May 1971. The remaining secretaries are for international affairs; agriculture; culture, science, and education; foreign trade and supply; agitation; economy; propaganda; questions of security; and party organization. Unlike the Politburo, which has no administrative responsibility, the Secretariat is responsible for the administration of the SED. There is an overlap between the Secretariat and the Politburo in the sense that several members serve on each organization. For example, Gunther Mittag is secretary of economy and is also a member of the Politburo. The Secretariat is responsible for providing the leadership for the professional party organization, which consists of a hierarchy of subordinate secretariats at the regional, district, and lower administrative levels. This hierarchy is responsible for ensuring the implementation of state economic policy by the various governmental organs. It is also responsible for the allocation and mobilization of manpower and other resources of the SED.

Other Levels of SED Organization

SED control extends down to the lowest control organs.[12] Below the national level come the district party organizations, which possess similar structural arrangements. For example, each district has a secretariat that consists of a first and second secretary and secretaries of economics, agriculture, agitation and propaganda, and science, education, and culture. Other members of the secretariat are the chairman of the district planning commission, the district agricultural council, and the district labor organization. District leaders are elected at congresses by delegates from town and county party units. After the district organization come the county and local party units. The basic party unit is at the place of work. The SED dominates all phases of economic and social activity. The primary objective of its members is to carry out its policies in all fields of activities.

A fundamental point to make with reference to East Germany is the interconnection of SED and government administrative units. Supreme authority in both party and government is vested in the leaders of the SED, who draw into their hands the main lines of command for both party and government. Party and government structure parallel each other. An interlocking relationship continues down to the lowest administrative level. Although inefficiency may result at lower administrative levels because of communication problems, there is no question but what the interconnection of party and government and

THE EAST GERMAN SYSTEM

party domination of the government confer on East German public administration exceptional unity of control and uniformity of ideological perspective.

THE EAST GERMAN ECONOMY

East Germany has a highly developed industrial economy with the highest per capita income and living standards of all of the Soviet bloc countries. The economy is run by the allocation of resources by administrative decisions rather than by a market mechanism; its operations are governed by a priority system that over the years has given preference to capital goods and military and scientific goods over consumer goods. The key economic questions concerning production and resource allocation are decided by economic planning. Predetermined tasks and resource allocation govern the operations of both industrial and agricultural enterprises. The state through the economic plan not only prescribes the objectives to be followed by all economic units but also the success criteria involved in evaluating performance. Flexibility in the operation of enterprises is permitted within the targets and resource limits set by the plan.

The organization of production and distribution in the East German economy can be divided into four categories. First, there are those production and distribution units that are state owned. The state enterprise is the most important economic unit in value of output and number of persons employed. Then there are the cooperatives, which are of particular importance in agriculture. The third type of economic unit is the semistate enterprise in which both state and private participation exist. Finally, there are private enterprises that continue to function under state supervision.

Table 8.1 presents a sector breakdown of the contributions of state-owned enterprises, cooperatives, semistate enterprises, and private enterprises to the East German economy expressed as a percentage of net product for 1970.

The East German economy can also be examined from the standpoint of the contribution of each economic sector to net product. The dominance of the industrial sector is rather pronounced. Agriculture, which contributed 28.4 percent of net product in 1950, has declined in importance to the point that in 1970 it only contributed 11.7 percent of net product.[13] In Table 8.2 the contribution of each sector is expressed as a percent of net product and also in value as represented in millions of Ostmarks.*

---

*The East German mark, or Ostmark, is strictly a domestic currency. It is not convertible into any foreign currency and is not

TABLE 8.1

Contributions to East German Net Product,
by Economic Unit
(percent)

Sector	State-Owned	Cooperative	Semistate-Owned	Private
Industry	79.6	3.4	11.4	5.7
Construction	54.9	27.5	9.0	8.6
Agriculture	14.2	81.1	0.1	4.6
Transportation and communication	93.0	—	3.8	3.2
Trade	63.7	23.6	7.1	5.6
Other sectors	92.1	1.8	3.0	3.1

Source: Staatliche Zentralverwaltung für Statistik, Statistisches Taschenbuch 1971 (East Berlin: Staatsverlag der DDR, 1971), p. 27.

TABLE 8.2

Contributions to East German Net Product,
by Sector, 1970

Sector	Million Ostmarks	Percent
Industry	68,580	60.9
Construction	9,247	8.2
Agriculture	13,140	11.7
Transportation and communication	5,723	5.1
Trade	14,181	12.6
Other sectors	1,682	1.5
Total	112,553	100.0

Source: Staatliche Zentralverwaltung für Statistik, Statistisches Taschenbuch 1971 (East Berlin: Staatsverlag der DDR, 1971), pp. 26-2

Industry

During the postwar period East Germany was forced to shift into production of its own heavy machinery and metallurgical products to make up for the loss of these supplies, which before the war were largely produced in West Germany. The cost of doing this has been considerable in an economy poor in resources. In addition East Germany has had to rely on the Soviet Union for a large proportion of the raw materials needed by its industry. Despite these disadvantages East Germany has attained a position among the world's foremost industrial countries. Its principal industrial products are partly traditional, partly new; they include basic chemicals, metal working, industrial and agricultural machinery, transport equipment, electronic equipment, and precision instruments. In particular, ferrous metallurgy has progressed rapidly since the war, far surpassing prewar levels. Improvement in technology was facilitated by the development of a process for reducing East German iron ores with lignite coke to produce pig iron.

The machinery and transport equipment industry is the most important industry in the GDR in terms of its contribution to the value of gross industrial production. In 1969 gross industrial production in the machinery and transport equipment industry amounted to 34.3 billion Ostmarks out of total gross industrial production of 137.7 billion Ostmarks. East Germany has become the most important quality machine producer in the Soviet bloc, and machinery accounts for about half of its exports to the Soviet Union. Second in importance is the food processing industry, which contributed gross industrial output valued at 24.2 billion Ostmarks in 1969. Of particular importance is the production of meat, animal fats, margarine, and edible oils. The chemical industry is third in importance, with a contribution of 19.7 billion Ostmarks in 1969. Since the war there has been great expansion into the field of organic chemistry, with concentration on solvents, acetic acid, and plastics. In the important inorganics—sulphuric acid, sodium carbonate, sodium hydroxide, and ammonia—output has almost tripled over prewar levels. Also of importance is the electronics industry, particularly the production of electrical

---

quoted in international monetary markets. Moreover, the laws of the GDR prohibit the movement of Ostmarks across the border. An unofficial exchange rate between East and West German marks as of June 1971 was four Ostmarks for one Deutsche Mark. The domestic value of the East German mark varies greatly, since internal prices are fixed by the planning authorities.

equipment. Table 8.3 presents the contribution of each industry to the total value of gross industrial production for 1969.

Agriculture

Agriculture's contribution to net domestic product has declined in importance. In 1960, for example, out of a net product of 73.1 billion Ostmarks the contribution of agriculture amounted to 12 billion Ostmarks. In 1969 net domestic product had increased to 107.2 billion Ostmarks, while the value of agricultural production had increased to only 13.4 billion Ostmarks.[14] Moreover, before the war the present area of East Germany was self-sufficient. It produced a grain surplus and was a major exporter of sugar beets and potatoes. Since the war the area has become a grain importer and a food-deficit region. In recent years the amount of investment going into agriculture has increased in an effort to improve productivity. In 1969 about 16 percent of total investment was in agriculture, compared to 13.5 percent in 1969.[15]

TABLE 8.3

Industrial Gross Production,
by Industry Group, East Germany
(million Ostmarks)

Industry Group	Value of Production
Energy and fuel	7,847.9
Chemical	19,654.2
Metallurgical	10,778.7
Construction material	2,656.8
Water power	722.1
Machinery and vehicles	34,307.6
Electrotechnical	12,572.7
Light industry	15,238.9
Textile	9,756.8
Food	24,174.3
Total	137,710.0

Source: Staatliche Zentralverwaltung für Statistik, *Statistisches Jahrbuch der Deutschen Demokratischen Republik, 1970* (East Berlin: Staatsverlag der DDR, 1970), p. 108.

THE EAST GERMAN SYSTEM

In terms of physical output potatoes are the most important food product, with sugar beets ranking second. In 1969 the production of potatoes and sugar beets as measured in metric tons amounted to 12.8 million and 5.8 million, respectively.[16] Wheat, rye, and barley also account for an important part of total output. From the standpoint of land utilization, shifts have occurred since the end of the war. The area devoted to grains has decreased, whereas oilseed and fiber plant acreage has increased. Priority has been given to the production of industrial crops, such as sugar beets and certain oil plants. In the area of animal husbandry, East German animal stocks were substantially depleted during the war. During the postwar period all stocks have been rebuilt to above prewar levels. In the area of meat production pork is the most important product, accounting for more than 60 percent of total production.

Foreign Trade

East Germany is a member of the Council for Mutual Economic Assistance (COMECON, or CEMA) which was created in 1949 as a counterpoise to the Marshall Plan. Its members are Bulgaria, Czechoslovakia, East Germany, Hungary, Poland, Romania, and the Soviet Union. The economies of these countries are linked together through bilateral trade agreements. One aspect of the development of the postwar East German economy has been its integration into the Soviet bloc economies. Today, the bulk of its foreign trade is with other members of COMECON. In 1969, for example, East German exports amounted to 17.4 billion Valuta Marks.[17] Of this amount, 11.8 billion Valuta Marks were with the COMECON countries.[18]

The GDR is strongly foreign-trade oriented. In fact foreign trade has increased at a faster rate than gross social product during the period 1960-69—an increase of 90 percent, compared to 45 percent. In 1969 exports amounted to around 20 percent of net domestic product and imports amounted to around 18 percent. On an international basis, in 1969 the GDR ranked thirteenth in the value of foreign trade. It contributed 1.6 percent of the world trade, compared to 9 percent for West Germany.[19] In terms of a comparison with other COMECON countries, the GDR ranks second only to the Soviet Union in terms of its position in foreign trade. Table 8.4 presents a breakdown of East German foreign trade by major export and import sources. A significant point to notice is the importance of trade with the Soviet Union.

East German trade with the Soviet Union conforms to the following pattern. Exports primarily consist of industrial goods and specialty equipment. The most important exports expressed in Valuta Marks are fishing vessels, tractors and agricultural machinery,

TABLE 8.4

East German Foreign Trade,
by Major Source, 1969

Country	Exports (million Valuta Marks)*	Imports (million Ostmarks)
Soviet Union	6,961.7	7,326.0
Czechoslovakia	1,740.7	1,544.3
West Germany	1,176.0	1,733.6
Poland	1,324.0	1,095.5
Hungary	779.2	875.0
Bulgaria	640.6	609.9
All exports and imports	17,443.0	17,239.1

*The Valuta Mark is only used in foreign trade and has the following conversion values: 4.2 Valuta Marks = $1; 4.667 Valuta Marks = 1 Soviet ruble. The Valuta Mark does not have the same value as the domestic East German Ostmark. The Valuta Mark is also expressed in terms of an official gold parity.

Source: Staatliche Zentralverwaltung für Statistik, Statistisches Jahrbuch der Deutschen Demokratischen Republik, 1970 (East Berlin: Staatsverlag der DDR, 1971), p. 296.

cranes and hydraulic lifts, cables and power lines, factory machinery, furniture, clothing, and optical equipment.[20] Imports consist of coal, gas, oil, steel, diesel machines, foodstuffs, radio receivers, and textile equipment.[21] It can be said that the terms of trade have favored the Soviet Union in that it has received highly complex industrial goods in exchange for raw materials.

ECONOMIC PLANNING

Economic planning involves the making of major economic decisions—what and how much is to be produced and to whom it is to be allocated—by the conscious decision of a central authority on the basis of a comprehensive survey of the economy as a whole. It represents an attempt to balance the supply and demand of resources in order to achieve an equilibrium. It is not only concerned with every branch

THE EAST GERMAN SYSTEM

of activity but embraces most aspects of economic life, including volume of output, wages, prices, location of industries, and employment. It is not content with merely making the system operate; it also has such objectives as increasing the national wealth or the rapid industrialization of the economy. It relies on orders for its implementation—it is controlled by a central planning agency, by financial organizations, and, above all, by the political authorities. The essential requisite for economic planning is the ownership of the agents of production by the state.

East German economic plans differ in their functional character. There are the physical output plans, which involve production, distribution, and investment goals, and financial plans, which are derivatives of these plans. Then, too, plans differ in terms of time limits. There are long-range plans, which may extend to a period of 30 years and which usually deal with a particular aspect of the economy. Then there are the medium-term plans, which cover a period from five to seven years and which develop targets or goals to be accomplished during this time. The normal frame of reference when one thinks of planning is the five-year plan. There are also annual plans that involve production plans to be followed by East German enterprises and other organizational units during the year. Annual plans can be broken down into quarterly or monthly periods. All economic plans are interrelated, and it is important and necessary for planning agencies to ensure their unification in order to establish a proper relationship between production and consumption and between national requirements and resources.

An outline of the East German plans is presented in Table 8.5. It is to be emphasized that they are the formally announced medium-term plans that provide the goals and guidelines to be followed during the time period involved. They are not the annual output plans. The greatest role is played by the medium-term plan, which is concerned mostly with changes in the capacity and rate of production of different industries or enterprises.

The Mechanics of Plan Preparation

The responsibility for the preparation of the economic plans is centered in four state organs: the Council of Ministers (Ministerrat), the State Planning Commission (Staatliche Plankommission), the Office for Prices (Amt für Preise), and the State Central Statistics Administration (Staatliche Zentral Statistische Verwaltung). The basic functions of each of these organs with respect to the development of the plans are as follows:[22]

TABLE 8.5

East German Plans Since 1949

Plan	Description
Two-year, 1949-50	Marked a transition to planned economy.
Five-year, 1951-55	So far only plan completed.
Five-year, 1956-60	After three years dropped in favor of a seven-year plan.
Seven-year, 1959-65	Planning period was modeled after the USSR; plan was dropped in 1962.
Seven-year, 1964-70	Plan was based on Ulbricht's report at SED party rally in 1963.
Five-year, 1966-70	Represented formal correction of seven-year plan.
Two-Year, 1969-70	Introduced long-term planning goals and corrected five-year plan.
Five-Year, 1971-75	Announced at meeting of the SED Party Congress in Berlin, June 1971.

Source: Bundesministerium für Gesamtdeutsche Fragen, Fünfter Tätigkeitsbericht (Bonn: Deutscher Bundesverlag, 1969), p. 89.

1. The Council of Ministers is the highest state organ responsible for the management of the economy. The plan is based on the policy directives of the Council, which also lays down the sphere of planning responsibility for each level of economic administration. The Council is responsible for the approval of the final draft of all plans.

2. The State Planning Commission is responsible for translating broad policy decisions made by the Council of Ministers into concrete programs. It has the responsibility for working out economic plans of all kinds and for their presentation for review by the Council of Ministers. It is also responsible for the supervision of the plans. Assisting the State Planning Commission are three advisory organs—the Council for Economic Research (Beirat für Ökonomische Forschung), the Secretariat for Research and Technology (Staatssecretariat für Forschung und Technik), and the Research Council (Forschungsrat). These organs are responsible for economic research and plan forecasting.

THE EAST GERMAN SYSTEM

3. The Office for Prices is attached directly to the Council of Ministers. It is responsible for the development of prices for product groups. On the basis of planning information the Office for Prices sets up a central price model that serves as a pricing guideline. The model is based on production costs, production volume, and the upper and lower limits of capital profitability, which are all used to determine pricing.

4. The State Central Statistics Administration is responsible for providing the State Planning Commission and the government ministries with a flow of information on all facets of economic activity. It is also responsible for providing plan indexes. Together with the State Planning Commission, it must make sure that the indexes in all reports agree with those in the planning documents in terms of content and value expressed. The State Central Statistics Administration possesses autonomy in that it is not attached to either the State Planning Commission or to the ministries, for its purpose is to serve as a means of control over planning. As is typical for any administrative apparatus in the GDR, there are counterparts to the Statistics Administration at the district, county, and local levels.

Development of the Five-Year Plan

The development of the five-year plan conforms to the following pattern. Control figures and forecasts are prepared by the State Planning Commission before the plan is drafted. These control figures cover the volume and distribution of national income, the overall volume of capital investment and industrial production in the more important branches of industry, the volume of output, and state purchases of farm produce, the volume of retail trade, expected increases in labor productivity, and the monetary income of the population. These control figures are based on the economy's achievements in preceding time periods and on forecasts of future manpower and progress in technology and labor productivity.

After the control figures have been developed, they are sent to the industrial, agricultural, and trade ministries. Each ministry is responsible for the application of control figures to its given area of jurisdiction. The control figures are also sent down to departments at the district, county, and local levels. These departments are subordinate to the councils at the district and county levels in the same way that the national ministries are subordinate to the Council of Ministers. For example, the agricultural plan, which is a part of the overall plan, would go from the State Planning Commission to the Ministry of Agriculture and Forestry. From there it is broken down by districts that have departments of agriculture. The departments are subordinate to the district council. Then the plan control figures are further broken down by counties that also have departments of agriculture. These departments are subordinate to the county councils.

The plan then goes down to the enterprise level. The purpose of this dissemination is to provide information that can be used as a basis for plan formulation by all production units. After the control figures have been made available to the various economic units and the lower echelons of government, there is a plan counterdesign that starts with the formulation of plans by industrial and trade enterprises, state farms, and other local economic units. These plans, which can be considered as target plans, cover all phases of their operations; they then travel upward to their eventual integration into the national plan. At each administrative level the plans cumulate into a larger whole. Also at each level the plans must be defended.

The process of reconciliation is the next step in the planning cycle. Once the plans have cleared the national ministries, they are merged into the draft plan in which the directives and policy objectives of the Council of Ministers is adjusted to the aggregation of plans from below. It is at this level that the various monetary plans are developed as a financial counterpart to the main, or physical output, plan. Included among the monetary plans would be the plans of the banking system. When the national economic plan is prepared, it is sent to the Council of Ministers and the Central Committee of the SED for approval. Once approved the plan in essence becomes law, and it passes down the administrative ladder until it reaches the enterprises. The plan specifies targets or goals to be obtained by each enterprise over the five-year period. It is to be emphasized that the plan is really a perspective or target plan rather than an operational plan. Its outline is presented in Chart 8.1.

It is necessary to emphasize the point that the five-year plan is more than a physical output plan. Included in the plan is a financial balance or plan that includes the revenues and expenditures of the state budget and the monetary flows of the banking system that show sources and uses of funds.[23] Also included in the five-year plan is a consumption model. The total computations for the plan involve a system of plan calculations in which the above-mentioned elements are incorporated into a mathematical model. Besides the model calculations, there are a number of expert assessments that are a part of the plan. These two parts are also called algorithmic and nonalgorithmic elements of the plan.[24]

One example of the various elements involved in planning pertains to the use of an industrial price model, which has been introduced for the first time in the 1971-75 plan.[25] A forecast of industrial prices has been made for the planning period. The purpose of the price forecast is to coordinate material production and financial planning procedures. An industrial price regulation system has been established within the range of the forecast. This system is designed to establish cost-price parameters for all enterprises in the GDR. Included is an average rate of profitability with upper and lower tolerance limits for all production groups in the GDR.[26] To accomplish pricing policies, central state organs, production groups, and individual enterprises are supposed to submit cost-price plans, which are integrated into the 1971-75 plan. These plans must conform to the cost-price parameters of the industrial price regulation system.

The state budget is also tied into the five-year plan. As the consolidated budget of all levels of government, it is the chief operational financial plan. Through it, the financial resources of the government, primarily the turnover tax and the profit tax, are collected and redistributed. A budget standard is based on the plan. This standard establishes the budget funds that are available to district, county, and local administrative units as their share of total state revenues for carrying out their planned tasks. The assemblies and councils of the districts, counties, and localities establish budget goals within the framework of the state budget standard. They base their own annual budgets on projected state budget expenditures and revenues. The state budget standard is utilized as a control parameter in such a way that financial resources are utilized in a concentrated manner so that a high degree of efficiency is achieved.

The state budget standard is based on the following plan indices:[27]

1. Basic budget figures for investment and maintenance.
2. Basic budget figures for goals in education and culture, public health and welfare, and physical fitness and sports.
3. Basic budget figures for local supplies, roads, and housing.
4. Basic figures for the development of local tax collection.
5. State standards for net profit and turnover tax payments and the production and trade taxes of local administrative units.

Chart 8.2 presents all of the components of the 1971-75 plan. Included are the price and consumption models that have been introduced for the first time.

The Annual Operating Plan

The annual plan is more directive than the five-year plan in that all enterprises have to prepare an operating plan that is supposed, among other things, to include the volume of output to be produced and sold and the assortment and quality of output to be produced and sold. The annual plan is supposed to be developed within the framework

CHART 8.1

Model for a Perspective Plan with Special Consideration
of the Planning of Structurally-Determined
Economic Objectives and Object-Planning, East Germany

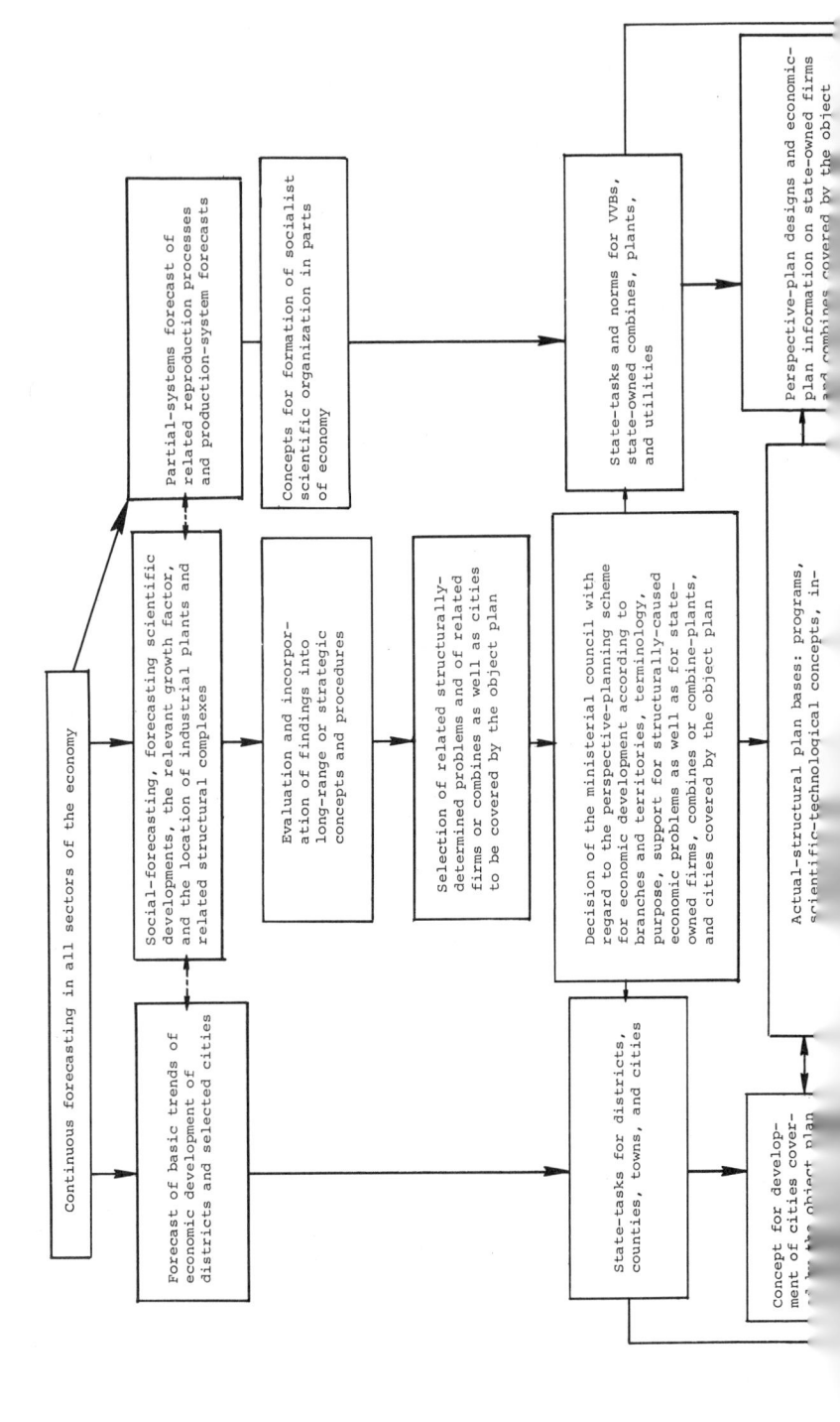

```
                        ┌─────────────────────────────────────────┐
                        │ Continuous forecasting in all sectors of the economy │
                        └─────────────────────────────────────────┘
                           │                           │
                           ▼                           ▼
         ┌──────────────────────────┐   ┌──────────────────────────────┐
         │ Forecast of basic trends │   │ Social-forecasting, forecasting scientific │
         │ of economic development  │   │ developments, the relevant growth factor,  │
         │ of districts and         │   │ and the location of industrial plants and  │
         │ selected cities          │   │ related structural complexes               │
         └──────────────────────────┘   └──────────────────────────────┘
                    │                              │           │
                    │                              ▼           │
                    │            ┌──────────────────────────────┐    ┌──────────────────────────────┐
                    │            │ Evaluation and incorpor-     │    │ Partial-systems forecast of  │
                    │            │ ation of findings into       │    │ related reproduction processes│
                    │            │ long-range or strategic      │    │ and production-system forecasts│
                    │            │ concepts and procedures      │    └──────────────────────────────┘
                    │            └──────────────────────────────┘                 │
                    │                           │                                 ▼
                    │                           ▼                    ┌──────────────────────────────┐
                    │            ┌──────────────────────────────┐    │ Concepts for formation of    │
                    │            │ Selection of related structurally-│ │ socialist scientific         │
                    │            │ determined problems and of related│ │ organization in parts        │
                    │            │ firms or combines as well as cities│ │ of economy                   │
                    │            │ to be covered by the object plan   │ └──────────────────────────────┘
                    │            └──────────────────────────────┘                 │
                    ▼                           │                                 │
         ┌──────────────────────────┐           ▼                                 │
         │ State-tasks for districts,│          │                                 │
         │ counties, towns, and cities│         │                                 │
         └──────────────────────────┘           │                                 │
                    │                           ▼                                 ▼
                    │            ┌──────────────────────────────────────────────────┐
                    │            │ Decision of the ministerial council with regard  │
                    │            │ to the perspective-planning scheme for economic  │
                    │            │ development according to branches and territories,│
                    │            │ terminology, purpose, support for structurally-  │
                    │            │ caused economic problems as well as for state-   │
                    │            │ owned firms, combines or combine-plants, and     │
                    │            │ cities covered by the object plan                │
                    │            └──────────────────────────────────────────────────┘
                    ▼                                    │
         ┌──────────────────────────┐                    ▼
         │ Concept for develop-     │     ┌──────────────────────────────┐
         │ ment of cities cover-    │     │ State-tasks and norms for VVBs,│
         │ ... object plan          │     │ state-owned combines, plants,  │
         └──────────────────────────┘     │ and utilities                  │
                    ▲                     └──────────────────────────────┘
                    │                                    │
                    ▼                                    ▼
         ┌──────────────────────────────────────────────────┐
         │ Actual-structural plan bases: programs,          │
         │ scientific-technological concepts, in-           │
         └──────────────────────────────────────────────────┘
                                                         │
                                                         ▼
                                    ┌──────────────────────────────┐
                                    │ Perspective-plan designs and  │
                                    │ economic-plan information on  │
                                    │ state-owned firms and combines│
                                    │ covered by the object ...     │
                                    └──────────────────────────────┘
```

[Flow chart, rotated 90°, showing the planning process of the GDR economy. Boxes and arrows represent the following elements:]

- the object plan
- Plan-drafts of districts, counties, cities, and towns, including proposals for multi-annual state plan norms economic plan information
- Complex plan drafts of the VVB, state-owned combines, firms, utilities. Economic plan information including funds
- Economic classification and budgeting of proposals for long-range state plans as well as for state-planning proposals of the object plan and preparation of the perspective plan of the economy through the SPK
- Resolution of Cabinet Council on perspective plan for development of economy of GDR
- State plans for VVBs, state-owned combines, firms, and utilities
- State plans for state-owned firms and combines included in the object plan
- Long-range state plans for structurally-determined economic tasks of ultimate producers, suppliers, local agencies, etc.
- State Plan norms for districts, counties, cities, and towns
- Long-range state plans for cities covered in the object plan
- Complex perspective and annual plans for districts, counties, cities, and towns
- Complex perspective and annual plans of VVBs, state-owned combines, firms, and utilities
- Permanent control and accounts, especially for realization of main tasks of economic structural policy

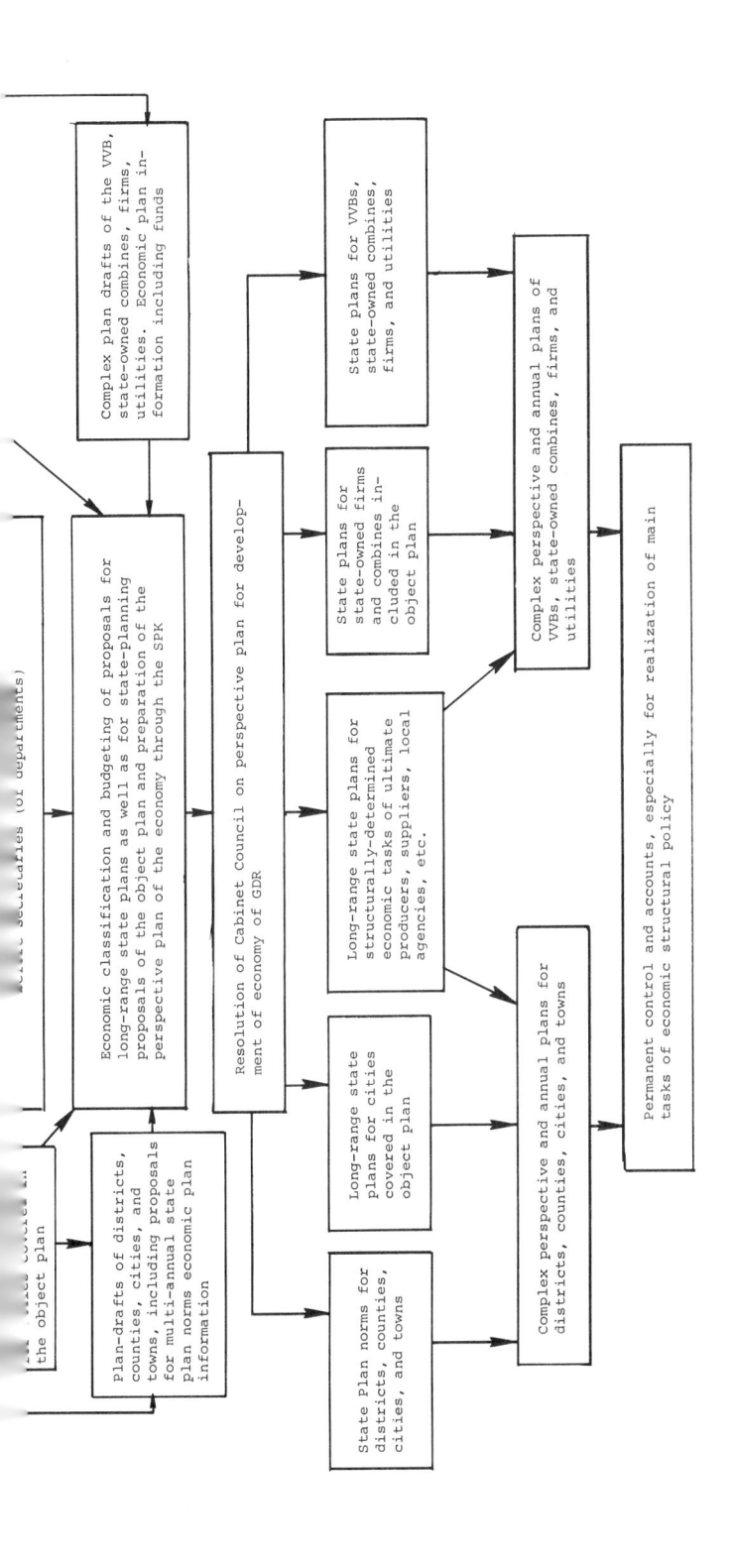

Source: Arbeitsgruppe für die Gestaltung des Ökonomisches Systems des Sozialismus, Zur Gestaltung des Ökonomisches Systems des Sozialismus in der DDR in den Jahren 1971-1975 (East Berlin: Dietz Verlag, 1970), pp. 147-65.

CHART 8.2
Components of East German Plan, 1971-75

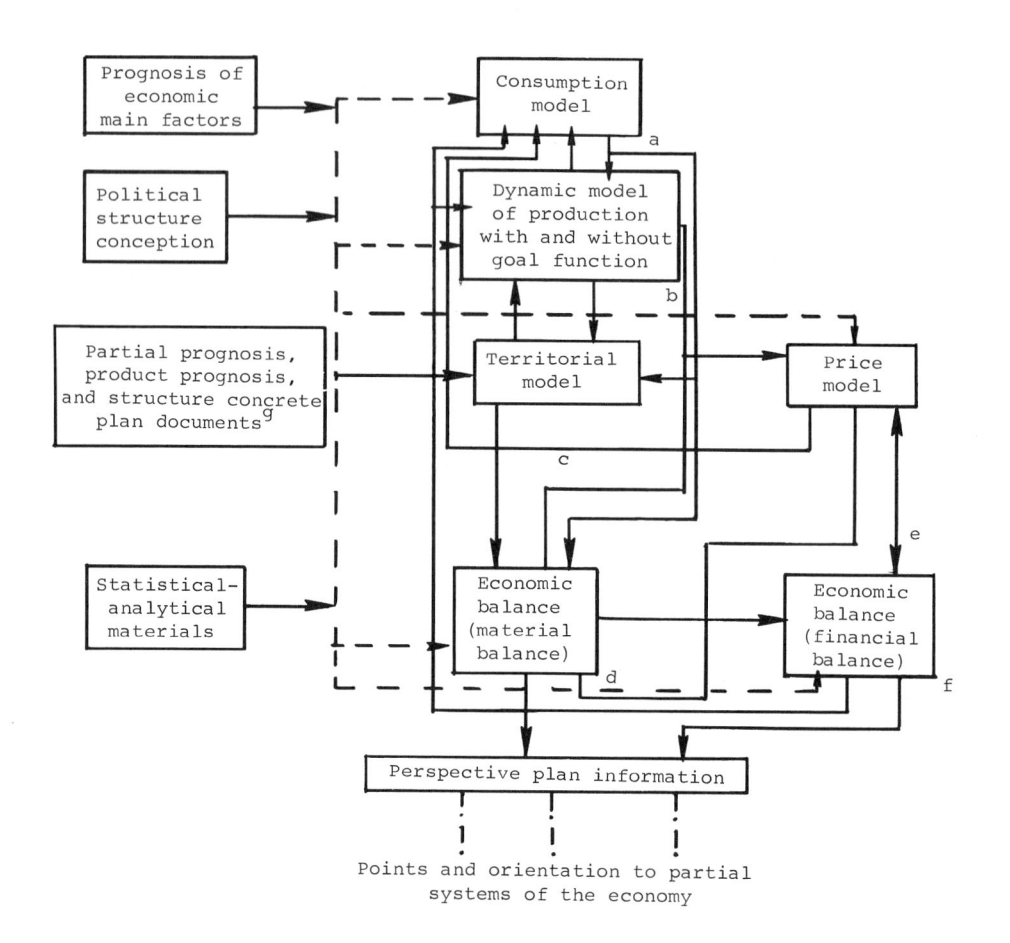

```
┌─────────────┐
│ Prognosis of│         ┌──────────────┐
│  economic   │- - - - →│ Consumption  │
│ main factors│    ┌ - →│    model     │
└─────────────┘    │    └──────────────┘
                   │           ↕   a
┌─────────────┐    │    ┌──────────────┐
│  Political  │    │    │Dynamic model │
│  structure  │────┼───→│ of production│
│  conception │    │    │with and without
└─────────────┘    │    │ goal function│
                   │    └──────────────┘
                   │           ↕   b
┌───────────────┐  │    ┌──────────┐       ┌──────────┐
│Partial prognosis,│───→│Territorial│ ←───→ │  Price   │
│product prognosis,│    │   model   │       │  model   │
│and structure concrete │           │       │          │
│ plan documents ᵍ│     └──────────┘       └──────────┘
└───────────────┘            ↓  c              ↕   e
                                               
┌─────────────┐       ┌──────────┐       ┌──────────┐
│Statistical- │       │ Economic │       │ Economic │
│ analytical  │──────→│ balance  │──────→│ balance  │
│  materials  │       │(material │       │(financial│
└─────────────┘       │ balance) │       │ balance) │
                      └──────────┘  d    └──────────┘  f
                           ↓                 ↓
                  ┌────────────────────────────┐
                  │Perspective plan information│
                  └────────────────────────────┘
                     ↓       ↓       ↓
             Points and orientation to partial
                   systems of the economy
```

    --- outside information, input
    ——— inside information, input and output
    -·- outside information, output

ᵃStructure of consumption.
ᵇAllowances for material consumption and changes in industry.
ᶜStructure of the net products, work force, basic funds, investments in territorial structures.
ᵈMaterial structure of the reproduction processes.
ᵉEffective prices per production group.
ᶠFinance relationship in the reproduction process.
ᵍFor example, scientific-technical conceptions.

Source: Ökonomisches Forschungsinstituts der Staatlichen Plankommission, Planung des Volkswirtschaft in der DDR (East Berlin: Verlag die Wirtschaftschaft, 1970), p. 154.

THE EAST GERMAN SYSTEM

of the five-year plan. In the annual economic plan the state prescribes the policies all production units are to follow. Enterprise managers, however, are permitted operation flexibility within the targets and resource limits set by the plan. The annual plan also functions on a quarterly and monthly basis.

To prepare the annual economic plan the State Planning Commission submits to the Council of Ministers a coordinated proposal for the assignment of government tasks.[28] On the basis of this ministries and other agencies are given goals and objectives, which they pass on to all production units. Each unit is supposed to work out its annual plan on the basis of government plan indexes, including the indexes of the long-range plan. The annual plan is then sent to an agency that is superordinate to the production unit. The plan is a draft that must be defended and justified by an enterprise before the agency. All plans go up to the central level to be justified by various government administrative agencies before the Council of Ministers. Then the State Planning Commission works out a consolidated draft of the annual economic plan. The draft, together with the state budget that is prepared by the Ministry of Finance, is submitted to the Volkskammer for debate. Approval is a foregone conclusion.

The directors of all government agencies, as well as the managers of state enterprises, combines, and other production units, are responsible for the execution of the annual plan. The ministries see that resources are utilized by production units on the basis of planning objectives. The State Central Statistical Administration is responsible for the accounting of the plan. Together with the State Planning Commission, it must make sure that the planning indexes in the reports of the production units agree with those in the planning document in terms of content and value expressed. The state enterprises, combines, and other production units have to provide an accounting of plan indexes.

Each East German enterprise has to prepare an annual operating plan. The keystone of the operating plan is the production plan, which is supposed to provide aggregate planned output. This output is divided into various production categories. Also included as a part of the operating plan is a statement of manpower needs required to carry out the production plan and a statement of material and technical supply needs. A financial plan breaks the operating plan down into monetary terms. It consists of a division of revenues and expenses and also presents a breakdown of the sources and uses of funds for the planned year. Included is a profit target that is determined by deducting all planned operating expenses from planned sales revenue.

The National Economic Plan, 1971-75

The main objective of the five-year plan is a further increase in the material and cultural living standards of the East German people, based on improvements in worker productivity and continued development of socialist production. The composition of the plan is based on the following indexes: [29]

1. National income is supposed to increase to 126 to 128 percent over the base period of 100 percent in 1970. In monetary terms, national income is to reach 136 to 138 billion Ostmarks.

2. Industrial production is to increase to 134 to 136 percent over the base period.

3. Total consumption, private and social, is supposed to increase to 121 to 123 percent over the 1970 base period. Real incomes are to increase to 121 to 123 percent over the base.

4. Construction is to increase to 127 to 129 percent over the base period.

5. The wage funds for the state-owned enterprises are supposed to increase by 21 to 23 percent, or from 65 billion Ostmarks in 1970 to around 80 billion Ostmarks in 1975. The net income of the population is to increase at around 4 percent a year. For certain professions and working groups special wage increases will be granted.

6. The construction of 500,000 apartment houses will be carried out in major industrial centers.

7. Social welfare expenditures, including expenditures for social security and education, are to increase by 30 to 35 percent over the period of the plan.

8. Exports are to be increased in order to compensate for the increased imports of basic materials and resources that are necessary for the growth of the economy.

Industry

The main objectives of industry during the plan period are to improve the technical base of the economy and to raise the technical level of production, especially through the use of improved research and production methods. Shifts are to be made in the use of energy for industrial production, with more reliance to be placed on the use of electricity; an increase of 38 percent in the mining of brown coal is anticipated. New power plants with increased energy-generating capacity are to be built. The geological industry is supposed to develop and open natural gas reserves and increase output by 32 percent during the plan period.[30]

The chemical industry is supposed to increase total output by 47 to 49 percent over 1970, and worker productivity is to increase 40 percent. The production capacity of tires for automobiles and trucks is to increase from 49 to 50 percent during the plan. The production of the pharmaceutical industry, with priority given to medical supplies, is to increase 70 percent. The production of sheet metal is to increase by 28 to 32 percent. Motor-vehicle production is scheduled to increase by 40 percent over the period of the plan. Priority is assigned to the production of electrical products, which are set to increase by 55 to 60 percent. Industrial production in the field of light industry is to increase 32 percent, while worker productivity in the same industry is to increase by 35 percent. The glass and ceramic industry has to increase its output by 45 to 48 percent. In the handicraft field, cooperatives and private enterprises have to increase their output by 26 to 28 percent.

Agriculture and Other Areas

In agriculture the output of slaughter animals is set to increase from 1,651 kilo tons in 1970 to 1,850-1,900 kilo tons in 1975; output of milk is set to increase from 6,492 kilo tons to 7,250-7,350 kilo tons; and the output of eggs is to increase from 3,505 million dozens to 3,650 million dozens. The production of food is to increase 18 percent over the plan period, while worker productivity is to gain by 20 percent. In transportation, 650 to 700 kilometers of railroad lines are to be completed, while passenger traffic is to increase by 10 to 15 percent. The postal and telephone services are projected to increase their services by 25 to 30 percent, while worker productivity is to increase by 23 to 27 percent. In forestry the production of timber is to increase by 12 percent during the planning period.[31]

Housing and Construction

In the directives for the 1971-75 plan the regime also plans the construction and remodeling of 500,000 housing units in another attempt to solve the housing shortage. During the previous five years only 365,000 housing units were completed, representing 91 percent fulfillment of the plan. Overall housing construction is to increase by 60 to 62 percent over the 1970 base period. In the field of construction, production is to increase by 27 to 29 percent, and the output of construction materials is to increase by 36 to 37 percent. The production of light metals used in the construction industry is to increase by 12 percent.[32]

Foreign Trade

Foreign trade is an integral part of the plan.[33] During the 1971-75 planning period about 75 percent of East German foreign trade is to be with other COMECON members. It is clear from the directive of the plan that one of the main aims of the next five years is the further integration of the GDR into COMECON, or, more accurately, its deeper economic involvement with the Soviet Union. The foreign trade and scientific-technical relations of the GDR with developing countries is also to increase. Foreign trade with capitalist countries will increase provided that it is in the interest of the GDR. The overall plan figures on foreign trade are very scanty and do not include any specific data on trade with Western countries.

Education and Social Welfare

During the planning period net income for the working population is to increase at an average of 4 percent a year.[34] The production of consumer goods is to increase by 30 percent; however, washing machine production is to increase by 65 to 70 percent, television production by 25 to 30 percent, and laundry and dry cleaning services by 28 to 31 percent. In education 16,000 to 17,000 classrooms are to be built. During the plan period, 900,000 students are to be trained for trades in the labor market, while 225,000 are scheduled to graduate from the universities and professional schools. In the overall student population, 90 percent are to finish the eighth grade, which is the equivalent of an elementary school education, and continue on into the polytechnical high schools. At the university level, 25,000 to 30,000 dormitory rooms and dining facilities to accomodate an additional 10,000 to 13,000 students are to be constructed.

District Development

The planning process extends down to the smallest administrative and economic units.[35] Although it is not necessary for the purpose of this book to carry the current five-year plan this far, its comprehensiveness can be shown in connection with the districts. For example, in East Berlin 30,000 new apartments are scheduled to be built. In the district of Cottbus, primary attention in terms of production is to be given to the chemical and light industries. Building construction is to increase by 24 percent. In the district of Dresden, the electronics and metallurgical industries have output priorities. Housing construction is supposed to increase by 27 percent. In the Gera district, priority in terms of performance is given to the electronics and chemical industries. Between 19,000 and 20,000 apartments

THE EAST GERMAN SYSTEM 217

are to be built. In the Halle district the objective is to increase the production of the potash, engine-building, and construction-materials industries. Some 40,000 apartments are scheduled to be built. In the Magdeburg district, total construction is to increase from 29 to 31 percent. Priority is to be given to the construction of chemical plants. Agriculture and food production in the Neubrandenberg district is supposed to increase from 30 to 32 percent. In the Rostock district priority is given to the shipbuilding industry.

SUMMARY

The territorial administration of the GDR is divided into districts, counties, and localities. For all practical purposes, however, real administrative power is centralized in the hands of the Council of Ministers of the GDR, for economic and political policies emanate from this body. As is true of the Soviet Union and other socialist states, one political party, the Socialist Unity Party of Germany (SED), is dominant, and its organizational structure parallels that of the government. Within the SED the Politburo and the Secretariat are the most important political organs. They are responsible for giving the party directions. There are minor political parties in the GDR that are tolerated and subsidized by the SED. They are firmly committed to SED policy and do little more than attract other voters to the support of the SED.

The economy of East Germany is planned and administered by the state. Most of industry and agriculture is state-owned. There is also a semistate sector in which the state participates as a partner with private enterprise, and a private sector, which accounts for around 5 percent of the total output of the economy. Industry accounts for around two-thirds of net national product, with chemical, electronic, and heavy industries being the most important contributors. Agriculture has declined in importance as a contributor. Foreign trade is important to the East German economy. The proportion of trade conducted with COMECON countries is quite high. Although the East German regime is interested in expanding its trade with the West, it is reluctant to do so at the expense of that with the COMECON countries.

Resource allocation in the GDR is done through economic planning. The most important plan is the perspective, or five-year, plan, which sets directives and goals. There is an annual plan, which is an output plan for all production units. Each enterprise has to prepare its production plan. Financial planning, which includes the money supply of the banking system and the state budget, is integrated with the physical output plans. In economic planning there is a new reliance on decentralized decision-making, business-type accounting procedures, interest-bearing loans, and profit incentives. These form a frame of reference in subsequent chapters. Nevertheless, it can be said that ultimate control over the economy is in the hands of the SED Council of Ministers.

CHAPTER

9

ORGANIZATION OF INDUSTRY, AGRICULTURE, AND TRADE IN EAST GERMANY

INTRODUCTION

In a socialist economy most productive and distributive enterprises are under the direct control of the state. There is some place for small-scale enterprises, particularly in Yugoslavia, but for the most part their operation is narrowly circumscribed. Some organizations are also left to local governments to operate on the grounds that their operation is largely of local importance. Such enterprises as public utilities, hospitals, theaters, and housing construction would fall into this category. Nevertheless, though the ownership and operation of these enterprises is entrusted to local governmental units, usually some agency of the central government has the ultimate responsibility for coordinating their operations within the general framework of the economic plans for the whole country.

The state exercises a virtual monopolistic control over all economic resources. It owns and operates large-scale industries, mines, power plants, railways, shipping, and various means of communication. It engages in farming on its own account through the institution of state farms, and it largely controls agriculture through the institution of collective farming. It has an exclusive monopoly of banking and foreign trade, and it controls the domestic channels of distribution in its role as manufacturer, farmer, merchant, shipper, and banker. In the field of labor relations, it is the sole employer of note and as such dominates bargaining between itself and the employees. Although trade unions are allowed to exist, their function is purely subsidiary to the interest of the state, and strikes are illegal.

The organizational structure of industry is complex because an extensive bureaucratic apparatus is necessary to plan and administer production and distribution policies. In the socialist countries there has been, however, a continual reorganization of the economic-administrative structure in an effort to promote greater operating efficiency. Control remains centralized, however, with the administrative and policy-making framework of industrial organization resembling a pyramid. At the apex is the central government and party hierarchy. There is an interlocking relationship between government and party, with party officials controlling the administrative structure of each organization. This merging of authority at the top continues with parallel lines of party and government organizations extending downward through the whole economic system.

The organization of agriculture has presented a problem in the socialist countries because the farmers have been hostile to efforts to collectivize and regiment them. For ideological and economic reasons it is regarded as imperative that agriculture be collectivized in some form. From an ideological standpoint the private ownership of land is supposed to foster acquisitiveness, which is supposed to be contrary to the instincts of a truly socialist society. Also, in the socialist countries the social and economic dichotomy between the large landowners and the rural masses has been sharp throughout history. For political reasons it was desirable for socialist regimes to expropriate large landholdings. But it is also necessary to point out that most land that was not in the hands of large landowners was farmed inefficiently. The need to industrialize required the use of farm labor in the newly developed industries. This was possible only if farms became larger so that they could be mechanized and operated by less, though specialized and trained, labor.

In the socialist countries agriculture is controlled by the state through national economic planning. The supply and price of inputs, the share of output marketed, the prices paid for agricultural products, and farm income and expenditures are regulated by the plan. The state exercises a monopolistic control over agricultural resources. It engages in farming on its own account through the institution of state farms. Through control of the state budget and the banking system it can control the allocation of monetary resources to agriculture. Overall procurement goals are established for agricultural products, and prices payable to farms are relatively low and differentiated according to natural conditions so that practically all differentiated rent is absorbed by the state budget. Retail prices of food are maintained by the state at fairly low levels to ensure a low cost of living for industrial workers. Similarly, industry benefits from cheap industrial raw materials such as cotton.

Agriculture has played a secondary role to the development of industry in the socialist countries. There are several reasons for this fact. First, faced with the urgent need for industrialization, agriculture becomes an obvious source of accumulation in these countries. Second, the rural masses have always been used to low incomes and are in a position to be exploited. Support on the part of pliable urban workers is gained through food subsidies, while the more individualistic farmers can be coerced to adhere to the interests of the state.

THE NEW ECONOMIC SYSTEM

The New Economic System (Neues Ökonomisches System) can be viewed as a series of reform measures developed in 1963. During most of the period leading up to 1963, economic policies were largely directed toward Soviet desires. Forced incorporation into the Eastern bloc had been accomplished. Production goals were based primarily on the construction and development of domestic basic industries and expansion of the production of capital goods, to the detriment of consumer goods. The substance of the first two five-year plans (1951-55 and 1956-60) was in accordance with these goals: predominant encouragement of capital goods accompanied by a clear neglect of private consumption. In the light of existing foreign-exchange deficits agriculture was expected to produce more of the high-quality products necessary for domestic consumption.

The consequences of these economic policies soon revealed themselves. The living standards of the East German population fell farther behind those of West Germany. The number of refugees, which included many skilled workers, increased from year to year. This continuous loss of manpower, with its consequent effect on the completion of production goals, was a major factor in formulating the goals of a seven-year plan, which began in 1958. The purpose of the plan was to bring the level of consumer goods up to the West German level. The planners hoped to reach this goal as early as 1961. The growth rate for the whole economy, however, dropped from 11 percent in 1959 to 6 percent in 1960 and 4 percent in 1961.[1] Difficulties with supplies—partly as a result of a bad harvest—were felt again and, together with the collectivization measures of 1960-61, led to a renewed surge in the outflow of refugees, which was finally turned off by the confinement measurements of August 1961.

This period of weakness caused by erroneous assumptions in the plan had simultaneously worsened conditions for future growth. Plant investments, which were already low in comparison to West Germany, stagnated; production and installations of new capacities were delayed; and supply deficiencies in raw materials and intermediate products lowered the use of those facilities that did exist. It became apparent to the East German authorities that economic planning so far had failed, and that planning methods and economic organization clearly no longer met the needs of a progressive industrial economy. The seven-year plan was dropped in 1961, and short-term annual planning, with newly formulated growth goals, was adopted.

Formal discussion of economic reforms began at the meeting of the Sixth Party Congress of the SED in January 1963. In the summer of 1963 the Guidelines on the New System of Economic Planning and Management were adopted. The focal points of the New Economic System were as follows:[2]

1. To change the structure of the management system and economic administration and improve planning methods;
2. To direct enterprise interests into the direction desired for the whole economy through the use of material interests in the form of a self-enclosed system of economic levers; and
3. To create necessary preconditions for more efficient monetary control.

The first effects of the reforms were revealed in the field of economic administration. The Associations of State-Owned Enterprises (Vereinigungen Volkseigener Betriebe, or VVBs) became independent accounting economic units whose accounts reflected the final balances of the state enterprises (Volkseigene Betriebe, or VEBs), so that they became the connecting link between the individual enterprise and the state budget. Since then they have become legally and economically independent and have their own funds available, which they balance themselves and which stem primarily from remittances from the VEBs. The principle of economic accounting leadership is supposed to induce the VVBs to plan, coordinate, manage, and control the production of all the enterprises in the industrial branch covered by them and to encourage interenterprise cooperation. In this way, their construction and management activities are similar to holding companies.

The development of a system of self-enclosed economic levers was of paramount importance within the framework of the New Economic System. Its effectiveness, however, was dependent on the reform of the price system. This system was still largely based on the prices of 1945 and was distorted, because state price formation offices set very low prices in order to hold down product costs. Raw materials were also subsidized. The result was that their prices, which were of secondary importance in a planned economy ruled by quantity thinking, generally prevented a substitution of other materials that would be favorable in terms of cost. Thus, profits achieved by the enterprises could not be the result of an optimal use of the factors of production.

In order to be able to determine cost-based prices that would approximately correspond to the shortages in the East German planned economy and in order to make the profitability of the enterprises visible for the first time, depreciations, which were much too low, also had to be recalculated by means of a revaluation of industry's permanent assets. In January 1964 a revaluation ordinance was decreed. The goal of revaluation was not only to achieve optimal use of undervalued assets; in addition, central planning authorities were to obtain a better idea of the distribution of fixed assets, for until the reforms it had not been possible to compare the structure of assets and capital formation. The result was false investment decisions and a rapid return marginal capital productivity. The revaluation increased gross fixed assets of GDR industry by 52 percent, to 105 billion Ostmarks.

A three-stage price reform was introduced in industry to encourage more rational assessment of costs and revenues and more economies in the use of scarce and imported raw materials that had been priced too low. The first stage of the industrial price reform started in April 1964. The objective was to raise prices in order to reduce budget subsidies to certain industries. Prices were raised, on the average, 70 percent for such products as coal, potash, ore, salt, nonferrous metals, pig iron, and rolling mill products.[3] The second stage began January 1, 1965. Again, the objective was to make enterprises more self-sufficient and less reliant on budget subsidies. Price increases averaging 40 percent were put into effect on such products as lumber, cut timber, pulp and paper, leather, hides, and chemical products.[4] About 3,000 enterprises were directly affected by the reform. The third stage began January 1, 1967. Price raises following the first and second stages averaging 4 percent were put into effect on building machinery, finished products of the chemical industry, products of the food industry, and other consumer goods.[5] Prices were still fixed and often reflected government priorities rather than real costs.

To decrease the use of direct government grants from the state budget to cover both investments and losses was a basic objective of the price reform. The goal of the third stage of the price reform was to improve the quality of output, eliminate the production of nonstandardized products, and to increase more economical use of resources. Before the price reform, subsidies to industry were approximately 13.5 billion Ostmarks yearly. These subsidies were particularly concentrated in the solid fuel, lumber, paper, building material, and metallurgical industries. For example, 50 percent of the operating costs of the lumber industry were subsidized by grants from the state budget.[6] The amount was 45 percent for the solid fuel industry and 55 percent for the metallurgical industry.[7] After the price reform, the amount of subsidies was reduced to 7.5 billion Ostmarks. These subsidies primarily take the form of support for the consumer goods and transportation industries and for housing construction.

Additional measures to promote efficiency were adopted to support the price reform. A system of management incentives was introduced in industry, including financial rewards for lowering costs and increasing profits and fines for subpar performance. In construction differentiated interest rates were used to shift priority from new starts to the completion of old projects and the modernization of existing installations. Foreign and domestic trade activities as well as industry were subject to new rigid contracts that fixed delivery deadlines and set higher standards of quality, styling, and customer service. Finally, procurement prices for agricultural products were increased in an attempt to induce greater output and better land use.

In 1969, two years after the third stage of the price reforms, new price policies were adopted.[8] First, price planning was introduced as a part of the total planning system; second, there was an attempt to develop more effective methods of price determination. The price reform had used cost-determined prices based on the value of labor as a variant of real value. This resulted in an average price that was too high for the labor intensive industries and too low for the capital intensive industries. Mechanization or automation was not stimulated; instead, labor-intensive production became more profitable and hindered technical progress. This called for a look at the price system, and it was realized that labor alone was not the sole source of value. Capital would also have to enter into the calculation, and the two together would have to determine prices.

The price reform also extended over into the field of agriculture. In October 1963 a new agricultural price system was developed.[9] Starting with the harvest of 1964 a uniform price system was used for grain products. Uniform prices for poultry and eggs based on wholesale delivery were also established in the same year. Prices of cattle and hogs were raised in 1965, and in 1966 uniform production prices for wool and other related products were introduced. In 1967 production prices for meat, poultry, and eggs were based on delivery from the yard. This change released agricultural enterprises from having to absorb the cost of transportation. Compulsory deliveries to state wholesaling organizations were also discontinued during the same year. In general, it can be said that with respect to agriculture the main thrust of the reform was to raise procurement prices for agricultural products in an attempt to induce greater output and better land use.

One measure that followed the price reform was an attempt to make planning more flexible by adopting a smaller number of enterprise planning coefficients. The New Economic System provided for four main plan indicators: the value of sales or, in some cases, output; the total wage bill; payments into the state budget; and investments. This was an improvement over the old system, which bound enterprises to detailed plans for virtually all phases of operation. The new indicators effectively maintained central control but left enterprise managers with more authority in determining the details of enterprise operations.

Another important aspect of the overall reforms was the acceptance of profit as the main criterion of enterprise performance. Prior to the reforms profit was used as an accounting device to ensure that enterprises covered costs out of their own resources and handed any surplus over to the state budget. To promote enterprise performance a system of incentives were tied to certain criteria. Incentives were based primarily on the volume of output, but efficiency of enterprise operations was affected adversely in that quantity was stressed at the expense of quality. When value of output was used as a measure of enterprise success, what usually happened was that only those articles containing the most expensive raw materials and components were produced. Incentives were based on the value of trade turnover; this criterion prompted trading enterprises to supply high-priced articles.

The New Economic System embraced the idea that the maximization of enterprise profit would ensure the quality and efficiency of production. Instead of tying incentive payments to the volume or value of output, payments are now based on profit. Given the tie between profit and performance, any increase in the profitability of an enterprise can be accomplished by producing what consumers and other enterprises want, on the one hand, and by reducing costs, on the other. Profit is now generally calculated on the basis of the output actually sold not merely produced. Moreover, improved systems of penalties are being adopted, whereby fines are deducted from profits, or receipts, for nonfulfillment of contracts, delays, poor quality, faulty specifications, and negligence.

The reforms of the New Economic System extended over into the field of banking. The objective was to give a greater role to the banking system in financing the flow of raw materials and intermediary and final products. Grants from the state budget to enterprises were downgraded, and if investments and working capital could not be financed from profits, bank loans could be obtained. Loans had to be justified to the banks on the basis of profitability. The ultimate purpose of the new arrangement was to achieve a more rational pattern of investment in productive capital and a reduction of the investment-output ratio. Financing from internally generated funds or through repayable loans—guided by the profit expectations of alternative projects—was expected to reduce the waste in real resources, which was a by-product of grant financing, and to provide a logical way for introducing the cost of capital as one of the factors of production.

The effects resulting from the price reforms were marked by numerous administrative difficulties.[10] Since consumer prices were supposed to remain unaffected by all of the price changes, the amount of subsidies were increased. The amount of the production tax had to be changed. The fact that the enterprises expected their activities to be directed according to unaccustomed economic criteria led to considerable uncertainty on the enterprise level. Their profit situation changed, which in turn affected investment financing, which also was regulated. Until then, investment decisions had been made by the central authorities and financed by subsidies from the state budget. The investment decree of September 1964 obligated the enterprises themselves to play a role in financing investments. Since profit determined the payment of enterprise surpluses to bonus funds and other income dependent upon performance, this increased delegation of responsibility to the enterprises also created one of the intended forms of economic levers.

As long as the ownership of capital and land is vested in the state in the name of the people, there are limits to the amelioration of the allocative and pricing processes. Moreover, as long as there is no market for these factors of production, any attempt to incorporate the cost elements of rent and interest rates can be made only in the form of arbitrary charges, meaning that they are not reflective of social costs. The device of a "pay-out period" may permit making better choices among potential investment projects, but the implied interest rates are not reflective of society's preference as between current and future consumption. Likewise, rent charges consonant with opportunity costs can be achieved only in a true market for land. Freedom of consumer choice is insufficiently provided for so long as the variety of spending outlets is centrally planned and the public can merely choose among what the plan prescribes in terms of quality, variety, and styles.

ORGANIZATION OF INDUSTRY

East German industry can be divided into four categories: state-owned, semistate-owned, cooperative, and private. The state-owned enterprise is dominant both in terms of the number of persons employed and the value of total output. For example, in 1969 state-owned enterprises accounted for 128.9 billion Ostmarks of industrial output, compared to 15.3 billion Ostmarks for the semistate enterprises, and 2.3 billion Ostmarks for the private enterprises.[11] The semistate enterprise can be regarded as an intermediate form of business organization in which the state is a shareholder. These are private businesses, the owners of which have been compelled to admit the state as a majority shareholder, the form of the business being turned into a limited partnership or, in rarer cases, a private partnership. In either case, the state is the dominant partner and sets the basic policy goals. As a result of the need for consumer goods and services, private enterprise is tolerated to a far greater extent than elsewhere in Eastern Europe. Between 1956 and 1965 emphasis was placed on reducing the size of the private sector. After 1965 the share of gross production contributed by private enterprise has declined slightly, from 6.5 percent to 5.8 percent.[12]

The organization of industry has to be considered as a basic part of the economic and political organization of the state. The state-owned enterprises form an integral part of the state economic organization and are indeed the foundation upon which this is built. Semistate and private enterprises are also closely associated with the state economic organization by means of a standardized system of contracts for purchases and deliveries, which they are bound to conclude. The structural principle on which both industry and the general economic system are organized is the same as that adopted in the machinery of government and in the operation of the SED, with its satellite organizations—i.e., democratic centralism. The essential features of democratic centralism are the leadership of the SED, the unqualified right of those who are at the head of the organization to issue instructions to those below, and the duty of the latter to obey.

The administrative and policy-making framework of industrial organization resembles a pyramid, with the top being the Politburo of the Central Committee of the SED and the bottom being the East German industrial enterprise. The Politburo is responsible for making major policy decisions, including those that affect industry. Then there is the Council of Ministers (Ministerrat) of the GDR, which is the most important governmental executive and administrative body in the country. It decides the basic questions and main proportions of the social and economic development of the GDR. To assist the Council of Ministers in coordinating economic activity there are a number of committees or organs whose responsibilities are to provide the information needed for decision-making. One important organ is the State Planning Commission (Staatliche Plan Kommission), which is responsible for the development of the national economic plans decided upon by the Council of Ministers. An advisory council for economic research (Beirat für Ökonomische Forschung) assists the State Planning Commission in plan preparation.

The direct links in the organization of production, however, are the national ministries and their subsidiary organizations. There are seven national ministries that are responsible for the following industrial areas: basic materials; metallurgy, ore, and potash mining; chemicals; electronics and electrotechnical industry; heavy machinery and construction; manufacturing machinery and vehicle building; and light industry. These ministries are responsible for the allocation of material and technical resources to industries in accordance with the objectives of the national economic plan. These resources are distributed according to plan through various central and regional supply organizations. Each ministry is divided into a number of administrative units that are responsible for the administration of different industrial sectors within an industry. Control over individual industries extends down to the regional and district councils.

The role of the SED in the organization and administration of industry cannot be minimized. Control over both the government and economic machinery in the GDR is in the hands of the SED. There is an interlocking relationship between government and party. The SED maintains firm control over every aspect of East German life through well-organized and disciplined organization. Members are assigned to all institutions and enterprises in East German society. In factories primary party units called cells operate to maintain discipline. There is a local unit of the SED in all enterprises that is supposed to act as the custodian of the nation's interest as opposed to the more narrowly circumscribed outlook of industrial managers. Most managers, however, are members of the SED, but despite this fact the party maintains its own independent hierarchy in each enterprise. At the head of this hierarchy is the party secretary, who shares responsibility with the enterprise manager for plan fulfillment. He is also supposed to keep the party informed of any adverse developments in the enterprise. Some ambivalence exists in defining his relationship with the manager and with the party. He can neither exercise excessive interference in the decisions of the manager, nor can he be too lax from the standpoint of control.

An organizational chart of industry in the GDR is presented in Chart 9.1. At the top is the Politburo, which is the supreme instrument of political power in the GDR. The control functions are readily apparent. There are two institutions at the intermediate level that serve as connecting links between the administrative and economic units. State-owned enterprises are grouped together under the VVBs. A VVB can be considered as a form of trust. Semistate-owned and private firms and producer cooperatives are grouped together under regional economic councils (Bezirkswirtschaftsrate). In a regional economic council, firms with similar production functions are grouped together. In addition there are other enterprises, usually utilities, that are under the control of county economic councils. Chart 9.1 reflects the reforms of the New Economic System in that all enterprises that are locally managed are subordinate to the regional economic councils, whereas all enterprises that are centrally managed are subordinate to the VVBs. The purpose of this arrangement is supposed to be better coordination of central and territorial planning.

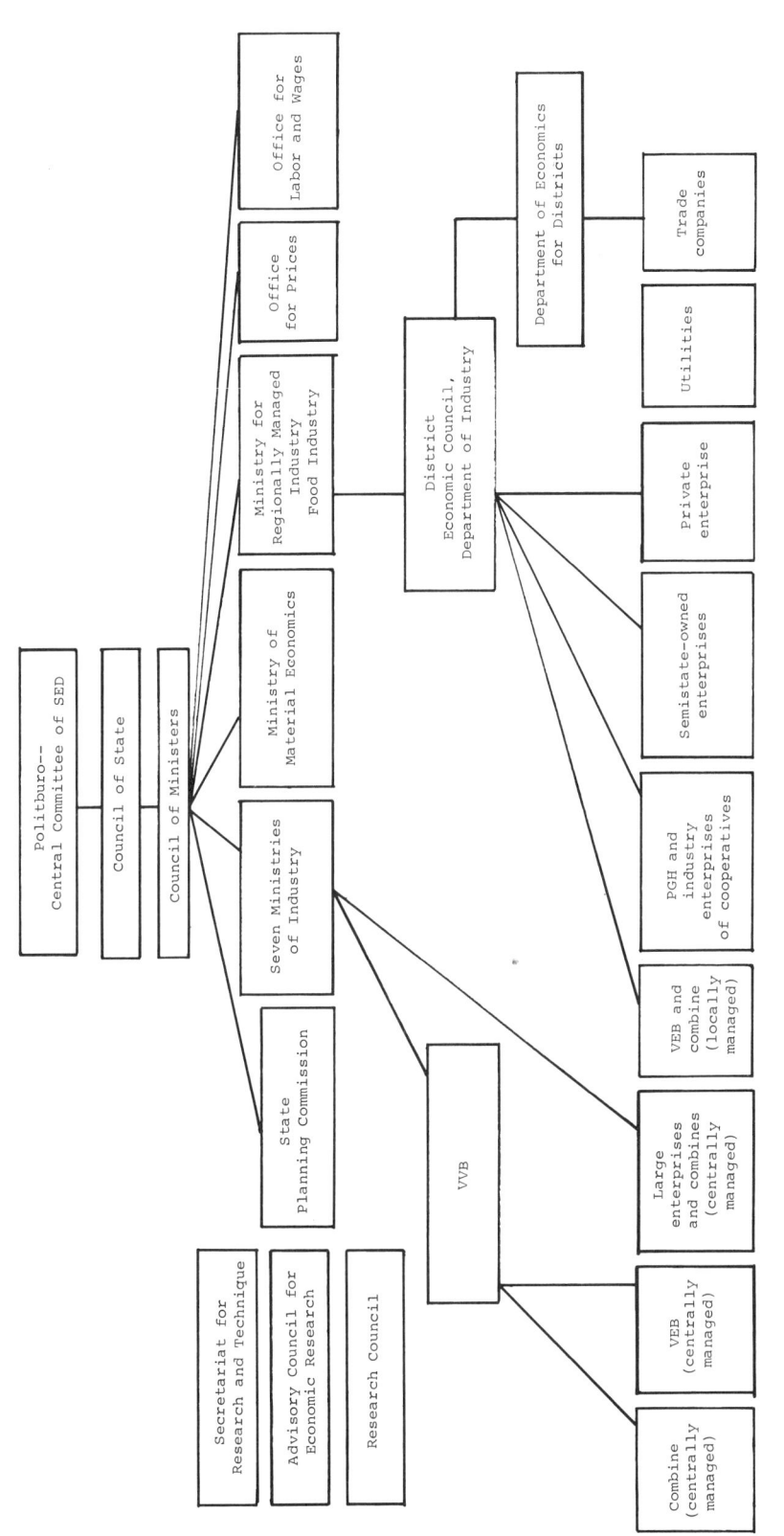

Simplified Survey of Organization of East German Industry

Source: Bundesministerium für Gesamtdeutsche Fragen, Fünfter Tätigkeitsbericht, 1965-1969 (Bonn, 1969), p. 75.

The VVB

The VVB represents the most important link between the administration of the industrial system and the basic enterprise units. VVBs were first established in 1958, when the industrial ministries were abandoned. The industrial ministries were reestablished in 1965, however, and the VVBs were subordinated to them. As a result of the reforms of the New Economic System, the role of the VVBs was changed from strictly an administrative unit to an economic leadership organ responsible for investment, production sales, and export goals. A VVB can be considered as a form of trust that has control over the operations of enterprises in a given economic field. In 1968 there were 110 VVBs covering all areas of manufacturing and distribution and having under their control not only state-owned enterprises but semistate-owned and private enterprises as well.[13] Each VVB is responsible for fulfilling that part of the economic plan over which it has jurisdiction and for facilitating the implementation of directives from the State Planning Commission and synthesizing the recommendations from the individual enterprises below.

A VVB is permitted to retain a share of its profit to finance working capital and investment. It is also allowed to use part of its own earnings to form its special funds, to finance industrywide investment and research programs, to establish central incentive and bonus funds, and to cover the deficits of its unprofitable subordinates—deficits that had been made up from the state budget before the reforms. As a scientific and economic managing organ it is supposed to have full responsibility for the production process over firms subordinate to it in its industrial field. One major unsolved problem, however, is the exact demarcation of competence between a VVB and the industrial enterprises, or VEBs. One of the reasons for this is the special situation created by the reforms. The VVB is supposed to function as an economic unit and financial control organ, with the authority to enter into contracts, and also to function as a guiding administrative unit of central economic management. In some respects it duplicates the functions of the enterprises over which it has jurisdiction. The actual rights of a VVB have not been clarified so far. An organizational chart of a VVB is presented in Chart 9.2. Some of its responsibilities can be ascertained from the framework.

As was pointed out previously, the industrial price reform did not adequately take into consideration the economics of capital goods. Price calculations for individual products were in essence based on production costs as reflected by the value of labor. Moreover, after the close of the third stage of the industrial price reform, production and sales conditions, as well as the rate of profit related to capital goods, in individual branches of industry developed differently. So

CHART 9.2

Organizational Structure of a VVB

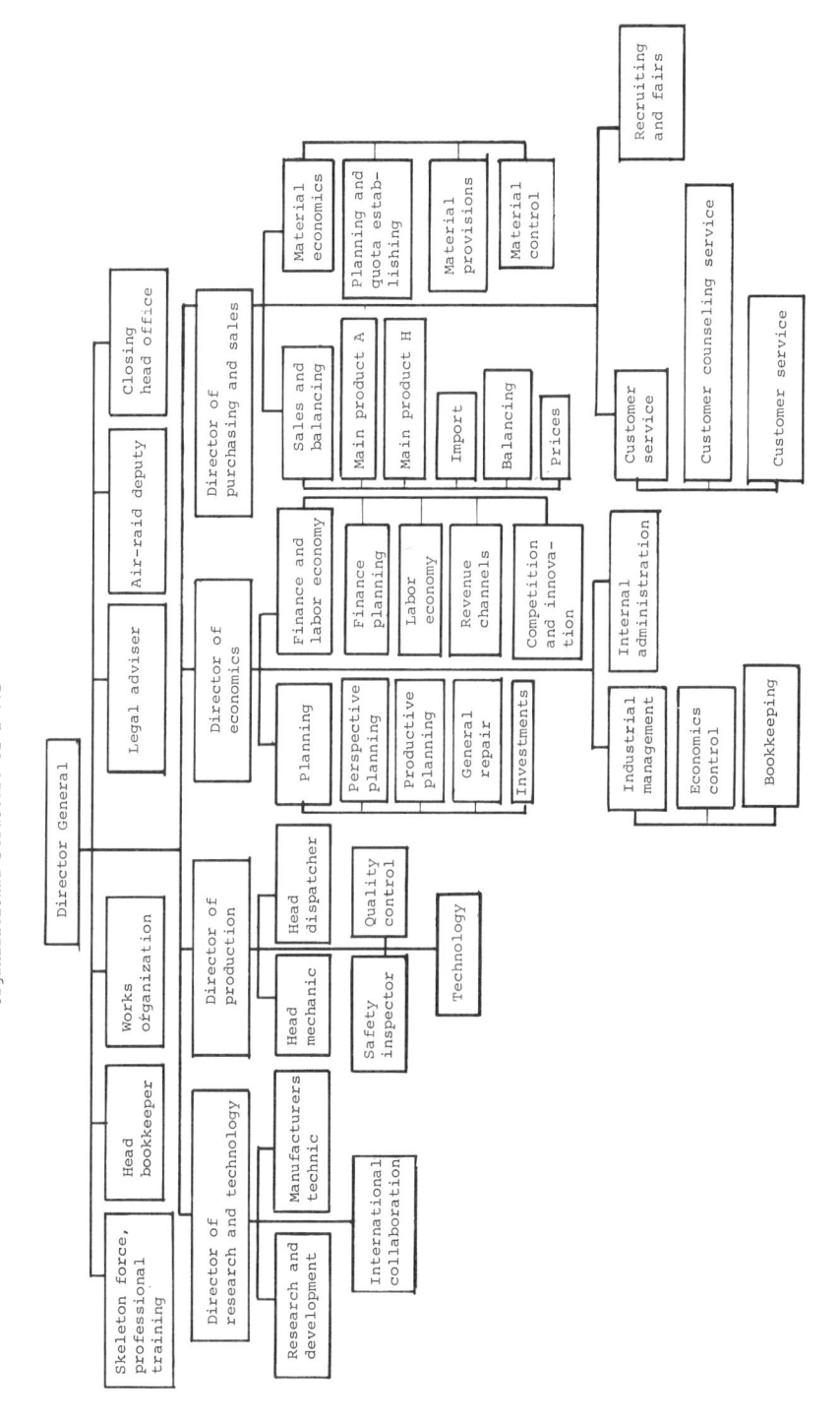

```
                                    Director General
  ┌──────────────┬──────────────┬─────────┴────────┬──────────────┬──────────────┐
Skeleton force,  Head         Works            Legal adviser  Air-raid deputy  Closing
professional     bookkeeper   organization                                     head office
training
  │
Director of                  Director of        Director of       Director of
research and                 production         economics         purchasing and sales
technology
  │                              │                  │                  │
  ├─ Manufacturers               ├─ Head            ├─ Planning        ├─ Sales and
  │  technic                     │  dispatcher      │                  │  balancing
  ├─ Research and                ├─ Head            ├─ Perspective     ├─ Main product A
  │  development                 │  mechanic       │  planning         ├─ Main product H
  ├─ International               ├─ Safety          ├─ Productive      ├─ Import
  │  collaboration               │  inspector       │  planning         ├─ Balancing
                                 ├─ Quality         ├─ General          └─ Prices
                                 │  control         │  repair
                                 └─ Technology      └─ Investments
```

- Material economics
- Planning and quota establishing
- Material provisions
- Material control

- Finance and labor economy
- Finance planning
- Labor economy
- Revenue channels
- Competition and innovation

- Internal administration
- Industrial management
- Economics control
- Bookkeeping

- Customer service
  - Customer service
  - Customer counseling service
  - Customer service
  - Recruiting and fairs

Source: Bundesministerium für Gesamtdeutsche Fragen, Fünfter Tätigkeitsbericht, 1965-1969 (Bonn, 1969), p. 73.

prices related to capital were introduced in 1969. This led to price reductions in industries with above-average returns on capital and to price increases in industries with lower returns on capital.

There has been a gradual transition of industrial prices related to capital goods. With respect to the VVBs the following principles are supposed to be observed:

1. In VVBs whose profits approximate centrally established rates of profit, industrial prices related to capital are being applied to new products introduced to production. As a rule, existing prices have not been changed.

2. In VVBs whose profits are significantly above the centrally determined rate of profit, industrial prices related to capital are being used in connection with the reduction of prices for product groups having the highest rate of profit.

3. In VVBs whose profits are below the centrally determined rate of profit, industrial prices related to capital are being applied in connection with improved rates of return on capital based primarily on a reduction of production costs.

The Combine

In the GDR the combine (Kombinat) is a consolidation of different firms on the bases of economic and administrative functions. Individual firms belonging to a combine lose their juridical independence. The rationale for the use of the combine is the improvement of profit through a continuous production process and through decreases in costs resulting from large-scale production. The combine is a result of the economic reorganization that took place during the 1960s, in which greater production efficiency was a basic policy desideratum. Efficiency was equated with large operations. Although a combine represents the merger of several firms, from an administrative standpoint it is subordinate to the VVBs or to the district economic councils.

The combine is responsible for developing its long-range and annual production plans and coordinating the plans of the enterprises subordinate to it. Fulfillment of the plan of the combine as a whole and in the main enterprises is used to evaluate the director and the department directors for bonus purposes. In giving bonuses to the directors of the enterprises of the combine plan fulfillment in the overall combine and their own enterprises are taken into account. In order to assess the production output and performances of the enterprises a production coefficient is calculated that covers the total of all industrial finished products and finished industrial services produced by the enterprises, regardless of whether these are directly intended for distribution outside the combine or whether they are processed or used in other enterprises of the same combine.

The Semistate-Owned Enterprise

The semistate-owned enterprise (Betriebe mit Staatlicher Beteiligung) represents another form of an industrial production unit. This type of enterprise involves mixed state-private ownership in which the share of the state is over 50 percent. It represents a sort of transitional form of production unit between the state-owned enterprise and the privately owned enterprise. Pressure on private enterprises to take the state on as a partner began in earnest in 1956 and has continued to the present. These pressures take the form of tax regulations that serve to reduce the amount of profits made by private enterprises and of limitations on the number of workers that they can employ. Private craftsmen and artisans have been subject to the same pressures in state efforts to get them to join producer cooperatives.

In 1969 semistate enterprises accounted for around 10 percent of gross industrial production.[14] Their importance in terms of contribution to production relative to the state and private sectors has increased slightly during the period 1965-69. Their importance, however, varies considerably from industry to industry. Semistate enterprises are of particular importance in light industry, where in 1969 they accounted for about 25 percent of the value of output; in the textile industry, where they accounted for 23 percent of total output; and in the food industry, where they accounted for 20 percent of total output.[15] On the other hand, semistate enterprises accounted for only 3 percent of the total value of output in the chemical industry.[16] Semistate enterprises are also typically medium- or small-scale employers, concentrated primarily in the light, textile, and food industries. In 1968 3,280 enterprises employed 50 or fewer workers, whereas 22 enterprises employed from 500 to 1,000 workers.[17] No semistate enterprise employed more than 1,000 workers.

Semistate enterprises are administered by the regional economic councils and by the ministries responsible for a given type of product. The state, as a partner, provides the capital and also takes its part of profits. The operation of semistate enterprises is governed by planning directives. Control and management, however, are usually vested in the original owner of the enterprise, who is given a salary plus a share in the profit. The owner is given autonomy in plant operation, particularly as long as a profit is being made. Semistate enterprises are often used as a yardstick for comparing production costs with state enterprises.

Production Cooperatives

Production cooperatives (Produktionsgenossenschaften des Handels) for artisans and craftsmen were created during the period 1958-60. During that time pressure was put on private artisans and craftsmen to join. This pressure, which still continues, takes primarily the form of tax discrimination against private artisans and material support on the part of the state for the cooperatives. Also, targets set by private artisan enterprises are increased by the regional economic councils each year. It can be said that the ultimate objective of the state is to get all private artisans into cooperatives. The reason is partly political and partly economic. The economic rationale for the cooperative is supposedly the economy of large-scale operations that is obtained when artisans are combined in large workshops, with state support in the form of marketing services, finance, and new production methods. The state also provides a unified network of receiving offices and customer service stations complete with coordinated transportation facilities. Despite unremitting state pressure, however, a substantial number of artisans continue to function outside of the cooperatives. In 1969 there were 127,687 private artisans and craftsmen.[18]

Cooperatives are concentrated primarily among the following trade occupations: carpenter, painter, plumber, electrician, shoemaker, watchmaker, auto mechanic, and television repair. To join a cooperative a craftsman must contribute his tools and pay an admission fee which is usually set at 1,000 Ostmarks. This contribution draws no interest, and members are liable for losses incurred by the cooperative. Each member draws a monthly salary, which varies from one trade to another and which can be bolstered by premiums, bonuses, and other rewards for high productivity. All profits over and above wages, premiums, materials, and other operating costs are banked and divided at the end of the year. A certain percentage is allocated for capital investment, accumulation of reserves, repair of plant and equipment, and amortization of property and also for job training for apprentices and for recreational and social facilities. The remainder is distributed to members of the cooperative on the basis of their contributions to total output. Each cooperative has a manager and a board of directors who are elected by secret ballot. Major decisions such as acquisition of property and setting of pay scales and service charges require the approval of two-thirds of the members of the cooperative.

The Enterprise

The enterprise (VEB) is the lowest production unit in the East German economy. It operates as a legal person engaged in production activity under the national economic plan. It is under an obligation to fulfill its own production plan, which contains certain targets or success indicators that should be attained. It is required to operate under a profit-and-loss accounting system and has fixed and working capital that form the basis of its statutory fund, the size of which is shown on its balance sheet. It can decide how best to use the fixed and working capital assigned to it, provided that each is used for purposes that are stipulated in the production plan. An enterprise also has the right to make capital investments from funds that are set aside for amortization purposes and to fix the prices of its products within certain prescribed limits as set by the economic plan.

In general a VEB is organized along the following lines. There is a director who is appointed by the state to run the enterprise. He is governed from above by directives and rules of behavior that guide his decisions. He is not rigidly circumscribed as to what he can do, however, but rather is free to operate as he thinks best as long as it is within the general framework of the national economic plan and his own operating plan. He can influence the contents of the operating plan because he is familiar with the resource needs and product specifications of his enterprise. Planning of necessity must permit a certain degree of managerial autonomy, for it is impossible to supervise in detail the operation of many enterprises.

In addition to the director there are assistant directors and a chief engineer or area manager who is responsible for overall production operations. There are various department managers who are responsible for the operation of individual departments. These departments are varied. Typically, there is a supply department, responsible for the procurement of materials. There are also departments that are responsible for accounting, wages, personnel, transportation, and finance. Below the departments come the various manufacturing shops. Authority extends downward from the director through several strata of managerial personnel to the shop foreman and the heads of work teams. Paralleling this organization is the party organization, which is supposed to see that the enterprise managers and workers act in accordance with the objectives of the SED.

Distribution of Profits

Profit is accepted as a basic criterion of enterprise performance and efficiency. Profit is significant because a direct link has been established between it and incentive payments, so that it is in the interest of the enterprise personnel to strive to maximize it. It is necessary to point out, however, that planning must be regarded as the main driving force behind production. Overall profitability for different branches of the economy is state determined, and individual enterprises are subject to other directive indicators that supplement profit considerations. Moreover, the prices of the factors of production and of the articles produced are not determined freely in the market to reflect scarcity-preference relations. For a variety of reasons the state fixes prices above or below production costs. By the very act of changing prices the state may make some products profitable and others unprofitable, even though the methods of production have not changed.

When an enterprise makes a profit, the first claimant is the state. A part of profit is allocated to the state budget, and the remainder is divided by the enterprise into a number of funds. Each fund is designed to accomplish a specific objective. There is a production development fund. Its purpose is to finance capital investment for the introduction of new technology, mechanization and automation, renovation of fixed assets, modernization of equipment, and for other purposes that are designed to develop and improve production. There is also a fund for social and cultural measures, which has as its purpose the improvement of worker morale and productivity. It provides revenue for the construction and maintenance of child-care centers, expansion of recreational facilities, support of athletic programs, and housing construction. There is also a reserve fund, which is used for the purpose of paying off long-term loans.

As far as individual members of the enterprise are concerned, however, the material incentives, or bonus, fund is the most important. The bonus system is supposed to link the total wages of all workers with the overall results of the enterprise. Deductions from profits to the material incentives fund are made at fixed rates. After state budget deductions 20 percent of net profit is allocated to the fund. Bonuses are subdivided into two categories—those paid to engineering, technical, and white collar workers and those paid to regular factory workers. In the GDR the size of the material incentives fund is based on formulas in which a distinction is made between planned and above-plan profits and, further, between profits made by exceeding production targets and those achieved by reductions in prime costs.

A simplified scheme of profit use for the individual state enterprise can be presented as follows:[19]

>   Gross profits of the enterprise
>   Less payments to the state budget and interest on bank loans
>   Equal net profits of the enterprise, which are divided into:
>   1. Production fund to finance fixed and working capital
>   2. Social and cultural fund to improve the social and intellectual life of the workers

3. Material incentive fund to stimulate worker productivity
4. Reserve or amortization fund
5. Profit residual that is not committed to any fund but that goes to the state budget.

The distribution of funds are based on certain formulas. For example, in 1969 the social and cultural funds amounted to 1.5 percent of the regular wage fund of a VEB.[20] The production fund is based as a percentage of fixed and current assets and is formed from a part of the amortization deductions earmarked for a full renewal of fixed production assets, from receipts from the sale of unused property, and from deductions from profits.

Pricing Policies

Prices set by enterprises in the GDR may take three forms. First, there may be a maximum price, which may be lowered in accordance with production and sales conditions. This price may be set by a VVB or enterprise on the basis of legal regulations. For example, to supply heat and electric power proposed prices are submitted by an enterprise to the state organ responsible for the examination and coordination of price proposals. This organ, which is the Office of Prices, must grant a price sanction to the enterprise. If subsidies are claimed, an enterprise does not have the right to lower maximum prices. When maximum prices are lowered, that part of net income that is to be transferred to special funds cannot be lowered. Normally, maximum prices are set for special products subject to rapid technological development.

Second, there are established prices, which are set down in contracts between buyers and sellers. These prices are stable and may not be changed. For example, the following prices may be charged by a state electric power enterprise: During daylight hours a charge of 5 pfennigs per kilowatt hour and during night hours a charge of 2 pfennigs per kilowatt hour.[21] For input of electric power from hydroelectric power plants into the public network the following prices apply: During daylight hours 3 pfennigs per kilowatt hour and during night hours 1.9 pfennigs per kilowatt hour.[22] Standard prices are normally used for important products with a wide volume of consumption. Included are basic materials and electric power.

The final type of price is arranged between buyers and sellers on the basis of a contract. State enterprises are legal corporate bodies, free to choose their markets and suppliers for many products. Arranged prices cover such products as construction materials and machinery and special services such as repair work. Subcontracting work is an area in which prices are arranged.

A normative upper limit of profitability is set by the state. Should this limit be exceeded by any production unit, VVB or otherwise, it is supposed to set off a responsive reaction. Management is supposed to immediately lower prices; if they do not have the authority to take such action, they are to recommend to the Office of Prices that prices be lowered. This normative limit is tied to the goal of a constant regulated lowering of prices. There is also the principle that prices for new products must be set in such a manner that any price regression forces producers to clear their assortments and offer new products.

Private Enterprise

A private sector continues to remain in East Germany even after two decades of a state policy of appropriating private industry. In fact East Germany is the only socialist country in the Soviet bloc that does have private enterprise. There is a certain ambivalence in the attitude of the state toward the existence of private enterprise. There still remains the immovable political-ideological principle of eliminating all forms of capitalist production in the GDR within a given time by the conversion of all private industries into socialist ownership. Private industries are insignificant in comparison to the nationalized economy and are still used for the gratification of many varied consumer needs, for the procurement of foreign exchange, and for supplying the nationalized industries. They are tolerated and even promoted in some fields of production. This toleration, however, is circumscribed, extending only to sometimes favorable treatment of the turnover and profit taxes.

In 1968 there were 3,638 industries in the GDR that were completely in private hands. They averaged an employment of 86,169 workers for the year, or about 1.5 percent of the total labor force, and 3.4 percent of all workers and salaried employees in industry.[23] Although 29.6 percent of all industry was in private hands in 1968, total operations accounted for only 1.6 percent of the entire industrial production of the GDR. With private industries it is almost exclusively a case of small- and medium-sized businesses.[24] In 1968 92 percent of all private industries employed no more than 50 workers and salaried employees.[25] These plants contributed about 75 percent of the entire gross industrial production of all private industries. In 1968 there were only three private enterprises remaining in the class employing 201 to 500 workers and salaried employees, and only one survived in the category of 501 to 1,000 employees.[26]

Private industries belong mostly to the industrial fields of light industry and the food and beverages industry. About 70 percent of the entire industrial production stemming from the private industries and sold in 1967 were dispensed by private enterprises in these two industrial fields.[27] In the branches of luxury goods, production of work uniforms and service clothing, linen, paper and pasteboard articles, clothing and sewing products, fur and leather goods, and similar products, one-third to one-half of all plants are privately owned. Accordingly, private industry is tolerated by the state in those industrial branches that serve the direct needs of the population and where considerable experience is necessary in the manufacture of certain special products in small quantities. Also, traditional relations of the private enterprises with foreign countries have a value of their own for GDR exports that should not be underestimated.

There are certain tax constraints placed on private enterprise in accordance with the political-ideological hostility on the part of the state toward this form of ownership. For example, income tax regulations applying to private industry practically disallow the formation of capital reserves. By a normative limitation of cost concepts recognized by the tax law and by assessment regulations that usually rate assets too high and liabilities too low, high taxable profits are shown, which are then subjected to a sharply progressive income tax. The consequence for private industry is a withdrawal of liquidity for emergency needs, economic stagnation, and a consumption of personal capital. Thus, private entrepreneurs have neither the chance for financing investments out of private capital formed out of private income nor the possibility of utilizing self-financing from their profit except for investments for replacements and certain small expansion and rationalization efforts.

Profit taxes allow for a much more differentiated application in order to permit an economic activity on the part of private enterprise desired only to an extent by the state than the taxes dependent on the proportional size of the capital allow. Moreover, as a consequence of the income and profit taxation in the GDR, the amount of capital of the private entrepreneur that is subject to property or capital taxation cannot reach any great level. Since the turnover tax appears in the pricing of products only as an element of calculation or as a price component, profits of individual private enterprises are affected only to a limited degree.

In addition to private enterprises individual craftsmen and artisans also function in the GDR. There is considerable control on the part of the state, and individual workers are encouraged to join cooperatives. The national plan itself is used to control the work of artisans. The 1971 plan sets higher targets for artisan enterprises, particularly with regard to repairs and services and to consumer-goods production, such as contractors to industry. Encouragement primarily takes the form of compensation for equipment brought into an artisan cooperative. There is also vocal pressure from the main artisans' cooperative (Production Cooperatives of Artisans) on individual artisans to join. To some extent the pressure has been successful, for the number of private artisan enterprises has shown a gradual decrease. In 1967 there were 132,610 private artisans in the GDR; the 1968 figures indicated a decrease to 127,455.[28]

There are also private retailers and innkeepers. Typically, these types of enterprises are limited to one family and may not be bought or sold. The annual average number of workers, as a rule, may not exceed three persons. Employing more than three full-time persons requires a prior permit from the Department of Trade and Supply of the appropriate district council. Each permit is valid only for a period of one year. Working family members are included only if a formal employment situation exists.

In general personal income tax rates are used to discriminate against persons who derive income from private enterprise. The tax schedule for certain occupational groups involving freelance operators, i.e., commercial artists, artisans, film producers, small retailers, and architects, was amended in January 1971 to include the introduction of a progressive income tax scale that starts with an income of 20,000 Ostmarks a year. This scale runs to a maximum rate of 60 percent, compared to a maximum rate of 30 percent on incomes in excess of 20,000 Ostmarks.

ORGANIZATION OF AGRICULTURE

There is a distinct similarity in the organization of agriculture and industry in the GDR. Agriculture is controlled by the state through economic planning. The supply and price of inputs, the share of output marketed, the prices paid for agricultural products, and farm income and expenditures are regulated by the plan. Overall procurement goals are established for agricultural products that are to be delivered to state purchasing agencies. Given the procurement goals that are supplemented by local requirements, each agricultural unit has to formulate a production plan. When this is done, each plan in conformance to planned goals goes up the administrative line to be examined and combined with other plans.

The administrative organization of agriculture is presented in Chart 9.3. At the top is the Council of Ministers. Then there are the Ministry of Agriculture and the State Committee for Purchasing. Control flows downward from the Ministry of Agriculture to the regional and district councils as well as the local councils. These councils have responsibility over the agricultural, production, and purchasing units under their jurisdiction. The State Committee for

CHART 9.3

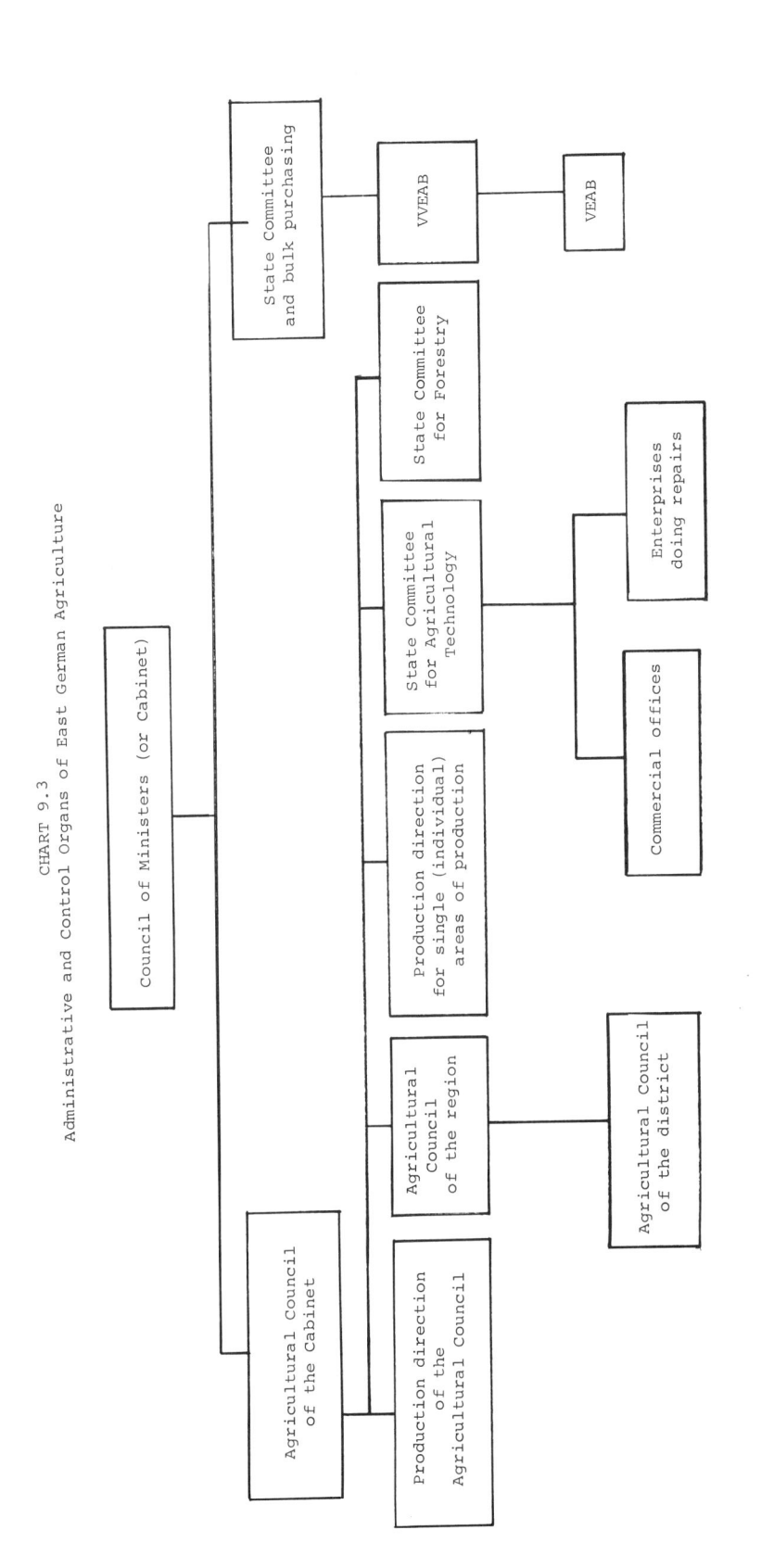

Administrative and Control Organs of East German Agriculture

aVVEAB--United National Inclusion and Bulk Purchasing.

bVEAB--National Inclusion and Bulk Purchasing Enterprise.

Source: H. Jorg Thieme, *Die Sozialistische Agrarverfassung* (Stuttgart: Gustav Fischer, 1969), p. 91.

Purchasing exercises control over the Vereinigung Volkseigener Erfassungs and Aufkaufbetriebe (VVEAB) and Volkseigener Erfassungs und Aufkaufbetriebe (VEAB). The former is the equivalent of the industrial VVB. It is a state procurement organization responsible for the purchase and distribution of agricultural products to state stores and other outlets. A VEAB is somewhat similar to a VEB in that it functions at a lower level relative to the VVEAB. It, too, is responsible for procurement of agricultural products at lower or local levels.

The basic agricultural production units are the state farm (Volkseigenes Gut) and the collective or cooperative farm (Landwirtschaftliche Produktionsgenossenschaft). Some private farms may exist but can be considered a rarity. It is, of course, a socialist article of faith that private ownership of land hinders development in agriculture. Private plots of land that are farmed by members of collective farms are permitted, however. In 1970 state farms contributed 14.2 percent of the value of agricultural output in East Germany, cooperatives contributed 81.1 percent, and the private sector, which includes basically the private plots, contributed 4.6 percent.[29] State-owned enterprises contributed 0.1 percent. Also, in 1970 the state and cooperative farms controlled 94.2 percent of all agricultural land in use.

The state farm or collective farm is usually a part of a production group. The involvement of many related enterprises is supposed to effect through vertical integration more efficient production methods. For example, a collective farm producing livestock can be a member of a production group that would also include a state enterprise (VEB) responsible for slaughtering and meat packing. One unit does the producing and the other does the processing. A system of cooperative management is supposed to coordinate production, processing, and distribution efforts. The trend is toward consolidation of agricultural enterprises producing identical products into a production group. An example of this trend is the organization of agricultural enterprises, meat processing enterprises, and distributive outlets into a cooperative group for the district of Jena. This arrangement is presented in Chart 9.4.

The state enterprise (VEG) for meat processing of pork receives the plan figures for the production of slaughtered animals, the profits to be achieved, production funds deductions, net profit to be derived, wage funds, bonus funds, and allowances for reserves. On the basis of these figures, the VEG sets up a production plan that is distributed to all of the enterprises involved in the production of hogs. These enterprises receive a production quota that they are expected to fulfill. The stockyards also receive plans regarding the slaughter of hogs by types and the use of intestines and other parts. Processing

CHART 9.4

Future Structure of Cooperative Management
of Hog Production in Jena

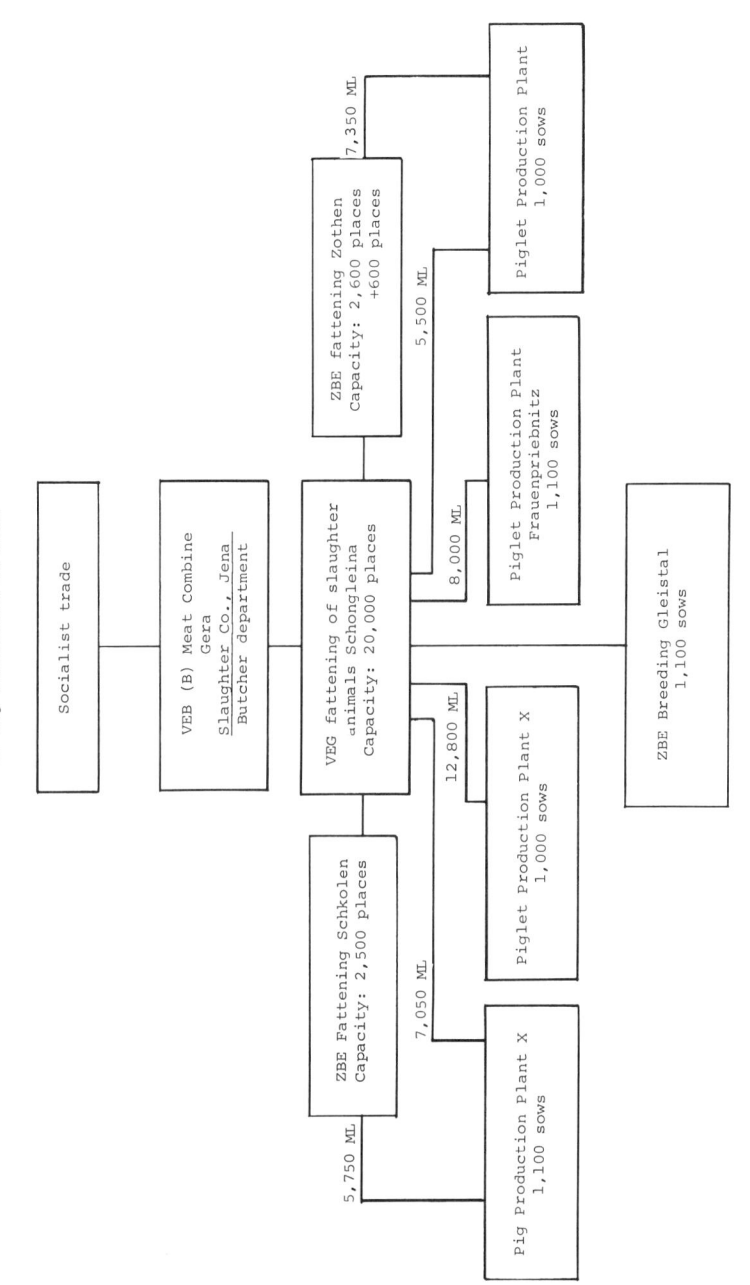

```
┌─────────────────┐
│ Socialist trade │
└────────┬────────┘
         │
┌────────┴──────────┐
│ VEB (B) Meat Combine│
│       Gera         │
│ Slaughter Co., Jena│
│ Butcher department │
└────────┬──────────┘
         │
┌────────┴──────────────┐         ┌──────────────────────┐
│ VEG fattening of      │─7,350 ML│ ZBE fattening Zothen │
│ slaughter animals     │─────────│ Capacity: 2,600 places│
│ Schongleina           │         │        +600 places    │
│ Capacity: 20,000 places│        └──────────┬───────────┘
└───┬────┬────┬────┬────┘                    │5,500 ML
    │    │    │    │                         │
 5,750 7,050 12,800 8,000                    │
   ML   ML    ML    ML                       │
                                 ┌───────────┴──────────┐
┌──────────┐ ┌──────────┐ ┌──────────┐ ┌──────────────────┐
│ZBE Fatten│ │Piglet    │ │Piglet    │ │Piglet Production │
│ing Schko-│ │Production│ │Production│ │Plant             │
│len       │ │Plant X   │ │Plant X   │ │1,000 sows        │
│Capacity: │ │1,000 sows│ │          │ │                  │
│2,500     │ │          │ │          │ │                  │
│places    │ │          │ │          │ │                  │
└────┬─────┘ └──────────┘ └──────────┘ └──────────────────┘
     │
┌────┴──────┐                  ┌─────────────────┐
│Pig        │                  │Piglet Production│
│Production │                  │Plant            │
│Plant X    │                  │Frauenpriebnitz  │
│1,100 sows │                  │1,100 sows       │
└───────────┘                  └─────────────────┘

                               ┌─────────────────┐
                               │ZBE Breeding     │
                               │Gleistal         │
                               │1,100 sows       │
                               └─────────────────┘
```

Notes: ZBE: Zwischenbetriebeliche Einrichtung; ML:
Mastläufer (suckling pigs); places: pig capacity.

Source: Bundesministerium für Gesamtdeutsche Fragen,
Fünfter Tätigkeitsbericht, 1965–1969 (Bonn, 1969), p. 274.

plants receive orders concerning the range of production of the finished product according to the assortment. A contract is entered into between the meat packing enterprise and the hog producers covering prices and delivery. Thus, every step in the production chain from the breeding of hogs to the production of the end product is integrated into the system of cooperative management.

State Farms

State farms (Volkseigene Guter or VEGs) are owned by the government and operated as regular industrial establishments with managers and hired workers. They have generally been established on confiscated large private landholdings and are supposed to serve as models of efficient farm management and production. Their annual budgets and operating plans are developed by the government, which is also responsible for the determination of wages paid to the workers and for the provision of livestock and equipment. The VEGs are also supposed to provide special services, including the maintenance of experimental stations, research institutes, and the teaching of agricultural students.

The VEGs sell their produce to government procurement offices for processing and distribution through state stores, for stockpiling, and for exports. The arrangement between the VEGs and the government takes the form of a contract that specifies the price to be paid for the commodity produced and the delivery date. There is usually a basic procurement price for each commodity. Prices can be used as incentives for changes in production. For example, if an increase in the production of dairy products or meat is desired, prices are raised. Prices are also set at levels that reflect, at least in part, differences in average production costs on state farms operating in different areas of the country. Lower prices are paid in better land areas, reflecting the fact that no charge is made for land rent.

State farms are managed by directors. In the past a director primarily responded to directives from above and exercised little individual initiative in the running of the farm. The reforms of the New Economic System, however, have broadened the responsibilities and autonomy of the director. He has the right to determine the number of workers to be used on the farm, the planned production cost, the planned labor productivity, and other general factors of managerial control. Although this has meant greater independence of state farm management from central control, the basic policies to be followed are determined by the state, and directors must operate according to these policies.

The VEGs received the bulk of their financial support from grants from the state budget before the reforms. Now they are expected to be going concerns in terms of their ability to support themselves out of internally generated funds and from bank credit. A basic part of the reforms, as extended to the field of agriculture, is the use of differentiated interest rates as economic levers. Banks serving agricultural enterprises not only can dictate the use of credit but also can differentiate interest charges based on the amount of internal funds put up by an enterprise and on the length of repayment period. A VEG is supposed to function like a state industrial enterprise (VEB), by operating profitably within a new cost-price framework and generating its own funds for investment.

Distribution of Profit

There are distinct similarities between state agricultural and industrial enterprises in the GDR. Each is run by a director who has similar managerial responsibilities. Wage payments are also similar in that there is a reliance on piece rates and bonus payments. Both types of enterprises operate within the framework of an annual production plan. Earnings are distributed in a similar manner in that both types of enterprises have special funds that are allocated income.

The starting point in the distribution of profit is gross sales, which is obtained by multiplying the planned volume of sales per product by the set state price. From gross sales production costs, including the cost of seed and fertilizer and depreciation, are deducted to get gross income. From gross income a deduction is made into the wage fund, and the remainder is called the socially clear income. This income may be considered as a residual that is divided between the state farm and the state. Since January 1, 1968, the VEGs are obliged to pay a land and production fund tax to the state. This tax is similar to a production tax, which is levied on industrial enterprises. The land tax is tied directly to the fertility of the land and extends to a maximum of 300 Ostmarks per hectare of cultivated land. The production tax ranges from 0.5 percent to 3 percent of the gross value of fixed and circulating capital. In addition there is a deduction from profit, which also goes to the state. The amount is set during the planning period. Remaining income is divided into various VEG funds. An example of the utilization of profit of a VEG is as follows:[30]

Total sales	1,000,000 Ostmarks
Less seed, fertilizer, and other costs, including depreciation	500,000

Equals gross income		500,000
Less wage funds		200,000
Equals social clear income		300,000
Less special costs	50,000	
Less production levy	40,000	90,000
Equals gross profit		210,000
Less land and production fund tax		40,000
Equals net profit		170,000
Less investment funds	80,000	
Less enterprise bonus funds	3,000	
Less social and cultural and reserve funds	37,000	120,000
Equals profit residual or remainder		50,000

Collective Farms

The collective farm (Landwirtschaftliche Productionsgenossenschaften, or LPG) or agricultural producers cooperative is the basic type of farm unit in East Germany. It may be defined as a form of agricultural organization in which varying numbers of individual farmers combine their resources and talents and operate on a collective basis. The collective farm is socially owned; that is, the land is held in perpetuity by the collective. Statutes permit a collective farm to use all land, farm equipment, and livestock contributed by its members for meeting obligations to the state. Collective farms provide their own working capital and fixed investment funds from the income of farm operations. In the past members were paid in cash and in kind, and their wages were usually tied to the actual earnings of each farm. Members were also residual claimants on the harvest; that is, they were paid from funds remaining after paying for the fixed obligations to the state, operating costs of the farm, investment reserves, and social costs. As a result of the reforms, however, minimum daily wages have now been established, and bonuses either in cash or kind are also used as labor incentives.

In 1970 there were 9,009 collective farms in operation in East Germany, compared to 511 state farms.[31] In terms of land area utilized collective farms had in use 5,392,400 hectares in 1969, compared to 442,600 hectares for the state farms.[32] The average state farm is somewhat larger than the average collective farm. Both collective and state farms have decreased in numbers over time and have increased in the average area of land in use. In 1960 there were 19,313 collective farms and 669 state farms.[33] By 1970 the numbers had decreased to 9,009 and 511, respectively.[34] Both collective and state farms have been consolidated for the purpose of increasing agricultural output.

East German collective farms are divided into three categories. Type 1 requires the collective ownership of farmland only. Type 2 requires the collective ownership of farmland, draft animals, and equipment, with private ownership and utilization of other livestock and meadows. Type 3, the most numerous in 1969, entails the complete collectivization of all means of production, except for a private plot of land of about half a hectare per farm family. The Type 1 collective farm was utilized primarily during the collectivization drive of the late 1950s. Many farmers chose to join this type of collective because it required the least amount of socialization of property. The Type 3 collective farm is regarded as the final type of collective, however. The number of Type 1 and Type 2 cooperatives has decreased from 12,976 in 1960 to 3,485 in 1970, while the Type 3 cooperatives have decreased from 6,337 in 1960 to 5,524 in 1970.[35]

Each LPG keeps what is called a land book, which serves as a basis for calculating the distribution of income. Entered into the book is the amount of land added to the LPG in the name of its owner. When a farmer enters an LPG, he in essence contributes his land for which he receives a land share that expresses the extent of his contribution to the cooperative. LPG members retain title to the land they contributed and have the right to sell it to the state, the LPG, or to other LPG members. The land may also be inherited, but it cannot be withdrawn from the LPG or used as its contributor sees fit. So it would be incorrect to say that the land is private property. Land may also accrue to an LPG from other sources. For example, the state may turn over to it land that was expropriated during the early agricultural reforms or land that has reverted to state ownership when its owners fled the country. The absence of landownership also does not preclude membership in a cooperative, for land can be rented to a farmer. The distribution of income to members is based on land shares and work units. The latter is based on the overall productivity of the cooperative and is determined at the end of each year.

LPGs may employ outside specialists, such as accountants, agronomists, and agricultural engineers, who are paid a salary. Internally, they are headed by directors, who are responsible for their management. The basic labor unit of the LPG is the brigade. It consists of 50 to 100 workers, headed by a brigadeer, or foreman, who is usually appointed by the director. An LPG may have a number of brigades. Some are responsible for cultivation and production of field crops and are kept together for the duration of the crop rotation period. Other brigades are responsible for livestock production. Each brigade is provided with the machinery and equipment necessary to perform its tasks.

The Distribution of Income

Like the VEBs, the LPGs set aside revenues into funds that are used for specific purposes. Profitability is the major criterion of performance, and capital needs are financed from profits. Out of revenues, a number of general expenditures have to be met.[36] These include contributions to a sociocultural fund, production expenses for such items as fuel and fertilizers, insurance that is designed to protect the LPG from the loss of its physical assets, and contributions to a capital fund for the purpose of acquiring capital goods. Wages paid to workers come out of a regular wage fund. In addition, there are bonus funds that are tied to profit and levies that go to the state.

Capital of an LPG can be divided into fixed capital and circulating capital.[37] Fixed capital consists of buildings and other installations, machinery and equipment, transport, breeding animals and livestock, land, and orchards. Circulating capital consists of production in process, provisions for production, and finished products destined for sale. Circulating capital may change in both quality and quantity. The use of circulating capital has assumed more importance in terms of the effectiveness of production. This capital passes through all phases of the LPG reproduction process—production preparation, production execution, and the realization of the final product. The gross product of an LPG is a result of productive work performed and includes circulating capital, consumption, and labor costs. Gross sales minus production costs gives the gross income of an LPG. This shows the new value (Neuwert) accomplished for the year. The reproduction process for the period has ended. Expanded reproduction, if there is any, then goes into fixed and circulating capital.

ORGANIZATION OF DOMESTIC TRADE

Domestic Trade

Domestic trade can be broken down into two categories—retail and wholesale. Retail trade is carried on by several types of establishments: state retail stores (Verkaufsstellen des Volkseigenen Einzelhandels); consumer cooperative retail stores (Verkaufsstellen des Konsumgenossenschaftlichen Einzelhandels); enterprises with state partnership (Betriebe mit Staatlicher Beteiligung); and private retail stores (private Einzelhändler), which may also include private food and specialty stores (privates Nahrungs und Genussmittelhandwerk).[38] Retail trade is characterized by the existence of small- and medium-sized stores with an average of four or five employees. Most of

CHART 9.5
Reproduction Process of East German Agricultural
Production Cooperatives

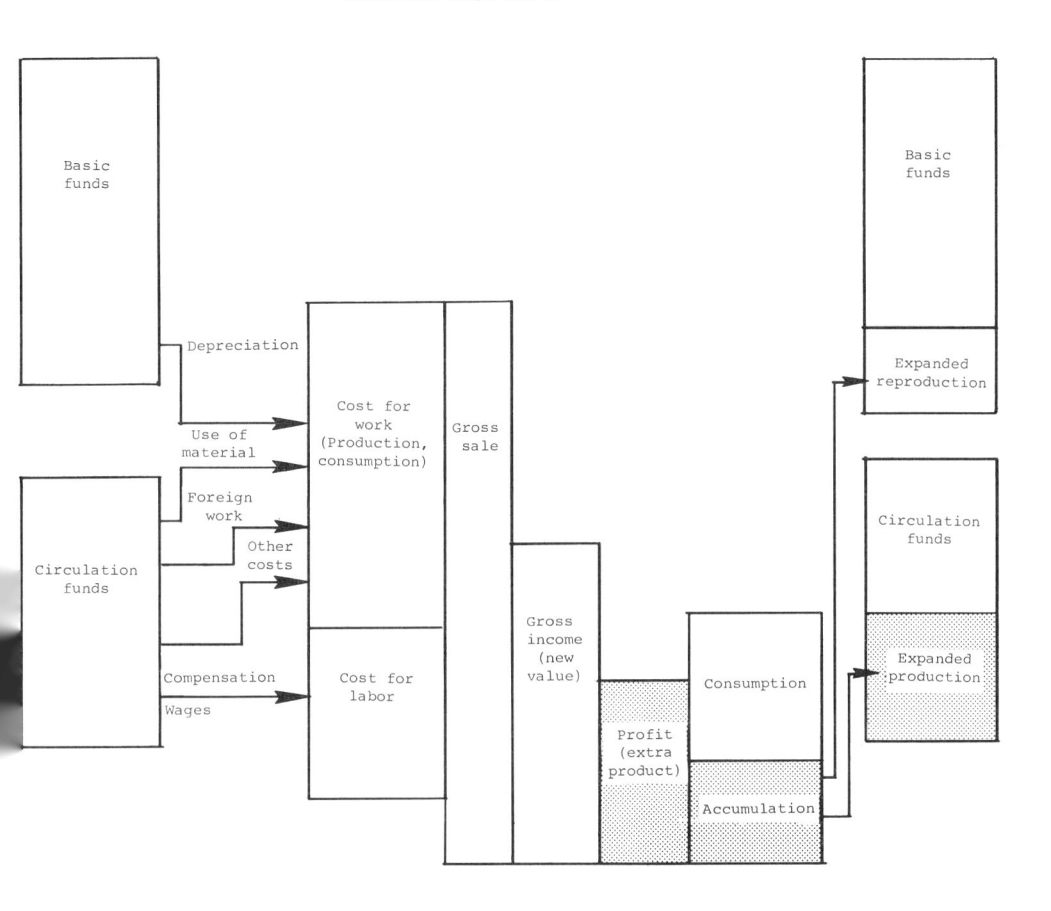

Source: Guther Mittag, *Politische Ökonomie des Sozialismus und ре Anwendung in der DDR* (East Berlin: Dietz Verlag, 1969), p. 871.

these stores are affiliated with state associations or trusts that function on a national or regional scale. For example, there is an Association of State Department Stores that functions as sort of a trust and has control over all individual state department stores in the GDR. The network of government stores is under the jurisdiction of the Ministry of Trade and Supply and its ancillary organs, which exist at the district, county, and local levels. Retail prices are, for the most part, fixed by the state at levels that attempt to equate supply with demand. The retail price consists of several elements—production costs, profit of the producer, the turnover tax, and wholesale and retail markups.

Wholesale domestic trade is handled by state distribution organs, which are responsible for virtually all commodity groups.[39] These organs are called Central Purchasing Bureaus (Zentral Einkaufe Buros). Among other current responsibilities they are supposed to work out assortment models on a long-term basis with the production enterprises. They are also charged with supplying industrial goods to retailers and with maintaining standards of quality and variety. Central wholesale organs are under the jurisdiction of the Ministry of Trade and Supply, and wholesale units affiliated with each organ are located all over East Germany. In some cases, however, the wholesaler is by-passed through the use of a direct sales link between producer and retailer or direct sales between two producers. The latter is fairly common when industrial goods are sold by one production enterprise to another enterprise.

The private commission broker (Kommissionshandler) can be considered as a part of the East German wholesale trade system. His purpose is to bring buyers and sellers together. For this, he receives a commission, which is usually set at 10 percent of the sales price of the good sold.[40] The private commission broker also takes goods on consignment; however, the producer retains title to the goods. The role of the commission broker is apparently of some importance in the GDR, particularly in the soft goods and textile areas.

An organization chart of domestic trade in the GDR is presented in Chart 9.6. Distribution is divided into three categories—wholesale, retail, and special forms. Each category is further subdivided on the basis of territorial organization.

A recent development in the GDR is the integration of retailing, wholesaling, and production into what can be called an economic federation or production-distribution group. For example, the Karl-Marx Stadt consumer cooperative enterprise, the Leipzig Centrum, the Textile Wholesale Trade Directorate, and eight associations of state enterprises in the textile industry formed a clothing federation in 1969 to serve the Leipzig-Karl-Marx Stadt area.[41] All partners in this federation are supposed to have equal rights. Its highest

CHART 9.6

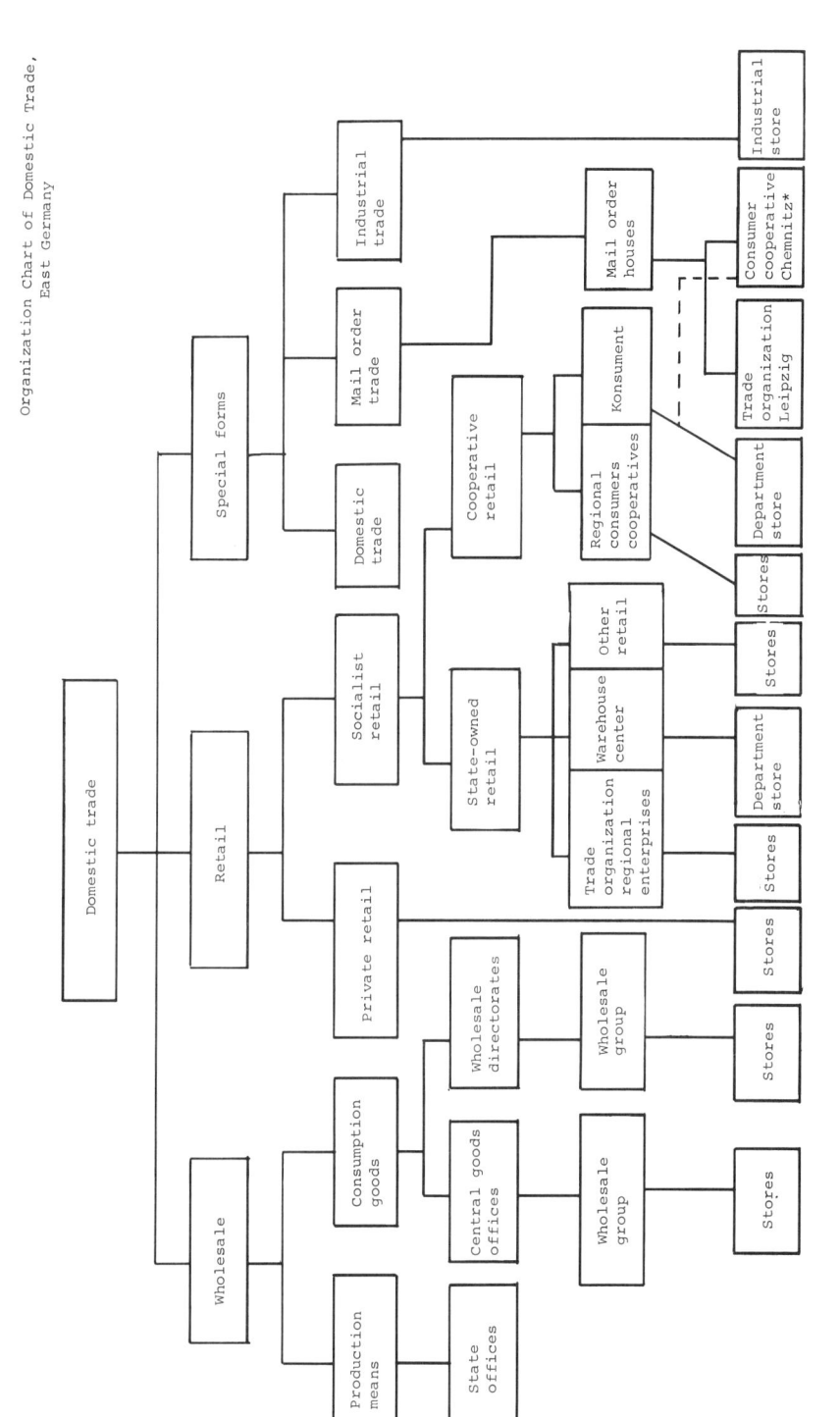

Organization Chart of Domestic Trade, East Germany

*Chemnitz is now Karl Marx Stadt.

Source: Hans Schlenk, Der Binnenhandel der DDR (Cologne: Wissenschaft und Politik Verlag, 1970), p. 72.

body is the federation council, which consists of the general managers of all of the participating production and distribution enterprises. For the 1971-75 planning period the federation is attempting to achieve optimal results in the preparation of clothing assortments. An assortment model has been developed that is supposed to select the most efficient use of material resources, research and production capacity, price developments, and sales organization.

Foreign Trade

Foreign trade is conducted within the framework of annual and longer-term plans drawn up by the Ministry of Foreign Trade (Ministerium fur Aussenwirtschaft) and the State Planning Commission.[42] Until recent years, foreign trade was separate from domestic trade. The actual trading between the GDR and other countries was handled by foreign-trade enterprises (Aussenhandelsbetrieben, or AHBs) under the jurisdiction of the Ministry of Foreign Trade. When the amount of available foreign exchange was determined by the plan, each enterprise engaged in foreign trade received an allotment to cover its import needs. Each organization was responsible for certain designated commodities or services and each was a juridically independent company.

Since 1968, however, changes have been made in the organization of foreign trade. Although the arrangement above has been maintained to a major degree, an attempt has been made to decentralize control. Apart from the foreign trade enterprises, which are still subordinate to the Ministry of Foreign Trade, there are also those enterprises that are subordinate to the industrial ministries or to the industrial trusts.[43] These enterprises are allowed to manage their own exports independent of the regular foreign trade organs. Market risks and incidental expenses are assumed by the production enterprise. In general, those enterprises that operate independent of the foreign-trade enterprises produce a unique and well-known product, such as Meissen china. Since 1971 all enterprises engaged in foreign trade receive the full Valuta Mark value for their exports.

The Ministry of Foreign Trade is responsible for developing foreign trade and marketing research. Responsibility for foreign trade is in the hands of the Institute for Socialist Economic Management of Foreign Trade, which is under the jurisdiction of the College of Foreign Economies, operated by the Ministry of Foreign Trade. The German Institute for Market Research is responsible for marketing research. It is a part of the Ministry of Foreign Trade. It is supposed to develop foreign markets for East German products, as well as to work on special problems in the field of foreign trade.

SUMMARY

In 1963 a series of economic reforms was undertaken in the GDR for the purpose of increasing economic efficiency. These reforms, which can be regarded as sort of a continuing process, involved several elements of the economic system. Producers' prices were brought closer in line with production costs in order to reduce the need for subsidies from the state budget. Similarly, procurement prices payable to state and collective farms were raised in relation to industrial prices, to encourage agricultural production. Enterprises have been charged with greater financial responsibility in that there is more reliance on internal financing. The profit criterion has been accepted as the main indicator of enterprise performance, while the number of plan directive indicators previously regulating enterprise activities has been greatly reduced. Increased importance has been attached to material, as distinct from moral, incentives. A portion of enterprise profit is distributed individually and collectively to the workers and other employees according to the quantity and quality of the work performed. Profit is now generally calculated on the basis of the output sold, not merely produced or handled, so that it is in the interest of both industry and trade to supply customers with what they want.

Industrial enterprises in the GDR may be divided into three categories. The first category is the state-owned and -operated enterprise. It operates on the basis of an annual production plan, which is integrated into the national economic plan. Its success is supposed to be judged primarily by the volume of its sales and profits. The state-owned enterprise is usually tied in with the operation of a VVB, which can be considered a form of state trust. The second category of enterprise is the semistate enterprise, in which the state and private individuals are partial owners, although the state has a controlling interest. The state prescribes the policies all state-owned enterprises are to follow in the national economic plan. Private enterprises represent the third category. They play a minor role, contributing about 5 percent of total production in the GDR, and are almost exclusively limited to small-scale industry, trade, and services. Private enterprises are subject to discriminatory taxation and usually have no assurance of material allocations from the state.

Agricultural land in the GDR is farmed by either state farms or collective farms. State farms are owned, managed, and operated directly by the state, and those who work on them are paid wages. They are similar to state industrial enterprises in that they operate under a profit-and-loss accounting system. State farms in the GDR are usually larger than collective farms in land size and number of workers employed, and they mostly concentrate on extensive farming or on experimental work. The collective farm is dominant in terms of numbers and the total amount of land farmed. It is collectively owned, managed, and worked by its members. Each farm is headed by a director who is responsible for its operations. Compensation of the members is based on the success of the farm and the quality and quantity of work contributed by each. Minimum wages are also applicable to members of collective farms.

CHAPTER

10

THE FISCAL SYSTEM OF EAST GERMANY

INTRODUCTION

The operation of any modern state requires the collection of large sums of money for the financing of various public services and for the general administrative functions of government. This is as true for the socialist countries as it is for countries with market economies. There is a great deal of difference in the ways in which the two forms of economic organizations acquire and dispose of their revenues, however. In the socialist countries government expenditures go for operating industry as well as carrying on its normal government functions. Since the government has provided the expenditures necessary for the operation of agricultural and industrial enterprises, it stands to reason that it would receive part of the proceeds derived from the sale of goods and services by these enterprises.

The role of taxes in a socialist country is significant. They provide the state with control over economic resources. In this respect they are similar to taxes in the capitalist countries. Their role goes one step further, however, they perform an important control function. The turnover tax, which typically is the most important tax in most socialist countries, can be used as an example. It can be used to inhibit consumption of certain articles. It is higher on luxury goods than it is on basic consumer goods. It is also used to maintain a balance between aggregate demand of the public and the supply of consumer goods that have been made available. When demand exceeds supply, the rate of the turnover tax is increased; when supply exceeds demand, the rate is lowered. The turnover tax is also used to regulate enterprise profit. Since prices are normally fixed for the producer, an increase in the rate of the turnover tax could lower the amount of profit.

An outstanding feature of the fiscal systems of the socialist countries is the predominance of indirect taxation over direct taxation. This is surprising in view of the fact that Marxist doctrine would hold that the use of such taxes discriminates against the working classes because they are regressive and inequitable. There is a purpose for this reliance on indirect taxation, however. First, indirect taxes are easier to administer and harder to avoid than direct taxes. They are collected from thousands of enterprises rather than millions of individuals, and in the early stages of socialist development this was important because the administrative machinery of government was not well developed. Second, the role of the government as reflected by the size of the national budget is more important in the socialist countries, so taxation by necessity must also be higher. Direct taxes would not provide the revenues that are necessary to support budgetary expenditures. The direct taxes would also have more of a negative impact on work incentives than indirect taxes.

The State Budget

In the socialist command economies the state budget is of paramount importance since it provides for the accumulation and distribution of much of the national income. The main function of the state budget is the reallocation of income within a command economy. This reallocation process involves not only the receipts of the central government but also of provincial and local authorities and other organizations and the balances of productive enterprises. The budget is the major instrument for financing many types of investment and for controlling the utilization of investment in accordance with planning objectives. Moreover, the budget is the key element in national economic planning and growth, and it links the requirements of the plan with the financial and production plans of the enterprises.

The state budget, as mentioned above, is interrelated to the process of economic planning in that its monetary allocations help distribute resources in accordance with the production programs set forth in the plan. It is a component part of the financial plan, which is integrated with the overall economic plan. Budgetary expenditures on investment, for example, represent a financial reflection of decisions pertaining to priorities that have been established in the economic plan. The monetary allocations of the budget are related to planned output and can serve as a check on the execution of the plan by enterprises since the allocation of funds for investment must be related to the output plans of each enterprise.

The state budget can be called a consolidated budget. This means that the budgets of regional and local government authorities form an integral part of the state budget. The reason for this is that in a socialist command economy the state budget provides an excellent control mechanism over the flow of financial resources. It enforces conformance on the part of all government entities with the state's overall financial policies. The proportion of state budget expenditures allocated to local and regional budgets ranges considerably among the socialist countries.* The federal system of administration and decentralization naturally enhances the role of regional and local entities, and as a result of recent economic reforms the proportion of funds passing through local budgets has tended to increase.

THE DEVELOPMENT OF THE FISCAL SYSTEM

In May 1945 the first public administrative units to resume the fiscal function of revenue collection were the town governments. They levied town taxes based on the old tax laws and also assumed the revenue sources that belonged to the county, state, and national governments. The first change in the tax system was made in the Soviet military decree of June 23, 1945, which set up special financial departments in states, counties, and towns. As Soviet-type large-scale enterprises were set up, levies in the form of payments from profits were paid to the state and county financial departments. Later, as the administration of the government became more centralized, payment was made to the state budget. In 1948 taxes on alcoholic beverages and cigarettes were introduced.

In 1949 important changes were made in the East German fiscal system. Article 119 of the constitution of the GDR transferred the authority to tax to the national government. The state budget became the most important financial organ in the GDR. The Länder, or former state governments, were deprived of their tax authority. They could collect taxes for the national government and regulate the finances of the counties and municipalities. The latter were allowed to keep the property tax and small-business tax. In 1951 the small-business tax was transferred to the national government, completing the process of centralization that had begun in 1949. The shift in taxing authority is reflected in Table 10.1.

By 1950 the framework of the present East German fiscal system had been established. The state budget became the key fiscal instrument

---

*The proportion of the state budget expenditures allocated to local and regional budgets ranged in the early 1960s from 15 percent in Romania, 60 percent in the Soviet Union.

TABLE 10.1

Changes in Distribution of Tax Income,
East Germany, 1946-50
(million Ostmarks)

Government Level	1946	1947	1948	1949	1950
National	—	—	375	2,354	12,253
States (Länder)	7,521	7,863	7,885	7,228	—
Countries and towns	937	1,114	1,167	1,125	1,251
Total	8,458	8,977	9,427	10,707	13,504

Source: Adelbert Kitsche, Das Steuersystem in der Sowjetischen Besatzungszone Deutschlands (Buersche Druckerei Dr. Neufang, Gelsenkirchen-Buer, 1960), p. 44.

of the economy. The Ministry of Finance was made responsible for its preparation. As the principal financial organ of the GDR, the Ministry of Finance was given jurisdiction over the budget system at all levels of government and was made responsible for the preparation of the financial plan. Until the economic reforms of 1964 the state budget was the basic source of financing in the GDR. Most measures in the economic plan were financed from it. The source of most enterprise funds for investment was the state budget. The reforms, however, attached major emphasis to internal financing and bank credits as sources of enterprises investment funds. This has tended to reduce the proportion of funds passing directly through the state budget. During the years 1960-63 around 70 percent of the national income was redistributed through the state budget for planning purposes; in 1968 and 1969 around 60 percent of national income was redistributed by the budget.[1]

THE ORGANIZATION OF THE FISCAL SYSTEM

The most important fiscal organ, as pointed out above, is the Ministry of Finance. It is subordinate to the Council of Ministers, which is responsible for the development of economic policy. The Ministry of Finance and the State Planning Commission are directly responsible for the preparation of the economic plan. It can be said that the Ministry of Finance is more responsible for the preparation

THE FISCAL SYSTEM OF EAST GERMANY 259

of the financial plan, particularly the state budget, and the State Planning Commission is more responsible for the physical output plan. The Ministry of Finance also exercises a very important control function over all financial organs in the GDR. It supervises and exercises control over the budgets of the district, county, and local governmental units. It also exercises control over the banking system by setting up policy rules and guidelines for banks to follow. It is responsible for supervising the cash and credit plans of the banks. The Ministry of Finance is responsible for the collection of all tax revenues in the GDR and for the printing of coins and currency.

The Ministry of Finance has branch finance departments in the districts, countries, and major cities. These departments play an important role in the fiscal system. They are responsible for the collection and disbursement of tax revenues. They assist in the preparation and execution of the state budget. They verify calculations of tax payments made by enterprises and other economic organs under their jurisdiction. The departments also are responsible for seeing that enterprises conform to objectives established in the national economic plan.

The state budget is very important, for through it flows a large part of national income. It is interrelated with the financial plan of the GDR, which is used primarily as a check on the basic plan, which is expressed in physical value terms. The state budget includes the budgets of all political and economic entities in East Germany—the national government, East Berlin, districts, counties, and municipalities and the balances of state enterprises. The fact that it is a consolidated budget means that the state budget is a very important control instrument. The rationale for consolidation is easy to understand. If the economic plan is to function properly, individual economic or political units cannot be permitted to act independently. Consolidation of all budgets enables the Ministry of Finance to see to it that all units are acting within the proper framework of the plan.

Table 10.2 presents a comparison of national income and state budget statistics for the period 1960-69. National income is a measure of income earned by resource owners by supplying the services of economic resources to the productive process. The purpose of comparing state budget expenditures to national income is to show the extent of the direct participation of the state in the economy. It is necessary to point out that the size of the state budget may be overstated to some extent. One reason is that intragovernmental transfers are doubly counted.[2]

The development of income and expenditures in the state budget has been influenced by various economic reforms since 1964. The most important reform has been the gradual introduction of the principle of self-financing, which obliges the state-owned enterprises to

TABLE 10.2

Comparison of State Budget Expenditures to National
Income, East Germany, 1960-69
(billion Ostmarks)

Year	State Budget Expenditures	National Income
1960	49.4	71.0
1961	50.8	73.1
1962	55.5	75.2
1963	56.1	76.7
1964	56.3	80.5
1965	55.8	84.2
1966	60.8	88.3
1967	59.0	93.0
1968	59.5	97.8
1969	65.0	102.8

Source: Staatliche Zentralverwaltung für Statistik, Statistisches Jahrbuch der Deutschen Demokratischen Republik, 1970, (East Berlin: Staatsverlag der DDR, 1970), pp. 17, 323.

finance investments largely from their profits or by obtaining credit from the banks. The purpose is to promote more efficiency and self-reliance on the part of the enterprises. Before the reforms the great bulk of enterprise investments were financed directly from the state budget. This reform has led to some relief for the state budget in that income and expenditures have been reduced. Profits from the state-owned enterprises have been increasingly credited to enterprise funds rather than to the state budget. Now only completely new investments deemed to have top state priority in terms of their improving the economic infrastructure are financed by nonrepayable grants from the state budget.

The reforms have also granted more autonomy to county and municipal governmental units with respect to the use of revenues. For example, more revenue in the form of certain taxes is turned back to the municipalities. Sharing is done in such a way to encourage assemblies and councils of these municipalities to raise their performance standards in terms of providing better facilities and services. In accordance with the principle that good management yields economic advantages, all additionally generated funds brought about by improved

THE FISCAL SYSTEM OF EAST GERMANY 261

services can remain with the municipalities. Districts and counties are to receive increased shares of the taxes paid by consumer cooperatives. Municipalities have been given the exclusive right to levy resort fees and luxury taxes to improve the level of resort and recreation activities and to implement cultural measures.

The Preparation of the State Budget

The state budget, as mentioned previously, is a consolidation of the budgets of all political and territorial units in the GDR. It is prepared by the Ministry of Finance basically as follows.

1. The councils of the municipalities develop their budget plans on the basis of planning directives issued by the Ministry of Finance. They must prepare their budgets and defend them before the state financial organs responsible for their jurisdiction.

2. The county councils and assemblies develop their plans also on the basis of planning directives, which they receive from the Ministry of Finance. They prepare the county budgets, listing sources of revenues and types of expenditures. When the budgets are prepared, they must be defended by the county councils before the financial organs of the state.

3. The district assemblies develop their budgets within the framework of state budget standards. The assemblies are also responsible for setting budget standards for the counties and municipalities under their jurisdiction. On the basis of state planning figures, the districts prepare their budgets and defend them before the district branches of the Ministry of Finance.

4. All state organs and state enterprises subordinate to the ministries must prepare their budgets. These budgets must also account for all income and proposed expenses. They are sent to the Ministry of Finance for approval. Also included at the state level is the social insurance budget.

5. The process of budget reconciliation is the responsibility of the Ministry of Finance and the State Planning Commission. The Ministry of Finance reviews all of the budget plans and compares them to the objectives of the financial plan. After the budgets are approved, the Ministry of Finance prepares a draft budget that is sent to the Council of Ministers for approval. The State Planning Commission is supposed to see that the draft budget conforms to the national economic plan. When the budget is approved by the Council of Ministers, it is then sent to the Volkskammer (People's Chamber). A budgetary committee is supposed to review the draft budget and make recommendations to the Council of Ministries. Acceptance of the budget by the Volkskammer, however, is a formality. The budget

is adopted and returned to the Ministry of Finance, where it is put in final form. The consolidated state budget then becomes the formal budget of the land.

The income and expenditures of the state budget are kept in state budget accounts in banks authorized to implement budget tasks. These accounts cover all budgetary transactions down to the local level. The finance departments of the districts, counties, and municipalities have to keep budget subaccounts for the entry of income to the credit of the state budget, as well as for payments charged to the state budget. Budget subaccounts are handled by branch banks at the district, county, and local levels.

The State Budget for 1971

The total revenues and expenditures of the GDR for 1971 are estimated to be 85.9 and 85.8 billion Ostmarks respectively.[3] These revenues and expenditures of the state are derived from two sources: the funds that must be deducted from profits and used in accordance with the objectives of the economic plan, by all state enterprises and combines; and the revenues and expenditures of the state budget. According to the plan for 1971 the VEBs, state-owned combines, and the VVBs must set aside, out of their profits, the amount of 10.1 billion Ostmarks for expanded capital investment, working capital, and personal material incentives.[4] This amount is in accordance with the principle that the means for expanded production must be self-earned. Since 1965 profit deductions for the above purposes are added to the total volume of state revenues and expenditures, although they are not included in the state budget. There has been a shift in the financing of current production and investments from the state budget to internal sources of financing and credit from the banking system.

The remaining amounts of 75.8 billion Ostmarks in revenues and 75.7 billion Ostmarks in expenditures is represented in the state budget. The state budget usually shows an annual surplus of revenues over expenditures. This surplus has two important functions: in terms of fiscal policy, it has an anti-inflationary effect on the economy in that more money is withdrawn from the economy than is put into it; and it is used to increase the resources of the State Bank (Staatsbank). The state budget can also provide a further fiscal policy effect on the economy through changes in revenues and expenditures.

The state budget can be broken down into categories expressed in terms of territorial organization. There is the national budget of the GDR, district (Bezirk) budgets, county (Kreis) budgets, and local budgets. The expenditures and revenues of these budgets are controlled by the state budget. There is a reason for this control. The state cannot be indifferent to the independent raising and spending of finance, as it might be in conflict with the state's overall financial policy, economic planning, and the utilization of resources. Typically, taxes and expenditures are centralized in terms of determination. The proportion of funds passing through district, county, and local budget has tended to increase as a result of the economic reforms, however.

Although it is difficult to be specific about the East German budgetary system, the following outline emerges: local, county, district, and national budgets comprise the state budget. Each individual budget reflects the responsibility of the political unit to which it is attached.

Local Budgets

In East Germany local governments have some autonomy in terms of revenue sources. The 1970 budget law permits local governments to receive revenue from the following sources:[5]

1. Net profit levy, production and service taxes, and the trade tax of enterprises under the jurisdiction of the local councils;
2. Community taxes and taxes from the LPGs (agricultural producer cooperatives);
3. Revenues of technical agencies under the jurisdiction of local councils;
4. Taxes from cooperatives, enterprises with government participation, private industry, commission merchants, professional persons, and miscellaneous taxes, unless specified by law;
5. Taxes on private craftsmen and artisans and craft cooperatives; and
6. Revenues from the state budget.

Local government expenditures provide goods and services in the form of police and fire protection, maintenance of roads, construction of public facilities, provision of fuel and water, and the provision of health and cultural services. Other expenses financed out of local government budgets include the support of athletic competition, awards to students and participants in competition, bonuses to exceptional workers, and subsidies to theaters and entertainment enterprises.

County and City Budgets

The county (Kreis) and city (Stadtkreis) budgets are similar in design to the local budgets. The sources of revenue for the counties and cities are varied. Taxes from the LPGs provide one source of revenue.[6] The cities and counties also share revenues with the municipalities from taxes on other types of cooperatives, such as craftsman and artisan cooperatives, and revenues of county agencies under their jurisdiction. The land acquisition tax and land tax also provide budgetary revenues. The bulk of revenue is obtained from the state budget.

The county councils are responsible for the development and repair of roads under their jurisdiction. They are also responsible for financing the provision of certain goods and social services. For example, they are responsible for maintaining and expanding state housing, communal facilities, and administrations on the basis of the state financial plan, to the extent that responsibility for state housing has not been assigned to other administrative units. In 1971 the county and cities will have the right to finance tasks that are to be carried out on a supplementary basis within state limits.

District Budgets

The district (Bezirk) budgets are supposed to contain planned expenditures of 15.4 billion Ostmarks in 1971.[7] Revenues are also planned at 15.4 billion Ostmarks. Revenues are set in the state budget and are designed to cover administrative costs of all district government units, as well as certain other functions over which the districts have jurisdiction. Revenues come from several sources, including funds of the state budget, shared taxes with county and local governments, loans, and charges of district government enterprises.

The National Budget

The national budget includes the receipts and expenditures of the central government. Included in the expenditures are defense, public administration, consumer subsidies, investment grants to enterprises, and social consumption expenditures. Total national budget revenues and expenditures for 1971 are approximately 60 billion Ostmarks.[8]

Government Expenditures

The state budget, as mentioned previously, is interrelated to the process of economic planning in that its monetary allocations help distribute resources in accordance with the production programs set forth in the plan. It is a component part of the financial plan, which is integrated with the overall economic plan. Budgetary expenditures on investment, for example, represent a financial reflection of decisions pertaining to priorities that have been established in the economi plan. The monetary allocations of the budget are related to planned output and can serve as a check on the execution of the plan by East German enterprises since the allocations of funds for investment must be related to the output plans of each enterprise.

A general idea of the overall planned expenditures of the state budget can be gathered from Table 10.3. The expenditures are expressed as a percentage of the total amount. The types of expenditures have certain objectives within the framework of the East German economy. It is possible to identify these objectives by examining the expenditure items listed under each category of expenditure.

Financing the Socialist Economy

Expenditures under this category would include allocations to state enterprises for capital investments and for working capital. Capital goods and construction industries are the major recipients of budget funds for investment purposes, for the government concentrates on growth-inducing investments in areas that constitute the base of economic power. Appropriations from the state budget are also used to finance the construction of transportation facilities, investment in state farms, and housing construction. State farms are government owned and operated, and they are a major recipient of state funds.

Expenditures on the socialist economy are projected to be 9.7 billion Ostmarks in the 1971 state budget. A general breakdown of these expenditures is as follows:[9]

1. Appropriations for investment grants, 6.5 billion Ostmarks;
2. Appropriations to finance selected scientific and technical operations of state-owned enterprises, 1 billion Ostmarks; and
3. Appropriations to promote productivity in agriculture, 2.2 billion Ostmarks.

Social and Cultural Measures

Included under this category are education, culture, health, and welfare. Expenditures on education include construction and maintenance costs of schools, payment of teachers' salaries, and provision of financial support for students. Also included would be the support of certain types of scientific research. Expenditures on culture include support for museums, expositions, and the fine arts. Health expenditures cover outlays for medical and hospital facilities, training of medical personnel, and medical research. Physical culture expenditures are also included under the general category of social and

TABLE 10.3

Structure of Expenditures in East German
State Budget, 1971

Expenditures	Percentage
Socialist economy	12.8
Education	10.1
Culture	2.0
Health and welfare	8.3
Social security	19.4
Housing construction	7.1
Defense	9.5
Miscellaneous	30.8
Total	100.0

Source: Deutsches Institut für Wirtschaftsforschung, Der Staatsplan der DDR 1971 (East Berlin, January 15, 1971), p. 16.

cultural measures and are used to support the athletic programs, which are carried on throughout East Germany. The following outlays for education and health are projected in the 1971 state budget:[10]

1. The sum of 6.4 billion Ostmarks is allocated to the East German educational system. This amount is to be supplemented by an additional 655.8 million Ostmarks from the state budget to replace and expand the basic funds of the educational institutions and also 582.7 million Ostmarks, which will be raised by loans.

2. A total of 6 billion Ostmarks is allocated to support health measures. To replace and expand the basic assets of the state health and social welfare institutions, an additional amount of 169.9 million Ostmarks is to be financed from the state budget and 117.3 million Ostmarks from credits.

Expenditures for social (including social security), cultural, and scientific measures are of great importance in the state budget of the GDR. In 1970 nearly 40 percent of total expenditures fall in the above categories. In 1971 30 billion Ostmarks are allocated in the state budget for social welfare purposes. Of this amount, 14.7 billion Ostmarks is allocated to social security, and the remainder to education, culture, and health.[11] An increase over 1970 expenditures is planned for education. In 1971 23.6 percent more money is to be put at the disposal of universities and technical schools than in 1970. Within this figure, expenditures on the construction of teachers' colleges, boarding schools, and student dormitories are to increase by 50 percent over 1970.[12]

Social Security

Social security expenditures, set at 14.7 billion Ostmarks for 1971, are the largest single item of expenditures in the state budget.[13] The amount is only partially covered by contributions from the insured; more than a third—approximately 5.8 billion Ostmarks—of the funds come from state budget subsidies.[14] Receipts and expenditures for social security are carried in a social insurance budget, which forms a part of the state budget. Contributions are collected by local tax offices of the Ministry of Finance. In the case of workers and members of families who assist in a business the person responsible for payment is the manager of the business; he has to pay over the contributions every month and deducts the insured person's contribution from his wages. Self-employed persons have to pay their own contributions and must make quarterly payments in advance.

Although social security benefits are part of the subject matter to be covered in the chapter on income distribution, the rudiments of the system are as follows:[15]

1. Old-age and invalidity pensions and survivors' benefits constitute one part of the system. Old-age pensions are provided to males over 65 and females over 60. Benefits are financed by levies on all insured persons and employers. Any deficit is supported by funds from the state budget. Fees are collected by local financial offices of the Ministry of Finance, and payments are administered by the trade unions or by the National Insurance Institution, which is responsible for the insurance of production cooperatives and self-employed persons.[16]

2. Sickness and maternity benefits are also payable to all persons under the East German social insurance system. Medical benefits involve payment of general and specialist care, hospitalization, laboratory services, maternity care, and out-patient treatment. Maternity benefits include cash payments, medical expenses, and home care.

3. Disability benefits are also paid to East German workers. Included are temporary disability benefits and permanent disability pensions. Also included are medical care, retraining, nursing allowances, survivors' pensions, and children's allowances.

4. Although unemployment is not supposed to exist in a socialist planned economy, unemployment compensation is part of the East German social insurance system. Benefits are based on need. No claim for relief can be made if an unemployed person has income in an amount greater than the unemployment benefit.

5. The family allowance represents another type of social insurance payment. It is paid to families with one or more children and is financed by general budget revenues rather than by contributions from workers and employers.

Housing Construction

Housing construction enjoys a high priority in terms of allocation of budgetary funds because there is an acute housing shortage, particularly in the large cities. Funds allocated to housing construction are of two types—funds that are made available to construction enterprises for building apartments and other dwellings and funds that are provided to individual home builders in the form of credit.

In 1971 5.4 billion Ostmarks have been earmarked for apartment construction.[17] This amount is supposed to provide 64,000 new apartments. In this connection it should be pointed out that the building of one-family homes is to be made more difficult by the alteration of conditions for obtaining mortgages. Until 1971 the building of one-family homes was promoted by the granting of state credits at very favorable rates. In the future, these conditions will no longer apply. This step may be explained in part by the paucity of construction capacity, which cannot be sufficiently rationalized in the building of one-family homes. There are also political implications, however. The state feels that it cannot justify the provision of above-average housing facilities for a small number of persons by providing subsidies that have to be paid for by all of the working people.[18]

Defense

Outlays for defense in 1971 are supposed to amount to around 7 billion Ostmarks, or around 9.5 percent of total budget expenditures.[19] This amount may well understate the amount that is actually spent for defense-related activities, however, because a substantial proportion of military research is carried out under other categories in the state budget. For example, expenditures for science include outlays for research and development of complex military equipment, such as aircraft and missiles. The general defense category includes monetary and material allowances for armed forces personnel, payment for supplies and repair of combat equipment, maintenance of military installations and schools, and military construction.

Miscellaneous Expenditures

Expenditures under the miscellaneous category are difficult to classify. Presumably consumer price subsidies is one item carried under it. In 1970 the following subsidies were financed from the state budget:[20]

1. Subsidies for the maintenance of low retail prices for milk, butter, bread, meat, and potatoes, 4.6 billion Ostmarks;

THE FISCAL SYSTEM OF EAST GERMANY

2. Subsidies for industrial products such as children's wear, brown coal briquettes, and coke, 0.8 billion Ostmarks;
3. Subsidies for passenger transport, 1 billion Ostmarks; and
4. Subsidies for living accommodations, including rent, 2.2 billion Ostmarks.

Budget expenditure for administration is another item that is presumably carried under miscellaneous expenditures. This includes financing for local and central government agencies such as planning and financial bodies, ministries, government departments, and the courts and judicial organs. In this connection it is necessary to remember that the East German state budget covers a scope of activities much broader than equivalent activities financed in the budget of West Germany. The state budget covers the planned expenditures for all levels of government in East Germany.

Government Budget Receipts

In the GDR the means of production belong to the state. Therefore, the state budget is supposed to influence, in accordance with political and economic objectives, the incomes of all economic groups. The budget is used to direct material consumption according to the objectives of the national economic plan. The economic plan, which is based on production, and the financial plan, including the budget, which is based on the distribution of the national income, are compiled and harmonized in similar fashion. Thus, the basis for the development of revenues are tax regulations and the financial plan. The framework of the East German revenue system is as follows:

1. All levies on the state-owned enterprises are set in the state financial plan.
2. Taxes on cooperatives are generally based on their financial plans.
3. Taxes on the incomes of white and blue collar workers and self-employed persons are based on the wage sums allocated in the financial plan.
4. Taxes on the private sector of the economy are generally based on indexes for production, partially the turnover of goods, as determined in the economic plan.
5. Taxes on craftsmen and artisans are estimated, based on the craft tax law.
6. Taxes levied on farmers are based generally on such indexes as the assessed value of animal and land production.

Total government revenues in the GDR are obtained from several sources—deductions from profits, turnover taxes, income taxes, and various other taxes, including excise taxes on tobacco and alcohol and property taxes. State enterprises provide the bulk of the receipts to the state budget. This is understandable for the reason that the state is the owner of the enterprises and contributes to their support out of the state budget. Thus, the first claimant upon enterprise profits is the state. It is also important to note that budget revenues consist of a large number of taxes, collections, and payments. An attempt will be made to classify the main sources of budgetary revenues. A distinction will be made, where possible, between state and local budget revenue sources. Certain state budget revenues are shared with local budgets, and certain types of taxes are the domain of county and local government units.

Deductions from Profits

This revenue source is not considered a profits tax but is regarded as a form of deduction from the surplus product created in the state sector by state enterprises. The distribution of profits falls into two categories—profits retained by enterprises and used to finance various internal funds, such as the material-incentives fund and the sociocultural fund, and profits paid into the state budget. These profits can be broken down into three categories: profits paid to the budget as capital charges; profits paid to the budget for financing investment, including credit repayment and expansion of working capital; and profits paid to the budget as a free or uncommitted remainder. To an enterprise this free remainder represents the proportion of funds that are not committed to any particular fund or budget charge. With increased emphasis in the GDR placed on internal sources of financing for enterprises, the proportion of profits going to the state budget has tended to decrease. An increase in profits brought about by the financial reforms, however, should increase the absolute amount of profits flowing into the state budget.

Deductions from profits are made by all state enterprises and combines. Excluded are consumer cooperatives, agricultural cooperatives, and private enterprises, which are subject to income taxation. Deductions are usually based on the actual rather than on the planned profits of enterprises and can vary from industry to industry. The rate for a particular enterprise is fixed on the basis of its financial plan for the year. The final selling price of products produced by the enterprise is designed to cover its cost of production and planned profit. The latter may or may not occur depending upon the efficiency of the enterprise. Each enterprise has the right to retain part of its profit for such purposes as expanding its fixed and working capital, and in setting the rate of the profit deduction the government takes this into consideration.

The rates of deductions from profits are set by the Ministry of Finance for a period of one to two years and are determined in such a way that they have the desired effect on the internal and external economic policies of the GDR. Enterprises that produce export goods of a high quality, thus contributing favorably to the balance of trade, pay rates that are set at around 35 percent of net profits. These rates are considered low and are designed to enable enterprises to utilize a higher percentage of their net profits for the modernization of plants and equipment and for contributions to the material incentive fund and other funds designed to increase plant productivity. Enterprises that do not enjoy high priorities in terms of their contribution to the improvement of the infrastructure of the economy have to pay a higher rate to the state budget out of net profits. For example, seven enterprises of the VVB (Association of State Enterprises) for Industrial Plant Assemblies and Steel Construction were assigned a deduction rate that ranged from 35 to 70 percent during the period 1969-70.[21] The differentiated rates were based upon the importance of the different enterprise operations to the structural development of the economy.

The Production Fund Levy

The production fund levy is applied to all state enterprises and combines and to industries managed or controlled by the districts, counties, and municipalities. It is expressed as a percentage of the gross value of capital goods and current material assets. The rate and volume of the levy are set in the state financial plan. Enterprises have to pay the levy out of their profits into the state budget. The levy is included as a part of the internal accounting of enterprises and is included in their financial plan as a direct payment to the state. Prior to 1971 the levy was differentiated according to the economic importance of the enterprise. In 1971, however, the levy was set at a flat 6 percent of the working capital of all enterprises.[22] Special exemptions must be obtained from the Ministry of Finance.

The Turnover Tax

The turnover tax (Umsatzsteuer) is the most important source of tax revenue in the state budget. The tax represents the difference between the total cost of production of a commodity and the price it brings as an article of general expenditures on the market. It represents a firmly fixed portion of the price and is delivered to the state budget in accordance with sales of goods on which the tax is levied. The tax is collected by wholesalers, retailers, individual enterprises, and procurement organizations dealing with consumer goods and foodstuffs. As a rule, the following procedure is followed: If enterprises making goods subject to the tax sell them directly to buyers or to trade organizations, then the turnover tax is paid by the enterprises themselves according to the place of production of such goods; if, however, goods are sold through the wholesale organizations, then the turnover tax is paid by the latter at the place of sale of the goods. The burden of the turnover tax ultimately falls on the East German consumer, so that it can be considered to represent a part of the flow of funds between the state and households.

There are certain exemptions from the turnover tax.[23] Imports of needed raw materials are exempted from the tax. Goods designed for export receive favorable treatment in that there is a rebate to producers for the amount of turnover tax claimed in the production process. The amount of water, gas, and electricity purchased by consumers is exempt. The self-use of products by agricultural and forest enterprises is exempt if the turnover is less than 6,000 Ostmarks a year. Property transactions are generally exempt from the tax. Medical services, provided they are covered by insurance, are exempt. Any payment in kind is exempt from the tax.

The basic rate of the turnover tax is 3 percent.[24] The rate of the tax, however, is differentiated by commodities and between enterprises producing similar goods. In general the following patterns of rates emerge.[25] The rate is 1.5 percent for products produced for internal use. The rate is also 1.5 percent of the retail price on basic foodstuffs. The rate is 3.75 percent on enterprises with a turnover of more than 1 million Ostmarks a year. The basic rate of 3 percent is levied on the retail price of most consumer products. Rates in excess of 4 percent are levied on products that have an inelastic demand schedule—beer, cosmetics, tobacco, and articles made of precious metals.

The turnover tax is complex. The rates vary from city to city and region to region, and they may be imposed in three ways, as follows:

1. As an absolute sum per unit of a commodity;
2. As a percentage of the full retail sales price of a commodity; or
3. As a difference between retail sales less the retail markup and the enterprise wholesale price.

The turnover tax is in actuality a broad-based sales tax since it applies, on a gross basis, to all transactions through which a tangible economic good passes. Thus, it exercises a significant influence on the distribution of income in East Germany. This is true because of its regressivity to income as a tax base. Since the marginal and average propensities to consume tend to be lower at higher-income levels, the purchase of items subject to the turnover tax is ordinarily a smaller proportion of the higher incomes. It should be remembered that the turnover tax is a "cascade" tax, the amount getting larger as the number of transactions increases. Therefore, the final market price of consumer goods could contain a number of turnover taxes. Since the turnover tax is normally the largest single source of revenue for the state budget, the potential effects on the nature of income distribution are significant. The progressivity of the state income tax, however, may have some neutralizing offset effect on the regressive distribution effects of the turnover tax. This would appear to be minor for the reason that progressivity in the income tax system extends down into the lowest income levels.

It is also necessary to mention the importance of the turnover tax as an instrument of state control. In addition to being a principal source of revenue for the budget it also serves to absorb the excess purchasing power of consumers. The production plans of the national government provide that a given amount of goods be made available to consumers annually. On the other hand, in order to maintain incentives and partly because of errors in planning, consumers may receive more purchasing power than can be absorbed by the goods made available to them at controlled prices. This excess of purchasing power is siphoned off by the turnover tax, which has the impact of an excise or sales tax, as it is applied primarily to consumer goods. It is not a fixed-rate tax, with the yield an independent variable, but, on the contrary, is a tax whose desired yield determines the rate, which also varies in response to particular supply and demand conditions. The turnover tax guarantees a steady inflow of funds to the budget and is easy to collect and inexpensive to administer.

Income Taxation

Unlike most socialist countries, East Germany places considerable reliance on income taxation as a source of revenue. The income tax is levied on the following sources: wages of individuals, income of agriculture and forestry, capital income, income from independent work, and income of small business enterprises.[26] Certain income is exempt from taxation, including social security payments, welfare payments, stipends for students paid from public sources, and rents and payments to "fighters against fascism."[27] There are also special forms of income exemptions. National prizes and awards are exempt from taxation. Interest on savings accounts and on the bonds of the district and national government is also exempt. Maternity payments and special benefits are not taxed.

In addition to personal exemptions there are deductions for various types of expenses.[28] Debt interest is deductible. Other deductions include property taxes, fees for professional associations, expenditures for travel between the home and the job, expenses for professional improvement, and expenses for tools and working clothes. Family deductions are also permitted. There are deductions of 300 Ostmarks for each child and 500 Ostmarks for the spouse. Support of parents is also deductible, provided that they are unable to work. Special provisions are also made for older workers. A man is entitled to a special deduction of 120 Ostmarks a year if he is 64 years or over, and a woman is entitled to the same deduction if she is 49 years or over. All of the family deductions are permitted only for taxpayers whose incomes are less than 20,000 Ostmarks a year.

An interesting phenomenon of the East German income tax is that the taxpayer can be taxed on his consumption expenditures, provided that they are more than 10,000 Ostmarks a year and are at least 50 percent higher than his actual income. The purpose of this provision is two-fold: there is a control function in that consumption over a certain amount is penalized, while savings are rewarded; and there is the attempt to get at expenditures based on capital income. Remnants of the rentier class still exist in East Germany.

The income tax is progressive, the rates depending on the source and size of income. Discriminatory rates are so designed as to inhibit the accumulation of excessive profits by nonstate enterprises and to prevent private enrichment. The degree of tax progression on incomes earned by free professionals, i.e., individuals not directly employed by state enterprises, is markedly greater than the progression on the income of wage and salary earners. For example, the tax schedule for certain occupational groups, including lawyers, artisans, engineers, architects, commercial artists, advertising experts, and other free-lance operators was amended in 1971 through the introduction of a progressive tax scale starting with an income of more than 20,000 Ostmarks a year up to a maximum rate of 60 percent.[29] The existing tax system is maintained for all freelance individuals with an income of up to 20,000 Ostmarks per year. The degree of progression is actually much greater for private craftsmen and entrepreneurs, extending to 90 percent of incomes in excess of 500,000 Ostmarks a year.[30] Personal income taxes are also levied on farmers selling privately grown produce directly to consumers and in addition on the private owners of buildings, rooms, and equipment.

The rates of the personal income tax are presented in Table 10.4. It is necessary to remember that there is discrimination in the use of these rates against freelance individuals employed indirectly by the state, private entrepreneurs, and farmers selling produce directly to consumers. The maximum effective tax rate on wage and

TABLE 10.4

Income Tax Rates, East Germany

Income Class (Ostmarks)	Tax Rate* Ostmarks	Percent
Less than 1,200	0 +	0
1,200 - 1,800	16 +	15
1,800 - 2,400	106 +	18
2,400 - 3,600	214 +	24
3,600 - 4,800	502 +	30
4,800 - 6,000	862 +	35
6,000 - 7,200	1,282 +	37
7,200 - 9,000	1,726 +	40
9,000 - 12,000	2,446 +	46
12,000 - 15,000	3,826 +	51
15,000 - 20,000	5,356 +	69
20,000 - 30,000	8,800 +	80
30,000 - 40,000	16,800 +	84
40,000 - 50,000	25,200 +	88
50,000 - 250,000	34,000 +	89
250,000 - 300,000	212,000 +	90
300,000 - 400,000	257,000 +	95
400,000 - 500,000	352,000 +	98
500,000 +		90

*Tax rate for any one income class is the sum of the Ostmark levy and the indicated percent of income in excess of the minimum income for each class.

Source: Gesetzblatt der Deutschen Demokratischen Republik, "Einkommensteuergesetz" (East Berlin: Staatsverlag der DDR, 1970), p. 12.

salary workers employed directly by state enterprises, combines, and cooperatives is 30 percent.

It is significant to note that the income tax reaches down into the lowest income levels. The minimum monthly wage in East Germany in 1970 was 300 Ostmarks, and the average monthly wage of industrial workers in 1969 was 734 Ostmarks. Despite the number of exemptions and deductions, most of which are also available in West Germany, the tax burden is considerable even at low income levels. Certainly, a graduated tax on personal income, particularly when coupled with government transfer and expenditure programs and perhaps with other government programs such as minimum wage laws, can at least erase some of the more glaring disparities in the distribution of wealth and income. But the redistributive effect of the East German income tax seems to be somewhat minimal when the tax is examined. In fact, when the turnover tax is also considered, the tax burden on individuals may be proportional or even regressive.

Table 10.5 presents changes in monthly incomes and changes in taxes for single persons, married persons with one child, and married persons with three children. A change in monthly income from 400 to 500 Ostmarks for a single person is accompanied by a change in income taxation of 24 Ostmarks. This is a marginal tax rate of 24 percent. The table indicates some sort of progressivity in reverse. For example, the marginal tax rate on an income change of 600 to 700 Ostmarks a month for a couple with one child is 34 percent compared with a marginal tax rate of 20 percent for a change of 3,000 to 4,000 Ostmarks a month. The corresponding rates in West Germany, given the same situation, are 19 percent and 34 percent, respectively.[31] It is apparent that at relatively low income limits, the progressivity of the income tax stops and proportionate marginal rates begin. These rates stop at 20 percent on the highest income levels.

The discussion of the East German income tax rate structure can be enhanced by comparing the average and marginal rates of tax. The average tax rate is computed by dividing the tax liability by the tax base. The marginal tax rate is computed by dividing the change in total tax liability by the change in the total tax base. If the tax rate structure is proportionate, the marginal rate must be equal to the average rate as the tax base increases in size. If the tax rate structure is progressive, the marginal rate must be higher than the average rate as the tax rate increases. If the tax rate structure is regressive, the marginal rate must be less than the average rate as the tax base increases. In Table 10.6 the marginal and average rates for single persons and married persons with one child are compared.

TABLE 10.5

Changes in Monthly Income and in Income
Taxation, East Germany
(Ostmarks)

Monthly Income	Single	Married with one Child	Married with three Children
400- 500	24.0	20.0	15.0
500- 600	30.0	24.0	20.0
600- 700	34.0	30.0	24.0
700- 800	22.5	34.0	30.0
800- 900	22.5	22.5	34.0
900-1,000	22.5	22.5	22.5
1,000-1,260	22.5	22.5	22.5
1,260-1,500	20.0	21.0	22.1
1,500-2,000	20.0	20.0	20.0
2,000-3,000	20.0	20.0	20.0
3,000-4,000	20.0	20.0	20.0

Source: Deutscher Bundestag, Materialien zum Bericht zur Lage der Nation 1971, Drucksache VI/1690 (Bonn-Bad Godesberg: Dr. Hans Heger Verlag, 1971), p. 338.

Social Insurance Taxes

Taxes to finance the East German social security system are levied as a percentage of wages and salaries. The revenue is paid into a state social insurance budget, which is consolidated with the state budget. Disbursement of social insurance funds is the responsibility of the trade unions. The financing of the social insurance system is as follows:[32]

1. Old-age pensions, health care, and maternity benefits are financed by a tax of 10 percent of earnings up to 600 Ostmarks a month on the workers and a payroll tax of 10 percent on employers. Self-employed persons pay a tax of 14 percent of monthly earnings up to 600 Ostmarks a month, and mining enterprises pay a payroll tax of 20 percent. There are special tax rates for members of cooperatives. Any deficit is supported by funds from the state budget.

2. Work-injury and unemployment compensation are financed by a tax on payrolls of employers, which ranges from 0.3 to 3 percent a month. Maximum earnings upon which contributions are based

TABLE 10.6

Comparison of Marginal and Average Income Tax Rates, East Germany
(percent)

Monthly Income (Ostmarks)	Single Person Marginal	Single Person Average	Married with One Child Marginal	Married with One Child Average	Married with Three Children Marginal	Married with Three Children Average
400– 500	24.0	9.5	20.0	4.5	15.0	0.8
500– 600	30.0	12.4	24.0	7.6	20.0	3.6
600– 700	34.0	15.3	30.0	10.3	24.0	6.3
700– 800	22.5	18.0	34.0	13.1	30.0	8.9
800– 900	22.5	18.6	22.5	15.8	34.0	11.5
900–1,000	22.5	19.0	22.5	16.5	22.5	14.0
1,000–1,260	22.5	19.4	22.5	17.1	22.5	14.9
1,260–1,500	20.0	20.0	21.0	18.2	22.1	16.4
1,500–2,000	20.0	20.0	20.0	18.7	20.0	17.3
2,000–3,000	20.0	20.0	20.0	19.0	20.0	18.0
3,000–4,000	20.0	20.0	20.0	19.3	20.0	18.7

Source: Deutscher Bundestag, Materialen zum Bericht zur Lage der Nation 1971 (Bonn–Bad Godesberg: Dr. Hans Heger Verlag, 1971), pp. 338–39.

amount to 600 Ostmarks a month. Any deficit is supported by funds from the state budget.

3. Family allowances are financed entirely from the funds of the state budget. There are no contributions from employers and employees.

It is significant to note that a major part of social insurance expenditures in East Germany are financed out of the general tax revenues of the state budget. The apportionment of these expenditures, however, varies for the different types of social welfare service. The cost of the family allowance is borne entirely by the state out of general tax revenues. Old-age pensions and sickness insurance benefits are financed by employee and employer contributions, with the state making up any deficit. Unemployment compensation is financed by employers, with the state financing any deficit.

Other Taxes

In addition to the turnover and personal income taxes, which constitute important sources of revenue to the state budget, there are other taxes that also provide revenue. Some of the more important are as follows:

1. There is a corporate income tax (Korperschaftsteuer), which is levied primarily on private corporations in the GDR. As there are few of these left, the tax is not an important revenue source. The tax is imposed on incomes from agriculture and forestry, trade, and other business activities. Certain expenditures, including depreciation, debt interest, and social security payments, are deductible. After deductions and exemptions the rate of the tax starts at 16 percent on an income of 1,200 Ostmarks and increases progressively.[33] The highest marginal rate is 95 percent on incomes in excess of 250,000 Ostmarks.

2. The small business tax (Gewerbesteuer) is levied on all unincorporated enterprises in the GDR. Included are individual entrepreneurs, joint partnerships, trade cooperatives, and mutual insurance companies. Forest associations, religious organizations, and fishing enterprises with less than seven employees are exempt from the tax. Deductions are permitted for debt interest, pension funds, and wages of employees. The rate of the tax is expressed as a percentage of business profits. The first 1,200 Ostmarks are exempt. On the next 1,200 Ostmarks the rate is 1 percent. For each additional 1,200 Ostmarks the rate increases by 1 percent until a maximum of 5 percent is reached on profits of 7,200 Ostmarks and over.[34]

3. There is a capital tax (Vermogensteuer), which is levied on persons, corporations, cooperatives, and other entities in the GDR. Consumer cooperatives, for example, are supposed to turn over a

capital tax and a net profit levy to the state budget. Exempt are all state enterprises that own their own capital shares. For persons the first 10,000 Ostmarks of value of capital is exempted for the spouse and each child under 15. The tax rates are .5 percent on taxable capital up to 25,000 Ostmarks, 1.5 percent on taxable capital between 25,000 and 500,000 Ostmarks, and 2.5 percent on taxable capital of 500,000 Ostmarks and over.[35] For corporations and other entities, capital exemptions from 20,000 to 50,000 Ostmarks are permitted. The tax rates are 2 percent on taxable capital up to 500,000 Ostmarks, and 2.5 percent on taxable capital in excess of 500,000 Ostmarks.[36]

4. The land tax (Grundsteuer) is an important source of local government revenue. Municipalities are entitled to levy a tax on the ownership of agriculture, forestry, and business properties. Exemptions are permitted for the property of a state enterprise, provided that it is used for business purposes. Properties of religious organizations are also exempt. Housing is exempt. To compute the tax, a rate, which is not uniform, is levied on the assessed value of property.[37] The actual rate is determined by the Ministry of Finance and not the localities.

5. The land acquisitions tax (Grunderwerbsteuer) is levied on the purchase and sale of land. Exempt are sales of land valued at less than 200 Ostmarks. The basis for the tax is the sales price of the land or, if ownership has changed hands without a sale, the value of the land. The rate of the tax is a flat 7 percent of the price of the land.[38] The county councils have control over this tax.

6. Other sources of revenue include a tax on the purchase of motor vehicles, an insurance tax, motor vehicle license plate charges, a lottery tax, amusement taxes, and an inheritance tax. Some of these taxes, such as the amusement tax, enter into the budgets of local and county governments. Nevertheless, overall control over local revenues remains with the state, although local and county units usually have some discretionary rights to differentiate tax rates within prescribed limits or to grant exemptions.

SUMMARY

The public finance system of the GDR is more comprehensive than the systems of the market economies. The most important instrument for the control and guidance of the finance system is the state budget, which is an integral part of economic planning. The financial plan, of which the state budget is a major component, is always prepared at the same time as the physical output plan. The relationship of the financial and economic plans is obvious. All financial flows are influenced by output plans. Each of the plans can

THE FISCAL SYSTEM OF EAST GERMANY

be realized only when the requirements of the other is fulfilled. The budget, as a part of the financial plan, is the most important vehicle for all payment flows. Through it flow funds to support the investments of state enterprises and transfers to finance many expenditures of lower governmental units. The bulk of collective consumption items, such as education and health, are also financed from the state budget.

The state budget is consolidated. This means that it includes the budgets of all governmental units in the GDR, as well as the budget for social insurance. The purpose of a consolidated budget is to give the state control over the financial activities of all economic and political units. Local government units, however, do have some control over certain types of revenues and expenditures. Local assemblies employ their financial resources in important projects in education and child-care facilities and in health, recreations, and sports activities for their citizens. Taxes paid by cooperatives and private traders can be turned over to the cities and larger communities within a county unit.

The bulk of revenue for the state budget is obtained from levies on what is called the "people-owned" sector of the economy. This term refers to the state enterprises and combines. The levies consist of payments from net profits of enterprises, production taxes, and other types of payments from the "people-owned" sector. The turnover tax is also another source of revenue. This tax applies mostly to consumer goods and some consumer services and represents the difference between producer and retail prices, excluding the wholesale and retail margins for the trading enterprises. There are also income taxes that are levied on cooperatives and private enterprises and on persons. These taxes are progressive, the rates depending on the source and size of income. The rates also vary according to occupations and type of work. Persons who receive an independent income from private sources are taxed at a much higher rate than persons who are employed solely by a state enterprise. Artisans and craftsmen who are self-employed have a separate scale of tax rates. In addition to the turnover and income taxes there are social security taxes, capital and land taxes, and other types of taxes.

CHAPTER 11

INCOME DISTRIBUTION IN EAST GERMANY

INTRODUCTION

Income distribution in the GDR is consciously modeled after the system that prevails in the Soviet Union. It is determined by the state rather than by the marketplace. Income policy has clear-cut aims within the broader compass of the national economic plan. The industrial and agricultural labor force is supposed to deploy itself where needed, to increase the fruits of its efforts, and to advance its skills continuously. Moving about forces workers to take jobs in greater numbers in favored branches of the economy and locations where goods are being produced. New skills must be learned as rapid technological changes develop. Increased production calls for constant attention to objective norms for output and costs. Income distribution is used to reward workers systematically, so that desired behavior is differentially compensated and serves thus as an incentive.

Specifically, income distribution in the GDR refers to the allocation of the national income by distributive shares, primarily in the form of wages and salaries. Since property is owned by the state, there is no income in the form of rent paid to landowners. Interest does figure in the national income to some extent, as a part of income received by individual producers may be considered as interest on the relatively small amounts of capital they own. Interest is also used as a device to encourage personal savings, which are regarded as necessary to put a brake on excess consumer demand, and interest rate differentials exist in favor of long-term savings deposits. Profits, which are distributed in the form of dividends or retained by corporate shareholders in a capitalist system, occupy a different role in the GDR. They are used as a criterion of enterprise performance and, up to a point, of the efficiency of production.

The basic Marxist principle, "from each according to his ability to each according to his needs," does not govern the distribution of income in any socialist country. This principle has been amended "to each according to his ability." Thus, piecework pay, wage differentials, and bonuses to outstanding workers have always been a part of the reward structure in the GDR and other socialist countries. This reliance on material incentives was justified by Lenin himself when he stated that socialism could be established "with the help of enthusiasm born of the great revolution, on personal profit, on self-interest, on economic calculation." The Leninist principle has been accepted ever since as being applicable to the transitional stage that can be called the lower phase of Communism, or socialism, while the Marxist ideal is still considered valid in the long run under full Communism. Whether that ideal is ever attained is debatable.

Wages are only one side of the coin, however. When various government expenditures for free and subsidized consumer services, such as medical benefits and family allowances, are taken into consideration, total income for most workers is increased. Large sums of money are redistributed in East Germany through such transfer payments as old age pensions, sickness and social benefits, and other forms of allowances. The extent to which incomes are redistributed through the medium of transfer payments must be examined carefully, however. First, it is necessary to point out that most transfer payments are made to people regardless of their income category. An example is the family allowance. Second, many transfers take place laterally within income groups. Single persons are taxed more heavily than married persons. The family allowance favors couples with children.

It is also necessary to mention the provision of free education, which provides the opportunity for qualified persons to prepare themselves to participate in the distribution of income. Unquestionably, free education has had an effect on the breaking down of class barriers and providing upward mobility for many persons. Education, as well as other benefits, can be lumped under the general heading of social consumption. All collective goods and services would come under this category. Social consumption is financed from the state budget, social insurance funds, special profit funds of industrial and agricultural enterprises, and resources of localities. The share of social consumption out of total consumption in socialist countries averages around 25 percent.

WAGE SYSTEMS

Wages constitute almost all of the income distributed in the German Democratic Republic and are determined by the government rather than by the market forces of supply and demand. There is a considerable similarity in the function of wages in East and West Germany, however. For one thing, wages constitute a reward for performance and an incentive for continued productive activity in both countries. Wages also constitute a device for evoking a distribution of labor among various occupations and industries. Both functions of necessity call for differences in wages rather than equal wages for all workers. Wage differentials exist to a considerable degree, and scarcity in a particular area or talent affects wage determination in East Germany the same way as in West Germany.

In looking at the wage system in East Germany it is obvious that considerable reliance is placed upon the use of material incentives to stimulate worker productivity. Wages are regarded as remuneration for work in proportion to its quantity and quality. A basic problem in any industrial society is how to motivate workers to perform with optimum efficiency. Regardless of whether enterprises are state-owned or privately owned, productivity is a necessary desideratum for economic development. Slogans, exhortations, shibboleths, and other forms of moral incentives designed to improve the social consciousness of the workers have largely proved inadequate in terms of work motivation.

The Leistungsprinzip

The basis for the East German wage system is codified in the Gesetzbuch der Arbeit in which the principle of performance (Leistungsprinzip) is formally recognized as the main determinant of wage payment.[1] Stated simply, the Leistungsprinzip means that wage payments are tied to the quality of work. Differences in wages are based on the quality of work done by each worker. Piecework pay, wage differentials, and bonuses to outstanding workers have always been a part of the East German reward system. According to the constitution of the GDR only work and its results can determine a person's material and social position.[2] Work is a duty and a matter of honor for every able-bodied citizen, in accordance with the principle, "He who does not work, neither shall he eat."

Industrial Wages

Wages are set by the government within the framework of the national economic plan. The wage system is based on the total wage funds (Gesamtlohnfonds), which is a part of the national economic plan. The computation of the funds is based on the number of employees of the GDR in one plan year; the average rate of increase intended for the average wage earner is figured according to the planned increase in production and productivity for the planning year.[3]

The total wage fund is partitioned into wage funds for all economic fields (Wirtschaftsbereich). Important considerations are national economic policies and enlargement or reduction in importance of certain industrial fields. For example, the plan may call for an increase in chemical output and a decrease in mining output. Then the wage fund of the chemical industry will be increased, and the wage fund of the mining industry decreased. This influences the management of both industrial fields; the chemical industry can create new jobs and the mining industry has to reduce them. The wage levels of the two industries are also influenced. In the chemical industry wages will be raised, and in the mining industry they will be lowered. The purpose of this procedure is to redirect the movement of labor to the chemical industry and also to increase worker productivity.

The wage funds for the various economic fields are then divided into funds for the individual firms. The wage fund for a particular firm consists of the following components:[4]

1. The basic wage including payments for overtime;
2. Wages for workers who are not directly involved in the production process;
3. Extra wages which are based on the difficulty of the work, including payments for night, holiday, and Sunday work; and
4. Additional wages for state holidays, vacations, and participation in public duties.

The unions have little influence upon the development of the wage fund, for procedures are worked out by the state planning commission in the development of the economic plan. The total system of the wage funds is organized from the national level down to the individual firm. This excludes pressure that can be exerted by the unions at the local, county, or district level. The unions can influence the form the wage fund takes at the firm level, particularly with respect to piece rates.

The wage fund actually takes two basic forms—piece wages and time wages. Both are based on work output indicators (Leistungskennziffern), which include a minimum work effort.[5] Then, technically based wage standards (Technisch Begrundete Arbeitsnormen, or TAN) are computed, forming the basis of the wage computation. Fulfillment of the TAN is necessary to receive piece and time wages. The work output indicators and TAN are the responsibility of enterprise management rather than central authority. In this respect, trade unions can have some influence over the wage structure, particularly with respect to piece wages. Usually, the unions will attempt to lower output standards so that overfulfillment is made easier.

One characteristic of the wage system in the GDR is the extensive reliance on the use of piece rates. It is estimated that piece rate payments comprise 50 to 70 percent of the total wages of all industrial workers in East Germany.[6] The merit of the piece-rate system is that it can be used to stimulate worker productivity and to distinguish between good and bad workers. Under this system a base rate is set for performing a given task; for example, workers assembling carburetors in a factory making automobile parts may be paid 1 Ostmark for each carburetor assembled. A slow worker may assemble only 5 carburetors a day, and his wage would accordingly be 5 Ostmarks. An average worker, assembling 8 carburetors a day, would receive 8 Ostmarks, and a superior worker, completing 12, would receive 12 Ostmarks. Each is paid according to his productivity, and the purpose behind this system is to get the workers to produce as large a daily output as possible.

Actually, there are a number of piece-rate arrangements. The arrangement used in East Germany is to establish a normal daily output for the average worker.[7] For example, the average worker may be expected to assemble 5 carburetors a day. The minimum payment is 5 Ostmarks. If a superior worker exceeds the norm, he receives payment in proportion to his productivity in excess of the norm. In addition to the regular piece rate there is a premium piece rate that is tied to factors other than quantity of output. For example, premium piece rates are paid when output meets special quality requirements. The purpose of the premium piece rate is to prevent concentration on quantity of output at the expense of quality.

The most important element of an East German worker's income is his wage, which is paid from the wage fund of each enterprise.[8] In addition to piece wages and time wages, however, there are also bonuses. In fact, piece rates or time rates plus bonuses cover most industrial wage earners. The rationale of the bonus is to tie personal interests of workers more closely to the interests of production. The bonuses are not paid from the wage funds but from incentive funds that are tied to enterprise earnings. Bonuses may be awarded on the basis of individual or collective performance. Individual bonuses are based on the performance of each worker as measured against other workers, while collective bonuses reward a group of workers as a whole and are divided uniformly among the workers. In East Germany incentive funds have averaged about 4 percent of the wage funds in production firms since they were first introduced in 1967. The bonus has ranged from one-third to twice a worker's monthly wage.[9]

Wage Groups

Wages are determined by government fiat. In the GDR the main state agency that is responsible for wage determination is the State Office for Work and Wages (Staatlichen Amt für Arbeit und Löhne). This office is responsible for examining prevailing wage structures and practices within East Germany. It has to approve all collective agreements between unions and management. It participates in the calculation of wages that are a part of the national economic plan, and it is responsible for the classification of workers into wage groups, which are as follows:[10]

1. For production workers, there are eight wage classifications. Classes 1 and 2 are for unskilled and part-time workers; classes 3 and 4 are for semi-skilled workers; class 5 is for skilled workers who passed a special examination, but who have no work experience; classes 6 and 7 are for skilled workers with work experience; and class 8 is for workers with extensive specialized knowledge and work experience. Thus, East German workers are paid according to a multiple wage-grade scale differentiated according to variations in skill from unskilled to highly skilled workers. There are also wage scales within classes. Wage scales by class are also differentiated by branch in line with the East German regime's priorities for differential industrial development.

A standard wage payment pattern is used as the basic pay mechanism for both piece- and time-rate workers in various industries. Each worker is classified by class according to skill and function. Overall satisfactory performance entitles the worker to the standard wage rate for his category. Wage differentials between the highest and lowest wage classes would vary according to the branch of industry. Industries with high priorities have a wage differential as much as 5 to 1 in standard wage payments. This excludes bonuses, superior work performance, and overtime. Wage differentials within classes are much narrower than between class differentials, averaging around 20 percent for the wage scales.

2. There are also eight wage classifications for white collar workers. Straight time rates, usually monthly, are paid to workers in the white collar category. A standard wage for each class is set, which depends upon education, years of service, and other qualifications. There are wage scales within class.

3. There are five wage classifications for management and members of the scientific and technical intelligentsia. The standard wage payment for each class depends on education and work experience. A college education or its equivalent is a basic requisite. Included in the wage groups would be commercial and technical firm managers, branch managers, managers and assistant managers of laboratories

and research branches of a firm, directors of institutes and educational institutions, and any type of person who performs some sort of managerial function.

4. There are four wage classifications for master workers. Included in this category would be electricians, carpenters, construction workers of different skills, and craftsmen of various types.

There are also those workers who would fall outside of the regular classification system. Public service workers have their own wage system, which is set by the state. There are also self-employed persons and workers who are employed by the few remaining private enterprises in the GDR. In this case wages also have to conform to standards set by the state. Wage agreements are concluded between these enterprises and the state.

In total there are 25 wage groups into which all workers, with the exception of public service employees, self-employed persons, and scattered other workers are classified. The wage system is developed and determined by the state. The German Confederation of Free Trade Unions (Freier Deutscher Gewerkschaftsbund, or FDGB) participates in the administration of wages but has little impact on their actual determination. It can make recommendations, but the decisions made by the State Office for Work and Wages are final and must be followed. There is a reason for central planning and decision-making concerning wages. The economic plan has to take into consideration all supply and demand factors, and regulate the distribution of wages, investment, and social income. There has to be a balancing of resources, which is the function of the national economic plan and its planning organs. Interference over wage matters on the part of unions would detract from the necessary balancing of resources.

Agricultural Wages

There is a distinct similarity between agricultural and industrial wages in the GDR in that both are directly tied to performance standards. The State Norm Commission sets the amount to be paid for the various kinds of jobs. Minimum yearly work standards are established at a general meeting of all members of an agricultural unit. Work is evaluated by various evaluation groups depending on the type and responsibility of the job and is calculated in terms of work units. The work unit is computed through the use of the following equation:[11]

$$\frac{(\text{actual work performed}) \times (\text{rating factor})}{\text{daily work norm}} = \text{work unit}$$

For example, the weeding of turnips may contain a rating factor of 1.2, the daily work norm may be 2,000 meters of turnips weeded a day, and the actual work performance may be 3,000 meters of turnips weeded a day. The work unit would be computed as follows:

$$\frac{3{,}000 \times 1.2}{2{,}000} = 1.8 \text{ work units per day}$$

The calculated work units are then adjusted according to the quality of work. There are three quality standards, which are as follows:[12]

1. Quality standard 1: not only has the work norm been fulfilled, but the quality of work is flawless.
2. Quality standard 2: the work is satisfactory. The quality of work is up to 80 percent of perfect performance.
3. Quality standard 3: a generally poor performance in terms of the quality of work.

Wages then are based on both the quantity and quality of work. The calculation of wages is as follows:[13]

1. The full wage is paid if the work performance falls within quality standard 1.
2. Eighty percent of the full wage is paid if the work performance falls within quality standard 2.
3. Fifty percent of the wage is paid if the work performance falls within quality standard 3.

Wages are paid out of the wage funds of agricultural enterprises. In addition, there are bonus funds that are distributed among the workers. These funds have assumed increasing importance during recent years. Bonuses are also based on performance and are distributed as follows:[14]

1. A type 1 bonus pays up to 60 percent per 100 work units and up to 40 percent of land shares.
2. A type 2 bonus ranges up to 70 percent per 100 work units and up to 40 percent of land shares.
3. A type 3 bonus amounts to at least 80 percent per 100 work units and up to 20 percent of land shares.

Nonmaterial Incentives

In East Germany, as is true of other socialist states, material rewards are combined with other types of noneconomic rewards in an attempt to achieve maximum effort on the part of the workers. Competitive contests between individuals or groups have been fashioned for such interrelated ends as increasing output, improving the quality of production, raising labor productivity, and reducing costs. Individual workers are spurred on by a variety of formal or informal rewards, all of which aim at raising the self-esteem of the honored and perhaps inspiring by example numerous unknown admirers to improve their work performance. The contests and campaigns in themselves motivate workers through their desire to win, but in addition this type of competition distributes a large number of nonmaterial rewards tied to outstanding performance. These include special vacation and travel privileges, titular honors, and opportunities for occupational advancement.[15] The play is on the desire to excel and surpass other individuals in the interest of the state.

Group competition is somewhat similar to individual competition. Factories or groups within factories challenge each other to socialist competition. This involves production contests, attempting to surpass previous records, trying to exceed a quota, and working with a backward unit to improve its levels of performance.[16] The success of the unit involved is rewarded, as with individuals, with a variety of honorary awards. Plants are given flags to fly from their roofs to show that their workers won in output competition, and extra compensation, free travel passes, and other benefits redound to the advantage of the workers.

Moral stimuli are also used to motivate East German workers. A major task of unions in the GDR is to promote what is called socialist emulation, which means the development of moral responsibility on the part of the workers to increase production for the interest of the state. Although glorious deeds of self-sacrifice on the part of workers may be resurrected from the past to spur workers on to greater activity, the unions are supposed to provide the stimuli, through techniques such as motion pictures and lectures, to make them strive for improved performances and increased output.

There is also worker participation in the management of production. Mass meetings are held to discuss and review production experiences and concrete programs for improvement of performance. In all industrial enterprises there are production conferences to which all types of workers—white collar, blue collar, engineers, and management—can be elected by their various departments. These conferences meet to consider production goals and can make recommendations to the enterprise director, who is supposed to consider them before making any final decision. Although useful suggestions may emanate from the conferences, there are obvious drawbacks in that management may ignore the suggestions and that workers often strive to obtain easier work norms.

Nonmaterial incentives attempt to capitalize on fundamental psychological needs of individuals for affection, for a sense of being included in important affairs, and for feeling some control or influence over events that shape their lives. The success of most nonmaterial incentives, however, appears to depend upon effective political indoctrination and education. Such propaganda is aimed at heightening personal awareness and putting a particular campaign or drive in proper perspective. Mass movements to achieve output goals are carefully organized to control production efforts through education and psychological pressure.

Income Differentials

Income differentials in the GDR exist to a considerable degree. The claim of a "classless society," which is commonplace in socialist countries, obviously does not apply to income classes but to exploitative classes. The reasons for income differentials are apparent. Income policy has clear-cut aims within the broader scope of economic growth strategy. Workers are expected to deploy themselves where wanted and to advance their skills. Income differentiation is based on pragmatic consideration of worker self-interests. Although, from an ideological standpoint, the East German regime would like to see productivity and economic growth based on the revolutionary fervor and enthusiasm of the masses, from a practical standpoint it finds it necessary to rely upon traditional motivational methods.

Income differentials primarily take the form of wages. There are wage differentials based upon skills. As has been pointed out previously, there are eight skill grades for industrial workers which are differentiated according to variations in skill from unskilled to highly skilled categories. The use of piece rates and bonuses also automatically causes considerable variations in earnings among workers, even in the same grade. Income disparities tend to be accentuated by the new role of material incentives. Salary differentials based on the skill requirements and complexity of the job and the importance of the industry relative to the national economy exist for white collar workers, engineers, and managers. As one would expect, average wages are higher in those industries where higher skills are required and work is difficult. Hazardous work commands a higher premium than less arduous work.

It is difficult to be specific about the exact extent of wage differentials in the GDR. There is obviously a considerable disparity between high and low incomes. One indication of this disparity is revealed in the scale of union membership dues. As previously mentioned, union dues range from 0.5 Ostmarks on monthly incomes of 100 Ostmarks or less to 35 Ostmarks on incomes of 2,600 Ostmarks or more. This would indicate a minimum wage disparity of at least 26 to 1. The lower and upper ranges of monthly income, however, may represent extreme situations as, for example, the minimum monthly wage was 300 Ostmarks a month in 1970 and has been raised to 350 Ostmarks a month in 1971. Unquestionably, income disparity is also reduced by taxes and transfer payments that redistribute income from one group to another. The extent of the redistribution may well be overrated, however, for the reason that the GDR relies extensively on consumption taxes. Moreover, there are certain privileges, expressed in nonmonetary terms, that redound to the advantage of the party elite, professional workers such as managers and engineers, and members of the intelligentsia. For example, special priorities are given for housing, automobiles, and travel.

Another measure of income differentials can be obtained by using the range of incomes subject to income taxation. The income tax in the GDR starts at a base yearly income of 1,200 Ostmarks and ends at a flat rate of 90 percent on yearly incomes of 500,000 Ostmarks or more. This only indicates a range of incomes, however, and tells nothing about the actual distribution of incomes within income classes. The range does indicate that a wide latitude in earnings potential exists. It is certainly true that successful enterprise managers and professional people and persons with special skills in short supply do earn large incomes in the GDR. The income tax range indicates that an income differential of at least 20 to 1 is probable.

Average monthly incomes by industrial classification also indicate wage variations. These averages do not show the difference between the highest and lowest wage in each industrial field, however, nor do they reflect the effect of bonuses on incomes. Table 11.1 presents the average monthly income for industrial fields in the GDR for 1969.

It is obvious, then, that the socialist system of the GDR has not succeeded in eliminating the privileged class, nor have any moves been made to equalize all wages and salaries effectively. To the contrary, an elite group consisting of the intelligentsia, scientists and technicians, and highly placed party members enjoys a very high standard of living. The difference between the income of the average worker and that of the privileged strata is striking and is enlarged by special contributions from the state, including such special benefits as private villas and personal limousines (also a common practice

TABLE 11.1

Average Monthly Incomes for Industrial Groups,
East Germany, 1969
(Ostmarks)

Industrial Group	Average Monthly Income*
Energy and fuels	810
Chemicals	763
Metallurgy	836
Building materials	746
Machinery	765
Electronics and instruments	740
Light industry	646
Textile	594
Food	677
Average	734

*The average is for all industrial workers.

Source: Staatliche Zentralverwaltung für Statistik, Statistisches Jahrbuch der Deutschen Demokratishen Republik, 1970 (East Berlin: Staatsverlag der DDR, 1970), p. 127.

in other socialist countries). In spite of such subsidies as extremely low rents and utility costs the wages of the typical worker are insufficient to enable him to afford many of the consumer durable products that are taken for granted by his industrial counterpart in West Germany.

This situation is changed, however, when the income amounts to several times the average wage, as would be the case for middle-echelon party and state functionaries, engineers, plant managers, and scientists, who frequently have a take-home pay of between 2,000 and 4,000 Ostmarks a month. These individuals also enjoy special economic advantages over lower-income workers, such as being able to take their leaves in cheaper vacation homes and being able to shop in special stores. Such bonuses, which are not apparent in the actual salaries, result in increasing the standard of living of such persons to a level far beyond that of the average worker.

Moreover, there is a category of wage earners in the GDR whose incomes are at least 10 times that of the average worker. For these persons, the state introduced in 1952 so-called individual contracts, which were to be concluded primarily with scientists, artists, and other persons who possessed special talents.17 In part these individual contracts were designed to keep persons with the talents needed by the state from fleeing to West Germany. When the decree was issued, an average number of 50 individual contracts, with salaries ranging between 7,000 and 15,000 Ostmarks a month, and an average number of 20 individual contracts, with salaries of more than 15,000 Ostmarks a month, were to be issued each year.18 Since 1952 there has been an increase in the number of contracts as well as the amount of the salaries granted.

In addition to their exceptionally high salaries selected persons also receive premiums and special awards that provide additional income. Walter Ulbricht, former chairman of the SED, has been awarded one Lenin Order, two Karl Marx Orders, three Hero of Work titles, and various other awards. The Lenin Order included an award of 10,000 rubles, the Karl Marx Order carried a gift of 100,000 Ostmarks, and each Hero of Work award amounted to 10,000 Ostmarks.19 The National Prize First Class, valued at 25,000 Ostmarks, is granted to various scientists, authors, and writers. Writers, actors, engineers, and scientists are therefore able to increase their incomes considerably Long-time members of the SED can also be counted among the elite class of East Germany. Not only do they frequently receive two or three times the normal pensions, but they are also given special awards that range from 1,000 to 25,000 Ostmarks.

It should be pointed out, however, that the education system in the GDR does provide considerable upward mobility for any talented person. The SED and the state have both provided substantial incentives for those persons who are capable of attending universities or technical colleges. A new elite social group has been created that consists of the managers and technicians who run the state enterprises. This group is a product of the educational system. Thus, it can be said that to a considerable extent income differentials are based on merit and performance in the GDR.

General education in the GDR is free and obligatory. It begins at the age of six and is based on a ten-year polytechnical school system. From the general educational system the student may elect, if he is qualified, to proceed to further schooling. The majority of students go on to vocational schools; the remainder go on to universities and technical schools. Professional and social advancement is the end result of a university education. Career-oriented subjects, particularly the applied sciences, are emphasized, as opposed to the liberal arts "frill" subjects in vogue in many Western universities. As is true in other aspects of East German life, the performance principle underlies the system of education, with monetary incentives being directly tied to performance in the classroom.

The fact that East Germany has one of the lowest birth rates in Europe, coupled with a shortage of labor, has forced the state to recruit, as a matter of public policy, as many women as possible for the labor force. In contrast to West Germany, the percentage of persons in the labor force has risen steadily in the last few years until at 51 percent it is one of the highest in the world. Just under one-half (46 percent) of the labor force is comprised of women, compared to 36 percent for West Germany.[20] East German women usually return to work after marriage and childbirth. The state has found it to be in its own interest to promote the training and employment of women to solve an acute labor shortage. One factor that has compounded this problem is the distribution in the age of the population. Reflecting the effects of two major wars, there is a sizable concentration of persons in the old and young age groups. In 1970, for example, 22 percent of the population was 60 years of age or older.[21] This means that wage earners in the GDR have to support a rather large unproductive segment of the economy.

As a result of the large number of women in the labor force, many East German households have two income earners. Despite this fact, incomes of East German households are on the average one-third lower than household incomes in West Germany. In 1967, average household income in the GDR was 1,001 Ostmarks compared to DM 1,473 in the FRG. In 1960, the comparable figures were 843 Ostmarks and DM 1,019 respectively.[22] Retired persons are at a particular disadvantage in the GDR since on the average they draw only about a third of the pensions paid in the FRG. Certain elements of the East German population are well treated with respect to pensions, however. Former employees of scientific, artistic, educational, and medical institutions draw what is called an "intelligentsia pension," providing a graduated income of up to 800 Ostmarks per month.

INCOME REDISTRIBUTION THROUGH TAXES AND TRANSFER PAYMENTS

Wage payments constitute only one side of the coin as far as income distribution is concerned. The initial distribution of income is subject to alteration by state use of taxes and transfer payments. Taxes provide the state with control over economic resources. Transfer payments are primarily concerned with the redistributive function of government. There are transfer payments that go directly to people in the form of money income. Family allowances, old age pensions, and unemployment compensation are examples. There also are transfer payments that can be considered as subsidies. Often these subsidies are designed to supply goods or services to particular groups at prices far below their actual costs. An example of a subsidy would be education, which is free and which is supported by grants from the general revenues of the budget. But regardless of the type of transfer, the initial pattern of income distribution has been altered.

Taxes also have a redistributive effect on income. A progressive income tax serves to redistribute income in the direction of greater equality because the proportionate share of the upper income groups in the total income is reduced and the proportionate share of the lower income groups is raised. The progressivity of the income tax structure brings about this result because the effective rate of taxation—the ratio of total taxes paid to income received—increases with the size of the income. This means, in other words, that the proportionate share of the total tax burden is greater for the upper income groups, hence, there is a redistribution in the direction of greater income equality. Any consumption based tax can have an offsetting effect to the progressivity of an income tax, however, in that usually it amounts to a larger part of the incomes of the lower income groups than for the higher.

The Effect of Taxes on Income Redistribution

The major problem in any attempt to determine the extent to which the East German tax structure brings about redistribution of income is that of determining the incidence of taxation. Since the GDR employs different types of taxes to obtain its revenue this is a problem of considerable complexity. The problem, moreover, has a dual aspect: It is necessary, on one hand, to identify the persons or groups upon whom the tax is nominally levied and, on the other, to identify the income recipients who actually pay the tax. The latter is the problem of the ultimate incidence of taxation.

In the GDR the important direct taxes, i.e., taxes levied directly on income, are the personal income and social security taxes. The problem of the incidence of direct taxation is relatively simple because it can be safely assumed that such taxes cannot be shifted. This is certainly true for the personal income tax and social security taxes paid by employees. Then, the problem becomes simply one of determination of the amount of direct taxes paid by particular income groups. Social security taxes on employers, who are typically state enterprises, are more difficult to analyze. From the employer's point of view social security taxes are simply a part of labor costs, and, like other costs of production, they will be borne eventually by the consumer. It is necessary to point out, however, that employers would have little effect on price determination, for prices are determined by state administrative decisions rather than by the marketplace

In setting prices an allowance is usually made for profit expressed as a percentage of average production costs for all enterprises producing a given commodity. Social security contributions are accounted for by employers as a separate production expense.

The personal income tax is levied on individuals in the form of wages and salaries or from self-employment. A separate scale of tax rates is established for various occupational groups, with workers directly employed by state enterprises favored with lower rates than self-employed persons and persons who receive an independent income from private employment. The rates of the personal income tax, at least as they apply to the vast majority of income recipients, are more proportional than progressive. Moreover, they reach down to the lower income levels, so that it would appear that few persons avoid paying at least some income taxes. The social security tax is also paid by the workers and is levied at a flat rate on monthly incomes up to 600 Ostmarks. This rate is also differentiated on the basis of occupational categories. When the personal income and social security taxes are combined, it is possible to get some idea of the burden of direct taxes in the GDR. It is necessary, however, to make the following observations.

First, the actual burden of the income tax is far less than the rates would indicate. Although it is true that the rates begin at a rather low level of income, there are many deductions and exemptions that reduce the size of the tax base. It is also true that certain income, i.e., prizes and pensions, are also free from taxation or taxed at reduced rates.

Second, social security taxes are set at proportional rates and stop when a certain level of income is reached. Incomes above the level of 600 Ostmarks a month are not subject to a tax. This means that a considerable part of total income is untaxed. Moreover, as incomes have risen, the amount not subject to the tax has also increased. The burden of social security taxes relative to total employee income has decreased from 7.5 percent to 6.3 percent during the period 1960-69.[23] Table 11.2 presents in a general way the burden of income and social security taxation in the GDR. Total personal income and average monthly income are used.

With respect to the incidence of indirect taxation there is strong presumption that their incidence is primarily on the consumer. Although it has been argued that the turnover tax is derived from the surplus product created in the state sector of production and does not come from personal income, and is thus not a tax, the generally accepted view is that it is a tax that does indeed fall on the consumer. This is so because the consumer will pay for a particular quantity of a commodity a price that is higher by the amount of the tax than he would pay for the same quantity in the absence of the tax.

TABLE 11.2

Personal Income and Average Monthly Income,
Taxes and Social Security Contributions,
East Germany, 1969

Income	Amount (billion Ostmarks)	Income	Amount (Ostmarks)
Personal income	57.3	Average monthly income	650
−Social security contributions	3.6	−Social security contributions	41
−Direct taxes	4.1	−Direct taxes	57
Net income	49.6	Net income	562
+transfer payments	4.2	+transfer payments	48
+other income	1.7	+other income	20
Gross net income	55.5	Gross net income	630

Source: Deutscher Bundestag, Materialien zum Bericht zur Lage der Nation 1971, Drucksache VI/1690 (Bonn-Bad Godesberg: Dr. Hans Heger Verlag, 1971), p. 333.

The turnover tax is the most important source of tax revenue in the East German state budget, accounting for around two-thirds of revenue. It can be said that the state depends upon indirect taxation not only for the bulk of general expenditures but a considerable part of welfare expenditures as well. Although no simple statement about the relationship of the turnover tax to the redistribution of income is possible, the implication is fairly clear. There is at best a very limited vertical redistribution of income between social and economic classes in the GDR. Whatever progressivity there is in direct taxation is counterbalanced by the turnover tax. With respect to social welfare payments, which are financed to a large extent out of general budgetary revenues, a considerable part of the real cost of these payments are borne, in the final analysis, by those who benefit by them.

There are other points of importance involved in the overall character of the East German tax system. There is, first, the vital question of equity in taxation. The regressive character of indirect or consumption taxes is widely recognized, and this is a factor that cannot be ignored in an evaluation of the incidence of the benefits and costs associated with the system of social insurance. Furthermore, the price effects allied with indirect taxation may have undesirable consequences in other sectors of the economy. Finally, it should be emphasized that indirect taxation tends to conceal the real costs of public activity because the diffusion of these costs throughout the economy makes it virtually impossible for the citizen to know precisely what proportion of his income is being absorbed for public purposes.

Some general observations are relevant in attempting to appraise the burden of taxation. The real burden on individual members of the economy arises from the transfer of resources to the national government through expenditure programs. Taxes do not impose an overall real burden but change the distribution of incomes among persons in the economy. The distributional effects of taxes are reflected in the resulting changes in real income positions among individuals. Those who have a relative decline in real income may be regarded as bearing the tax. Although it is difficult to measure the extent to which real income is modified by taxation in the GDR, the likelihood is that any modification or change between income classes is minor.

Social Insurance

The social insurance system in East Germany provides benefits in money and kind to augment the wages of industrial and agricultural workers. Under its provisions, workers are covered for sickness, injury, and disability; death and maternity; retirement; and miscellaneous other benefits. The system is contributory with workers and employers contributing a fixed percentage of earnings and payrolls for the various social insurance categories. The state finances deficits out of general budgetary revenues. The social insurance funds are administered by the trade union organizations and, in some cases, by insurance agencies of the state. There is a built-in incentive element in the social insurance system in that most benefits are graded according to wages. There are also negative incentives in that eligible workers who are not members of trade unions usually receive lower benefits during sickness and old age. The purpose is to keep the number of nonunion members low.

A series of social security reforms occurred in the spring of 1968.[24] These reforms concerned all forms of payments made under social security laws. Minimum social security benefits were raised, and changes were made in voluntary supplementary social security contributions. Benefits were set at a minimum of 150 Ostmarks a month, including cost-of-living supplements. Old-age pensions were increased by 21 Ostmarks a month and widows' pensions by 31 Ostmarks a month. Additional changes were made in other types of benefits in an effort to raise the amounts paid to some groups up to a national average.

The GDR actually has several social security organizational arrangements. In this respect it is somewhat similar to France and other European countries in that it is fragmented in terms of its operation. There is the social security system proper, which is administered by the trade unions and which covers the vast majority of white and blue collar workers. There is also a national insurance organization, which covers the self-employed and small-scale private enterprises with five or fewer employees. In addition, there are also several special social security groups, such as the ones for the people's police, customs administration, employees of the state railways, and the postal service. Additional old-age pensions and other benefits are given to the academic intelligentsia, artists, scientists, engineers, and members of medical establishments through insurance contracts with the national insurance organization of the GDR.

The social security system is financed by employer and employee contributions of 10 percent on payrolls and earnings up to 600 Ostmarks a month. These rates, as of 1970, have been unchanged for a period of 20 years. Self-employed persons pay a rate of 14 percent and members of the LPGs contribute 9 percent. The share of state funds necessary to finance the difference between contributions and expenses was estimated to be around 50 percent in 1969. In this connection it is necessary to point out that family allowances are financed out of general state revenues. The framework of benefits payable in the East German social insurance system is outlined below.[25]

Old-Age and Invalidity Benefits

Old-age pensions are provided to males 65 and over and females 60 and over. Miners are allowed to draw pensions at the age of 50. Workers must be insured for a minimum of 15 years to draw a full pension. The amount of the pension is calculated by multiplying 1 percent of average monthly earnings times years of insurance, plus 30 Ostmarks a month. There are dependents' supplements, which amount to 39 Ostmarks a month for the surviving spouse and 40 Ostmarks a month for each child under the age of 15. Disabled workers receive 1 percent of average monthly earnings times years of insurance, plus 30 Ostmarks a month. There are also dependents' supplements of 39 Ostmarks a month for a spouse of 60 years or over, or who is caring for small children, and 40 Ostmarks a month for each child under 15. In the event of accidental death there is a widow's pension, which amounts to 60 percent of the base pension of the insured. There are also orphans' pensions, which amount to 25 percent of the base pension of the insured for each person under 15. Maximum survivor pensions can amount to 100 percent of the pension of the insured. A lump sum payment of 20 days' earnings is available for funeral expenses.

Sickness and Maternity Benefits

Sickness benefits involve the cost of medical expenses and the payment of an allowance to compensate for the loss of earnings during the period of illness. Persons covered by sickness benefits are reimbursed for the cost of hospitalization and drugs and the fees of physicians. Sickness benefits amount to 50 percent of average earnings for the calendar year, payable from the first day of confinement and extending for six weeks. This base payment continues for 39 weeks; however, after the six weeks additional payments are provided for dependent children. Workers with two or more children receive from 65 to 90 percent of average earnings for the calendar year for the seventh to thirteenth week of confinement. Benefits are paid up to the thirty-ninth week of confinement, but only if recovery is assured. Medical benefits, including general and specialist care, hospital and laboratory services, and appliances, are also covered under the social insurance system.

Maternity benefits are available to all women covered by social insurance proper; they are to be distinguished from other maternity benefits that are a part of the system of family allowances and are paid to all women after a pregnancy. Maternity benefits for women covered by the social insurance system include coverage of all medical expenses plus payment of all or part of earnings lost as a result of pregnancy. Working women are entitled to 100 percent of earnings for six weeks before birth and eight weeks after birth. Nonworking women receive lesser amounts that are based on the extent of social insurance contributions. Nursing mothers receive 10 Ostmarks a week additional assistance for a period of 6 months. Moreover, there is additional financial support based on the number of children in the family. For example, two children would provide a lump sum grant of 600 Ostmarks for home care.

Employment-Injury Benefits

The third facet of the East German social insurance system consists of a program designed to provide care for the victims of industrial accidents or occupational disease. The coverage of this program extends to all employed persons. Four types of benefits are provided for those eligible under the program—payments for medical care, allowances in lieu of wages for temporary disability, pensions in the event of permanent disability, and annuities for the dependents of the victim of a fatal accident. All medical expenses incurred as a result of work injury are covered. Temporary disability benefits are similar to sickness benefits. Pensions for permanent disability amount to two-thirds of average monthly earnings for a calendar year, plus supplements for children of 10 percent of the pension. For partial disability, pensions are pro rated on the basis of loss of work capacity. Widows and other dependents of workers killed in an accident receive survivors' pensions that range from 40 percent to 100 percent of the earnings of the insured.

Unemployment Compensation

Unemployment compensation is similar to employment-injury compensation in terms of financing. Each is financed by a payroll tax on employers. On an a priori basis it can be concluded that the rate of unemployment in the GDR is extremely low. In the past it was generally assumed that the only unemployment that can be tolerated is of the frictional type, which, owing to economic planning, should not exceed 1 percent of the total work force. In recent years, however, economists have argued that optimal employment is below maximum employment as the latter may in fact lead to lower national income. Unemployment benefits in the GDR amount to 10 percent of earnings based on 26 weeks of coverage during the last 12 months before unemployment. There are also supplements for dependents. Benefits are payable after a seven-day waiting period for a period up to 26 weeks.

Family Allowances

The family allowance system differs from other social insurance programs in that the benefits do not depend upon the actual wage or salary of the worker, and all benefits are in the form of cash payments. Family allowances consist of a monthly cash payment to each family with dependent children. The monthly payment is 20 Ostmarks a month for the first and second child, 50 Ostmarks for the third, 60 Ostmarks for the fourth, and 70 Ostmarks for the fifth and subsequent children. The allowance is limited to children under 15 and to students. In addition to the family allowance there are birth grants of 500 Ostmarks for the first birth, which rise progressively to 1,000 Ostmarks for the fifth and subsequent births.

Other Welfare Expenditures

The welfare expenditures referred to above are all made within the framework of the East German social insurance system. In addition to these expenditures, however, there are several other types of expenditures for welfare purposes that are financed out of budgetary expenditures. Housing subsidies are provided for families with low, fixed incomes. Welfare and charitable expenditures are made by local governments for such things as aid to the aged and infirm, medical care for the insane, and aid to children. In general such assistance is directed to persons who, for one reason or another, are not eligible for benefits or assistance under the existing social security programs. There are also a variety of forms of assistance to war victims and "fighters against fascism" and their dependents. These include not only special pensions but such things as medical care, homes for the aged and disabled, financial aid for vocational training, scholarships, and the care of war orphans.

It is also important to point out that industry has certain responsibility as far as social welfare measures are concerned. Industry has the responsibility for maintaining high safety standards to protect workers from industrial accidents. Safety enforcement standards are strict, and industrial accidents are far lower in East Germany than in West Germany. Industry is also responsible for the provision of medical care and work hygiene. In enterprises with less than 200 workers medical care is provided voluntarily by the East German Red Cross. In companies with 200 to 500 workers medical care is provided by a nurse who has undergone a state examination. Companies with 500 to 2,000 employees are required to have the services of a physician and a registered nurse. Companies with 2,000 to 4,000 workers must maintain a company clinic run by a full-time physician with additional laboratory and medical equipment required. Large companies, with 4,000 or more workers, are required to maintain a full-time outpatient clinic.

The GDR provides for all insured persons' coverage for the cost of medical care. Home treatment, hospital care, and health spas are covered. A patient is free to choose his doctor and hospital. Only in the case of orthopedic shoes is a small monetary contribution required from the patient. Visits of private nurses and doctors in the homes of patients are usually limited to a period of 26 weeks. Otherwise, there is no time limitation on the amount and extent of medical treatment a patient can receive.

A significant feature of the East German social security system is that benefits are often based on the importance of the individual to the state.[26] Persons who are working in occupations where there is a shortage of manpower, or who provide unusual or vital services are provided with a better degree of social security than most workers. Special allowances, which are sometimes supplementary to ordinary social insurance payments and sometimes independent of them, are granted to workers in key industries, members of the intelligentsia, and to specially deserving persons. For example, members of what can be called the "scientific and technical elite," including professors, engineers, and architects, receive a further payment in addition to ordinary social insurance benefits when they are disabled or reach old age. These benefits amount to between 60 and 80 percent of an insured person's average earnings in the last year before disability or retirement. Additional payments are also given to dependents. Persons who have provided outstanding services are paid honorary pensions that range from 600 to 1,500 Ostmarks a month. Workers in key industries are paid additional allowances of 5 percent of average net monthly earnings for the last five years prior to disability or retirement.

PRICES

Given the public ownership of the means of production and the absence of the free market mechanism, the East German economy has no automatic or simple mechanism for determining rational prices. A fixed and variable price arrangement exists, fixing prices applied to many consumer necessities, setting ceiling prices for less essential consumer and industrial goods, and allowing free prices, in some cases, for farm products and certain other items. The level of prices for basic necessities is below the level of cost, including both production and distribution costs, to the government. On the other hand, prices for many other consumer goods are set well above actual costs of production and distribution, and the difference in part captured by the turnover tax. In East Germany, the size of the turnover tax is determined by the required level of the retail price.

The use of prices to regulate the distribution of real personal income is considered wasteful and thus undesirable. Regulation can be effected by regulating nominal wages, social services, and personal taxes. There is a case against frequent changes in the price of necessities in that such goods represent a large proportion of the incomes of lower income groups, and price changes produce a haphazard redistribution of real income. So price stability has become a prime desideratum of East German economic policy. It is reflected in the consumer price index, which has shown a remarkable stability during the period 1960 through 1970. With 1960 set as a base of 100 percent, the consumer price index increased to 100.9 percent in 1970.[27] This increase was accompanied by increases in per capita income and general living standards. Average monthly real income increased by 35 percent during the period 1960-70—this increase does not reflect the fact that increases in wages were far less than increases in productivity during the period.[28]

SUMMARY

Income distribution in the GDR takes primarily the form of wages, which are regarded as a part of the social product, the distribution of which is the business of the state. The basis for distribution is performance. For the worker's work and his wages, the basic socialist principle holds good: "From each according to his ability, to each according to his performance." This means that there is considerable difference in incomes between workers, which tends to be accentuated by the important role assigned to the use of material incentives. The purpose of material incentives is to provide a further stimulus to output. They are tied closely to the performance of enterprises as measured in terms of profits. A part of profits is channeled into a material incentives fund, from which bonuses are paid to workers to reward them for performance. Thus, profits and bonuses are tied together; the larger the one, the larger the other.

Wage scales for different branches of industry are as a rule divided into eight groups. The allocation of workers to their appropriate wage group is determined by wage and salary classifications, which are prepared for each branch of industry. These classifications are arranged according to the character of the work done, and the demands made on the qualifications of the workers. Within each wage group, a standard wage payment is set. If a worker is to receive the stipulated payment, he must perform his alloted task with respect to both quality and quantity. If performance is above the standard work norm, an efficiency bonus is paid. If output is below the prescribed norm, wage payments are lowered accordingly.

A form of wage payment commonly used in the GDR is the piece rate. The great advantage of the piece-rate payment is that by means of the simplest calculation the relationship between the work done and the payment received can be made clear. Typically, piece-rate payments are proportional, in which the payment is related to the fulfillment of a norm. Piece-rate bonuses are also used. Under this system, index figures related to the quality of the product or to the amount of material used are set. If the work, as represented by the index figures, is satisfactorily done, then bonuses are paid. Piece rates, as well as time rates, are also supplemented by bonuses that are also tied to performance. These bonuses are paid out of special funds of enterprises.

The tax-transfer payment system in the GDR follows a pattern similar to other socialist countries. Income and social security taxes, however, account for a larger proportion of state revenue than is usually the case. Nevertheless, the turnover tax is the single most important source of state tax revenue. Transfer payments are distributed primarily through the social security system, which has as its objective to guarantee all citizens some minimum standard of material well-being. Compulsory insurance against sickness, accident, and old age is normally extended to cover all workers, all self-employed persons who do not employ more than five workers, members of cooperatives, and special categories of professional persons. Responsibility for the administration of social security benefits for the masses of industrial workers falls on the unions affiliated with the FDGB, while the National Insurance Institution is responsible for the insurance of self-employed persons and business and professional men.

Social security benefits are financed by contributions received from insured persons and employers and from subsidies from the state budget. Insurance contributions vary from group to group; this is due partly to actuarial considerations, particularly in the case of miners, and partly to political motives. The typical rate of contribution is 20 percent of earnings subject to insurance. Of this amount, the insured person and the employer each pays one half. For miners and persons in similar employment the rate is higher. Different rates are also paid by self-employed persons. Receipts and expenditures relating to social security are set out in a social insurance budget, which forms a part of the state budget.

CHAPTER

12

**MONEY AND BANKING
IN EAST GERMANY**

INTRODUCTION

One might ask to what degree money and monetary institutions are able to influence resource allocation, consumption, investment, incentives, and the like in an economy that relies heavily on the supremacy of a centrally determined plan and on administrative controls. The ability of money and monetary institutions is circumscribed to a greater degree in East Germany than in West Germany due to a more extensive control exerted over economic decisions by the East German planning and administrative apparatus. Nevertheless, the East German economy can be viewed as a monetary economy in which money does perform certain functions, although policies exercised by such monetary institutions as the Staatsbank (State Bank) play a subservient role to the direct controls exercised by the complex administrative apparatus of the government.

Money in the East German economy possesses many of the same functions as money in the capitalist countries. Within and outside of the state sector money serves as a unit of account; that is, all goods and services that are bought and sold are valued in monetary units. Money also functions as a medium of exchange in East Germany in that wages and salaries are paid in currency, and receivers of money can use it to purchase goods and services. The ownership of money, however, does not give individuals command over the allocation of resources as it does under a capitalist system, for resource allocation is determined by the national plan and not by the price system.

Similar to the control over other aspects of the East German economy, there is a plan to control the monetary aspects—the financial plan—which parallels and is coordinated with the production and distribution plans for each period of time. The three essential components of the financial plan are the following: the state budget, which is responsible for resource allocation between consumption and investment; the credit plan, which regulates the granting of credit by the banking system to the enterprises during a stipulated period of time; and the cash plan, which controls the amount of money in circulation. By use of the components of the financial plan, the planners seek to coordinate the operations of the monetary and financial aspects of the economy with the production of physical goods and services. The financial plan is calculated after the production plan because it determines the income and expenditure patterns of all important sectors of the East German economy.

The East German banking system possesses the following characteristics:

1. Banking is centralized as a monopoly of the government. This means that through the direct operation of the banking system the government can control the volume of credit and hence the money supply.
2. The banking system is subordinate to the economic plan and serves as an instrument of control through the verification of planned transactions.
3. Banks specialize according to functions: There are banks for savings, investments, and foreign trade.

THE DEVELOPMENT OF THE BANKING SYSTEM

The first period in the development of the East German banking system began in May 1945. All credit institutions, including the Reichsbank, were closed by the Soviet occupation forces and all deposits were blocked. Although there was no formal liquidation of deposits, for all practical purposes they were dissolved by the action of the Soviet occupation authorities. In July 1945 formal organization of the East German banking system began. In the five German states in the Soviet occupation zone, state-owned banks (Landeskreditbanken) were created as instruments of the public law (Anstalten des Öffentlichen Rechts). These state banks were permitted to start branch banks in the larger towns. Town banks and savings banks were also created, in many cases taking over the buildings and equipment of former banks. In Berlin the Berliner Stadtkontor, a separate banking institution, was also created in July 1945. Mutual loan societies were established in November 1945, and Volksbanken for tradesmen were created in 1946.[1]

Only the cooperative banks, the prewar Raiffeisenkassen, were allowed to take up their former functions of providing farm credit. Some private banks, particularly those that were operating in the western parts of Saxony and Thuringia, were also allowed to operate. These banks were in the part of East Germany originally occupied by United States troops. Most were taken over by the state after the monetary reforms of 1948, with some minor exceptions.

In February 1947 Emissions and Girobanks were established in Dresden, Halle, Weimar, Potsdam, and Schwerin. Each bank took the name of the corresponding state in which it was located. The banks were responsible for regulating the supply of money and providing a clearing system for commercial transactions. They could only perform banking functions for other monetary institutions or state agencies. In May 1948 a central authority, the Deutsche Emissions and Girobank, was established with its place of operations in Potsdam. This bank was created to coordinate the operations of the five Emissions and Girobanks of the German states and to regulate the circulation of money and the credit and clearing system. It did not have the authority to issue bank notes, however.

The Monetary Reform of 1948

The most important aspect of the East German monetary reform of 1948 was the creation of a central banking system. This reform was introduced by the German Economic Commission on June 21, 1948. The Deutsche Emissions and Girobank was renamed the Deutsche Notenbank. Private savings, except for small amounts, were devalued at a ratio of 10 to 1, but savings of state organizations were converted at a ratio of 1 to 1. The basic idea was to distribute the money according to priorities set in the national economic plan, introduced in the second half of 1948. This change to a centralized economic plan required a change to a centralized banking system. In 1948 an Investment Bank (Deutsche Investitionsbank) was also created for the purpose of long-term investments of plants in the national economy. Also in 1948 a new currency unit was issued, which became the Mark der Deutschen Notenbank, or MDN.

All regional banks were centralized under the Deutsche Notenbank. The Deutsche Notenbank was given the responsibility for currency issue, the provision of short-term credit, and the regulation of the clearing system. It was also made responsible for the development of the cash and credit plans. In 1952 the Deutsche Notenbank was given the authority to manage the accounts of all of the state-owned enterprises, of all private firms with more than 10 employees, and of all farmers with more than 20 hectares of land. The purpose of this provision was to give the Notenbank complete control over production and trade in the GDR. Since all financial transactions of enterprises were legally required to be accomplished through the Notenbank, this afforded the bank an opportunity to view their economic performance with regard to plan fulfillment. The very status of an enterprise's account at the bank became an indicator of its efficiency. If it broke even on its operation, its account would neither increase nor diminish. If it made a profit, its balance at the bank would grow; if it operated inefficiently and sustained losses, its balance would decline.

Following the monetary reforms of 1948 other banks were created. In February 1950 the Deutsche Bauernbank, or Farmers' Bank, was established as a financial institution to finance agricultural production. Independent regional farm banks were merged into the Deutsche Bauernbank in 1952. In addition to the Bauernbank, other banks were created in 1950. A network of banks for artisans (Banken für Handwerke und Gewerbe) were established to provide credit and banking facilities to small producers and tradesmen in the private sector. Savings banks were permitted to function under local authority, subject to the general supervision of the Ministry of Finance. Guarantee and credit banks were created for the purpose of handling the money of the Soviet occupation authorities and trading companies.

By the end of 1952 the formal banking system of the German Democratic Republic had been devised. The banking system was supposed to act as an instrument for the building of the socialist state. The organization of socialism was decided upon and announced at the second party conference of the SED. The banking system was set up in the following arrangement, which was maintained until the banking reforms of 1967-68:

1. At the top of the East German financial system was the Ministry of Finance. It maintained control over the financial organs of the state—the state budget and the banking system. It was responsible for the preparation of the consolidated financial plan, which would include the state budget, the cash and credit plans of the banks, and the financial plans of state agencies. As the principal financial agent of the East German government, the Ministry of Finance managed the budget system at all levels of government, supervised the financial system of the country, and was responsible for carrying out government economic policy.

2. The Deutsche Notenbank was the central bank in the banking system. It acted as the fiscal agent of the government in that it received all tax revenues and paid out budgetary appropriations to enterprises and institutions. It was responsible for granting short-term credit to all types of enterprises. It prepared the credit and

cash plans, which are a part of the financial plan, and it carried the accounts of most enterprises in the country, thus exercising an important control function. It was also responsible for the emission of currency and for holding all precious metals.

3. The Deutsche Bauernbank was the specialized banking institution for agriculture. It was responsible for granting both short- and long-term credit to agricultural cooperatives, state farms, forestry enterprises, and other agricultural enterprises. It was responsible for the preparation of the cash and credit plans with respect to agriculture. It kept the accounts of all cooperatives and state farms. In 1962 it was given responsibility for payment of state budget funds to agricultural enterprises and for the receipt of taxes.

4. The Deutsche Investitionsbank was primarily responsible for providing investment funds to industrial enterprises. It assumed most of the functions of the banking system for long-term investments. Its activity was limited to special areas, such as investment in the production and installation of capital goods, and it received its funds from the state budget and from the savings of individual enterprises. Its importance as a grantor of long-term credit diminished as the Deutsche Notenbank began to assume this function.

5. There were other types of banking institutions in East Germany. The Berliner Stadtkontor was created in 1945 as a special banking institution to serve the Soviet sector in Berlin. Later it became the East Berlin branch of the Deutsche Notenbank. There was the Deutsche Handelsbank attached to the Notenbank, which was responsible for foreign-trade transactions. This bank became the Deutsche Aussenhandelsbank in 1966. The Berliner Volksbank and the Banken für Handwerk und Gewerbe represented a network of cooperative banks designed to provide credit to craftsmen and artisans. There were also farm cooperative banks and savings banks (Sparkassen).

Some changes were made in the East German banking system between 1952 and the banking reforms of 1967-68. The Deutsche Bauernbank became the Landwirtschaftsbank in 1963. The most important change, however, occurred in the size and status of the Deutsche Notenbank. Special industry banks (Industrie-Bankfilialen) were created as special branches of the Notenbank. Each bank was supposed to serve as a special bank for a given industry. The Deutsche Notenbank also assumed more responsibility for the granting of long-term credit. An element of flexibility was also introduced in banking policy in that banks were given more initiative in promoting the development of projects of social importance. This flexibility extended over into the area of credit. Although the use of credit had to conform to plan objectives, banks and enterprises were given latitude in working out credit terms.

The Banking Reforms of 1967-68

In December 1967 basic changes were made in the organization of the East German banking system. These changes were a concomitant of the 1963 economic reforms that attempted to change the administration of the economy from rigid to more flexible control. The institutional structure of banking did not differ from the banking systems of other socialist states with regard to their essential features until 1967, even though it was more varied because of the greater articulation and weight of individual sectors of the national economy. But functional and institutional changes have been brought about in accordance with the application of the economic reforms. These changes, which were codified in the Law on the State Bank of the German Democratic Republic, may be summarized as follows:[2]

1. The functions of the Deutsche Notenbank were diverted to new banking institutions. The Staatsbank was created as the new central bank and assumed the functions of currency emission, granting credit to specialized banks, and participation in the preparation of the economic plans. The Industrial and Commercial Bank (Industrie und Handelsbank) was also created from credits and deposits of the Deutsche Notenbank and the Deutsche Investitionsbank, which was dissolved at the same time. The basic function of granting credit to industrial firms was assumed by the Industrial and Commercial Bank.

2. In addition to the Industrial and Commercial Bank, other specialized banks were revised to handle credit and deposit activities as well as other functions. These banks were the Agricultural Bank (Landwirtschaftsbank), the German Bank for Foreign Trade (Aussenhandelsbank), and cooperative banks (Genossenschaftsbanken für Handwerk und Gewerbe). These banks carry out the economic and credit policies of the state and are responsible for them. Decentralization of banking responsibility gives the commercial banks greater responsibility for the operation of the national economy.

3. An important reform pertained to the changing of all specialized banks from purely administrative entities to financially independent units. Through a stated principle of economic bookkeeping, banks must cover all of their costs and gain a profit through various interest charges and charges for services. To encourage greater personal interest on the part of bank employees, special funds were created for bonuses. The yearly amount of these funds were set at 1.5 percent of the wage fund for each bank. In addition, there may also be a further increase of up to 2.75 percent of the wage fund based on a determined performance.

4. The responsibility of banks with respect to the granting of credit was increased. When the banks grant loans to enterprises,

they must now act primarily on the basis of economic criteria of efficiency. Banks can refuse to grant loans to enterprises or support effective proposals. Criteria established for loans include measures of profitability of production funds, growth of wage funds in relation to the growth of profit, and the relationship of taxes to production funds and contributions from net profits. An important role has been assigned to bank credit, particularly in the investment sphere, where it is supposed to help in controlling the enterprises in order to bring the economic plan to the optimum level and make it as effective as possible.

Until the end of 1964 the financing of enterprises was done primarily from the state budget. The percentage of financing from internal enterprise sources, such as profits and amortization, and from bank credit was quite small. In order to facilitate a comprehensive control of all financing procedures, including internal financing, the amount of profit and depreciation that did not go to the state budget was sent to the Deutsche Notenbank. Credit-financed investments were centrally controlled by the state. Credit was a plan-bound advance of money from the state to the enterprises. A state partnership in credit form existed, with the state supplying the credit.

In the new banking arrangement the direct intervention of the state in terms of control has been changed. Responsibility for financing investments has been delegated more to the banking system and to the VVBs. Only special types of investment that enjoy high priority are supposed to be financed by the state from the state budget. Most investments are supposed to be financed by loans from credit institutions, or from internal sources, such as accumulated amortization and net profit. What has happened is a decentralization of control over credit. The most important credit-control organs are the banks rather than the central bank and the state budget. The control of the banks over credit-financed investment is comprehensive. It extends from the purpose of the investment to its control and use. Important projects carry favorable priorities, such as lower interest rates and longer repayment terms.

Probably the most important function of the East German banks is the control function. The banks not only have the task of supplying enterprises with funds for investment but must also enforce compliance with planning objectives. The control functions of the banks may be summarized as follows:[3]

1. All enterprises may withdraw cash from the banks only for wage payments. This regulation is designed to guarantee control by the banks over all money transactions.

2. The banks keep the accounts of all enterprises and economic organizations and are responsible for the clearing and collection of checks and other financial payments.

3. The banks have the authority to control uses of enterprise funds in the interest of plan fulfillment. They are supposed to take part at an early stage in enterprise planning, advise enterprises in their credit and investment policies, and use credit and interest as a leverage to enforce the most effective use of resources in terms of planning objectives. The banks can enforce or reverse investment policies over the objections of an enterprise. Although credit terms to the enterprises may be more flexible than before the banking reforms, there is a much greater element of control on the part of the banks.

During the period 1961-68 there has been a marked shift in the sources of investment financing. In 1961 the bulk of investment financing came from the state budget. Bank credit accounted for less than 10 percent of the total amount of investment funds. Then a shift in financing sources occurred in 1964. More emphasis was placed upon the self-sufficiency of the enterprises. An increase in the use of both internal and bank credit occurred. By 1968 funds from the state budget had declined to less than 25 percent of total investment funds, while internal financing had increased to 50 percent. The shift in the sources of investment over the 1961-68 period can be seen in Table 12.1.

TABLE 12.1

The Financing of Investment, by Sources, East Germany
(million Ostmarks)

Year	Investment Total	Investment State	State Budget Payments	Internal Sources	Bank Credit	State Budget (%)	Internal (%)	Bank (%)
1961	15,575	12,760	9,130	2,430	1,200	71.6	19.0	9.4
1962	15,862	13,060	9,060	2,664	1,336	69.4	20.4	10.2
1963	16,721	14,340	10,033	2,868	1,434	70.0	20.0	10.0
1964	18,100	15,518	9,310	3,523	2,675	60.0	22.8	17.2
1965	19,390	16,625	7,480	5,715	3,430	45.0	34.4	20.6
1966	20,800	17,826	6,600	7,126	4,100	37.0	40.0	23.0
1967	22,600	19,390	4,847	9,695	4,847	25.0	50.0	25.0
1968	26,200	22,400	5,600	11,200	5,600	24.8	50.2	25.0

Source: Sibylle May Lang and Maria Elisabeth Roban, "Veränderungen im Bankensystem der DDR," Sonderdruck aus Vierteljahrshefte zur Wirtschaftsforschung, 1968 (Deutsches Institut für Wirtschaftsforschung), p. 407.

THE ORGANIZATION OF THE EAST GERMAN BANKING SYSTEM

The banking system of the GDR resembles a pyramid. At the apex is the Staatsbank. Then there is a system of commercial banks that handle credit and deposit activities as well as other functions, of which the Industrial and Commercial Bank is the most important. It is responsible primarily for the provision of credit to industrial and construction firms. The Agricultural Bank, the former Deutsche Bauernbank, is the second-most-important credit institution.* It is responsible for the provision of credit to the agricultural, forest, and food industries. The Foreign Trade Bank is responsible for foreign-trade transactions, including those with the socialist countries. Formerly, all foreign-trade transactions were the responsibility of the Deutsche Notenbank. Then there are the cooperative banks, which are responsible for the provision of credit to small retailers, craftsmen, and private enterprises with less than 10 employees. Finally, there are the savings banks. In addition to serving as a repository for savings, the savings banks are responsible for providing housing credit and credit to retailers, self-employed persons, and special types of enterprises.

Control over the banking system runs from the top to the bottom (see Chart 12.1). At the top are the Staatsbank and the Ministry of Finance, which are responsible for setting policy within the framework of the economic plan. Then there are the major banks that are responsible for the financing of a particular economic activity. Each bank has numerous branch banks organized on a regional, county, and municipal basis. Branch banks are often specialized in that they are responsible for the financing of a particular type of industry.

The Staatsbank

The Staatsbank is the central bank of the GDR. Within the planned economy of East Germany, it performs a number of functions, as follows:[4]

1. It acts as the fiscal agent of the government in that it receives all tax revenues and pays out budgetary appropriations to enterprises and institutions.

---

*The full title of the Agricultural Bank is the Bank für Landwirtschaft und Nahrungsgüterwirtschaft.

CHART 12.1

Structure of Banking System, East Germany

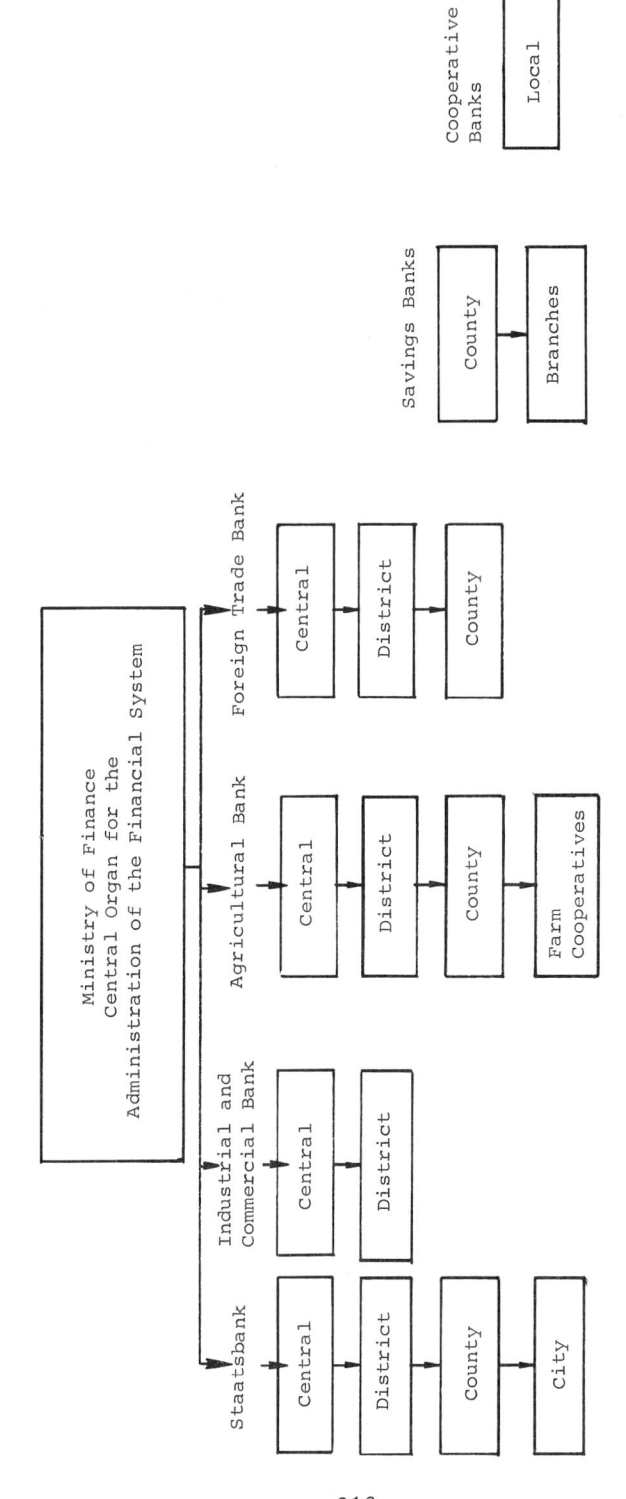

```
                    ┌─────────────────────────────────────┐
                    │        Ministry of Finance          │
                    │   Central Organ for the             │
                    │ Administration of the Financial System │
                    └─────────────────────────────────────┘

   Staatsbank      Industrial and      Agricultural Bank      Foreign Trade Bank
                   Commercial Bank

   ┌─────────┐     ┌─────────┐         ┌─────────┐           ┌─────────┐
   │ Central │     │ Central │         │ Central │           │ Central │
   └────┬────┘     └────┬────┘         └────┬────┘           └────┬────┘
        ▼               ▼                   ▼                     ▼
   ┌─────────┐     ┌─────────┐         ┌─────────┐           ┌─────────┐
   │District │     │District │         │District │           │District │
   └────┬────┘     └─────────┘         └────┬────┘           └────┬────┘
        ▼                                   ▼                     ▼
   ┌─────────┐                         ┌─────────┐           ┌─────────┐
   │ County  │                         │ County  │           │ County  │
   └────┬────┘                         └────┬────┘           └─────────┘
        ▼                                   ▼
   ┌─────────┐                         ┌──────────────┐
   │  City   │                         │     Farm     │
   └─────────┘                         │ Cooperatives │
                                       └──────────────┘

                          Savings Banks              Cooperative
                                                       Banks
                          ┌────────┐  ┌──────────┐    ┌───────┐
                          │ County │─▶│ Branches │    │ Local │
                          └────────┘  └──────────┘    └───────┘
```

Source: Based on data compiled by the author.

2. It is responsible for the preparation of the cash and credit plans, which are a part of the financial plan. In this capacity, the bank is exercising a planning function that involves currency needs and credit expansion.

3. It is also responsible for the emission of currency and for holding all precious metals and foreign currencies owned by the government. As the bank of issue, it can issue money and withdraw it from circulation, thereby helping to regulate the supply of money available to enterprises and individuals in accordance with the cash plan.

4. It exercises control over other banks within the East German banking system. It determines credit policies to be followed, sets the interest rates to be charged, and controls legal reserve and liquidity requirements.

One of the most important functions of the Staatsbank involves economic planning. As mentioned previously, the Staatsbank has the responsibility for the preparation of the cash and credit plans. These plans are approved by the Ministry of Finance. The purpose of the cash and credit plans is to adjust the supply of money to the real output goals of the national economic plan and to prevent expenditures outside of planning purposes. The cash and credit plans are used to implement the physical output plan and to preserve price stability.

The cash plan controls the amount of money in circulation. It is prepared quarterly and consists of a balance statement that shows the inflows and outflows of money. The inflow of money represents deposits in the Staatsbank. These deposits represent currency receipts from a wide variety of sources—tax payments, rents and municipal services, post office and savings banks receipts, and receipts from railroad, water, and air transportation. Monetary outlays under the cash plan go for wage payments, pension allowances and insurance payments, payments for agricultural products and raw materials, consumer loans, expenditures for individual housing construction, and cash outlays by various economic organizations. The outflow side of the balance statement represents most of the money income payments in the GDR. Withdrawals for wage payments constitute most of total monetary outflows of the cash plan. Inflows into the Staatsbank represent the deposits of receipts of consumer expenditures that result from wage and other income payments on the outflow side. Thus, the cash plan is an instrument that is used to control the performance of the consumer sector in terms of the use and disbursement of money.

The credit plan determines the amount of short- and long-term credit that is to be allocated to all industrial and agricultural enterprises in the economy during the period of the national economic plan. It is broken down into two categories—a short-term and a long-term credit plan. The short-term credit plan is designed to provide loans to the various sectors of the economy for such purposes as financing the acquisition of inventories by enterprises. The sources of funds used to provide short-term credit are budgetary contributions, bank reserves and profits, balances of credit institutions such as savings banks, and net changes in currency in circulation. The uses of funds include loans for the payment of wages, loans for temporary needs, loans against drafts in the process of collection, and loans for technological development. It can be seen that the purpose of the plan is to collate the short-term needs of enterprises with the supply of credit.

The long-term credit plan is prepared on an annual basis and is designed to provide loans for both productive and nonproductive investments that have completion dates of several years or longer. It, too, shows the sources and uses of funds during the year. The funds to finance fixed investment are obtained from several sources: funds from the state budget, which include allocations for such purposes as construction, home building, and agriculture, and also temporary Treasury loans; loan repayments by collective farms, consumer cooperatives, and various enterprises; and various subsidies. The funds are used to provide loans to collective farms, consumer cooperatives, individual enterprises, and to repay temporary Treasury loans.

The Staatsbank is directly responsible to the Ministry of Finance. Its affairs are administered by a president, vice president, and a board of directors who are appointed by the Ministry of Finance and who have the responsibility for guiding the general policies of the bank.[5] The president is responsible for the presentation of drafts of the cash and credit plans of the bank to the Ministry of Finance. The president is also responsible for the implementation of central-bank policy in accordance with the principles of socialist performance. He is assisted in this responsibility by the board of directors.

The Industrial and Commercial Bank

The Industrial and Commercial bank assumed various functions of the Notenbank and the Investment Bank in 1968. It is a commercial bank for industry, construction, trade, and transportation and possesses the following functions:[6]

1. It is responsible for keeping the accounts of enterprises. In this manner it is in the position of exercising an important control function. Since all financial transactions of the enterprises are required to be accomplished through the Industrial and Commercial Bank, this affords the bank an opportunity to view their economic performance with regard to real and financial plan fulfillment.

Inasmuch as most transactions between enterprises are in terms of money through bank transfers, the flow of goods is necessarily accomplished by a counterflow of funds. By requiring that all purchases and sales of goods be matched against authorized payments and receipts, it is possible for the bank to exercise control over the budget of an enterprise as a regulator of production. The very status of an enterprise's account at the bank is an indicator of its efficiency. If it breaks even in its operation, its account should neither increase nor diminish. If it makes planned or unplanned profits, its balance at the bank will grow, if it operates inefficiently and sustains losses, its balance will decrease.

2. The Industrial and Commercial Bank provides both short- and long-term credit to enterprises and other organizations. The most important purpose of short-term credit is to finance accumulations of inventories by enterprises. Another important use of short-term credit is to finance accounts receivable. This provides working capital to the seller of goods while payments are in the process of collection. Short-term loans must be for purposes consistent with the credit plan. Interest rates, which may vary as to borrower, are applied to all short-term loans, and penalty rates are charged on overdue loans. Interest proceeds are used as a source of revenue to cover the operating expenses of the Industrial and Commercial Bank. Long-term credit is normally granted for the acquisition of machinery or equipment embodying advanced technology.

3. It is responsible for participating in the development of the economic plan in the area of finance. Here, it must cooperate with the Ministry of Finance and the State Bank. It participates in research and compiling data that is to be used in the development of the plan. Responsibility is given to the bank for the prediction of both long-term and short-term credit needs. It is also responsible for the training of bank personnel and for the introduction of economic accounting in all subsidiary banks.

The Industrial and Commercial Bank has a very extensive system of branch banks. The organization of the branch banks is set up partly along territorial lines and partly along production and technical lines. On a territorial basis there are district, county, and municipal branches; on a production basis there are special banks for the individual VVBs. These banks assumed the financing function of the Deutsche Notenbank for the VVBs when it was dissolved in 1967. Altogether, 50 special branch banks were formed for the VVBs. These banks may serve one or several VVBs in industry or construction. They keep the accounts of individual enterprises and are responsible for the clearing and collection of funds. They are responsible for the provision of credit and the supervision of all budgetary relations between VVB-enterprises and the state.

The Agricultural Bank

It can be said that the Agricultural Bank is to agriculture what the Industrial and Commercial Bank is to industry. It is the business bank for agriculture, forestry, and related industries. Its customers include the agricultural cooperatives, state farms, state forest enterprises, consumer cooperatives, and enterprises of the food industry. It is under the jurisdiction of the Ministry of Finance and is organized on both a territorial and production basis. There are agricultural banks extending down to the local level, and banks that are designed to deal with a specific industry. The Agricultural Bank has the following responsibilities:[7]

1. It exercises the all-important control function over enterprises by keeping their accounts and serving as a clearing system.
2. It is responsible for the collection of agricultural revenues for the state budget and for the distribution of budget funds to the agricultural enterprises.
3. It is responsible for the granting of short- and long-term credits to enterprises and for enforcing the proper use of credit.
4. It assists the Staatsbank in the preparation of the cash and credit plans as they are relevant to agriculture.
5. It holds the idle money of enterprises and promotes savings on the part of the population.

The role of the Agricultural Bank in the preparation of the annual credit plan is worthy of mention.[8] All branches of the bank receive the annual credit plan drafts of enterprises under their jurisdiction. The branches examine the credit plans and make suggestions for improvement based on overall planning indexes. The directors of each branch bank either approve or disapprove the enterprise credit plan. Then each branch bank drafts the credit plan to cover its own field of competence. These plans go up the chain of command to the Agricultural Bank. The national credit plan for agriculture is then developed, reconciled with the credit plans for industry and foreign trade, and submitted to the Ministry of Finance for approval or disapproval.

Economic indexes for plan fulfillment in agriculture are developed by the Agricultural Bank, the Agricultural Council of the GDR, and the State Committee for the Procurement of Agricultural Products. Assistance in developing and implementing these indexes runs up and down the following chain of command:

1. Directors of the VVB bank branches and the directors of the VVBs and other organizations on the same level;
2. Directors of district (Bezirk) bank branches and chairmen of the district agricultural councils; and
3. Directors of county (Kreis) bank branches and chairmen of the county agricultural councils.

The Agricultural Bank receives its financial support from 250 million Ostmarks in stock of the Deutsche Notenbank, payments from the state budget, and net profits from banking operations. Fifty percent of net profits have to go to the state budget, however, and the remainder to special reserve funds.

The Foreign Trade Bank

The Foreign Trade Bank is responsible for financing East German foreign trade and for carrying out a large part of international settlement operations. It was formed from the dissolution of the Deutsche Notenbank, and its original capital structure consisted of 300 million Ostmarks of the Notenbank. The bank has its main office in East Berlin and branch offices throughout the GDR and in other countries. It is organized as a shareholding bank with the Staatsbank controlling the majority of the shares.

The functions of the Foreign Trade Bank can be presented as follows:[9]

1. It conducts commercial banking operations with other countries, including West Germany, and finances East German foreign trade enterprises and the foreign trade operations of other firms.
2. It takes checks, bills of exchange, and other documents of payments from both inside and outside of the GDR.
3. It is responsible for the purchase, sale, and holding of foreign exchange.
4. It is responsible for the maintenance of the accounts of all enterprises directly involved in foreign-trade transactions.
5. It is responsible for participation in the preparation of the national economic plan, particularly with respect to foreign-trade transactions, which would include assistance in the preparation of the credit plan.

The Foreign Trade Bank is administered by a president, vice-president, and board of directors. The president is responsible for the preparation of the credit plan of the bank. He also represents the bank in business with other financial institutions inside and outside of the GDR. The board of directors acts as an advisory board to the president and sees that the objectives of national policy are carried out. The top administrative hierarchy is also responsible for the preparation of the annual balance sheet and profit-and-loss statements.

Funds to support the bank come from three sources: share capital, which is represented primarily by the 300 million Ostmarks of the Deutsche Notenbank and also by purchases of the Ministry of Finance; reserve funds, which come from annual net profits; and special funds, which come from other internal sources. By law the bank is required to retain at least one-tenth of its annual net profits in its reserve funds up to a certain level.

The Cooperative Bank for Handicrafts and Industry

A distinctive feature of the East German banking system is the existence of cooperative banks that have the responsibility of providing credit and banking facilities to small producers and traders. The Cooperative Bank for Handicrafts and Industry (Genossenschaftsbank für Handwerk und Gewerbe) heads a network of some 230 cooperative banks that function throughout the country. Membership in the cooperative banks consists of both public and private craftsmen and firms. Although membership is supposedly voluntary, pressure is placed on private organizations to become members.
The functions of the Cooperative Bank for Handicrafts and Industry are as follows:[10]

1. It is responsible for the development and strengthening of socialist performance principles. This means that the bank and its affiliates are supposed to stress conformance to the objectives of the national economic plan. The banks are to stress work productivity and cost savings on the part of their members.

2. It is responsible for assistance in the preparation of the financial plan as it is relevant to the areas of the economy that it serves. Based on the objectives of the plan, the bank is supposed to elaborate proposals for its own credit plan.

3. The bank participates in the development of the planning projects of all producers that are affiliated with it. It makes proposals for the management of enterprises, based on its own analysis and experience.

4. It is responsible for granting both long- and short-term credit to artisans and craft enterprises. The granting of credit has

to be consistent with the objectives of the credit plan. In the credit contract interest differentials are used to achieve the most effective use of the credit funds.

5. The bank takes savings deposits from the general public. It purchases and sells securities and administers and deposits of its customers.

Savings Banks

The savings banks are responsible for the reception of savings and other deposits from the population, especially in the form of contract savings. These savings accounts carry a uniform interest rate of 3.25 percent per annum. Savings can be deposited and withdrawn in any amount, except that withdrawal notice must be given. The savings banks hold about three-fourths of all savings deposits in East Germany, but such facilities are also available at the postal savings system (Deutsche Post) and at branch agencies of the Agriculture Bank and banks for artisans. The network of offices at which savings accounts are made available to the population is widespread, and the savings banks and other savings institutions provide facilities for the transfer of funds.

The savings banks also have other functions, as follows.[11] They manage the accounts for private crafts and trading firms with at least 10 employees. They grant long-term credit, particularly for housing construction, and short-term credit to individuals and small enterprises. Loans to individuals are typically restricted to a maximum limit of 2,000 Ostmarks and are made available for such purposes as the purchase of consumer durable goods. Loans to small enterprises are usually to finance inventories. The savings banks also manage the accounts of the state budget in areas where branch banks of the Staatsbank do not exist. In addition, they are responsible for loan subscriptions and the purchase of mortgage bonds.

A standard interest rate of 4 percent per annum is charged by the savings banks to finance new housing, maintenance, modernization of living quarters, and other types of personal expenditures. The income from the interest has to be used to cover the 3.25-percent interest for savings depositors and the business costs of the savings banks, which include administration, maintenance of facilities, and the provision of other services. It might be added that the uniform interest rate of 3.25 percent on savings deposits represents a departure from the differentiated rates that prevailed up to January 1, 1971. These interest rates ranged from 3 to 5 percent, depending on the size and length of maturity of deposits. With interest payments at 4 and 5 percent on a portion of total deposits, however, the costs of the savings banks were not being met.

The Role of Credit in East Germany

As has been mentioned previously, the credit plan is an integral part of the financial plan. The credit plan, which controls the outlay of short- and long-term credit, is prepared by the Staatsbank. The total amount of credit and the proportions allowed to different branches of the economy are centrally determined according to planned economic needs. Otherwise, the microeconomic distribution is left to the judgment of the banks and enterprises concerned. Loans are extended on the condition of good management and the soundness of the purpose for which credit is to be used. Although interest rates are of little significance in programming investment at the central level, they are used at the microeconomic level as an important instrument of promoting the most efficient distribution and application of credits.

The credit and interest policy regulations for the 1971-75 planning period specify that enterprises may be granted credit for the implementation of certain types of capital investments. In accordance with the plan, credit priority is to be given to investments that are designed to improve the infrastructure of the economy, especially with respect to automation. Priority is also granted to projects that are designed to facilitate improvements in enterprise reorganization. Enterprises may also be granted credit for the financing of projects designed to improve working and living conditions, such as the construction of company housing. Research and development projects also enjoy high priority. Credit is also made available for the financing of inventories and the construction of warehouse facilities.

Guidelines for Granting Credit

Credit guidelines are worked out within the framework of the credit plan. The most recent guidelines, which were established in December 1970, are as follows:[12]

1. Credits for science and technology are granted on the basis of the state plan index figure and the financial plan based on it. Credit can be granted for advance financing of science and technology, particularly to support concentrated or early completion of projects. Repayment of credit must be made from a special fund set aside for this purpose.

2. Credit for investment projects is based on state planning index figures. These figures include the material volume of all investment projects, including construction and equipment. Index figures for efficiency are established for each project. These include the time required for the investment to pay for itself and the amount of capital invested per unit of productive capacity created. These

indexes are established by the State Planning Commission in cooperation with the banks. Adherence to them is a prerequisite for the granting of credit. Also as a prerequisite to the granting of credit, an enterprise must participate with its own assets in the financing of the investment project, at least in the amount shown in the state plan index figure for net profit. Allowance is made for setting up bonus funds for employees and for other planned uses for profit. Moreover, no credit will be granted for any new investment project unless it is in the list of items included in the national economic plan.

3. Credit for working capital is granted on the basis of enterprise plans for working capital. The enterprises must guarantee that the credit will lead to a more rapid increase in output and performance compared with the existing rate of economic growth. As a prerequisite to the granting of credit, enterprises must participate with their own assets to a minimum amount of 50 percent of the amount of the working capital.[13] Interest rate reductions to a rate of 1.8 percent per annum for a period of one year can be granted in order to promote the setting-up of economic reserves or stockpiles of important products.

Interest

To implement the credit policies to be followed during the 1971-75 plan period, changes have been made in the use of interest. The interest rates used prior to 1970 were low in comparison with international interest rate levels. As a result, the cost accounting of enterprises did not reflect the true expenditures incurred in connection with the use of credit. Consequently, the production cost of goods was valued too low by international standards. As a result, enterprises were not sufficiently forced to reduce their production costs.

For this reason the regulations for the 1971-75 planning period provide for the uniform application of a 5-percent basic economic interest rate for capital and operating credits, including credit for receivables from the delivery of goods and credit for science and engineering. The basic interest rate is supposed to set uniform standards for the return from funds financed by credit. Banks can use additional differentiated interest rates, however, which are designed to achieve greater flexibility in the implementation of credit policy. Interest rates are differentiated by the duration of the investment period—2 percent for a period of 12 to 24 months, 3 percent for a period of 24 to 36 months, and 4 percent for 36 months and more.[14]

Banks may grant interest rebates down to a total interest rate of 3 percent when enterprises surpass specified criteria for credit use, such as the use of their own funds or an above-average rate of return on investment.[15] Conversely, penalty interest rates can be charged up to a total rate of 7 percent when enterprises do not meet the criteria for effectiveness as set by the credit guidelines but the deviation is within a tolerable range. Differentiated additional interest charges up to a maximum of 15 percent can be charged by the banks in all cases in which the credit terms are not followed in the process of plan implementation. Interest rate rebates down to a minimum of 1.8 percent can be granted when high economic returns are realized by enterprises, particularly in connection with rationalization processes.

All enterprises are required to keep monetary assets earmarked for various purposes in specific bank accounts in their corresponding commercial banks. Any deployment of the assets must be embodied in the plan of the enterprise and must be contractually agreed upon with the commercial bank. Deposit monetary assets, however, can earn higher rates of interest the longer they remain on deposit in order to stimulate their more effective use. The interest rate is 2 percent per annum on deposits kept for 12 to 24 months, 3 percent on deposits kept for 24 to 36 months, and 4 percent on deposits of 36 months or more.[16] Any deposits that accumulate contrary to plan objectives earn no interest. Moreover, banks can exercise control functions over deposits. For example, they can force advance repayment of credit. They can also force the use of deposit assets in the place of planned state budgetary funds.

Agricultural Credit

To promote a gradual transition to an industrial form of organization in agriculture and the food industry, the Agricultural Bank has been given wider latitude over the granting of credit.[17] Priorities have been established for the granting of credit. In particular, credit will be granted for measures that will increase the productivity of the soil. This would include the purchase of modern tilling equipment, construction of agricultural chemical centers, and the construction of installations producing organic fertilizers on an industrial scale. Credit will also be granted for the acquisition of modern production equipment for agriculture and the food processing industry and the mechanization of existing structures when it is possible to greatly reduce the amount of human or animal labor. Credit priority is also extended to investments designed to improve canning and storage facilities.

The terms of credit are agreed upon by the Agricultural Bank and the individual enterprise. Maximum credit terms are as follows:[18]

1. For investments to increase soil fertility, 90 percent of normal productive life.
2. For investments for canning and storage and for large industrial type installations, 90 percent of normal productive life.
3. For measures to mechanize old structures, a payoff period of 5 years.
4. For all other investments, 50 percent of normal productive life.

Interest rates are graduated in accordance with the importance of the investment to the national economy, the extent of commitment of the enterprise's own resources, and the terms of credit. For example, variations in interest rates for some types of investments are presented in Table 12.2.

Investments to increase the fertility of the soil enjoy high credit priority in comparison to other types of investments. For example, for low priority investments, firms have to put up a minimum of 25 percent of the total value of the investment from their own internal sources. Interest rates vary from a minimum of 2 percent per annum to a maximum of 4 percent. To receive the minimum of 2 percent, an enterprise must use at least 75 percent of its own resources,

TABLE 12.2

Investments to Increase Fertility of the Soil
(percent)

Term of Credit	Interest Rate		
One-fourth of the maximum term	1.00[a]	1.00[b]	1.00[c]
One-half of the maximum term	1.00	1.00	1.00
Two-thirds of the maximum term	1.00	1.50	2.00
Over two-thirds of the maximum term	1.50	2.00	2.00

[a]Enterprises in this column use 40 percent or more of their resources.

[b]Enterprises in this column use between 20 and 40 percent of their resources.

[c]Enterprises in this column use up to 20 percent of their resources.

Source: Gesetzblatt der Deutschen Demokratischen Republik, II, 112 (East Berlin, November 6, 1968), p. 884.

compared to 40 percent for preferred investments.[19] The repayment period of the credit is also shorter.

The control functions of the agricultural banks are important. The banks are authorized to increase the rate of interest retroactively for the entire credit in the event that an enterprise fails to comply with stipulated conditions in the credit contract. Currency balances of enterprises must be maintained with their corresponding bank. A portion of enterprise financial resources are maintained on deposit in a special "funds for investment" account. Interest is paid by the banks on this account. The rates range from 1 percent on deposits of less than a year, 2 percent for deposits of two years' duration, and 3 percent for deposits of over two years.[20] Banks can compel withdrawal and use of these deposits for specified plan purposes.

It is hoped that the banking and credit reforms will improve the position of agriculture relative to other parts of the national economy. There has been an increase in the outlay of capital funds for agriculture. The reforms are attempting to encourage maximum efficiency in the utilization of buildings and machinery. Credit priority is being given to investment projects that are designed to increase the productivity of labor and land and reduce the amount of materials used. Such investments are supposed to increase the profits and improve the performance of agricultural enterprises so that they may be able to return to the economy more funds in Ostmarks and foreign currency. Thus, these funds become available for a more rapid repayment of credit and for expanded reproduction. It is too early, however, to judge the effect of the credit reforms on the performance of the agricultural sector.

SUMMARY

The structure of the East German banking system is easy to define. The overall banking policy in the GDR is laid down by the Ministry of Finance with the assistance of the State Planning Commission and the Staatsbank. The latter is the central bank and performs functions similar to the central banks in the capitalist countries—emission of currency, carrying out the financial policies of the government, refinancing other banks, supervising foreign payments, and servicing the state budget. It also prescribes the rules governing bank deposits, the extension of credit, and bank accounting and statistics. There are two major functions that differentiate the Staatsbank from capitalist central banks. It serves as a control mechanism to ensure that the flow of funds between enterprises is in accordance with the objectives of the national economic plan; it also plays an important role in economic planning in that it prepares the credit and cash plans, which are a part of the financial plan.

In East Germany there has been a trend toward functional specialization on the part of banks to service the particular needs of industry, agriculture, and foreign trade. Certain responsibilities have been taken away from the central bank and given to the specialized banks. The Industrial and Commercial Bank is responsible for granting short- and long-term credit to industry. Also, under the banking reforms of 1967-68 it has been given greater control over the operation of enterprises. There is also an Agriculture Bank, which has the responsibility of providing short- and long-term credit to agricultural and forestry enterprises. Both banks keep the accounts of enterprises under their jurisdiction. In addition, there is a Foreign Trade Bank, which is responsible for financial transactions between the GDR and other countries. There is also a comprehensive network of savings and cooperative banks, which serve as a repository for savings and a source of credit funds.

One of the principles adopted in the East German financial reforms is that enterprises must rely more on internal financing as a source of investment funds. This means that enterprises, even in the sphere of investment, have to rely basically on their own resources instead of allocations from the state budget. The purpose of this reform is to make individual firms more self-reliant and efficient. Banks have also assumed a more active role in that in essence they can see to it that enterprises use their own internal funds. The amount of credit granted by the banks has also increased relative to the total amount of investment financing in the GDR.

Under the banking reforms there is much more reliance on financial incentives and disincentives rather than on directives to accomplish economic performance. The most important financial instrument consists of differentiated credit terms, which can affect enterprise profits and incentive payments. Banks participate with enterprises in planning investments. Projects that enjoy favorable priorities in terms of their credit to overall output receive lower interest rates and larger repayment periods. In cases in which credit is not used for the approved purpose or a project is not finished on time, banks can undertake certain sanctions against an enterprise. A penalty interest rate can be charged for the period originally approved. Banks can also require the repayment of credit before maturity.

The banking reforms also brought about a change in the operation of banks. Banks are supposed to operate as financially independent entities rather than administrative authorities. Through the principle of economic accounting, banks are supposed to at least cover operating costs and try to make profits. Banks have been given more guidance over the economy and are supposed to pursue economic efficiency through active credit policies and consultations with enterprises.

CHAPTER 13

LABOR UNIONS AND THE EAST GERMAN STATE

INTRODUCTION

The role of labor unions in a socialist state is relatively easy to define. They exist and workers are not only permitted but encouraged to belong to them. Unlike their counterparts in the industrial countries of the West, they do not enjoy a significant sphere of autonomous action. They do not have the right to strike, and decisions on wage rates, output norms, hours of labor, and similar matters are prerogatives of the government rather than the unions. These decisions are made on a national scale, typically by a state committee on labor and wages. Such powers that unions do possess are in relationship to the operation of an enterprise. Although it was originally intended that important managerial decisions would be made by a troika of management, union, and party representatives, the role of the union has declined in importance as the drive for industrial efficiency strengthened managerial authority. It can be said that in terms of a constellation of power, unions rank behind both management and party in a socialist enterprise. They have certain functions, which can be enumerated as follows:

1. They have the right to participate with management in the development of the economic plan for an enterprise.

2. They are responsible for the maintenance of worker discipline by discouraging tardiness, absenteeism, and worker turnover and by promoting measures to encourage productivity.

3. Management is required to obtain their permission in assigning workers to wage categories and in introducing regulations on piecework and bonus systems.

4. Unions play an important role in the area of social insurance and carry out a variety of activities in connection with vacations,

education, recreation, and culture. They are responsible for the collection of social security contributions from enterprises and disbursements of cash benefits.

5. They have the right to express opinions on candidates nominated for management positions and to oppose discharges of workers initiated by management.

Nevertheless, the basic collective bargaining function, which unions perform in the Western democracies, has been emasculated in the socialist states. Unions are supposed to cooperate with management and function in the state and its national objectives. Although they have specific powers and responsibilities, they are subservient to the interests of the Communist Party.

Socialist unions are organized on a vertical, industrial basis, i.e., according to the branch of industry. For example, in the Soviet Union there are 25 unions, each of which includes all workers in a particular industry of the national economy. There is a union for coal miners, for railway workers, for agricultural workers, and for municipal service workers. At the apex of the union pyramid in each socialist country there is a Central Council of Trade Unions consisting of representatives who, like other trade union leaders, are elected. Membership in unions is voluntary and includes both workers and persons of managerial status. The union funds are derived partly from members' contributions and partly from state grants.

The basic unit of the socialist trade union structure is the local union, which is made up of all wage and salary earners, including management personnel, in a particular enterprise. Union members can elect a factory committee that represents all workers on questions related to their work and welfare. This committee, which may include management personnel, participates in an advisory capacity in drafting the enterprise's production and construction plans. Standing committees are also formed that deal with production, work norms of the labor force, social insurance and services, and cultural activities. A major purpose of the committee is to increase the workers' responsibility for production. It is supposed to organize competition based on emulation of individual workers and groups and to encourage inventions and rationalization proposals.

The role of trade unions in a socialist state is prescribed by the Communist Party. Supreme authority in both Party and government is vested in the hands of the Communist Party, which draws into its hands the main lines of command. The Party constitutes itself as the leading force of the working class generally and of state and social organizations; this entitles it to use mass organizations to transmit its will to the masses. Adherence to Party objectives is enforced by Party members who belong to unions and by Party statutes, which impose upon the members the duty to carry out directives and decisions within the other organizations to which they belong. It is the responsibility of the Party to stimulate the interests of the workers in achieving higher levels of production, as well as promoting their political and ideological education. The structure of the trade unions corresponds to that of the Party on all levels; union leaders usually belong to the corresponding leadership echelon of the Party, so that its dominant role is always assured.

LABOR UNIONS IN EAST GERMANY

In May 1945 efforts were made by former Social Democratic Party (SPD) members and trade union leaders to form a united socialist workers' party. These efforts were rebuffed by leaders in the KPD (Kommunistische Partei Deutschlands). The KPD wished to ally itself with various antifascist circles in Germany in order to exert influence in the other occupied zones. In 1946, however, the KPD and the SPD were merged into the Socialist Unity Party (SED). State control over the unions dates pretty much from this merger. Works councils, acting as the representative of the workers, frequently opposed the SED's efforts to introduce politics into industry; however, they were abolished in 1948 and replaced by trade union councils. In 1948 the German Confederation of Free Trade Unions (FDGB) was established as a single organization subdivided on an industry basis. Any primacy that the FDGB hoped to claim for itself as the representative of the workers was renounced in favor of the SED. According to FDGB statutes the SED is entitled to use all mass organizations to transmit its will to the masses.

The constitution of the GDR was passed in 1949 and guaranteed the exclusive monopoly of the FDGB in Article 14.[1] The constitution provided the right for everyone to belong to unions. This does not include the right to establish unions separate from the FDGB, however, The right to strike was made illegal. In 1950 the FDGB was declared a social mass organization of the SED. The role of the SED in union affairs then became all-pervasive. The trade unions then set for themselves the goal of helping the SED win the entire working class for the building of socialism.

The objectives of the FDGB were succinctly stated in a labor statute of 1955, which was as follows:

> The labor unions in the DDR are schools of democracy and socialism. Their goal is the socialistic state order. They organize the socialistic competition of blue and white collar workers and the intelligentsia for the fulfillment and overfulfillment of the national economic plans. They

are responsible for raising worker productivity. They help to introduce new progressive working standards based on technology. They help the blue and white collar workers and members of the intelligentsia to increase their political and professional qualifications, and to promote progressive work experience and methods especially after the example of the Soviet innovators of science, production, and technology.[2]

The first collective agreements were introduced in East Germany in 1951. These agreements were of two parts: a framework agreement for a branch of industry concluded by the appropriate economic ministry and the central board of the industrial union and a plant agreement, based on the framework agreement, concluded by the plant management and the shop union committee. The agreements were geared to both the industry and the individual plant relationship to the overall economic plan. The plant directors obligated themselves to create the necessary conditions for smooth production, to establish technical work norms, and to classify the plant workers according to eight basic work categories. The unions agreed to organize work competition, to cooperate in the setting of work norms, and to explain to the workers the necessity of labor discipline.

Included in the agreements were all of the ramifications of the Soviet work system. Socialist work competition within one plant and between plants was established. Emphasis was placed on programs that were designed to stimulate competition among individual workers, or among groups of workers, to see who could produce the most. A system of piece rates tied to worker performance was introduced. Trade unions were to promote what is called socialist emulation, which means the development of moral responsibility on the part of the workers to increase production for the interest of the state.

Work statutes in the GDR were codified into public law in April 1961 in the formal Gesetzbuch der Arbeit der Deutschen Demokratischen Republik. Paragraph 4 gives the workers the right to belong to labor unions.[3] The right of workers to belong to unions independent of the FDGB is prohibited, however. Paragraph 4 also states that an objective of the FDGB is to lead the workers toward the further development of socialism. Unions are to lead the fight toward achieving a high socialist moral, increasing worker productivity and mobilizing the whole working class for the general fulfillment of the national economic plans. In Paragraph 89 the FDGB is given the authority to manage the entire social security system.[4] With respect to strike action, which the FDGB does not possess, the Gesetzbuch states that the working class of the GDR owns the means of production. To strike under this condition would be against their interest. In a socialist society there is no need for a paragraph on the freedom to strike, for there are no opponents to strike against.

Major Characteristics of the FDGB

Trade unions in the GDR are a curious mélange of a survival from the past and modern adaptations to the needs of the state. In some respects the trade unions are reminiscent of medieval guilds in that they embody the employer, who is the representative of the state, and the employees, who are the workers. In some ways they are like the unions of the advanced capitalist countries in that they try to safeguard the interest of the workers against management, send elected delegates to the national trade union congress, and are affiliated with the World Federation of Trade Unions. But the most distinctive feature is that, while providing protection against management and the bureaucracy, they cooperate with the employer, the state, and assist in the implementation of the national economic plan on the labor front. In this respect East German unions may be considered to be a transmission belt for the economic programs of the state to the masses.

Union Membership

More than 90 percent of the East German labor force belong to unions affiliated with the FDGB. Membership, although ostensibly voluntary, is in reality based on pressure upon the worker to join. Without membership, advancement in a given occupation is rarely possible. Monetary and nonmonetary rewards for performance are usually given only to FDGB members. Union membership also gives other advantages, especially preference in some of the social insurance benefits. For example, nonmembers receive only one-half of the regular rates for nonoccupational sickness benefits. Union members receive extra allowances for sick pay as well as lower rates in rest homes. Union members can also take advantage of low cost vacations. In addition, the FDGB has also created funds that can be used as loans to union members at little or no interest charges.

The revenues of the FDGB consist of membership fees and revenues from various cultural and business activities. Membership fees are based on monthly earnings and range from 0.50 Ostmarks on monthly incomes of 100 Ostmarks or less to 35 Ostmarks on monthly incomes of 2,600 Ostmarks or more.[5] In addition to the monthly dues special assessments can be levied against union members. The greatest percent of the dues remain at the local union level, where they are used to finance educational, cultural, physical culture, and sports activities and for other services to members. The remainder of the dues are remitted to the national union, where they are used for administrative staff and organizational purposes.

The rights of union members are specified in the Gesetzbuch der Arbeit.[6] The rights include participation in elections and in discussion at union meetings, with the right to criticize and raise questions in union organs or on the work of unions and administrations and to bring in any proposals. Every union member may elect and be elected to all union bodies, conferences, and congresses. He may propose or oppose any candidate, as well as criticize him. Elected officials are answerable for their actions to the union members. Members are entitled to be present at any union meeting where their own activity is being discussed and may present to the union proposals concerning their activities and the protection of their rights. No member can be discharged without the sanction of the trade union committee representing the enterprise at which he is employed.

There is a reverse side of the coin, however, in that rights also entail responsibilities on the part of the workers, which are also spelled out in the Gesetzbuch der Arbeit. First, most important, a trade union member must contribute to the fulfillment of the plan of the enterprise and participate actively in socialist emulation. Second, a member is obliged to advance systematically his educational and cultural level as well as his political outlook. Third, a member should work for strict observance of labor discipline and the full use of work time. Fourth, a member is supposed to attend union meetings, fulfill union assignments, and pay his dues promptly. Finally, a union member is under an obligation to oppose any "antisocial manifestations" on the part of other workers and to observe the rules of the socialist community.

In spite of their numerous activities the East German labor unions have no real power of independent action, for they are completely dominated by the SED. It is only fair to point out, however, that organized labor was completely emasculated by the Nazis, and so the SED can hardly be accused of depriving the German worker of any previously existing rights. In any case the Communists insist that the government of the GDR is a dictatorship of the proletariat, and for that reason completely independent labor organizations would be an anomaly. This is an argument of doubtful validity, for it is quite clear that the present government of the GDR is not a dictatorship of the proletariat.

Functions of the FDGB

The formal functions of the FDGB are expressed in Article 12 of the Gesetzbuch der Arbeit.[7] The main functions can be enumerated as follows:

1. The promotion of socialist competition: The goal is the socialist state order. Socialist competition means that individuals and groups are obliged to fulfill or overfulfill production plans in definite respects and compete with others for good records. Unions are supposed to organize and promote the socialist competition of blue and white collar workers and members of the intelligentsia for the purpose of increasing worker productivity and fulfilling the plans of the national economy.

2. The application of more modern methods of production: Unions are to promote worker discipline and assist in the development and introduction of methods designed to increase total output. Unions are to consider methods designed to decrease costs and to increase the productivity of the workers.

3. Collaboration in collective agreements: Collective agreements on the part of unions and management in the GDR are obligatory. Both parties are supposed to pursue the same aim of advancing production and improving the material standards of society. Collective agreements are based on approved state plans for production, wages, and construction and on established wage standards. In a collective agreement the union assumes an obligation to help fulfill the production plan. Management is obliged to consult with the union over any changes in wage payments. Unions and management have joint jurisdiction over the use of material incentives. Unions also have some jurisdiction over working conditions and the development of an appropriate wage scale within the framework provided by the economic plan.

4. The development of cultural and sports activities: This may perhaps be considered one of the more important union functions. In conducting this function East German unions exercise a great deal of influence over the welfare of all workers, spend large sums of money, and employ many persons in the process. Programs of sports, recreation, and cultural activities reflect the interlocking aims of the SED for increasing health and morale, group loyalty, understanding of party aims and for raising the level of education and culture of workers and their families.

5. The administration of social welfare benefits: Unions in the GDR are directly concerned with the administration of social insurance for wage earners and salaried employees. They supervise the medical care of workers and their families, determine temporary disability compensation and maternity and other allowances, and send workers to health resorts and rest homes. Through their representatives unions participate in the granting of pensions by social insurance authorities and supervise the construction of health centers. Unions organize public councils of active union members to assist and check on all medical institutions. Social insurance operates under centralized governmental policies and budgetary controls, but with administration through the unions at all levels.

6. The supervision of safety measures in enterprises of all kinds: In the field of safety and working conditions the unions share in decisions for improvements and in the state function of inspections. Unions can check on observance by management of the safety regulations and on the state of safety instruction in enterprises.

The Organization of the FDGB

Before presenting the organization framework of the FDGB, it is necessary to make two observations concerning the relationship of the FDGB to the East German system as a whole. The most basic observation is that the unions carry on all of their work under the leadership of the SED. Second, the structure of East German unions is based on the principle of democratic centralism. Each of these observations may be expounded upon as follows:

1. East German trade unions are governed by principles established by the SED and reaffirmed in party and trade union documents. Initiative for major developments in union work comes from SED directives. Party groups in the unions and the power of the party to control appointments to union positions assures that party policy will be followed. There are party groups in the shops and enterprises, and the party often has its office conveniently near the offices of the director of an enterprise and of the union committee. The influence of the SED also is supposed to come through its members who are members of the trade unions and through persuasion and education. Party groups are established in the trade union congresses and conferences and in the elected organs of these sessions, with the duty to promote policies. The FDGB and SED are not only related by statutes and groups but also through the top leadership. The first secretary of the SED, Walter Ulbricht is also on the managing board of the FDGB. The leader of the FDGB, Herbert Warnke, is a member of the Politburo of the SED.

2. Democratic centralism is the basic organizational principle of the FDGB. This means, according to the trade union statutes, that all union organs from bottom to top are elected by the members and report to them, that union organizations decide all questions in accordance with the union statutes, that decisions are made by majority vote, and that lower union organs are subordinate to the higher. Invariably the decisions at the highest level of union management are binding at all union levels. Democratic centralism includes the concept of collective leadership and of democratic elections by secret ballot, with some exceptions, after open criticism and discussion of party work and open nomination and discussion of candidates. It involves also the idea of wide participation of the rank and file in trade union work. Initiative and independence are to be disciplined, however, within the limits of approved policy.

The FDGB is organized on the principle of one firm to one trade union. The industrial principle of organization is supposed to eliminate the division of labor into craft unions, thus securing unity of action in achieving stated national goals. Each national union has jurisdiction over all who work in one industry or in a group of related industries. There is logic in the industrial form of unionism in that the process of economic planning and control is based on the particular industry—for example, machine tools, textiles, coal, oil, and metallurgy—with general coordination among industries at the government level. There is also the territorial principle, which devolves planning and operational powers to regional authorities.

There are 15 unions affiliated with the FDGB, each of which includes all workers in a particular industry of the national economy. These unions are as follows: the metal workers union; the chemical workers union; the building construction union; the mining and energy workers union; the printing and paper workers union; the transportation and communication workers union; the textile and leather workers union; the state and local civil servants union; the agricultural, food processing, and forestry workers union; the scientists and technicians union; the medical workers union; the artists union; the teachers union; commercial workers union; and metallurgical workers union.

In addition to being organized on a national industrial basis, unions affiliated with the FDGB are also organized on a territorial basis. Territorial organization refers to the organization of unions into district, county, and local units. At the local, or village, level there are local unions that include members of national unions who are not in firms with their own trade unions, self-employed workers, and service workers. Also at the local level, is the plant union (Betriebs Gewerkschafts Leitung, or BGL). The branches of a particular union are then combined into county, district, and finally the national union itself. Integration of the industrial unions is accomplished at all territorial levels through the use of conferences that select policy-making boards.

Chart 13.1 presents the organizational scheme of the FDGB. The structure is pyramidal. The primary unit is the plant or village group. Through conferences, which are held from time to time, delegates elect committees responsible for operating the union affairs at the local, county, district, and national levels. At the apex of the pyramid is the FDGB congress, which includes delegates from all East German trade unions. Policy-making then starts from the top and flows downward to the local level through a series of policy-making bodies that exist at all territorial levels. Decisions made by the highest policy-making body are binding on all bodies subordinate to it.

CHART 13.1

Organizational Scheme
of FDGB*

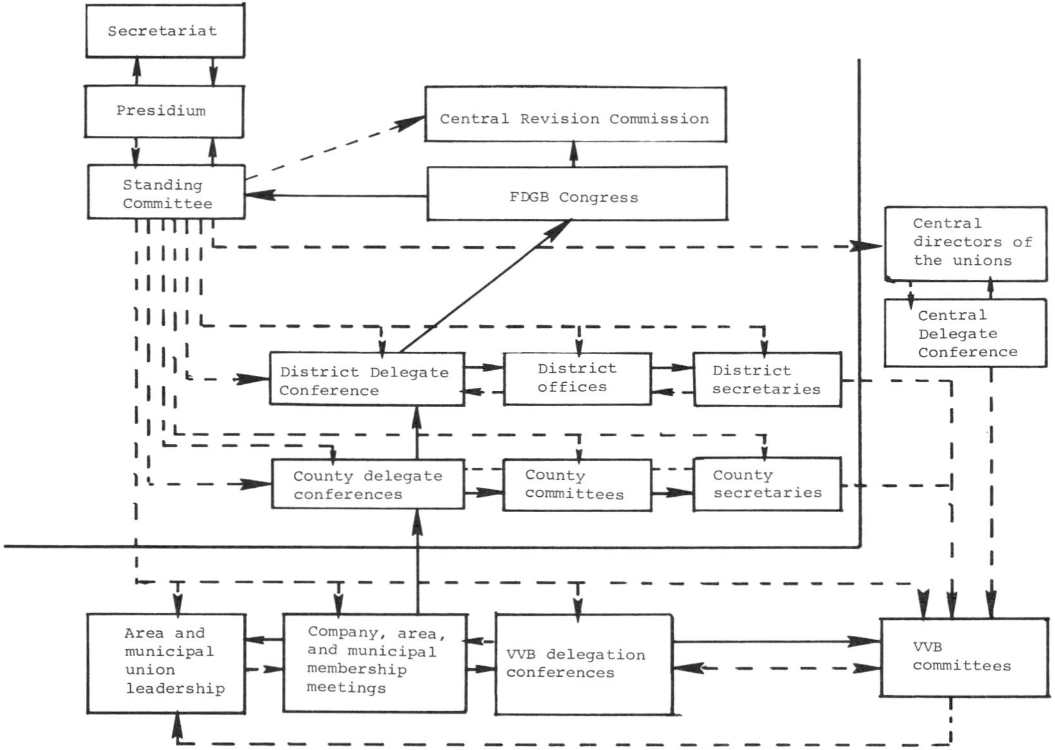

*Solid lines indicate election; broken lines indicate direction.

Source: Der Freie Deutsche Gewerkschaftsbund, Geschichte und Organisation (Bonn: Neue Gesellschaft Verlag, 1971), p. 61.

The highest organ of the FDGB is the Congress, which is supposed to meet at least once every four years. It is composed of delegates who are elected at the regional trade union conferences (Bezirksdelegierten Konferenzen). Delegates to the regional conferences are elected from district conferences (Kreisdelegierten Konferenzen), and delegates to the district conferences are elected from local union conferences. As the leader of the mass organization of East German workers the Congress has an important position in German society in that it speaks for workers at high levels of the party and government when policies are being considered. It is not an independent decision-making body representing the union members, however. Meetings are dominated by party policy, and top leaders of the party and government participate in the activities.

The major functions of the Congress, as defined at its seventh meeting held in 1968, are as follows:[8]

1. It receives the reports of the Executive Committee (Bundesvorstand) and the Central Revisions Commission (Zentrale Revisionskommission);
2. It elects the members of the Executive Committee and the Central Revisions Commission;
3. It establishes the policies to be followed by the FDGB unions during the period between the holding of congresses;
4. On intraunion matters the Congress determines the structure and staffs of all union organizations and approves their budgets; and
5. Members of the Congress provide communication from the top of the union structure downward when they return home and explain the decisions of the Congress at workers' meetings.

The Executive Committee of the FDGB consists of 200 members. It is managed by a Presidium of 26 members elected by the Executive Committee and a Secretariat of five members selected from members of the Presidium. Day-to-day work is directed by the Secretariat, which makes many decisions subject to the approval of the Presidium.[9] The Executive Committee has the following functions:[10]

    1. It is responsible for the overall implementation of labor union policy that has been developed by the Congress.

    2. It participates in the development of the national economic plan and is responsible for seeing that unions and union members cooperate in the fulfillment and overfulfillment of planning objectives.

    3. It is responsible for the introduction of new work methods at all levels of union activity.

4. It is responsible for the supervision of union administration of social security. The Executive Committee works out the social insurance budget, which is included in the state budget, and determines the rates of contributions for social insurance by enterprises in different fields. It issues regulations for administering the extensive systems of rest homes and sanitariums that are the responsibility of individual unions.

5. Staff departments in the Executive Committee deal with such areas as propaganda, housing and living conditions, physical culture and sports, work laws, work protection, and international relations. Altogether there are 13 departments. They make studies and carry on the detailed activities involved in directing the large union structure and in relations with government decision-making bodies.

The Review Commission (Revisionskommission) is the control organ of the FDGB organization. Its members are elected by secret ballot of the Executive Committee. The Review Commission is responsible for the ratification of the labor policies established by the Executive Committee.[11] It is responsible for the enforcement of labor statutes and the carrying out of democratic centralism. It is also responsible for the auditing of the funds utilized by the Executive Committee.

Below the Congress in the pyramidal structure of the FDGB come the district trade union conferences (Bezirksdelegierten Konferenzen). These conferences, too, are supposed to convene at least once every four years. The functions of the district conferences are to elect delegates to the national congress, elect members to the district executive committees (Bezirksorstände), hear reports from the district executive committees and secretariats (Bezirkssekretariate), and establish the labor union policy to be followed at the district level.

Each district has an executive committee (Bezirksvorstand) and a secretariat (Bezirkssekretariat). The size of the executive committee and secretariat varies with the size of the district. Executive committees are responsible for the social insurance budgets for their areas.[12] They are also responsible for the implementation of union policy set at the national level in their districts. They assist in the introduction of new work methods and are responsible for seeing that economic planning objectives are fulfilled. Secretariats are selected from members of the executive committees and are responsible for day-to-day work.

Below the district trade union conferences come the county trade union conferences (Kreisdelegierten Konferenzen). These conferences are responsible for the election of delegates to attend the district conferences and the election of members to the county executive committees. The executive committees (Kreisvorstande) are responsible for the implementation of the decisions of the federal and district executive committees within each county unit.[13] They are responsible for the social insurance budgets in their areas and assist in the implementation of planning objectives. County executive committees are also responsible for the election of county secretariats, who have the responsibility of the day-to-day running of county union activity between meetings of the conferences. All individual union units are subordinate to the control of the county executive committees of the FDGB.

There are also city and town conferences. These conferences elect delegates to the county conferences and also select city or village executive committees and secretariats. The executive committees and secretariats are responsible for union matters in their areas, particularly with respect to the implementation of planning objectives.[14] They are also responsible for the organization of socialist work competition.

The basic organization of the trade unions exists at the local level, where there is the plant union committee (BGL). The plant level of organization is extremely important because it is there that the productivity drives and enlightenment campaigns take concrete form.[15] Each committee has a chairman, secretary, and permanent commissions. In large plants elected delegate conferences are used to select the committee. The shop union committee has the following functions, which are codified in the Gesetzbuch der Arbeit:

1. In rule-making and the application of rules affecting workers the BGL has authority that limits to some extent the plant manager's right of unilateral action. On certain points his decision must be made jointly with the BGL, and on others he may issue orders only in accordance with general union regulations.

2. The BGL has the right to participate in the plant's planning for production or construction, whether in the plant or of housing, cultural, and service facilities.

3. It represents all plant workers on all questions of labor, living conditions, and culture.

4. It possesses certain control functions. For example, it has the right to check on the observance of labor laws and the collective contracts, on the progress of construction, and on the provision of services. It can take suggestions for improving the work of the plant to higher union organs, which are obliged to consider its proposals and inform it of their conclusions.

5. It takes part in the administration of the social insurance system, provides passes to rest homes and vacation resorts, and checks on the provision of medical services.

In firms with more than 500 workers there are department union committees. They are responsible for the organization of all union activity in their departments and secure the implementation of the decisions of the plant trade union. Department union committees also choose their officers and organize commissions similar to those of the plant committee. Committee functions include the protection of labor, the handling of social insurance, and representation on the plant labor disputes commission.

To ensure an active participation of as many union members as possible, union organization is further broken down into brigades. At the head of the brigade is the shop steward, who is selected in an open election. The brigade also elects representatives for culture, social security matters, and safety. The shop steward is responsible for the work performance of the brigade and also for the protection of its interests. He is responsible for the collection of union dues and for bringing new workers into union membership. In the brigade the worker has the closest connection with his union. It is at this level that basic attitudes and loyalties toward the union are formed. Loyalties are also carried over to the brigade, where socialist work competition with other brigades is stressed. Even at the brigade level an extension of the party structure exists to maintain work discipline, to carry on political education, and to promote fulfillment of production plans.

Collective Agreements

Collective agreements (Kollektivvertrage) between labor and management in the GDR bear little resemblance to standard bargaining procedures in the capitalist countries. Wage levels are set by the government within the framework of the national economic plan. Work conditions are regulated by the government and do not reflect negotiation between management and the union. Concluding collective agreements is one of the most important trade union functions, however, and the signed agreement becomes a legal document that management is supposed to honor. The collective agreement has both political and economic objectives. Both union and management agree to pursue the aim of fulfilling the production plan of the enterprise. The union agrees to promote socialist competition. Management is obliged to consult the union on all matters concerning the distribution of incentive funds and the provision of housing and social insurance. Norms of production are also established by management and the union under the collective agreement.

Collective agreements between union and management are regulated by the Gesetzbuch der Arbeit.[16] At the firm level, the union agrees to the following responsibilities:

1. To develop socialist competition among the workers;
2. To promote health and safety standards and to foster the cultural and sports activities of the workers;

3. To maintain labor discipline within the firm;
4. To introduce advanced work methods in the production process;
5. To enforce the socialist work principle, based on technical work standards, and to contribute to cost reductions; and
6. To agree with management over wages and production norms to be maintained by the workers.

In the collective agreement, the union does have jurisdiction over many aspects of worker activity. For example, it participates in formulating the distribution of various wage and incentive funds. It has jurisdiction over social welfare measures. It can enforce safety standards and protect the workers from abusive working conditions.

At the national level collective agreements are concluded between the FDGB and its union affiliates with the national planning commission, with central and district organs of the government, and with management, as represented by the VVBs.

Included in the collective agreements are wage-payment standards and working conditions for all economic fields in the national economy, for workers and firms within each field of activity, and for particular geographic regions. Wage agreements are related to national planning objectives and are binding in each field or region. Thus, it is impossible for individual firms in a particular region to offer higher wages than are called for in the national agreements.

There is no doubt that most of the regulations contained in union and firm collective agreements are intended to enhance the fulfillment of the national economic plan and not to increase the incomes of the workers. It is argued that the fulfillment of the national plan is good for the whole economy and will increase the consumption of society and also that of the individual. This societal consumption would include all that the state can offer, from education to health services.

Labor Disputes

The major issues that prompt labor disputes in the capitalist countries are largely absent in the socialist countries. Wage determination is outside the scope of labor-management decisions in the East German economy. Money wages are fixed by the planners as an important element in the total planning of prices, costs, and incomes, which must take into account the plans for consumer goods and services. Wages are not involved in union disputes, except for details in the application of central standards. Moreover, the main union weapon in a labor dispute, the strike, is not permitted. Socialist theory holds that in a system of public ownership of the means of production there are no contradictory class interests to cause labor conflicts.

For the most part, labor disputes are concerned with complaints involving worker rights. For example, a worker may have been transferred to another job against his will. Disputes may also involve the application of wage standards and safety measures or managerial attitudes that are not felt to be in the best interests of the workers. Disputes, however, may involve workers who are guilty of gross breaches of discipline. But whatever the reasons for the dispute the government plays a dominant role in determining the rules for settlement. These rules are codified in the Gesetzbuch der Arbeit and in regulations issued by the central committee of the unions, with governmental authority.

Labor disputes in the GDR are handled at three levels.[17] At the lowest level is the plant labor dispute commission, comprised of union and management representatives. The union representatives, who serve for one year, are appointed by the BGL. The commission considers disputes with respect to labor legislation, discipline, collective agreements, and factory or office regulations. At the meeting the duties of secretary and chairman are performed alternately by union and management representatives, and all decisions are made not by voting but by joint agreement. If the parties in the dispute are not satisfied with the decision of the labor dispute commission, they can apply to the BGL, which may either confirm the decision of the commission or reject it and render a new decision. The latter, however, is infrequent. The People's Court of Justice represents the final level of appeal. Both union and management may appeal a decision to the People's Court. Technically, the court decision is binding, although there can be appeal all the way to the national court level.[18]

There also may be disputes between labor and management over the terms of a collective agreement, particularly at the plant level. In the event that a dispute occurs, the union and management would appeal to their corresponding bodies at the next-highest administrative level. It is possible for a dispute between labor and management to go all the way up the administrative ladder to the executive committees of the national union and the VVB. Here, at least in theory, disputes are finally resolved.

SUMMARY

Unions in the GDR are organized into the FDGB. The supreme executive body of the FDGB is the Executive Committee, composed of 200 members elected at a national convention of delegates from all trade unions held every four years. It announces general policy and determines and checks on the functions of the affiliated unions. The day-to-day operations are carried on by a Secretariat composed of five members, including the FDGB president. For greater control over the affiliated unions a Presidium, consisting of the Secretariat and the presidents of the more important unions, is responsible for policy functions. Executive committees are also elected in each of the administrative-political district, county, and local units of the GDR.

The constituent unions, subordinate to the FDGB, range in geographical subdivisions from the national union level to the individual plant. At a national conference of elected delegates, also held every four years, an executive committee is elected that in turn elects one of its members as union president. The plant level of organization is extremely important because it is there that the productivity drives and "socialist enlightenment" campaigns take concrete form. In each plant, a plant union committee (BGL) is formed, constitutionally by election but often by appointment from above. In large plants there is a central union committee that provides more unified control, as well as department union committees.

Collective agreements in the GDR are of two parts: a framework agreement for a branch of industry concluded by the appropriate economic ministry, the VVBs, and the Executive Committee of the national industrial union; and a plant agreement, based on the framework agreement, concluded by the plant management and the shop union committee. The basis for both types of agreements are formulated in the Gesetzbuch der Arbeit. The agreements are geared to both the industry and the individual plant relationship to the overall economic plan. Management obligates itself to create the necessary conditions for smooth production and the establishment of technical work norms. The union obligates itself to organize socialist competition and to cooperate in the setting of norms.

Labor unions in East Germany differ from their counterparts in the Western capitalist countries in many respects. Their primary function is to see to it that workers perform within the framework of national economic policy goals. Socialist competition is organized between workers and enterprises for the purpose of increasing worker productivity and fulfilling the state plans. Unions also conclude collective agreements with enterprises that usually include the establishment of work norms and the improvement of safety standards. The administration of social insurance funds is also a union responsibility. Unions do not have the right to strike against the employers, however. Their influence upon the centralized formulation of wage policy and decisions regarding the distribution of the national income is small and presumably is never at variance with state policy. Moreover, when contradictions arise between the demands of increased production and workers' interests, it is the former that usually wins.

CHAPTER 14

COMPARATIVE OPERATING RESULTS OF THE EAST AND WEST GERMAN ECONOMIES

INTRODUCTION

The purpose of this chapter and the one that follows is to compare the accomplishments of the East and West German economic systems, with particular emphasis placed on the decade of the 1960s. The two countries afford an interesting comparison of two very different countries that were formerly a part of the Third Reich. The West German economic system today is basically a mixed system in which the influence of the government sector in terms of its impact on resource allocation is considerable. This impact involves taxes and expenditures that force a diversion of resources through the public sector and also direct government participation in the economy through the ownership of industry. Nevertheless, the market system is the dominant allocator of resources and the private sector contributes the bulk of the GNP. The East German economy, on the other hand, is state managed and directed, and the state-owned enterprise is the basic type of production and distribution unit.

Both countries have had to overcome considerable handicaps during the postwar period. Of the two countries, East Germany had the greater transitional problem in that it had to contend with the dismantling and reparation policies of the Soviet Union. The migration of millions of persons to the West also forced a curtailment in the implementation of its economic programs. It was not really until 1960 that the final development of the socialist planned economy occurred. West Germany had the benefit of a much less punitive occupation policy imposed by the Allied authorities. Marshall Plan aid contributed to the recovery of the West German economy. So, to some extent West Germany was given an initial advantage in the development of its economy.

A command system such as the East German economy possesses certain inherent advantages over a market economy. The state owns practically the whole of industry and the transport system and controls all agricultural activity. This widespread public ownership naturally lends itself to central economic planning. It may be considered that it is the public ownership that is fundamental to socialism, but what gives the East German economy its particular stamp is planning, with its emphasis on stimulating production and productivity and on their corollary, the system of priorities and controlled prices. What all of this means is that the centrally planned, publicly owned East German economy can shift resources around as it sees fit. It enjoys a considerable advantage, particularly in investment and in the control of social services and wages. Resources can be diverted from consumption to investment. The state has the authority to assemble the funds required for social services by means of indirect taxation, without having to face political criticism. The same applies to the allocation of investment and other types of state expenditures. Moreover, wages can be kept lower than productivity gains, and the difference is appropriated by the state in the form of saving for capital formation.

In East Germany trade unions are controlled to an extent that would neither be attempted nor tolerated in West Germany. Although East German workers are not completely debarred from using unions as a means of attaining improvements in working conditions and pay, the fact remains that the unions are the creatures of the state. They act as its agent in enforcing the prescribed wages and hours and in the promotion of increased productivity. There is little question of the workers using the strike threat and none at all of official strikes. East Germany, then, is virtually free of a problem that confronts West Germany and other market economies, namely, an inflationary spiral contributed to by union wage demands. State control over wages makes it easier to maintain a planned balance between private purchasing power and the supply of consumer goods and services. In practice, however, a degree of semirepressed inflation has been experienced, attributable in part to agricultural problems and to a heavy influx of workers into the cities.

These inherent advantages have been counterbalanced by defects in the system of planning, however. Development has been dogmatically determined and economic rationality has been subordinated to political expediency. Consumer sovereignty and the free play of supply and demand would limit the area of political decision-making, but these normal guides to optimizing production have been discarded. This has led to a waste of resources. Moreover, so far no workable pricing system has been devised. Prices do not fully reflect factor costs, as rent and interest are not necessarily fully accounted for in them, and, furthermore, different criteria for price-setting are used for different categories of products. As a result, prices do not and cannot perform a rational allocative function. Certainly, there are not the same built-in disciplines as in a market economy.

In comparing the economic development of East and West Germany, primary attention is placed on the decade of the 1960s. It was during this period that the self-imposed isolation of the GDR from the West took place through the erection of the Berlin Wall. By 1961 agriculture had been collectivized and the economic organization of the socialist state had been created. In 1963 the New Economic System of planning and management was introduced. In an attempt to stimulate increased production, the concepts of profit, cost, price, and economic cost accounting were accepted as principles of industrial management in the GDR. Also accepted was a new reward structure based on the performance principle (Leistungsprinzip), which tied wages and bonuses to the performances of workers and industrial enterprises. In addition the New Economic System attempted to create greater flexibility in economic decision-making through a decentralization of the bureaucratic and industrial structure.

It certainly cannot be stated that East Germany was an underdeveloped country upon which a Stalinist growth model imposed a policy of forced economic development. In Chapter 1 it was pointed out that the area that now comprises East Germany was as well developed economically as the current area of West Germany.[1] In addition to having a stronger agricultural base than West Germany, East Germany had a well-defined industrial structure. There was specialization in such areas as basic chemicals, machine tools, synthetic rubber, and office equipment. Moreover, the investment policies of the Third Reich had concentrated on increasing industrial output in the eastern part of Germany. In 1939 industrial output per capita in East Germany was 16 percent higher than in West Germany. Therefore, what actually happened after World War II was that East Germany was cut off from its prewar markets and had to readjust its economy toward fitting in with the far-less-industrialized countries of the Soviet-bloc. The mix of foreign trade was disadvantageous to the East Germans in that it was weighted with machinery items and chemicals, which the industrializing countries, such as Poland and Hungary, began to produce for themselves.

There are a number of ways in which the East and West German economies can be compared. One way is to compare the total output of the two economies over a period of time to see if increases favored one or the other. Then the output can be divided on the basis of source. Industrial and agricultural output for each country can be compared. Industrial output can be subdivided on the basis of contributing sources, and comparisons of growth can be made for each source. The contribution of capital to output can also be made to see which country is making a more efficient utilization of capital resources. It is also possible to compare labor productivity to see which country is able to combine its labor and capital resources more efficiently.

Income distribution is also a critical area of comparison. Money wages can be compared in terms of increases over a period of time for each country to see if differences are widening or narrowing. Then it is desirable to make a comparison of income distribution by income classes for the purposes of ascertaining which country has achieved a more uniform distribution. Real wages, or the actual purchasing power of money income, must also be examined. With respect to the purchase of basic necessities, how does the purchasing power of the average worker compare? It is assumed that in a socialist system disparities between rich and poor are eliminated through a more equitable state distribution of income. Also, social welfare in the form of pensions, medical care, and other benefits is supposed to be a hallmark of socialism. It is necessary to look at the tax-transfer payment structure in each country before a comparison of social welfare measures can be made. The tax structures of each country must be closely examined in terms of the redistributional effect on income.

A COMPARISON OF OUTPUT

A general comparison of the East and West German economies can be obtained through the use of national income and product aggregates. It is necessary to point out, however, that East and West Germany use different income and product concepts. In the GDR the appropriate concept to measure output is national income. The East German concept of national income includes material production only. The concept must be differentiated from the concept of gross product. The official East German output index is a price-weighted aggregate of the value of industrial output of all enterprises.[2] Considerable double-counting occurs in that the value of intermediate products transferred from one factory to another is added to the value of the final products. The total volume of production is therefore made to look far larger than is the actual case. For example, gross product in the GDR for 1970 amounted to 275.1 billion Ostmarks, and net product or income amounted to 108.3 billion Ostmarks.[3] The difference is comprised by the consumption of intermediate goods in the production process plus depreciation and rent allowances. The comparable West German income and product concept is net social product.

Table 14.1 presents a comparison of national income and net social product in the GDR and FRG for the period 1961-70. Both concepts are presented in real terms. Real social product for West

TABLE 14.1

Comparison of Real National Income and Real Net Social Product, East and West Germany, 1960-70

	East Germany National Income Expressed in 1962 Prices		West Germany Net Social Product Expressed in 1962 Prices	
Year	Billion Ostmarks	Yearly Growth Rate (percent)	Billion DM	Yearly Growth Rate (percent)
1960	71.1		300.3	
1961	73.5	3.4	315.6	5.1
1962	74.4	1.2	326.6	3.5
1963	76.7	3.1	336.1	2.9
1964	80.5	4.9	358.0	6.5
1965	84.2	4.6	376.8	5.3
1966	88.3	4.9	385.7	2.4
1967	93.0	5.4	381.4	1.1
1968	97.8	5.1	409.3	7.3
1969	102.8	5.1	442.4	8.1
1970	108.0	5.0	463.2	4.7

Sources: Staatlichen Zentralverwaltung für Statistik, Statistisches Taschenbuch, 1971 (East Berlin: Staatsverlag der DDR, 1971), p. 26; Statistisches Bundesamt, Statistisches Jahrbuch für die Bundesrepublik Deutschland, 1970 (Wiesbaden: W. Kohlhammer Verlag, 1970), p. 490.

Germany is equal to total goods produced and services performed less price increases that occurred during the period. The base period in comparable prices is 1962. Also presented is the yearly growth in national income and net social product for the GDR and FRG. The growth rates for each country were rather close together. Between 1960 and 1969 the growth rate for the FRG averaged 4.8 percent a year compared to 4.5 percent for the GDR. The recession of 1966-67 had an adverse effect on the West German growth rate as evidenced by the table, while the East German low of 1.2 percent in 1962 can undoubtedly be attributed to the problems experienced in the collectivization of agriculture. Unfortunately, preoccupation with the rate of economic growth tends to obfuscate the real issue of quality of output produced. In an attempt to achieve superior growth rates to the

TABLE 14.2

Comparison of Yearly Growth in
Gross Social Product and
Investment, East and West
Germany, 1960-70

	East Germany		West Germany	
Year	Yearly Growth of Gross Social Product in Comparable Prices (billion DM)	Investment of Previous Year per DM 1,000 Growth in GSP (DM)	Yearly Growth of Gross Social Product in Comparable Prices (billion DM)	Investment of Previous Year per DM 1,000 Growth in GSP (DM)
1961	2.9	5,550	30.30	2,398
1962	1.3	12,546	27.50	3,056
1963	2.6	6,425	23.90	3,923
1964	4.3	3,975	36.90	2,685
1965	4.3	4,359	39.50	2,873
1966	4.6	4,454	30.30	4,034
1967	5.2	4,228	3.90	2,387
1968	5.9	4,069	43.90	2,607
1969	6.0	4,412	63.70	1,959
1970	6.1	4,987	76.00	1,924
Total	43.2	4,824	385.70	2,465

Sources: Staatlichen Zentralverwaltung für Statistik, Statistisches Jahrbuch der Deutschen Demokratischen Republik, 1970 (East Berlin: Staatsverlag der DDR, 1970), pp. 17-18; Statistisches Taschenbuch, 1971 (East Berlin: Staatsverlag der DDR, 1971), p. 26. Statistisches Bundesamt, Statistisches Jahrbuch für die Bundesrepublik Deutschland 1970 (Wiesbaden: W. Kohlhammer Verlag, 1970), pp. 490, 502.

market economies, the socialist countries have often concentrated on quantity at the expense of quality.

The rate of growth of national product depends not only on the size of investment but also on the effectiveness of its use. A comparison can be made of capital investments to total output in both the FRG and GDR to ascertain the degree of efficiency on payoff of input to output. In other words, how much investment does it take to generate a unit of national product? In table 14.2 a comparison is made of investment and gross social product in the FRG and the GDR for the period of 1961-70. East German national income has been converted into gross social product for the purpose of comparison. The table indicates that over the period in consideration in order to achieve a DM 1,000 increase in gross social product, the FRG had to invest DM 2,465 compared to DM 4,824 for the GDR. Also, the table shows a lagged relationship between investment and growth of the gross social product, with the latter being related to investment of the preceding year.

Table 14.3 presents gross industrial production in the GDR and FRG for the period 1960-68 in Deutsche Marks. Gross industrial production in the GDR increased from DM 72 billion in 1960 to DM 112.5 billion in 1968, while gross industrial production in the FRG increased from DM 313.3 billion in 1960 to DM 455.3 billion in 1968.[4] There is little change in the ratio of industrial production of East Germany to West Germany during the period. In 1966 and 1967 industrial production remained constant in the FRG, reflecting the recession that began in late 1966 and continued through 1967. During the two-year period the ratio was narrowed to 1:4; however, in 1968 and in the subsequent two years industrial production in the FRG increased at a substantial rate, while industrial production in the GDR reflected a period of consolidation. So by 1970 the ratio of industrial production

TABLE 14.3

Gross Industrial Production,
East and West Germany,
1960-68
(in 1962 prices)

Year	East (million DM)	West (million DM)
1960	72.0	313.3
1961	76.3	331.1
1962	80.7	344.1
1963	83.4	355.3
1964	89.4	388.3
1965	94.3	410.3
1966	100.0	415.7
1967	106.2	406.6
1968	112.5	455.3

Source: Deutscher Bundestag, Materialien zum Bericht zur Lage der Nation 1971, Drucksache VI/1690 (Bonn-Bad Godesberg: Dr. Hans Heger Verlag, 1971), p. 272.

between the GDR and the FRG was about the same that it was in 1960.

When industrial production is broken down by industry classifications, a comparison between the FRG and GDR can be made on an industry-by-industry basis. Table 14.4 presents the percentage increase from 1960 to 1968 in industrial output for the 16 industry classifications in the FRG and GDR. In general the performance was better in the GDR, particularly in the metal manufacturing industries. During the period 1960 to 1968 output in these industries increased 86 percent in the GDR compared to 37 percent for the FRG. On an absolute basis East German output in the metal manufacturing industries increased from 15.3 percent of the West German output in 1960 to 20.8 percent in 1968. Although the East German economy starts from a lower value base, the gains it has made in certain industrial fields cannot be minimized.

Total production for all industries showed a minor gain in the position of the GDR relative to the FRG during the period 1960-68. In 1960 industrial production in the GDR was 23 percent of the total for the FRG; in 1968, it had increased to 24.7 percent of the total. The most significant gain was made in the metal manufacturing industries, which increased in the GDR from 15.3 percent of the comparable FRG total in 1960 to 20.8 percent in 1968. Within this industrial classification, the largest gains in the GDR relative to the FRG were made in the shipbuilding, machinery, and optical equipment industries. The machinery industry, including machine tools, increased from 18.3 percent of the FRG's output for the same industry in 1960 to 27.6 percent in 1968. The precision machinery and optical equipment industry increased from 14.9 percent of the output for the FRG in 1960 to 23.4 percent in 1968.

Despite a high level of East German output in mining total production in the basic materials industries showed a percentage decline in the position of the GDR relative to the FRG. In 1960 total output of the GDR in the basic materials industries was 24.5 percent of the FRG total; in 1968, the output in the GDR had declined to 23.9 percent of FRG total. In the GDR the leadership has been preoccupied with expanding output of basic materials. The expansion of capacity in fuels, power, and metallurgy for years absorbed most of the increase in construction. In pushing the expansion of the basic materials industries, the GDR has been prompted by the fact that there are shortages of imported materials from other countries within the Soviet bloc. Within the basic materials industries the greatest gain in the GDR relative to the FRG has been made in the mining industry. Output in this industry increased from 42.2 percent of the FRG's total in 1960 to 58.5 percent in 1968. This gain, however, is attributable in part to the policy in the FRG of closing down many

TABLE 14.4

Comparison of Relative Gains
in East and West German
Industry, 1960-68

Industrial Classification	Percentage Change 1960-68 West	East
Basic industries	61	58
Energy	75	60
Mining	-9	26
Metallurgy	24	42
Chemical	128	85
Construction	39	57
Metal manufacturing industries	37	86
Electrotechnical	61	99
Shipbuilding	14	52
Other industries	31	83
Light industries	34	39
Woodworking	39	62
Textiles	26	30
Clothing	36	30
Leather, shoes, hides	6	44
Pulp and paper	47	41
Polygraphic	50	29
Glass and ceramic	39	58
Food industries	40	38
Industry average	45	56

Source: Deutcher Bundestag, Materialien zum Bericht zur Lage der Nation 1971, Drucksache VI/1690 (Bonn-Bad Godesberg: Dr. Hans Heger Verlag, 1971), p. 278.

unprofitable mines. The chemical industry in the GDR, on the other hand, showed a decline in the GDR relative to the FRG, with 22.5 percent of FRG chemical output in 1968 compared to 27.7 percent in 1960.

There was no gain in the position of the light and food industries in the GDR relative to the FRG during the period 1960-68. Overall, there has been a lag in the development of these industries, even in comparison to prewar East German levels. One reason for the continued lag in the development of the light and food industries is the fact that their exports have remained far below prewar levels. Within the light industries, the greatest gain of the GDR relative to the FRG was made by the woodworking industry, with 31.1 percent in 1968 compared to 26.6 percent in 1960, and the leather and shoe industry, with 23.5 percent in 1968 compared to 17.3 percent in 1960. The clothing industry showed a decline in output in the GDR relative to the FRG. The food industry also showed a decline in the GDR from 33.3 percent of the FRG total in 1960 to 32.8 percent in 1968.

During the period 1960-68 there were shifts in the contributions of industries to total industrial production in both the GDR and FRG. The share of consumer-oriented industries in the GDR declined from 40 percent of total industrial output in 1960 to 36 percent of output in 1968; in the FRG, the share declined from 32 percent of total output in 1960 to 30 percent of total output in 1968. The share of basic industries in total industrial production increased from 37.9 percent in 1960 to 38.3 percent in 1968 in the GDR compared to an increase from 35.6 percent in 1960 to 39.5 percent in 1968 for the FRG. The metal manufacturing industries in the GDR contributed 21.7 percent of total industrial output in 1960 compared to 25.9 percent in 1968. In West Germany there was a decline from 32.6 percent of total output in 1960 to 30.7 percent in 1968.

A comparison of industrial production in the GDR and FRG can also be made within a frame of reference of industrial investment. When industrial investment is compared to industrial production, an index of capital productivity can be developed. In other words, the return in terms of industrial output from capital investment can be measured. In Table 14.5 gross industrial investment in the GDR and FRG are compared for the period 1960-68.

In comparing Table 14.5 to Table 14.3 a gross production value of DM 1,347 per DM 1,000 of industrial investment was achieved in the FRG in 1960, compared to a gross production value of DM 1,026 per DM 1,000 of investment in the GDR. In 1968 the respective production values for the FRG and GDR were DM 1,171 and DM 1,003. The industrial capital productivity in the GDR had increased from 76.2 percent of the FRG total in 1960 to 85.7 percent in 1968. The bulk of this gain occurred in the recession year 1967 in the FRG. On an individual industry basis the greatest productivity per monetary unit of investment capital was achieved by the GDR in the clothing industry, where in 1968 a production value of DM 6,794 was achieved for each DM 1,000 of investment.

In Table 14.6 capital productivity for the 16 industry classifications is presented in the GDR and FRG for 1968. The relationship is industrial production to industrial investment. For each industry DM 1,000 of invested capital yields a certain amount of industrial product. So for the chemical industry DM 1,000 of investment brings

TABLE 14.5

Gross Industrial Investment,
East and West Germany, 1960-68
(in 1962 prices in million DM)

Year	West	East
1960	232,525	70,190
1961	252,121	74,060
1962	272,544	78,720
1963	292,108	83,930
1964	311,479	90,570
1965	332,548	95,860
1966	353,408	101,130
1967	371,929	106,600
1968	388,732	112,260

Source: Deutscher Bundestag, Materialien zum Bericht zur Lage der Nation 1971, Drucksache VI/1690 (Bonn-Bad Godesberg: Dr. Hans Heger Verlag, 1971), Tables A-50 and A-51, pp. 276-77.

forth DM 1,435 in chemical production in the FRG compared to DM 958 in the GDR.

With respect to capital productivity it can be said that the GDR has made a solid gain both on an industrywide and individual industry basis relative to the FRG during the period 1960-68, particularly in the metal manufacturing industries. For example, the electrotechnical industry in the GDR relative to the same industry in the FRG increased from 100.5 percent in 1960 to 122.9 percent in 1968. On the other hand, capital productivity in the chemical industry in the GDR decreased from 74 percent of the capital productivity for the chemical industry in the FRG in 1960 to 66.8 percent in 1968. It is necessary to remember, however, that 1968 represents only one point in a period of time. Industrial production in the FRG was in a cyclical upswing from the recession of 1967. It is extremely likely that the choice of 1969 or 1970 would have afforded perhaps a more accurate capital productivity comparison between the two countries. Nevertheless, it can be said that a capital productivity gain in favor of the GDR relative to the FRG has indeed occurred.

Another method of comparing East and West German industrial production is through the use of a capital intensity (Kapitalintensität) index in which the ratio of capital to labor is computed. In this comparison the total amount of capital invested relative to the size of the

TABLE 14.6

Comparison of Capital Productivity,
by Industry, East and
West Germany, 1968

| | Capital Productivity | |
Industry Classification	West	East
Energy	361	421
Mining	553	481
Metallurgy	1,175	666
Chemical	1,435	958
Construction	907	714
Electrotechnical	1,698	2,086
Shipbuilding	1,134	1,110
Other metal industries	1,422	1,198
Woodworking	1,761	1,879
Textiles	1,339	1,011
Clothing	3,227	6,794
Leather, shoes, hides	2,130	1,075
Pulp and paper	1,253	1,031
Polygraphic	1,237	2,260
Glass and ceramics	1,225	618
Food	1,666	2,350
Industry Average	1,171	1,003

Source: Deutscher Bundestag, Materialien zum Bericht zur Lage der Nation 1971, Drucksache VI/1690 (Bonn-Bad Godesberg: Dr. Hans Heger Verlag, 1971), Table A-57, p. 283.

labor force in both countries forms the basis of the capital intensity index. It can be said that the more units of capital used relative to a unit of labor, the more advanced is a nation's industrial capacity. With respect to the capital intensity of the FRG and GDR during the period 1960-68, both countries increased their capital investment. The gap between the two countries widened, however. Capital intensity in the FRG increased by 71 percent, while capital intensity in the GDR increased by 56 percent. In 1960 the capital intensity for all industries in the GDR was 87.4 percent of the capital intensity of the same industries in the FRG; in 1968, the capital intensity ratio of the GDR relative to the FRG had declined to 80 percent.

In examining the capital-labor mix in both countries one important factor comes to mind—the static labor supply that exists in both countries. Unlike the United States, neither country has to worry about providing job opportunities for a constantly expanding labor force. In the FRG the industrial labor force numbered 8.3 million workers in 1960; by 1968 this number had dropped to 8.1 million persons. In the GDR during the same period the industrial labor force remained virtually unchanged: in 1960 it amounted to around 2.9 million workers; in 1969 it also amounted to around 2.9 million workers. Capital investment, on the other hand, increased from DM 232.5 billion in 1960 to DM 388.7 billion in 1968 in the FRG; in the GDR capital investment increased from DM 70.2 billion to DM 112.3 billion for the same period. Capital investment in the FRG increased by 67 percent over 1960, while the industrial labor force declined by 200,000 workers; in the GDR, capital investment increased by 60 percent, while the labor force increased by 50,000 workers.

Table 14.7 presents the labor force and amount of capital investment in the 16 industrial classifications for the FRG and GDR for the period 1960-68. As the table indicates, shifts have occurred in the pattern of employment in both countries. In the FRG employment in the chemical industry accounted for the bulk of the employment gain for all industries that showed gains. On the other hand, the mining industry showed a decline of 50 percent during the period.

In Table 14.8 capital intensity ratios are presented for the GDR and FRG for the period 1960 and 1968 for each of the 16 industry classifications. Also presented in the table is a comparison of the amount of capital per unit of labor in absolute terms for both the GDR and FRG for 1968. These amounts are expressed in Deutsche Marks and are obtained by dividing total capital investment in an industry into the labor force in the industry. For example, capital investment for the FRG in the chemical industry in 1968 amounted to DM 57.8 billion, and the size of the labor force was 837,000. In the GDR the amount of capital investment in the chemical industry for 1968 was DM 19.5 billion, and the size of the labor force was 304,000. This comes out to DM 69,060 of invested capital per unit of labor for the chemical industry in the FRG compared to DM 64,020 of invested capital per unit of labor in the GDR.

In absolute terms the combination of production factors of capital and labor, or capital intensity, averaged DM 28,100 for the 16 industries in the FRG for 1960 compared to DM 24,600 for the same industries in the GDR. In 1968 the average for all industries in the FRG had increased to DM 47,980 compared to DM 37,380 for the GDR—gains of 71 percent and 56 percent, respectively. On a relative basis the gap in capital intensity was widened during the 1960-68 period in 13 of the 16 industries, narrowed in 2, and remained constant in 1.

In comparing East and West German industrial production over

TABLE 14.7

Comparison of Capital Investment and
Labor Force Employment,
East and West Germany,
1960 and 1968

| | West Germany ||||
| | Investment (million DM) || Labor Force (thousands) ||
Industrial Group	1960	1968	1960	1968
Energy	15.5	27.1	191.0	202.0
Mining	15.7	14.3	616.3	337.4
Metallurgy	34.8	43.1	685.3	615.9
Chemical	36.4	82.9	697.5	836.9
Construction	9.0	12.5	258.5	229.3
Electrotechnical	22.5	36.2	843.6	926.3
Shipbuilding	2.8	3.2	98.4	77.6
Other metals*	77.0	100.3	2,289.7	2,462.4
Woodworking	10.6	14.7	365.3	337.0
Textiles	17.3	21.7	619.5	489.1
Clothing	9.0	12.3	355.5	366.5
Leather, shoes, hides	4.7	5.0	179.2	144.5
Pulp and paper	7.5	11.0	196.2	196.1
Polygraphic	5.3	7.9	186.1	211.8
Glass and ceramics	3.9	5.4	183.5	163.3
Food	41.2	57.5	506.2	505.2
Total	313.3	455.3	8,271.9	8,101.3

| | East Germany ||||
| | Investment (million DM) || Labor Force (thousands) ||
Industrial Group	1960	1968	1960	1968
Energy	4.5	7.2	67.4	72.5
Mining	6.6	8.4	197.2	193.5
Metallurgy	4.0	5.7	160.7	172.5
Chemical	10.1	18.6	280.9	304.0
Construction	2.0	3.1	95.0	91.0
Electrotechnical	4.3	8.6	222.5	261.0
Shipbuilding	.7	1.0	41.4	42.0
Other metals*	10.6	19.4	713.9	809.0
Woodworking	2.8	4.6	154.7	144.0
Textiles	5.1	6.6	340.8	283.0
Clothing	2.6	3.4	122.2	108.0
Leather, shoes, hides	.8	1.2	71.4	69.0
Pulp and paper	1.9	2.7	63.2	59.0
Polygraphic	1.4	1.8	41.0	36.5
Glass and ceramics	.8	1.2	68.9	70.5
Food	13.7	18.9	215.4	209.5
Total	72.0	112.5	2,856.6	2,925.0

*Includes machinery and machine tools, transportation equipment, fine instruments, and optical equipment.

Source: Deutscher Bundestag, Materialien zum Bericht zur Lage der Nation 1971, Drucksache VI/1690 (Bonn-Bad Godesberg: Dr. Hans Heger Verlag, 1971), Tables A-46 through A-49, pp. 272-75.

TABLE 14.8

Comparison of Capital Intensity, by
Industry, East and West Germany, 1968

| | Capital Intensity in 1968 in DM || East as percent of West ||
Industrial Classification	West	East	1960	1968
Energy	372,140	236,476	66.6	63.7
Mining	76,920	90,170	117.2	117.2
Metallurgy	59,500	49,670	93.4	93.0
Chemical	69,060	64,020	93.0	92.7
Construction	60,200	47,560	108.0	79.0
Electrotechnical	23,030	15,910	72.7	69.1
Shipbuilding	35,980	22,100	71.0	61.4
Other metal industries	28,670	20,050	86.5	69.9
Woodworking	24,730	16,890	80.9	68.3
Textiles	33,230	23,060	82.4	69.4
Clothing	10,420	4,590	41.3	44.1
Leather, shoes, hides	16,150	15,770	130.2	97.6
Pulp and paper	44,890	45,020	123.9	100.7
Polygraphic	30,220	21,700	67.0	71.8
Glass and ceramic	27,090	28,260	127.6	104.3
Food	68,330	38,340	71.9	56.1
Industry Average	47,980	38,380	87.4	80.0

Source: Deutscher Bundestag, Materialien zum Bericht zur Lage der Nation 1971, Drucksache VI/1690 (Bonn-Bad Godesberg: Dr. Hans Heger Verlag, 1971), Table A-55, p. 281.

the period 1960-68 the salient point that comes through is that there was little change in the relative position of the two countries. Although industrial production expressed in 1962 prices increased by 45 percent in the FRG compared to 56 percent in the GDR, the GDR total remained at less than one-fourth of the FRG total in 1968. The gain on the part of the GDR during the period can be attributed to the recession of 1967 in the FRG. In fact, any gain made by the GDR during the 1965-67 period was canceled out by the rapid expansion in industrial production during 1968-69. In using measures of capital intensity and capital productivity there was also little change in the relative position of the two countries. Within industry groups, some changes did occur, with some GDR industries closing an output or productivity gap and a wider gap occurring for others. It must also be mentioned that in terms of resource allocation the GDR placed more emphasis on the development of certain industries over others. This was particularly true of the energy and capital-goods industries, whose performances were superior to the consumer-goods industries.

Labor Productivity

The Deutsches Institute für Wirtschaftsforschung (DIW) has made a comparison of labor productivity in East and West Germany.[5] Admitting difficulties in comparing statistical data of the two countries, the DIW evaluated the quantitative industrial output of each country in monetary terms. For each branch of industry, production was divided by employment to obtain comparable productivity values for the two countries. The production of nearly 200 products in the GDR was compared to the corresponding production in the FRG. A coefficient of comparison was computed for each product that, when multiplied by West German output, provided a Deutsche Mark value for the gross product of manufacturing in the GDR. Production values were then arranged on the basis of the industrial composition of the FRG to facilitate comparison. The end objective was to rearrange West German production statistics to make them correspond to a breakdown of similar East German production statistics.

The results of the comparison are for 1967. This base year was to some extent unfavorable for the reason that the turnover tax was still in effect in West Germany. The West German economy was starting an upswing from the recession that began in 1966. With 1967 as the year, the following points can be made:[6]

1. Although relatively more persons are employed in industry in the GDR, net per capita output in 1967 was 83 percent of that of the FRG.

2. Labor productivity in East German industry is one-third below the corresponding West German rate. The difference in labor productivity varies considerably from industry to industry, however. Relatively good results were obtained for industries that were located in the present area of the GDR before the war, even though those industries have been largely neglected by postwar state investment policies. These industries include food, beverages, tobacco, and light industry.

3. Those industries that were given priority in terms of the allocation of investment funds did not achieve productivity anywhere near the West German level. This can be attributed in part to the fact that the degree of automation is considerably lower in the GDR industries than in West German industries. Improvement on the part

of certain East German industries in relative output and productivity has become noticeable, however.

4. In the course of the 1967-68 economic recovery in West Germany the output and productivity lag of East German industry grew larger. Moreover, it is likely that this will also apply to the 1969-70 period. West German productivity increases have continued to be high; in East Germany not only have weather-caused difficulties brought on production losses but production bottlenecks in certain industries have also occurred to restrict economic growth and labor productivity. Plan shortcomings attributable to a lack of flexibility and information gaps have also contributed to the productivity differential between East and West German workers. Automation is being pushed hard, however, in those East German industries that show the greatest lag in labor productivity.

Table 14.9 presents a comparison of gross production and productivity in East and West German industry for the years 1967 and 1968. The 1968 figures represent an extrapolation of the 1967 figures.

TABLE 14.9

Output and Productivity in East and West German Industry, 1967 and 1968

Industry	Gross Production Comparison East : West West = 100 1967	1968	Percent Change	Productivity Comparison East : West West = 100 1967	1968	Percent Change
Power, coal, fuels	34.5	32.5	- 5.9	95.4	91.0	- 4.6
Chemicals	26.1	24.6	- 6.0	53.3	53.3	+ 0.1
Metallurgy	11.8	10.8	- 8.1	49.6	43.4	-12.6
Construction materials	24.7	24.8	+ 0.3	64.1	62.6	- 2.5
Machinery and vehicles	19.0	18.4	- 3.2	60.5	53.9	-10.9
Electrical and optical equipment, precision instruments	25.2	23.1	- 8.4	70.3	68.5	- 2.5
Light Industry	24.6	26.2	+ 6.6	79.2	76.8	- 3.0
Textiles	34.6	30.2	-12.8	60.5	54.0	-10.6
Foods, beverages and tobacco	32.6	32.1	- 1.6	80.4	75.9	- 5.6

Source: Deutsches Institute für Wirtschaftsforschung, Wochenbericht, VII, 6 (West Berlin, 1970), pp. 53-56.

AGRICULTURE

The development of agriculture in East and West Germany following the end of World War II has resulted in a diametrically opposite pattern. The Federal Republic has furthered the development of family farming with the provision of various forms of subsidies. In the GDR the structure of agriculture has been completely changed through the combination of many small farms into large-scale enterprise units—the state and collective farms. The difference in the size of the average agricultural enterprise in the FRG and GDR is significant. In 1969, for example, the average size of an agricultural enterprise in the FRG was 11 hectares compared to an average size of 564 hectares for enterprises in the GDR.

Tables 14.10 and 14.11 present a comparison of the agricultural systems in East and West Germany. Table 14.10 presents the number of agricultural enterprises in East Germany by type, the total agricultural land in use, the percentage of land farmed by each type of enterprise, and the average land size of each type of enterprise.

TABLE 14.10

Land Use by Type of Agricultural Enterprise, East Germany, 1970

Types of Enterprises	Number	Land Use In Hectares	Percent	Average Land Size
VEG[a]	511	442,638	7.0	866
LPG[b]	9,009	5,392,416	85.8	599
GPG[c]	346	20,758	0.3	60
Other socialist enterprises	—	65,969	1.1	—
Private	—	364,611	5.8	—
Total		6,286,392	100.0	

[a] Volkseigene Güter
[b] Landwirtschaftliche Produktionsgenossenschaften
[c] Gartnerische Produktionsgenossenschaften

Source: Staatliche Zentralverwaltung für Statistik, Statistisches Taschenbuch 1971 (East Berlin: Staatsverlag der DDR, 1971), pp. 79-81.

Table 14.11 presents the number of farms and the amount of land in use in West Germany. As has been already pointed out in Table 3.4, the great majority of West German farms are 10 hectares or less. Only 2,800 farms out of 1.3 million farms had a land area of more than 100 hectares.

In 1970 the total value of agricultural output in West Germany was DM 32 billion, or about 4 percent of the GNP.[7] Out of the 61 million inhabitants of the FRG, approximately 7 million live on farms. The population density on German farms is high in comparison to other countries. In 1969, for example, 448 persons on the average live on 100 hectares of farmland compared to 47 persons per 100 hectares in the United States and 270 persons per 100 hectares for other EEC countries. This density of 448 persons per 100 hectares can be compared to a population density of 282 persons per 100 hectares during the 1935-38 period. What this means is that there were more people on less land in 1969 than during the prewar period, despite government efforts to get them off of the land.

Despite increases in agricultural production, the FRG can only supply about two thirds of its needs. If the products derived from imported fodder are included, the amount goes up to three-fourths of

TABLE 14.11

Number of Farms and Land in
Farms, West Germany, 1969

Number of Farms (thousand)	Land in Use (thousand hectares)
185.3	131.6
177.6	235.8
279.2	928.8
252.3	1,834.9
169.1	2,088.3
111.6	1,925.9
99.7	2,395.7
49.5	1,839.8
15.2	980.7
2.8	474.4
1,342.1	12,853.8

Source: Statistisches Bundesamt, Agrarstatistische Arbeitsunterlagen, 1969-70 (Wiesbaden, 1970), p. 24.

total requirements. Only 30 percent of all land used for agricultural purposes provides food directly for consumption purposes; the remainder is used for fodder and other types of production. Government agricultural policy has concentrated on increasing the size of the farm unit and on improvement in the volume of output. Some success has been accomplished, for food production has expanded considerably in the last decade.

East German agriculture has also encountered certain difficulties. In contrast to the small farms they mainly superseded, the state and collective farms were expected to enjoy the advantage of large-scale operations. When the units are large, it is possible to invest in machinery and equipment that small individual proprietors cannot afford; there are also important economies in the division of labor. Despite the advantages, many of which are clearly indicated by the great and extensive farms of the United States, East German agriculture has had its problems. To some extent these problems began when collectivization was pushed to the limit in the early months of 1960. Serious food shortages developed that had to be relieved by increased imports.

In comparing East and West German agricultural production it is necessary to remember that East Germany was the most important agricultural area of Germany before World War II. Thus, East Germany had certain advantages in land fertility to begin with. The base for agriculture was established. It is also of importance to note that many of the East German farms are self-sustaining units in that agricultural equipment, agronomists, and other types of specialists are employed. The farms also receive assistance from agricultural colleges, which have been created to provide research and trained personnel for the state and collective farms. Support has been given to agriculture from the state budget, but with the economic reforms state and collective farms are supposed to operate as self-supporting business units.

One feature of East German agriculture is the extensive use of tractors and other equipment. In 1970, for example, there were 148,865 tractors in use, or one tractor per 40 hectares of land area.[8] These tractors are used in arrangements similar to the old machine tractor stations in the Soviet Union, except for the fact that the East German government has delegated control of the tractor stations to collective farms. In addition, there were 17,911 manure spreaders in 1970, or one manure spreader per 123 hectares of farmland; 12,000 potato combines, or one combine per 52 hectares of farmland; and 5,276 sugar beet combines, or one combine per 36 hectares of farmland. The extent of mechanization is indicated by the fact that in 1960 the number of tractors amounted to 72,170, or one tractor per 254.5 hectares of farmland, compared to 148,865 tractors in 1970, or one tractor per 40 hectares of farmland.

One basic objective of agricultural policy in East Germany has been to raise production to a comparable level with West Germany. Political and ideological considerations have dictated that the method of achieving this goal is through the socialization of agriculture. Since socialization was accomplished in the spring of 1960, a facet of East German policy has been to concentrate on the consolidation of Type II and Type III collectives. It was through the operation of the large-scale collective farm that the East Germans planned to match West German agricultural production by 1965. This objective has not been achieved.

In Table 14.12 a comparison is made of the application of commercial fertilizer in East and West Germany in kilograms per hectare of arable land. Three time periods are used—1938-39, 1961-62, and 1969-70. The use of fertilizer has increased much more in the GDR than in the FRG in recent years.

Some results of agricultural production are presented in Table 14.13. In this table vegetable production is compared for the same three time periods. Although yields have shown improvement in both countries over the last years, they are significantly higher in West Germany in comparison to East Germany.

Performance in terms of animal production of foodstuffs can also be compared for the GDR and FRG. In both countries improvements in performance have occurred over a prewar period. There

TABLE 14.12

Use of Commercial Fertilizer, East
and West Germany, Selected Years
(use per hectare in kilogram nutrients)

Fertilizer	1938-39 East Germany	1938-39 West Germany	1961-62 East Germany	1961-62 West Germany	1969-70 East Germany	1969-70 West Germany
Nitrogen	32.8	23.6	59.8	43.7	78.7	79.7
Phosphate	27.3	28.3	33.0	44.6	65.3	62.9
Potash	48.7	43.4	77.3	72.9	101.8	82.3
Calcium	78.1	56.4	118.4	38.2	177.5	47.5

Sources: Staatliche Zentralverwaltung für Statistik, Statistisches Jahrbuch der Deutschen Demokratischen Republik, 1970 (East Berlin: Staatsverlag der DDR, 1970), p. 199: Statistisches Bundesamt, Agrarstatistische Arbeitsunterlagen, 1969-70 (Wiesbaden, 1970), p. 18.

TABLE 14.13

Vegetable Production, East and
West Germany, Selected Years
(1 Doppelzentner per hectare)*

	1935-38	1961-66	1969	1970
East Germany				
Grain	23.9	25.9	29.5	28.2
Potatoes	194.3	168.8	146.2	195.7
Sugar beets	301.2	254.7	253.2	320.1
West Germany				
Grain	22.4	29.8	36.5	33.0
Potatoes	185.0	248.5	271.4	272.3
Sugar beets	327.2	381.5	438.7	440.1

*1 doppelzentner = 100 kilograms.

Sources: Staatlichen Zentralverwaltung für Statistik, Statistisches Jahrbuch der Deutschen Demokratischen Republik, 1971 (East Berlin: Staatsverlag der DDR, 1971), p. 203: Statistisches Bundesamt, Agrar-statistische Arbeitsunterlagen, 1969-70 (Wiesbaden, 1970), pp. 22-24.

is a significant gap between the two countries in favor of the FRG, however. Table 14.14 compares results in each country over four time periods. The comparison uses the performance of milk cows in total milk output in kilograms and also in fat content of the milk. The average yield of laying hens as measured by the number of eggs laid is also used.

The volume of agricultural production in East and West Germany can also be compared. There are, however, some factors that would affect output that should be mentioned. First, the amount of total investment in agriculture in the GDR ranged between 12 and 15 percent during the period 1960-69, compared to an amount in the FRG that ranged between 6 to 8 percent of total investment over the same period. Although a detailed comparison of investment figures is not possible, due to insufficient information about the definition of gross investment in the GDR, the relatively high share of agriculture in gross investment should be the highest among the industrial nations. Second, the provision and use of manufactured products in agriculture has increased constantly in both countries. Both the GDR and FRG are among the top 10 countries in the world that fertilize the most intensively. In

TABLE 14.14

Performance Comparisons per
Animal Unit, East and
West Germany, Selected Years

		1938	1962	1969	1970
Average milk performance per cow per year, with a 3.5 percent fat content	East	2,549	2,448	3,363	3,314
	West	2,436	3,710	4,070	4,109
Average fat content per cow per year	East	87	86	118	116
	West	84	130	142	144
Average yield of eggs per hen per year in single units	East	105	127	163	168
	West	105	166	211	216

Source: Staatliche Zentralverwaltung für Statistik, Statistisches Jahrbuch der Deutschen Demokratischen Republik, 1971 (East Berlin: Staatsverlag der DDR, 1971), pp. 222-23: Deutscher Bundestag, Materialband zum Agrarbericht 1971 der Bundesregierung (Bonn, 1971), pp. 190-95.

this connection it is noted that since 1965 the GDR uses more fertilizer per hectare of agricultural land than the FRG.

In Table 14.15 various measures of agricultural production and land use are compared in the FRG and GDR for two periods, 1957-61 and 1968. As the table indicates, there was little change in the position of the GDR relative to the FRG over the time period involved. For example, food production in the FRG increased from an average of 46.2 million tons in grain units in 1957-61 to 59.8 million tons in grain units in 1968. In the GDR the increase in grain units was from an average of 16.2 million tons in 1957-61 to 20.1 million tons in 1968. The FRG registered a gain of 29.8 percent compared to 24.7 percent for the GDR.

Table 14.16 presents the structure of food production in the FRG and GDR using two time periods, 1957-61 and 1968-69. The significant thing to note is that in many areas of production the position of the GDR relative to the FRG has declined. For example, in 1957-61 vegetable production in the GDR averaged 42.7 percent of the output for the FRG. In 1968 production had declined to 39.6 percent of the output for the FRG. Animal products in the GDR averaged 32.7 percent

TABLE 14.15

Comparison of Agricultural Production, East and West Germany, 1957-61 and 1968

Production	Unit	West Germany 1957-61	West Germany 1968	East Germany 1957-61	East Germany 1968	East as percent of West 1957-61	East as percent of West 1968
Land in use	million hectares	14.26	13.87	6.44	6.30	45.2	45.4
Total livestock	million GV[a]	11.89	12.44	5.06	4.96	42.6	39.9
Domestic cattle	million GV	11.02	12.17	4.50	4.77	40.8	39.2
Number of workers	thousands	3,794	2,630	1,416	1,068	37.3	40.6
Tractors and motors	million	15.15	30.98	2.30	6.25	15.2	20.2
Used fertilizer	thousand tons	602	933	239	502	39.7	53.8
Phosphate used	thousand tons	652	802	209	370	32.1	46.1
Potash used	thousand tons	1,017	1,046	511	582	50.2	55.6
Gross land production	million tons GE[b]	48.05	58.01	19.17	23.35	39.9	40.3
Performance in cattle breeding	million tons GE	42.62	52.36	14.57	17.46	34.2	33.3
Food production	million tons GE	46.21	59.83	16.19	20.10	35.0	33.6
Net food production	million tons GE	40.82	49.50	13.95	17.86	34.2	36.1

[a] 1 GV = 500 kg. live weight animal unit
[b] GE = 1 doppelzentner in grain units

Source: Deutscher Bundestag, Materialien zum Bericht zur Lage der Nation 1971, Drucksache VI/1690 (Bonn-Bad Godesberg: Dr. Hans Heger Verlag, 1970), p. 289.

TABLE 4.16

Structure of Food Production, East and West Germany, Selected Years

Product	West Germany 1957-61	West Germany 1968-69	East Germany 1957-61	East Germany 1968	West Germany 1957-61 %	West Germany 1968-69 %	East Germany 1957-61 %	East Germany 1968 %	Growth West 1957-61 to 1968	Growth East 1957-61 to 1968	East % of West 1957-61	East % of West 1968
Vegetable products	10,688	12,696	4,566	5,024	23.1	21.2	28.2	25.0	18.8	10.0	42.7	39.6
Grain	4,321	5,140	1,772	2,183	9.3	8.6	10.9	10.9	19.0	23.2	41.0	42.5
Food legumen	11	8	30	17	—	—	0.2	0.1	-27.3	-43.3	272.7	212.5
Rape-seed	71	196	189	295	0.2	0.3	1.2	1.5	176.1	56.1	266.2	150.5
Potatoes	1,770	1,572	793	710	3.8	2.6	4.9	3.5	-11.2	-10.2	44.8	45.2
Sugar beets	2,171	2,625	1,230	1,327	4.7	4.4	7.6	6.6	20.9	7.9	56.7	50.6
Vegetables	308	419	145	138	0.7	0.7	0.9	0.7	36.0	-4.8	47.1	32.9
Fruits	1,204	1,694	329	278	2.7	2.8	2.0	1.4	36.6	-15.5	26.5	16.4
Hops, tobacco, must, flax, and hempstraw	796	1,042	78	76	1.7	1.8	0.5	0.3	30.9	-2.6	9.8	7.3
Animal products	35,521	47,129	11,621	15,078	76.9	78.8	71.8	75.0	32.7	29.7	32.7	32.0
Slaughter animals												
Beef	9,400	12,168	1,818	3,228	20.3	20.3	11.2	16.1	29.5	77.6	19.3	26.5
Calves	977	864	218	126	2.1	1.5	1.3	0.6	-11.6	-42.2	22.3	14.6
Sheep	183	126	258	180	0.4	0.2	1.6	0.9	-31.1	-30.2	141.0	142.9
Pigs	11,507	15,865	4,248	5,465	24.9	26.5	26.2	27.2	37.9	28.7	36.9	34.5
Poultry	719	1,596	384	612	1.6	2.7	2.4	3.0	122.0	59.4	53.4	38.3
Goats	46	6	51	24	0.1	—	0.3	0.1	-87.0	-52.9	110.9	400.0
Cow milk	9,760	11,890	2,976	3,743	21.1	19.9	18.4	18.6	21.8	25.8	30.5	31.5
Goats milk	130	4	177	67	0.3	—	1.1	0.3	-89.2	-62.1	136.2	478.6
Eggs	2,031	3,930	866	1,095	4.4	6.6	5.4	5.5	93.5	26.4	42.6	27.9
Wool	171	132	322	320	0.4	0.2	2.0	1.6	-22.8	-0.6	188.3	242.4
Livestock changes	597	538	303	218	1.3	0.9	1.9	1.1	-9.9	-28.0	50.8	40.5
Total food production	46,209	59,825	16,187	20,102	100.0	100.0	100.0	100.0	29.5	24.2	35.0	33.6

Source: Deutscher Bundestag, Materialien zum Bericht zur Lage der Nation 1971, Drucksache VI/1690 (Bonn-Bad Godesberg: Dr. Hans Heger Verlag, 1971), pp. 290 and 291.

of production in the FRG during the base period and 32 percent during the year of comparison. There was a gain in the position of the GDR in certain areas, such as in the production of slaughter animals. Total food production in the GDR was 35 percent of the FRG total in the base period; in 1968 the GDR total had declined to 33.6 percent of the FRG total. Overall during the two time periods it can be said that the position of the GDR relative to the FRG in the production of food has declined.

The structure of agricultural production in both the FRG and GDR is dominated by animal products. The share of animal products in total production in 1968 was 79 percent in the FRG and 75 percent for the GDR. Within the production of foodstuffs the most important single item was the production of grain. In 1968 it amounted to 9 percent of food production in the FRG compared to 11 percent for the GDR. Sugar beets followed in importance, accounting for 4 percent of 1968 food production in the FRG and 7 percent of food production in the GDR.

THE WEST GERMAN ECONOMY, 1960-72

Although the main part of this section is devoted to the performance of the West German economy during the last decade and into the decade of the 1970s, a resumé of the development of the economy up to 1960 is in order. In 1948 the planned economy inherited from the war was eliminated and a drastic currency reform that revalued the mark was instituted. Progress made after 1948 took place under what was called a "social market economy." By this was meant an economic system directed toward combining free enterprise with social progress on the basis of competition. In the social market economy the function of the state was primarily one of maintaining order—that is, it had to formulate the conditions under which the market system would perform. Freedom of private enterprise and ownership, both guaranteed under the Basic Law, were to interract competitively to increase productivity and ensure industrial progress. The state was supposed to intervene only when it became necessary to promote competition.

The last few years, however, have seen German economic policy undergo a radical change. This change, which actually had its origin in the fall of 1966 with the resignation of Ludwig Erhard as chancellor, introduced more government direction into the economy. Even under the social market policies of Erhard and Adenauer the government's influence on the economy had not been negligible in terms of its contribution to the gross social product. After Erhard's resignation measures were taken in 1967 to provide for medium-term planning of the state budget and to stimulate the economy through more government spending. Ever since, economic policy has been Keynesian in nature.

Using two time periods, 1950-62 and 1950-64, and using real national income valued at factor cost as a growth-rate measure, the West German economy exhibited the highest growth rate in Western Europe.[9] In the period 1950-62 German real national income increased at a rate of 7.3 percent a year, compared to 3.3 percent for the United States, 4.9 percent for France, and 2.3 percent for the United Kingdom. In the period 1950-64 the German growth rate in terms of real national income increased at a rate of 7.1 percent a year, compared to 3.5 percent for the United States, 4.9 percent for France, and 2.6 percent for the United Kingdom. Italy ranked second to West Germany among Western European countries in growth rate, accomplishing a 6-percent-a-year increase in 1950-64.

There are extenuating circumstances that contributed to this high rate of economic growth. For one thing, West Germany had a very low base from which to start after the end of World War II. The economy had to do a large amount of technological catching up, drawing upon American expertise. Moreover, with a huge rise in the world demand for machinery, West Germany went into a massive boom in 1951 that has set the pattern for its economic success ever since. It was an export-oriented boom. A great concentration of effort on capital-goods industries was directed toward meeting profitable sales in world markets. The industrial structure established during the 1950s is a major explanation for Germany's continuing economic expansion.

During the period 1950-62 the West German growth rate increased at an average rate of 7.3 percent a year. This increase can be attributed to the following sources: employment, which accounted for 21 percent of the increase during the entire period; nonresidential structures and equipment, 14 percent; postwar recovery, 11 percent; advances in knowledge, 10 percent; shifts of resources from agriculture, 10 percent; economies of scale associated with income elasticities, 13 percent; and economies of scale associated with national market growth, 9 percent.[10]

The growth rate, however, declined sharply in the 1965-67 period to an average annual increase of less than 4 percent.[11] The slowdown in growth was particularly marked in government expenditures and business investment. In 1966 government expenditures increased at a rate of 0.3 percent in real income over 1965. This was attributable to the use of restrictive budgetary and monetary policies that were utilized to correct an internal and external imbalance that had developed in 1965. Real fixed-asset formation in 1966 increased at a rate of 0.9 percent compared to 6.5 percent in 1965.[12]

The recovery from the recession of 1965 was rapid. With the

support of fiscal and monetary policies that raised the level of aggregate demand the economy entered into a boom period in 1968. During the year gross investment increased by DM 23 billion over the preceding year. Government consumption increased by DM 3 billion, private consumption increased by DM 17 billion, and exports increased by DM 14 billion.[13] Total aggregate demand increased by DM 57 billion over 1967. The prime contributing factor to the recovery was a boom in investments that could be attributed in part to various financial incentives, including tax considerations that operated with an anti-cyclical effect particularly in connection with equipment investment. Large amounts of liquidity accruing to enterprises from abroad and relatively low interest rates also contributed to decisions to invest.

The boom carried over in 1969. If anything, the total gain in aggregate demand for 1969 over 1968 was more spectacular than the gain of 1968 over 1967. Gross investment increased by DM 25 billion, government consumption by DM 10 billion, private consumption by DM 31 billion, and exports by DM 17 billion. The increase in both domestic and foreign demand plus a labor shortage contributed to price instability. Moreover, despite the internal boom the balance of trade and services continued to show large surpluses, so that domestic market tensions were not reduced. In particular, foreign customers in anticipation of a revaluation of the Deutsche Mark felt it expedient on speculative grounds to place additional orders in West Germany. An internal imbalance between supply and demand also occurred in 1969. The orders reaching industry, and before long the building trade also, constantly exceeded deliveries. By the end of September 1969 the industrial order backlog, already very large by the end of 1968, had grown by a full month's output.

In October 1969 the Deutsche Mark was revalued. Its external value rose by 9.3 percent vis-à-vis the currencies of other countries. The immediate consequences of revaluation were that foreign money placed in Germany for speculative purposes flowed out again. This caused a decrease in central-bank monetary reserves. The domestic consequence of foreign-exchange outflows was that bank liquidity was reduced by some DM 31 billion during the three months following revaluation. Conditions in the domestic credit market became tighter.[14] This was clearly shown by a rise in interest rates. The Bundesbank raised its advance rate to 9 percent. At the same time there was also a rise in interest rates for bank loans and deposits as well as in the yield on securities. In order to restore internal and external equilibrium the Bundesbank, with federal fiscal policy directed to the same object, continued restrictive measures during the first part of 1970. West Germany began to experience something that other industrial countries had already learned, namely, that in a period of declining economic activity it is easier to decide on and implement measures to stimulate the economy than to apply the brakes in time during a boom.

Economic Growth, 1968-72

Recovery from the recession was rapid. In 1968 gross social product had increased by 8.8 percent in monetary terms over 1967. The 1969 gain over 1968 was even more spectacular—11.7 percent. The 1969 increase over 1968, however, was offset to some extent by rising prices. The real increases for the two respective years were 7.2 percent and 8 percent. In 1970 gross social product increased by 13.2 percent in monetary terms. In real terms, however, the growth in gross social product was less spectacular, at 5.4 percent.[15] This rate was behind the French real growth rate of 6 percent and the Japanese real growth rate of 11 percent but far in excess of the real growth rate of -1 percent for the United States. In 1971 money gross social product increased by an estimated 9.5 percent, but real gross social product increased by 2 percent. In general real growth rates declined for all of the Western industrial countries. In France the real growth rate increased by 5 percent and in Japan by 7 percent.

The index of industrial production increased by 11.8 percent in 1968 over 1967, and 13 percent for 1969 over 1968.[16] During the two-year period the index of production for the investment-goods industries increased 12.5 percent and 19.4 percent, while the index for the consumer-goods industries increased by 14.4 percent and 11.4 percent. In 1970 the index of industrial production showed an increase of 6.1 percent over 1969. The investment-goods index increased by 9.3 percent, while the consumer-goods index increased by only 2.4 percent. In 1971 the index of industrial production, particularly after the middle of the year, reflected a general downturn in the level of economic activity. The investment-goods index in particular showed sharp declines of 7 percent in August and 5.2 percent in November over the same months in 1970.

Table 14.17 presents the index of industrial production for the period 1962-70. This index is also broken down into a basic production-goods index, an investment-goods index, a consumer-goods index, and a construction index.

Inflation has become a problem in the West German economy. In 1970 the general price level, as measured by the gross social product deflator, increased by 7.6 percent, or about twice the highest rate experienced since the upsurge connected with the Korean War boom.[17] Industrial production prices increased by 6 percent in 1970, while the consumer cost of living index rose at a more moderate rate of 4.5 percent. This index reflected a cyclical lag and a number of

TABLE 14.17

Index of Industrial Production,
West Germany, 1962-70
(1962 = 100 percent)

Year	Industrial Index	Basic-Goods Index	Investment-Goods Index	Consumer-Goods Index	Construction
1962	100.0	100.0	100.0	100.0	100.0
1963	103.4	104.3	102.5	101.9	103.6
1964	112.3	118.1	110.2	108.6	118.8
1965	118.2	124.8	117.8	115.6	118.9
1966	120.3	129.2	117.3	118.4	123.7
1967	117.4	132.7	109.1	113.2	115.0
1968	131.2	151.6	122.7	129.5	121.8
1969	148.2	170.0	146.5	144.2	127.5
1970	157.2	178.6	160.1	147.7	138.6

Source: Deutsche Bundesbank, Monatsberichte der Deutschen Bundesbank (Frankfurt am Main, January 1972), Appendix, p. 65.

special factors. But it began to accelerate in 1971. In the first eleven months of 1971 the index increased by 5.5 percent, with a decline registered in August but with increases of 0.5 percent for each of the three subsequent months. The cost-of-housing index showed an increase of 14.9 percent for 1970 and an estimated increase of 18 percent for 1971.

During the period 1968-71 wage increases also accelerated. In 1968 wage increases including those attributable to wage drift amounted to 6 percent.[18] As an aftermath to the recession that for the first time since the early 1950s had produced a considerable drop in employment, the rise in wages remained moderate in relation to the expansion in economic activity, and profits rose sharply. In 1969 wage increases averaged 12.8 percent. Most of this increase occurred during the second half of the year. During the first half of 1969 this rise in wages caught up with the profit rise, and in the second half it clearly exceeded the increase in profits. In the second half of 1969 the share of gross wages and salaries in national income was roughly back to the 1965 level. In 1970 wage increases averaged 16.7 percent—the highest during the postwar period. These increases coincided with a slowdown in productivity growth. During the first three quarters of 1971 wages tended to show a decrease. In the first quarter wages increased by 16.2 percent compared to 17.2 percent for the first quarter of 1971. In the second and third quarters wage increases amounted to 13.2 percent and 12.2 percent.

As the West German economy heads into 1972 a situation of "stagflation" can be said to exist. In 1972 the index of industrial production is projected to decrease by -1 percent over the preceding year.[19] The main contributors to this decline are the investment-goods industry, with a projected decline of -3 percent over 1971, and the construction industry, with a projected decline of -6.5 percent. Total gross domestic investment is estimated to decline by DM 4.3 billion in 1972. Real gross social product is projected to increase by 1.5 percent—one of the lowest increases in the last 20 years—while money gross social product is projected to increase by 7 percent.[20] One significant point in this connection is the deterioration in the growth rate of the West German economy compared to the French economy. In all three years of the 1970s the French real growth rate has exceeded or is expected to exceed the West German real growth rate. In 1972 the real increase in French gross social product is projected to be 5.5 percent, compared to 1.5 percent for West Germany.

The general leveling off of economic activity in West Germany may be attributable in part to a decrease in world trade in 1971. With the medium-term effects of the 1969 revaluation of the Deutsche Mark and its subsequent floating in May 1971 on Germany's competitiveness aggravated by a continuing high rate of price increase, volume losses in export markets occurred. The position of German exports in world trade was exacerbated further in 1971 by the "new economic" policies of the Nixon Administration, which, among other things, placed import duties on goods coming into the United States. Since Germany is a major exporter of cars to the United States, its volume of car exports was adversely affected. In 1972 export growth in real terms is expected to reflect the problems of 1971, with an increase of 4.5 percent compared to a 1971 increase of 7.1 percent.[21] Real imports for 1972 are projected to increase at a rate of 3.5 percent.

Gross money social product is projected to increase from an estimated DM 749.2 billion for 1971 to an estimated DM 800.2 billion for 1972.[22] Most of this increase will come from the public sector, given the government's commitment to increase public expenditures should full-employment conditions be seriously threatened and given official plans on public infrastructure investment. Private consumption is also expected to provide some stimulus to economic activity in that it is projected to increase in monetary terms by 8.5 percent for 1972. The outlook for gross private domestic investment, however, is linked to the development of profits and liquidity, both of which are depressed in comparison to previous levels. An increase in profit margins will depend on how well business firms succeed in passing on wage costs in increased prices. Much will also depend on the scope for domestic and export price increases provided by price increases abroad.

The basic economic position of West Germany remains strong in comparison to other industrial nations, however. The main problem during the 1967-72 period was that the recovery from the recession was very rapid, and it began from a low starting point. At the peak of the recovery excessive pressures were placed on available resources. The labor market in particular was very tight, with a situation of more jobs than available labor. Distortions in income distribution also helped to create a situation that, when coupled with pressures on resources, upset the pattern of wage-price determination that had contributed to the high degree of price stability that existed in the economy in previous years. In addition, in terms of government demand management policies the period marks the first time that flexible policy-making arrangements were made available. The policy measures adopted in 1967 and 1968 contributed to the boom that followed, but an inflationary spiral developed with a momentum of its own. The problem became one of restoring price stability without creating a recession.

THE EAST GERMAN ECONOMY, 1960-72

The single most important development in the East German economy during the period 1960-71 was the reforms, begun in 1963, that were designed to stress economic efficiency. These reforms included, among other things, a reform of the price system, the introduction of a new system of managerial incentives in industry, a reduction in the number of planning goals to be met by enterprises, and an increase in the role of the state banking system. The reforms of the New Economic System extended over a considerable part of the 1960s. It is difficult, however, to tie the performance of the East German economy during the latter part of the decade to the reforms. Some of the features of the New Economic System were put into effect only on an experimental basis, some were postponed or modified, and some never got past the discussion stage. Administrative controls were tightened, particularly after 1965, reflecting the unwillingness of the leaders to grant more than minimal autonomy to regional and local authorities.

It can be said that economic growth in the GDR since 1963 has been accomplished despite the reforms that have been introduced, for implementation of the reforms has undoubtedly led to short-term frictions that have hindered growth. The reforms are designed to have more of a long-range effect on the economy in that they are supposed to trigger impulses that are supposed to have positive effects on its operation. Internal structural changes in the organization of agriculture, banking, and industry are not immediately felt in terms of their impact on the economy, and their end result is difficult to quantify. Reforms in the distribution of goods and services also may generate a positive though not quantifiable effect.

During the period 1960-70 produced national income in the GDR increased from DM 71 billion to DM 108.3 billion.[23] Shifts in the contributions of various sectors to produced national income occurred, with industry contributing 61.9 percent in 1970, compared to 56.4 percent in 1960, while the contribution of agriculture declined from 16.4 percent in 1960 to 11.7 percent in 1970.[24] In particular, the gain in net social product was minor during the period 1960-63—DM 71 billion in 1960 and DM 76.7 billion in 1963. This period was somewhat transitional in that it marked a definite change in the structure of the economic system. The Berlin Wall was created to stop the exodus of persons from east to west, and the conversion of East German agriculture to a collective form of organization was consummated. The reforms were developed in 1963, and gains averaging around 5 percent in real national income were recorded through 1970. The East German economy was far from being free of internal economic problems, however. A general shortage in the quantity and quality of housing and consumer goods has existed, and agriculture, despite efforts to increase its efficiency through large-scale operations, has lagged behind other sectors of the economy. In this connection it is interesting to note that the contribution of agriculture to national income in 1970 is not much different from what it was in 1955—DM 13.1 billion to DM 11 billion.

Economic Growth, 1968-72

There has been a negative consequence of concentration on structurally decisive sectors and projects, which has become more visible. Utilization of new capacities in these sectors has often been delayed because the supply of raw materials and semifabricated goods at lower, and neglected, levels has not increased at a sufficient rate. In 1970 in particular other interruptions occurred because the production of certain items was discontinued at one plant in the course of planned specialization but was not resumed at another factory at the time foreseen.[25] Capital investment suffered progressively from poor achievement of the construction industry due to unfavorable weather, lack of raw materials and equipment, and technical and organizational weaknesses. This made for delays in the completion of numerous investment projects; it also involved considerable cost overruns in some cases. New plants frequently failed to achieve the projected level of production or sometimes worked at less than 75 percent of capacity. This in turn was often the result of interruptions and damage caused by handling and servicing errors committed by insufficiently trained and unqualified personnel. The hope for a rise in productivity was therefore not achieved.

Industrial production in 1970 suffered numerous negative influences.[26] Factories were only partially successful in their attempts to make good the plan arrears incurred during the first quarter. By fully utilizng all capacity industrial output was increased in the second quarter. In the second half of the year, however, growth declined considerably and was accompanied by increasing diseconomies of production. Production even stopped completely in some sectors, e.g., metal working, by reason of missing parts deliveries, such as roller bearings and armatures. Even in those industrial sectors that have been promoted for years, such as chemicals, electronics, heavy machinery and equipment, and machine tools, production did not increase at the planned rate, partly due to delays in getting new plants producing. In addition, problems arose in the supply of power. The mining of brown coal was much impeded by weather conditions. Electricity and gas plants were badly overloaded in response to increased private and industrial consumption, and many power and pressure reductions took place.

Production growth in the construction industry was up 4 percent over 1969, compared to a planned increase of 8.6 percent. There were several reasons for the failure to match planned growth. There were delays in the delivery of building materials, and fragmentation of effort on too many sites. Above all, low efficiency of many construction enterprises in planning, managing, and executing important building projects is the reason for a low rise in building construction. Housing targets were the only ones to be achieved in 1970, but pressing shortages continue to exist.

In 1969, 1970, and 1971 agriculture in the GDR was affected by a low production, particularly of grain, vegetable oils, and sugar beets. In 1971 the agricultural harvest is reported to have fallen 20 percent short of the previous year's.[27] The poor harvest, due primarily to drought, cost the equivalent of fodder sufficient to produce 1 million tons of milk and 500,000 tons of meat and necessitated the importation of grain to avoid slaughtering cattle. Although the production of slaughter animals has remained steady during the 1969-71 period, milk yields have tended to decline.[28] Compounding the agricultural problem are a shortage of labor, which has been flowing to industry, and a lack of agricultural machinery.

The low expansion rate of 1970 meant the failure of the transition to a greatly increased growth rate for the five-year plan of 1971-75. The level of production achieved in 1970 on the whole just managed to attain the amount stipulated in the 1966-70 economic plan. Both total economic growth and growth in industrial production, however, only managed to reach the lower band of the plan spectrum. The increase in industrial production was achieved largely through increased productivity; however, the growth of 32 percent lagged behind plan projections of 40 to 45 percent.[29] The construction industry achieved an increase of 47 percent over the planning period, compared to planned growth of 40 percent. In both sectors the labor force employed had to be greater than planned in order to achieve the minimum production targets.

In general, investment planning for 1971 was marked by the concentration of gross capital investment in sectors, which caused bottlenecks, loss of production, and interruptions during the period 1969-70. Whereas investment volume was to be lower by 1.5 percent than in 1970, investment in industry was to increase by 3 percent, with the greatest increase planned for the power, parts-supply, and chemical industry.[30] Other industrial sectors were supposed to suffer some curtailment in investment. Efforts to exploit native raw materials, particularly natural gas, were to be encouraged. At the same time investment activity was to be much more closely supervised than before by the central planning bodies; investment decisions at the plant level were to virtually cease to exist in 1971.

Private consumption for 1971 was supposed to increase at a rate of 2 percent, and this increase was to be primarily for the benefit of low wage earners.[31] In March 1971 minimum gross wages in the GDR were fixed at 350 Ostmarks; certain work positions in the service industries, and also those positions with particularly low wages, were granted increases in wages. At the other end of the income spectrum tax increases were imposed upon those persons who are self-employed, members of the free professions, or employed by cooperatives. Prices for basic foodstuffs were to be held constant, but those for newly developed industrial consumer goods of higher value were to be fixed according to costs. An above-average increase in public consumption was ruled out.

Domestic consumption has been held in check as a matter of economic policy. The objective is to promote foreign trade. The plan target for foreign trade in 1971 called for an expansion of exports by 16 percent within a total foreign-trade expansion of 8 percent. While imports on the whole were to be held down, exports to socialist countries were to be increased by 14 percent and to Western industrial countries and developing countries by as much as 25 percent. Achievement of high export targets was given top priority by the 1971 economic plan. What this means is that goods are in essence rationed to the East German consumer. High prices are set internally on various specialty goods that are in demand in foreign markets. Taxes are also used as an instrument of rationing policy. Thus, the East German consumer is subsidizing the foreign trade of the GDR.

The transition to an increased pace of economic growth in the 1970s, which was the goal of the leaders of the GDR in 1969, can be regarded as a failure. There were several reasons for this failure, which are as follows:

1. The framework of the technical infrastructure, power, and transportation was too narrow and constricted industrial expansion.

2. The planning and balancing system was unable to cope with the increasingly complex economic process, nor was it flexible enough to react quickly to unexpected difficulties.

3. The neglect of those supply industries that were not structurally decisive, such as raw materials and semifinished products, has been detrimental to production as a whole.

4. In addition, many interruptions caused by shifts in production took place in 1970. Weaknesses of achievement in the construction industry hampered investment activity. Extreme weather conditions led to poor agricultural harvests and added another burden to the economy. There were reductions in electric power, lowered gas pressure, shortages in supplies of industrial goods, and a lack of fuel.

A decline in growth occurred during the second half of 1970, so that only two-thirds of the planned annual increase in production was achieved. The growth of investment at 7 percent was only half as great as planned for the year; even industrial investment, which was up 13 percent, was lower than the planned increase of 24 percent. During the year it became necessary to import more, while an unexpected decline of exports also occurred. Although exports increased during the last two months of 1971, a deficit of 1 billion Valuta Marks was anticipated for the year. A poor agricultural harvest also occurred in 1970 and contributed to a decline in overall total output of 4.5 percent from the projected goal of 6.3 percent.

The annual economic plan for 1971 reflected a rather conservative approach. Its main objective was to improve the infrastructure of the economy. Priority was given to the improvement of the raw material base. Except in the chemical industry, investment was restricted to a necessary minimum. Exports also were accorded top priority in the 1971 plan.

The two years 1970 and 1971 marked a caesura in the development in the economy of the GDR since the growth crisis at the beginning of the last decade. A consolidation phase encompassing many parts of the economy occurred at the expense of an increased rate of economic growth. This phase meant only a temporary pause, however, because there are many pressing needs. In particular, there is a need to increase exports. There is a shortage of labor and material reserves.

The period of consolidation in the 1971 plan was reflected in the scaling-down of some goals. During 1971 real national income increased by 4.5 percent over the preceding year. This rate was less than the rate projected in the 1971 plan. Labor productivity amounted to 4.5 percent in comparison to the plan goal of 5.4 percent.

The 1972 Plan

General economic uncertainties that marked the year 1971 delayed the setting-up of the 1972 economic plan. There was also a problem of its incorporation into the five-year plan, with its long-term goals for economic development. In general, however, the 1972 economic plan follows the pattern of the 1971 plan.32 The produced national income in 1972 is supposed to be 4.6 percent higher in 1972 and reach a projected 118.3 billion Ostmarks. To achieve this 4.6 percent goal, given a static labor force, an increase in labor productivity of 5 percent is essential. Industry is expected to expand at a rate of 5.5 percent, as in the preceding year. The growth goals of the various branches of industry are expected to follow the rate of development marked out in the five-year plan. The goal for light industry, however, already has been increased for 1972 over the average for the five-year plan. The planned increase in the construction industry for 1972 is set at 3.6 percent. Most construction is set for the building of 67,500 apartments and the repair of other housing units. In agriculture a total use in production of 4.8 percent is planned. This figure counts on a better harvest than was yielded in 1971. The services of the traffic, postal, and communications systems are expected to increase by 5.5 percent in 1972.

Private consumption, an area generally neglected by East Germany and other socialist countries, also comes in for attention. It is to be increased in 1972, and the quality of consumer goods is to be improved. In particular, increased imports of consumer goods are supposed to provide the basic goods, such as foodstuffs, but are also supposed to broaden the choice of goods available to consumers. An increase of 4 percent in the retail turnover of consumer goods is built into the 1972 plan. Services are also projected to increase by a greater amount. For example, an increase of 15 percent in the service repair of washing machines, refrigerators, and gas appliances is set for the plan. This is attributed to sharp criticism, reflected in the East German press, regarding long periods of waiting for service.

General investment activity is to be restricted to a 2-percent increase in 1972. Included among various types of investment projects are joint ventures with other socialist countries. A Polish-East

German cotton spinning mill is to be built in Poland. A natural gas connection line linking East Germany to Czechoslovakia is to be built, and the construction of a second petroleum pipeline linking East Germany to the Soviet Union is also scheduled for completion. Within the GDR priority is given to the continued expansion of energy facilities.

Average income for 1972 is set to increase by 4 percent. Incomes above this average are to increase for workers in coal mining, foundries, and power stations, however. Increases in salaries above the average are to be permitted for certain categories of workers. Bonus standards are also to be revised during 1972. Public consumption is to be increased, but no specifics are given. Travel is to be promoted with the neighboring countries of Czechoslovakia and Poland.

The State Budget, 1972

Total income and expenditures of the state in 1972 are set at 93 billion Ostmarks.[33] Of this amount, 82 billion Ostmarks will go to the state budget and the remaining 11 billion Ostmarks will go to the state-owned enterprises and combines. The bulk of this amount consists of the profits of state-owned enterprises. The amount of funds scheduled to go to the enterprises shows a decline over previous years. The reason for the reduction in these enterprise funds is tied to the attempt to give more decision-making and to provide more incentives to enterprises in order to make them more self-sufficient.

Revenues for the state budget reflect the current position that it is necessary to achieve higher profits through increased production, lower costs, and lower taxes. In this connection the minister of finance of the GDR has announced stronger control by the state over enterprises to ensure that profits are not illegally obtained by illegal price charges or shifting to more profitable selection lines. Tax payments from the so-called peoples-owned sector are set to increase by 5 percent in 1972, compared to 13 percent in 1971. Social security contributions are set at 10 billion Ostmarks in 1972, or approximately 12 percent of budget revenues.

On the expenditure side of the budget, expenditures for social and cultural purposes constitute the largest single component. Excluding social security subsidies, social and cultural expenditures are set at 22.7 billion Ostmarks. Of this total, 9.2 billion Ostmarks are allocated as subsidies for consumer retail prices. This is an increase of 530 million Ostmarks over 1971. Consumer goods that are subsidized include the milk, bread, butter, meat, poultry, fish, potatoes, children's clothing, heating coal, and fares of public transportation. The subsidy element is an important part of the state budget. Education expenditures are set at 6.4 billion Ostmarks. Health expenditures, set at 2.7 billion Ostmarks, include the provision of new office spaces for 780 physicians and dentists.

Chart 14.1 on the following page presents the relationship of the 1972 economic plan at the enterprise level to the various funds and to the state budget. Excluded from the chart are special funds formed by enterprises, such as the cultural and social fund. As the chart indicates a part of profits flows to the state budget through various levies, and the remainder goes to various enterprise funds for specific purposes—payment of bonuses, repayment of debts, and amortization.

SUMMARY

The purpose of this chapter has been to compare the development of the East and West German economies for the period 1960-71, with special emphasis placed on industry and agriculture. The year 1960 is significant not only because it forms the base of comparison for the decade but because it also marked the final drive toward the socialization of resources in East Germany. Thus, two countries, both of which were part of the same country, exist side by side with different economic systems. In East Germany resource allocation and the production process is determined by economic planning; in West Germany the same process is determined by the market mechanism. By virtue of its control over the means of production, a socialist economy such as East Germany should have an advantage in terms of industrial development and a sustained rate of economic growth. This, however, has not always proved to be the case. For one thing, given the nature of economic planning a certain rigidity is built into the socialist economic system that makes it unwieldy and not easily adaptable to the changes demanded by modern developments.

It can be said that the performance of both East and West Germany during the 1960s was quite good taking into consideration various events, such as the recession in West Germany in 1967. Both countries, reflecting their industrial heritage, rank among the top 10 industrial countries in the world—with West Germany ranked fourth and East Germany ranked ninth as of 1970. When the two countries are compared to each other for the decade of the 1960s, the gap between the two countries in terms of total output, industrial output, and other related measures has not been narrowed to any significant degree. Industrial output in the GDR has held at around 24 percent of the output of the FRG during the period. In general, industry in the GDR in comparison with the FRG is three years behind the FRG in capital intensity and more than seven years behind in

CHART 14.1

Profit Building and Profit Application
in Industry and Construction Enterprises,
East Germany

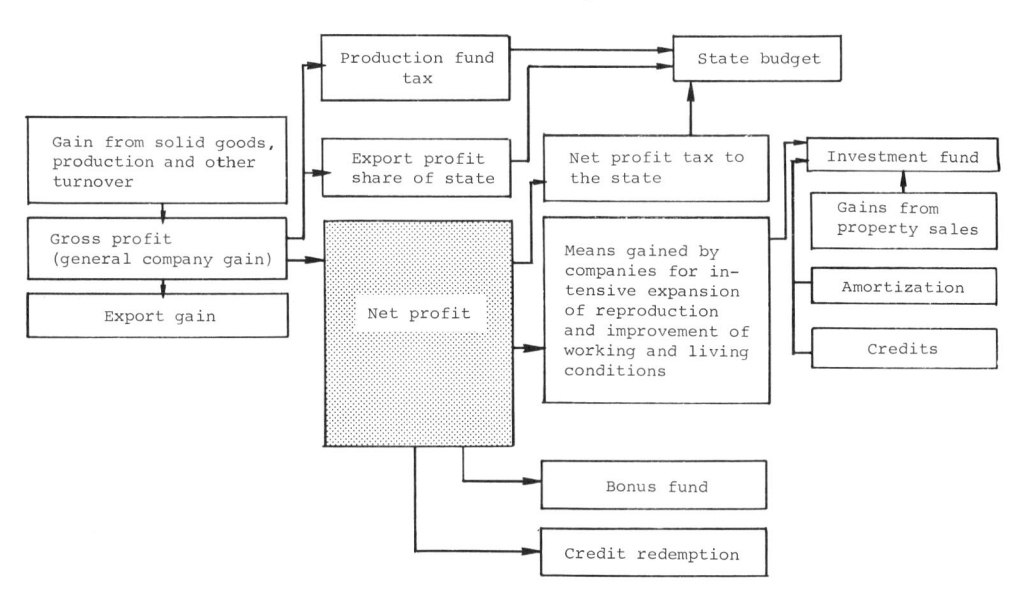

```
                          ┌─────────────────┐         ┌─────────────────┐
                       ┌─►│ Production fund │────────►│  State budget   │
                       │  │ tax             │         │                 │
                       │  └─────────────────┘         └─────────────────┘
                       │                                       ▲
┌─────────────────┐    │  ┌─────────────────┐    ┌─────────────────┐    ┌─────────────────┐
│ Gain from solid │    │  │ Export profit   │    │ Net profit tax  │    │ Investment fund │
│ goods,          │────┼─►│ share of state  │    │ to the state    │    │                 │
│ production and  │    │  │                 │    │                 │    └─────────────────┘
│ other turnover  │    │  └─────────────────┘    └─────────────────┘             ▲
└─────────────────┘    │                                  ▲                      │
                       │                                  │            ┌─────────────────┐
┌─────────────────┐    │                                  │            │ Gains from      │
│ Gross profit    │────┤                         ┌─────────────────┐   │ property sales  │
│ (general        │    │                         │ Means gained by │   └─────────────────┘
│ company gain)   │    │                         │ companies for   │            ▲
└─────────────────┘    │                         │ intensive       │            │
                       │   ┌─────────────────┐  ►│ expansion of    │   ┌─────────────────┐
┌─────────────────┐    │   │                 │   │ reproduction    │   │ Amortization    │
│ Export gain     │────┘   │  Net profit     │   │ and improvement │   └─────────────────┘
│                 │        │                 │   │ of working and  │            ▲
└─────────────────┘        │                 │   │ living          │            │
                           │                 │   │ conditions      │   ┌─────────────────┐
                           │                 │   └─────────────────┘   │ Credits         │
                           │                 │                         └─────────────────┘
                           └─────────────────┘
                                   │
                                   │         ┌─────────────────┐
                                   ├────────►│ Bonus fund      │
                                   │         └─────────────────┘
                                   │
                                   │         ┌─────────────────┐
                                   └────────►│ Credit redemption│
                                             └─────────────────┘
```

Source: Based on the financial direction for executing the economic and state budget plan of 1972 from Gesetzblatt der DDR, II, 78 (November 29, 1971). It contains special regulations for surplus plan profits, which are not due to self-performance, and for financial debts. Not mentioned here are funds also formed by the enterprises from costs, i.e., science and technique fund, repair fund, and culture and social fund. The chart is also published in Neues Deutschland, February 22, 1972.

work productivity. Capital intensity in the GDR, however, rose 71 percent in the period 1960-68, compared to 56 percent in the FRG, and gains in the productivity of capital were registered by the GDR relative to the position of the FRG.

In agriculture almost diametrically opposite patterns of development have occurred in the GDR and FRG. In the GDR agriculture has been completely changed through the process of socialization of land. Through the combining of many small agricultural units into large-scale enterprises, the GDR hopes to increase the efficiency and potential of agriculture. The GDR, however, has not succeeded so far in achieving optimal factor combinations based on the size of its agricultural enterprises. The FRG, on the other hand, has favored family farms, although pushing for the consolidation of small, uneconomical farms into larger units. The average size of the West German farm is much smaller than the average size of the East German farm—a ratio of 1 to 50. The performance of the East German agricultural sector, however, given a superior base from the prewar period from which to work, has generally been inferior to the performance of agriculture in the West German economy. For example, net food production per hectare of land has been lower in the GDR than in the FRG.

During the decade of the 1970s it is difficult to predict whether or not the differences in total output will be narrowed. When the period 1968-70 is taken into consideration, all gains made by the GDR as a result of the 1966-67 economic downturn in the FRG had been eliminated, and, if anything, the gaps in many fields were widened. The years 1969 and 1970 marked sort of a consolidation phase in the GDR. In 1971 and 1972, however, the picture has changed on balance to favor the GDR. The year 1971 witnessed an overall decrease in the rate of growth of the West German economy over the preceding three years, and the prognosis for 1972 is even less salutary. In the GDR, on the other hand, a solid gain of around 4.5 percent in real national income can be expected to occur in 1972. It is likely then that differences between the GDR and FRG in total output have been narrowed in 1971 and 1972.

CHAPTER 15

A COMPARISON OF INCOME DISTRIBUTION AND LIVING STANDARDS IN EAST AND WEST GERMANY

INTRODUCTION

In some respects there are similarities in the pattern of income distribution in the capitalist and socialist countries; in other respects the pattern is quite dissimilar. In both systems there is reliance on income differentials to allocate labor and to provide the incentives necessary to stimulate productivity. Moreover, the socialist countries use incentives not greatly dissimilar to those used in the capitalist countries—piece rates, higher salaries for persons engaged in work regarded as more useful by the state, and status symbols such as automobiles and better housing for government officials. A major difference between income distribution in the capitalist and socialist countries lies in the fact that the state rather than the marketplace is the prime determinant of income distribution in the socialist countries. But it is necessary to point out that in the capitalist countries there has been considerable modification of income distribution through state intervention in the marketplace. Indeed, through the use of income taxation and transfer payments, income inequality after taxes in a country like Sweden is probably less than income inequality after taxes in the Soviet Union.

In the socialist countries income is primarily limited to wages. It has been an article of faith, which has been subject to question only recently, that labor is the only factor of production endowed with the capability of creating value. Therefore, labor should be remunerated to the exclusion of land and capital. The total amount of wages to be paid, and the production counterpart to support wages, depends on the division of the national income between accumulation and consumption and, further, of consumption between the social consumption fund and the wage fund. It would stem from this that there would be as a matter of necessity a high degree of centralization and control over the determination of wages.

In the capitalist countries income is derived from two sources—labor and property. The latter takes the form of rent, interest, and profit, which are derived from the ownership of capital equipment or natural resources. There is a fundamental division between labor and nonlabor income that affects the relative share of income that accrues to the owners of human and nonhuman resources. Thus, income distribution in a capitalist country depends on the quantity of economic resources each individual owns and the price he obtains for each unit of such resources supplied to the productive process. The price depends on the extent to which the economic resources are being utilized.

Income distribution is altered in both the capitalist and socialist countries through the use of taxes and transfer payments. When various government expenditures for free and subsidized consumer services, such as medical benefits and transfer payments, are taken into consideration, total income can be altered considerably for the average worker, regardless of the system. As a matter of fact, government expenditures and transfer payments in the form of family allowances amount to around 50 percent for the average French worker. In the Soviet Union expenditures and transfer payments amount to 35 percent of average monthly earnings for wage and salaried workers. Even in the United States fringe benefits can represent a significant part of total income for many workers, particularly in unionized industries, and government expenditures and transfer payments can also add to total income. It can be said that neither capitalism nor socialism has a monopoly on the provision of social welfare measures to benefit workers and society.

It is real income, however, that is the important desideratum. In other words, it is not monetary income that should be considered, but what it will buy in terms of goods and services. Real income is tied to living standards and the material well-being of society. What is important from a welfare standpoint is the availability of goods and services per person; it is reasonable to talk of an improvement in the material well-being of a people only if, over time, each person has a growing volume of goods and services at his disposal. Thus, the most meaningful measure of material well-being is the level of real income, or real per capita consumption. Increases in a nation's total output of goods and services do not necessarily imply that the individual's standard of living has improved; an expansion of total output may involve investment goods and public goods that do not contribute directly to the material well-being of the individual.

The tax factor cannot be ignored, for obviously taxes are the reverse side of the coin from transfer payments and government expenditures. An international comparative analysis of almost any aspect of taxation is extremely complex, however. Attempts at simplification run the risk of inaccuracy and distortion. This is particularly true of tax burdens. Every major characteristic of personal income taxation varies widely among countries. Exemptions, allowances, and deductions are all treated differently. No accurate account can be taken of the tendency toward compliance on the part of the taxpayers or of the efficiency of collection on the part of governments. Moreover, simple comparisons of tax payments make no allowance for the multitude of concessions or transfers that can radically alter the amount of net income.

Some general remarks can be made about the types of taxes used in the capitalist and socialist countries, however. It can be said that there is far more reliance on direct taxes, particularly the personal income tax, in the capitalist countries than in the socialist countries. Conversely, indirect taxes are far more important in the socialist countries. Moreover, taxes perform several functions in countries such as the Soviet Union and East Germany. In addition to providing revenue for the state budget, the turnover tax is not only used to maintain a balance between the purchasing power of the consumer and the supply of goods but is also manipulated to regulate the amount of profits allowed to consumers. An agricultural income tax is also used to discourage collective farmers from spending too much time on their private plots at the expense of their regular work on the collective farm.

A reallocation of income in both the capitalist and socialist countries has been effected through the taxing and income-transfer processes of government. In looking at the capitalist countries in particular, the participation of the state in all phases of economic life is considerable. This is reflected to a major extent in the growth of income transfers, with a concomitant increase in the amount of income redistribution among different population segments. Taxes have also increased to finance transfers, but in analyzing the tax-transfer arrangement it is difficult, if not impossible, to sort out those taxes that more or less bear directly upon individual households, as opposed to those taxes that, at least in the first instance, fall upon business. There is the well-established principle, however, that business taxes are largely passed on to the consumer in the form of higher prices.

The use of forms of sales taxation in both the capitalist and socialist countries tends to obfuscate the whole concept of income redistribution through the tax-transfer arrangement. The value-added tax, which is the most important indirect tax in most of the major capitalist countries, is no more than a sales tax, although the fact that it appears in the price of a product rather than as an identifiable tax has the character of obscuring its true nature. It is assessed at each stage of the fabrication of products, from raw materials to finished goods, as a percentage of the value-added to the product at each stage. Any sales tax, including the value-added tax, tends to bear most heavily upon low- to middle-income families who spend a larger proportion of their incomes upon goods that would be subject to the tax.

The personal income tax as an instrument of income redistribution has far less impact in the socialist countries than in the capitalist countries. For one thing, the rates are much lower. This fact is made abundantly clear in comparing the personal income tax rates in the United States, Sweden, and the Soviet Union. In the United States the rates range from 14 to 70 percent; in Sweden the rates range from 10 to 65 percent. Moreover, it is also necessary to point out that these rates are only for the national income tax and do not take into consideration the fact that both countries also have state or local income taxes. In the Soviet Union, on the other hand, the rates as of 1967 ranged from a minimum of 0.15 percent to a maximum of 13 percent of monthly earnings, withheld by enterprises.[1] The personal income tax was supposed to have been abolished in the Soviet Union by 1965. This has not come about, although some liberalization in the amount of income exempted from the tax has occurred. Since 1967 the amount of income exempted from the tax was 60 rubles ($66.66) a month.

INCOME DISTRIBUTION

There is a greater disparity in the range of income distribution in the FRG as opposed to the GDR. This fact stems from the reason that income from property contributes a far greater amount to total income in the FRG than in the GDR. This income would accrue primarily to those persons situated in the upper income groups. As there is also a correlation between income and wealth, there is a much greater concentration of wealth in the hands of a small minority of individuals in the FGR than in the GDR. Although data on wealth ownership is unavailable for the GDR, available data for the FRG indicates that there is a concentration of property ownership in the FRG in the hands of a minority of individuals. In 1966, for example, there were 15,200 private households with taxable property of DM 1 million or more out of a total of 21.3 million private households. These households controlled 3.7 percent of all agricultural property, 3.2 percent of other land property, 7.7 percent of savings, 49.6 percent of stocks and bonds, and 38.1 percent of capital property.[2] The top 1 percent of private households classified by property ownership controlled approximately 7 percent of all agricultural property, approximately 13 percent of other land property, approximately 16 percent of savings, approximately 65 percent of investment securities, and approximately 65 percent of other forms of investment capital.[3]

Table 15.1 presents a distribution of property ownership by property classes. Property subject to taxation is also listed. For the sake of conciseness, the various types of property have been combined into a total. The number of property owners listed in the table account for about 4 percent of the total number of private households in the FRG. This 4 percent owns 73 percent of investment securities, 80 percent of other investments, 11 percent of agricultural property, 16 percent of other land property, and 21 percent of total savings.

Obviously, the quantity of economic resources held by an individual or household will have an impact on income distribution. Human labor is only one resource. Income also depends on the ownership of capital and land. In Table 15.1, the significant point is that approximately DM 221 billion in taxable property out of a total of DM 728 billion in taxable property was owned by a little less than 4 percent of all households in the FRG. Whether this is good or bad depends on one's point of view. There is no question, however, but what the concentration of property ownership results in a greater degree of income

TABLE 15.1

Property Ownership Based on Property Classes,
West Germany, 1966

Taxable Property by Classes (DM)	Number of Households	Total Taxable Property (billion DM)
0 and under 50,000	73,600	12.5
50 and under 100,000	143,100	28.1
100 and under 250,000	150,000	50.3
250 and under 500,000	50,000	34.5
500 and under 1,000,000	21,500	26.2
1 and under 5,000,000	13,600	40.4
5 and under 10,000,000	1,000	9.5
10 and under 50,000,000	540	11.9
50 and under 100,000,000	28	2.2
100 and over	22	5.3
Total	454,500	220.9

Source: Jürgen Siebke, "Die Vermögensbildung der privaten Haushalte in der Bundesrepublik Deutschland" (Bonn: Forschungsauftrag des Bundesministeriums für Arbeit und Sozialordnung, May 1971). (Unpublished document sent to the author.)

inequality than would exist if the property were more broad based in ownership. This concentration of property ownership also results in concentration of power in other areas in the hands of a small minority of households.

In many respects, however, there are similarities in the reward systems of East and West Germany. The practice of giving material incentives to workers, usually in the form of extra pay, is common in both countries. Piecework pay, differentiation in wages, and money incentives in the form of bonuses to outstanding workers are a part of the reward structure in each country. If anything, the East Germans carry the reward system further through the use of the piece rate, a device originated by, but virtually abandoned by, the capitalist countries to stimulate output. The piece rate is based on an output norm setting the number of units of production a worker is to turn out during a given time period and is multiplied by the payment per unit of output to get the wage. This payment may be fixed per unit of output or progressive in that the rate is fixed until the norm is reached and then increases per unit of output in excess of the norm.

There are other ways in which similarities exist in the wage structures of East and West Germany. Within factories and other forms of business units there are wage differentials based on skills. Salary differentials also exist for other types of workers not associated with factories. These differentials are based on the skill requirements of the job and the complexity of work. Wage differentials are also based on conditions of work, with hard or hazardous work commanding a higher premium than less arduous work. And, of course, regional differentials in wages and salaries exist to attract workers. So in the main there are structural similarities that are found in common technological phenomena, reflecting the place of science and the size of the industrial enterprise in both countries.

One method of comparing income differentials in East and West Germany is to examine the wage structure of different industries in both countries. Average wages in industries in both countries can be used as a rather rough measure of comparison. Unfortunately, absolute ranges in earnings for each industry are not readily available, but it should be apparent that the use of piece rates, bonuses, and other types of incentives can cause wide variations in the earnings of workers, even among those with similar skills, in the same place. It can be concluded that in an advanced industrial country, such as the GDR, the spread in wages from the highest to the lowest occupational level may be as high as 5 to 1 in complex industries, but lower in industries requiring less technological skills.[4] This spread does not take into consideration bonuses for successful plant managers and other rewards based on performance. A similar spread in wages and salaries would also exist in the industries in the FRG.

INCOME DISTRIBUTION AND LIVING STANDARDS

Table 15.2 presents average gross monthly earnings for industrial workers in the FRG for 1970 broken down for different industries. The average monthly earnings of all workers amounted to DM 1,164. The highest average monthly earning of DM 1,350 was recorded in the iron and steel industry, and the lowest monthly earning of DM 801 was recorded in the clothing industry. The ratio of average monthly earnings between the two industries is 1.7 to 1.

The distribution of average monthly income can also be compared by industry and trade for white collar and clerical workers. In 1970 the average monthly income for all white collar and clerical workers was DM 1,263.[5] The highest average monthly income of DM 1,650 was recorded in the mining industry, and the lowest average monthly income of DM 950 was recorded in retail trade. The range in incomes between top and bottom was 1.7 to 1. This range may also be presented

TABLE 15.2

Average Monthly Earnings
for Industrial Workers, West Germany, 1970
(DM)

Industry	Average Monthly Wage
Iron and steel	1,350
Stone and earth	1,345
Publishing	1,330
Transportation	1,310
Energy	1,250
Machinery	1,220
Mining	1,200
Chemicals	1,200
Glass	1,120
Woodworking	1,100
Food	1,050
Electronics	1,010
Textiles	950
Clothing	801
Average for all industries	1,164

Source: Statistisches Bundesamt, Statistisches Jahrbuch für die Bundesrepublik Deutschland, 1971 (Wiesbaden: W. Kohlhammer Verlag, 1971), p. 459. The figures should be accepted as approximations based on the chart that appears on page 459.

on a within industry basis.[6] For example, the average monthly income for male clerical workers within industry, trade, and banking in 1970 was DM 1,432, and the average income for male technical workers was DM 1,672. But these averages can be subdivided into income groups (Leistungsgruppe). The averages for these groups ranged from DM 982 to DM 1,887 a month for male clerical workers, and DM 1,064 to DM 2,029 a month for male technical workers. For each group the ratio between the highest and lowest average was 2 to 1. For female workers, however, there was a wider disparity in the ratio between the highest and lowest average. Average monthly income by performance groups ranged from DM 706 to DM 1,497 for nontechnical female workers, and from DM 758 to DM 1,804 for female technical workers. For both groups the ratios were better than 2 to 1 between top and bottom averages.

It is necessary to emphasize that these incomes are only averages and have nothing to do with ranges within income groups. Excluded are Christmas bonuses, which normally are equal to or more than a month's pay for many workers. Also excluded is payment for overtime work, which provides a minimum of 25 percent above base pay. Moreover, supplementary benefits from other sources average around 40 percent of wages or salaries for the typical worker. Included in the category of supplementary benefits are family allowances, rental allowances, and other forms of transfer payments. So comparisons of income differentials among wage or salary earners are made difficult by the exclusion of other benefits that also affect incomes.

More specific data is available for civil service employees. There are 16 income groups for federal civil servants. The range between the highest and lowest monthly salaries is better than 5 to 1.[7] As of January 1971 the lowest salary was DM 703 a month and the highest salary was DM 3,698 a month. This range does not include special civil servants whose salaries are above the quoted maximum of DM 3,698. The salaries of state employees are also not taken into consideration. By including this group of employees the ratio between the highest and lowest income is reduced to about 4.5 to 1.

So far the discussion of income differentials has been limited to white and blue collar workers in industry and trade and to civil servants. Data for other occupational groups also sheds some light on income distribution and income differentials. When the self-employed category of workers are included, a comparison can be made of the four major income groups—blue collar workers, white collar workers, government employees, and the self-employed—on a percentage basis for monthly incomes. In Table 15.3 self-employed workers account for the bulk of net income in the highest income group. In the self-employed group the highest incomes among professional groups are made by doctors.

TABLE 15.3

Net Income for Major Occupational Groups
Expressed as Percentage for Income Class,
West Germany, 1970

Income Class (DM)	Self-Employed	Government	White Collar	Blue Collar
0- 150	1.6	0.0	3.5	4.7
150- 300	2.9	0.0	6.9	7.6
300- 600	9.0	3.4	18.0	23.3
600- 800	12.3	10.6	20.0	32.9
800-1,200	23.8	40.4	29.8	28.9
1,200-1,500	21.6	31.8	16.0	2.6
1,800 and over	28.8	13.4	5.8	0.1
Total	100.0	99.6	100.0	100.0

Source: Statistisches Bundesamt, Statistisches Jahrbuch für die Bundesrepublik Deutschland, 1971 (Wiesbaden: W. Kohlhammer Verlag, 1971), p. 127.

The bulk of income in the GDR comes from two sources—the wage funds (Gesamtlohnfonds) and the premium funds (Prämienfonds). Both are determined with the framework of the national economic plan. Wages, particularly for industrial workers, take the form of piece rates and time rates, both of which are tied to output standards. The piece rate, as would be expected in a system that stresses performance, is the most common form of compensation. But regardless of whether piece or time rates are used, standard wage patterns are set by the state based on job classifications. From these classifications come 25 wage groups into which most East German workers are placed.[8] Income differentials vary between wage groups and within wage groups. These differentials can be raised or lowered as the state sees fit.

A rudimentary comparison can be made of average monthly incomes in industry and agriculture in the GDR for 1969. For example, in the state-owned construction industry (Volkseigene Bauindustrie) average wages for blue and white collar workers amounted to 805 Ostmarks, while average wages in the state-owned sector of agriculture (Volkseigene Landwirtschaft) amounted to 654 Ostmarks.[9] Average wages in the socialized sector of industry, i.e., that sector in which both the state and private industry participate collectively, amounted to 734 Ostmarks, while average wages in forestry amounted to 674

Ostmarks. These averages do not reflect differentials between incomes for blue collar and white collar workers. When white collar workers are excluded, the averages are lowered. Moreover, these averages do take into consideration income from the premium funds.

The premium funds are designed to reward performance in the fulfilling or overfulfilling of planning objectives. The amount of the funds is built into annual state planning figures and is based on the amount in the year preceding the plan. Calculation of the funds is tied to net profit after deductions that go to the state budget. For an individual enterprise the premium fund is raised or lowered when the state planning figures of total goods produced and net profit are either overfulfilled or underfulfilled during the plan period.[10] For every percentage point goods are produced over the plan quota set for the enterprise, the premium fund increases by 1.5 percent; for every percentage point the plan is underfulfilled, the premium fund decreases by 1.5 percent. In other words, if the plan figure of total output for the enterprise is exceeded by 2 percent, the premium funds increase by 3 percent. Moreover, for every 1-percent increase of net profit over planned net profit the premium fund increases by 0.5 percent, and for every 1 percent decrease of net profit from planned net profit the premium fund decreases by 0.5 percent. Additional amounts from the premium fund can also be paid for overfulfilling the state planning figure for goods production if work productivity norms are increased or if the goods are exported to certain economic areas.

Comparison of Wage and Salary Differentials

When wages and salaries are compared as averages or broken down into income categories, there is a more equal distribution of income in the GDR than in the FRG. This becomes first apparent when average incomes for individual industries are compared for the two countries. When Table 15.2 is compared to Table 11.1, there is a greater range in average incomes for individual industries in the FRG than in the GDR. The range in averages is DM 549 for the FRG compared to 242 Ostmarks in the GDR. It is necessary to point out, however, that to some extent the groupings in the two tables are not comparable. Nevertheless, this fact does not negate the point. A ratio of about 1.4 to 1 exists between the monthly averages of the highest and lowest industrial incomes in the GDR, compared to a ratio of 1.7 to 1 for the FRG. Moreover, there is a greater dispersion in average incomes from the industrial average for all industries in the FRG than is the case for the GDR. In 1970 the average monthly income for all industrial groups in the FRG was DM 1,164, with the

INCOME DISTRIBUTION AND LIVING STANDARDS

highest average of DM 1,350 for iron and steel workers and the lowest average of DM 801 for clothing workers. In the GDR the average monthly income for industrial groups in the GDR was 734 Ostmarks, with the highest average of 836 Ostmarks for the metallurgical industry and the lowest average of 594 Ostmarks for the textile industry.

More comparable data is presented in Table 15.4. In this table East and West German average monthly gross income is presented for blue and white collar workers in various industrial groups in 1969. Also presented are variations from the average wage for all industry groups expressed in percentages. There is actually a greater percentage range in averages for the GDR than for the FRG—33 percent as opposed to 27 percent. It is necessary to point out, however, that these industrial groupings are more circumscribed than the groups used in the preceding comparison.

The difference in average monthly incomes in the FRG and GDR widened considerably during the decade of the 1960s. For example, average monthly income in the GDR and the FRG for all industrial workers was virtually the same in 1960—571 Ostmarks as opposed to DM 575.[11] By 1970, however, average gross monthly income for

TABLE 15.4

Comparison of Gross Monthly Income, by Industrial Group, East and West Germany, 1969

Industry Group	Average Wage West	Average Wage East	Percentage Difference West	Percentage Difference East
Energy and fuels	1,133	810	107	110
Chemicals	1,129	763	107	104
Metallurgy	1,162	836	110	114
Building materials	1,127	746	107	102
Machinery	1,135	765	108	104
Electronics and industry	984	740	93	101
Light industry	934	646	86	88
Textiles	871	594	83	81
Food	994	677	94	92
Average	1,055	734	100	100

Source: Deutscher Bundestag, Materialien zum Bericht zur Lage der Nation 1971 Drucksache VI/1960 (Bonn-Bad Godesberg: Dr. Hans Heger Verlag, 1971).

industrial workers in the FRG had increased to DM 1,164 compared to 750 Ostmarks.[12] Average money gross earnings of East German industrial workers were 50 percent behind those of West German workers in 1970. Even after allowing for the price inflation that occurred in West Germany in 1970 the difference in real terms is not significantly altered. When the base is shifted to 1966, average gross monthly money earnings for East and West German industrial workers were 656 Ostmarks and DM 866, respectively.[13] Over the five-year period 1966-70 gross monthly money earnings had increased by 34 percent in the FRG, compared to 13 percent in the GDR.

The analysis so far has taken into consideration only average gross monthly incomes of industrial workers. Other groups of workers have been omitted, including the self-employed. In 1965 the gross monthly income of self-employed workers, including members of cooperatives, in the GDR was one-half of the amount for self-employed workers in the FRG—1,190 Ostmarks to DM 2,067.[14] Net income after income taxes and social security contributions was 1,040 Ostmarks to DM 1,661, with the East German net income two-thirds of the West German net income. In both countries the average gross income of a self-employed worker was twice as much as that of a regular worker. In the FRG the comparison was DM 2,067 to DM 852; in the GDR the comparison was 1,190 Ostmarks to 629 Ostmarks. Net income differentials, however, were lowered by personal income and social security taxes to DM 1,661 for self-employed workers and DM 710 for regular workers in the FRG, and 1,041 Ostmarks for self-employed workers and 551 Ostmarks for regular workers in the GDR. When old-age pensions are included in comparisons of average gross income, the difference between East and West Germany was almost 3 to 1, with West German pensions averaging DM 474 compared to an average of 164 Ostmarks for East Germany.

Differences in average monthly family incomes widened during the period 1960-67.[15] In 1960 average monthly gross family income in East Germany was 81 percent of average monthly gross family income in West Germany—843 Ostmarks compared to DM 1,019. In 1967 average monthly gross family income in East Germany had declined to 68 percent of West German average monthly gross family income—1,001 Ostmarks compared to DM 1,473. Net average monthly family income after personal income taxes and social security contributions can also be compared. One significant point to notice is that direct taxes, which are much higher in the FRG than in the GDR, reduced the net income differences between the two countries. In 1960 average monthly net family income in the FRG was DM 879 compared to 745 Ostmarks for the GDR. The GDR average was 85 percent of the FRG average. In 1967 the net average family incomes were DM 1,245 for the FRG and 878 Ostmarks for the GDR. The GDR average was 71 percent of the FRG average.

Average monthly net incomes for white and blue collar families in the FRG and GDR can also be compared for the period 1960-67. In Table 15.5 average monthly net incomes for various types of households are presented for both countries in 1960 and 1967. The differences in net income widened for all households regardless of size. Also presented in the table are percentage comparisons in each country of the relative position of individual households to the average for all households.

Income differentiation can also be measured by income classes in both countries through the use of the Lorenz curve. If incomes were absolutely uniformly distributed, the lowest 20 percent of income earners would receive exactly 20 percent of the total income; the lowest 80 percent would get exactly 80 percent of total income; and the highest 20 percent would get only 20 percent of the income. In using a Lorenz

TABLE 15.5

Average Monthly Household Net Income for Blue and White Collar Workers, by Household Size, East and West Germany, 1960 and 1967

	1960		1967	
Household	West (DM)	East (Ostmarks)	West (DM)	East (Ostmarks)
1 person	540	417	857	486
2 persons	704	665	1,109	813
3 persons	825	839	1,291	988
4 persons	947	913	1,464	1,058
5 and more persons	1,206	992	1,830	1,120
Average	852	758	1,307	899
Average = 100%				
1 person	63.4	55.0	65.6	54.1
2 persons	82.6	87.7	84.9	90.4
3 persons	96.8	110.7	98.8	109.9
4 persons	111.2	120.4	112.0	117.7
5 and more persons	141.5	130.9	140.0	124.6
Average	100.0	100.0	100.0	100.0

Source: Bundesminister für Innerdeutsche Beziehungen, Bericht der Bundesregierung und Materialien zur Lage der Nation 1971 (Bonn), p. 385.

curve the curve of absolute equality would actually be a straight line extending upward from left to right showing that 20 percent of income earners on the horizontal axis receive 20 percent of the income shown on the vertical axis, 40 percent of income earners receive 40 percent of the income, and so on. Any departure from this line is a departure from complete income equality. The measure of the degree of inequality in income distribution is the convexity of the Lorenz curve relative to the straight line indicating complete equality.

Table 15.6 presents a distribution of net income by quintiles in the FRG and GDR for the years 1960 and 1967. This income is limited to wage and salary earners in both countries. As the table indicates, there is a more even distribution of income by quintiles in the GDR than in the FRG. During the period 1960 to 1967 there has been a slight shift toward greater income equality in both countries. In 1967 the top 20 percent of wage and salary earners in the GDR received 30.4 percent of net income, compared to 32 percent in 1960. In the FRG the top 20 percent of wage and salary earners received 38.2 percent of net income in 1967, compared to 39.8 percent in 1960. Income of individual enterpreneurs is not reflected in the comparison; however, all income indicators support the assumption that its inclusion would increase the percentage of income in the top quintile in the FRG much more than the top quintile in the GDR.

TABLE 15.6

Comparison of Distribution of Net Income
by Quintiles for White and Blue Collar Workers,
East and West Germany, 1960 and 1967
(in percent)

Household Quintiles	1960 West	1960 East	1967 West	1967 East
First quintile	8.4	9.8	8.7	10.5
Second quintile	12.6	15.5	13.0	15.8
Third quintile	16.4	19.3	17.1	19.7
Fourth quintile	22.8	23.4	23.0	23.6
Fifth quintile	39.8	32.0	38.2	30.4
Total	100.0	100.0	100.0	100.0

Source: Deutscher Bundestag, Materialien zum Bericht zur Lage der Nation 1971, Drucksache VI/1690 (Bonn-Bad Godesberg: Dr. Hans Heger Verlag, 1971).

When Table 15.6 is presented in the form of a Lorenz curve, there is a shift to the left for both countries from 1960 to 1967 indicating a movement toward a more even distribution of household income. The curve representing the GDR is also closer to the line of income equality. For the mass of East German households there is less income inequality that for the mass of West German households. Nevertheless, the fact remains that income extremes exist in both countries. It was pointed out in Chapter 11 that certain groups in the GDR enjoy special privileges and a high level of income. Party functionaries, scientists, technicians, and other persons with special talents receive perquisites and benefits that place them in a class by themselves.

Real Wages

Although living standards in the GDR have improved over the last ten years, the promise first made by party leader Walter Ulbricht in 1958 to give East Germans higher living standards than their counterparts in the Federal Republic remains far from being fulfilled.

Although by 1969 East German industrial workers had the highest wages and living standards of all the countries in the Soviet-dominated COMECON, their average gross money earnings of 721 Ostmarks a month were well below average gross earnings of DM 1,026 a month for West German workers. Moreover, the gap in average monthly earnings had widened since 1960, when average monthly earnings for East and West German industrial workers were 571 Ostmarks and DM 575, respectively. The gap particularly widened during the period 1966-69, when average monthly earnings increased from 656 to 721 Ostmarks in the GDR, compared to an increase from DM 866 to 1,026 in the FRG.

In fact, since 1961 East Germany has raised productivity substantially without a corresponding increase in wages. During the ten years ending in December 1969 industrial gross production per man-hour rose by 87 percent while wages rose by only 30 percent.[16] An important factor in this performance was the closure of the last escape route to the West in August 1961, when the Berlin Wall was raised; another is that strike action on the part of unions has been prohibited since Soviet troops put down the strikes in June 1953.

When money wages are translated in terms of real wages, which represent the purchasing power of money wages, some goods cost less in East Germany than in West Germany, while other goods cost more. For example, rents, fares, and public services cost less in East Germany. A second-class railroad ticket in 1969 cost 2.5 Ostmarks per 15 kilometers in East Germany compared to DM 9 in

CHART 15.1

Lorenz Curve Comparing East and West German
Income Distribution by Quintiles, 1960 and 1967

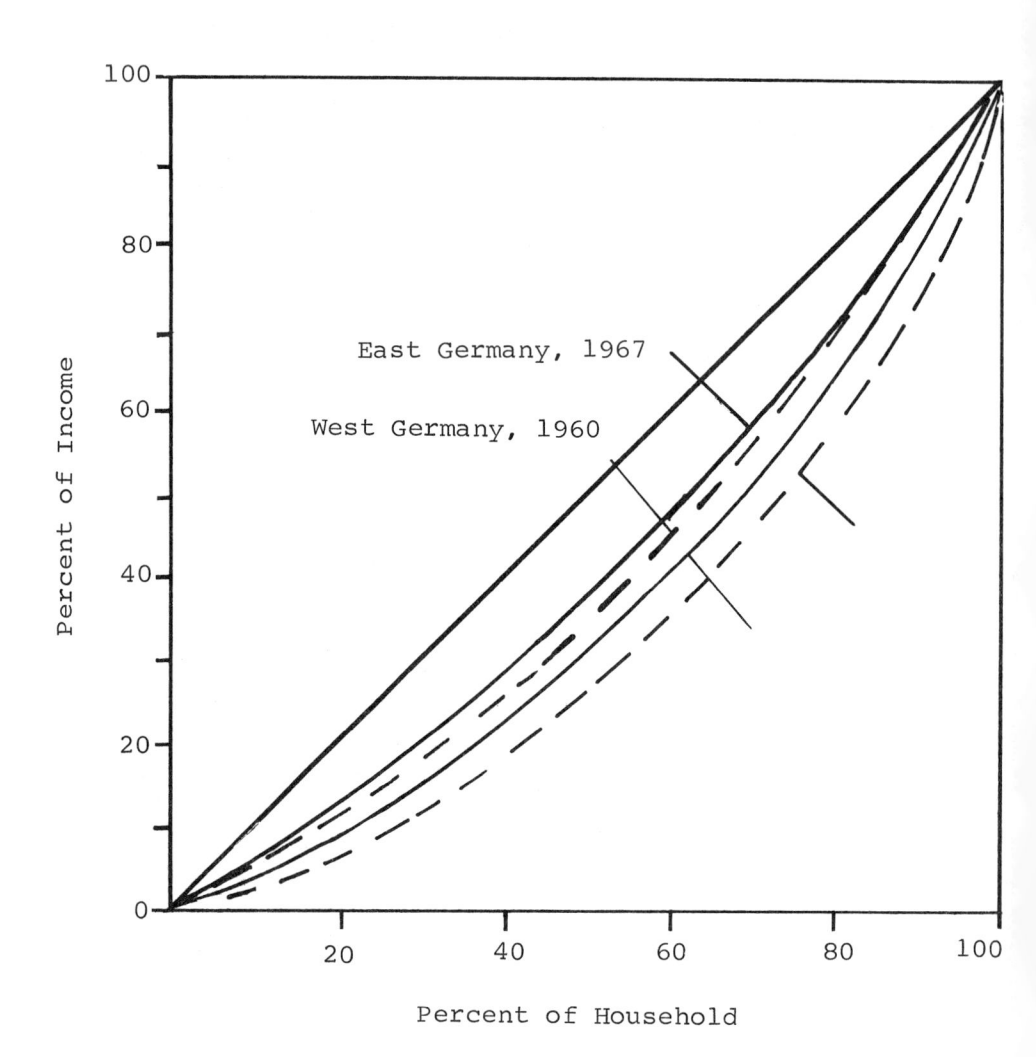

West Germany.[17] Basic foodstuffs show little cost differences between East and West. Some items, such as rye bread, margarine, milk, and potatoes, are less expensive in East Germany, while other items, such as sugar, eggs, and cheese, are more expensive. Butter, however, costs 10 Ostmarks per kilogram on the average for the East German compared to DM 7.72 per kilogram for the West German. Moreover, the East German takes 2 hours and 38 minutes to earn the kilogram of butter compared to 1 hour and 27 minutes for the West German. Meat in general costs more to the East German than to the West German. For example, port cutlets cost 8 Ostmarks per kilogram in the GDR, compared to DM 7.79 in the FRG.

Imported commodities, however, show a considerable difference in purchasing power between East and West. In 1969 oranges were priced at DM 1.56 per kilogram in West Germany, compared to 5 Ostmarks in East Germany. More important, in terms of working hours, 17 minutes were required to earn the oranges in West Germany, compared to 1 hour and 19 minutes in East Germany. A much wider disparity existed with respect to the importation of coffee. One kilogram of coffee in 1969 cost the West German DM 15.46, compared to 70 Ostmarks for the East German. In working hours the times were 2 hours and 54 minutes and 18 hours and 25 minutes, respectively. Other imported items, including lemons, cocoa powder, chocolate, tobacco, and cigarettes, also showed a wide disparity in favor of the West in terms of cost and the amount of working time required to purchase them.

Living standards in East and West Germany drew further apart during the last decade. Although the buying power of the East German Ostmark rose relative to the West German Deutsche Mark, it was not enough to offset West German wage increases. The difference in real income of households headed by workers in the GDR to those in the FRG increased from about 32 percent in 1960 to 45 percent as of 1970. A typical East German four-person household spends a much higher proportion of its real monthly income on food than its West German counterpart. This happens because, apart from most basic foods like bread, potatoes, and root vegetables, such staples as cheese, butter, margarine, eggs, meat, fruit, and coffee are usually much more expensive in the GDR than in the FRG. For example, fruits and coffee are four to five times more expensive in the GDR. As prices for clothing, household goods, and practically everything beyond the strictest necessities are also higher in the GDR, lower prices for rents, utilities, and public transportation furnish only a partial offset to the East German consumer. Table 15.7 presents a comparison of prices and purchasing power in East and West Germany as of 1969.

It is necessary to point out with respect to Table 15.7 that the price structure in East Germany, particularly for food and basic

TABLE 15.7

Prices and Purchasing Power of Hourly Wages, East and West Germany, 1969

		West Germany		East Germany	
Commodity	Quantity	Retail Price (DM)	Hours/Minutes to Earn	Retail Price (Ostmarks)	Hours/Minutes to Earn
Foodstuffs and Semi-luxuries					
Rye bread	1 kg.	1.18	0/13	0.52	0/08
Wheat flour	1 kg.	1.04	0/12	1.32	0/21
Noodles	1 kg.	3.16	0/36	2.80	0/44
Sugar (refined)	1 kg.	1.21	0/14	1.64	0/26
Butter	1 kg.	7.72	1/27	10.00	2/38
Margarine (cheapest)	1 kg.	2.98	0/33	2.00	0/31
Eggs (2d grade)	10	2.00	0/23	3.60	0/57
Milk (3% fat content)	1 litre	0.74	0/08	0.68	0/11
Cheese (Gouda type)	1 kg.	6.48	1/13	7.20	1/54
Beef (for stews)	1 kg.	9.74	1/50	9.80	2/35
Pork cutlets	1 kg.	7.79	1/28	8.00	2/06
Game sausage	1 kg.	7.83	1/28	6.80	1/47
Pickled herring (Icelandic)	1 kg.	2.80	0/32	1.76	0/28
Potatoes (late, best quality)	5 kg.	2.42	0/27	0.85	0/13
White cabbage	1 kg.	1.16	0/13	0.40	0/06
Oranges	1 kg.	1.56	0/17	5.00	1/19
Lemons	1 kg.	1.64	0/18	5.00	1/19
Cocoa powder	1 kg.	8.32	1/34	32.00	8/25
Coffee (medium quality)	1 kg.	15.46	2/54	70.00	18/25
Brandy (blended 38%)	0.7 litre	7.75	1/28	14.40	3/47
Chocolate (35% cocoa)	100 gr.	0.59	0/06	3.85	1/01
Tobacco (fine cut)	50 gr.	1.50	0/17	3.00	0/47
Cigarettes (medium priced)	10	1.11	0/12	1.00	0/16

		West Germany		East Germany	
		Retail Price	Hours/ Minutes to Earn	Retail Price	Hours/ Minutes to Earn
Commodity	Quantity	(DM)		(Ostmarks)	
Clothing, Textiles, Shoes					
Man's suit, 50 percent wool		171.00	32/05	188.00	49/28
Man's shirt, non-iron		15.68	2/57	58.50	15/24
Woman's dress, 50 percent wool		68.30	12/49	77.60	20/25
Man's tie, artificial fiber		3.90	0/44	12.50	3/17
Woman's stockings, Perlon, pair		2.51	0/28	6.40	1/41
Bed linen, damask, 1 set		36.80	6/54	42.50	11/11
Man's outdoor shoes, leather soles, pair		35.20	6/36	48.20	12/41
Woman's sports shoes, porous soles, pair		32.80	6/09	38.80	10/12
Durable Consumer Goods					
Man's cycle, 28 inch with lighting set	1	179.00	33/35	242.00	63/41
Small typewriter	1	205.00	38/28	430.00	113/09
Man's wrist watch stainless steel, 17 jewels, shockproof and waterproof	1	80.90	15/11	156.50	41/11
Vacuum cleaner, upright model, with tools	1	159.00	29/50	195.00	51/19
Electric cooker, 3 rings, oven, with automatic control	1	296.00	55/32	642.00	168/57

(Continued)

TABLE 15.7 (Continued)

		West Germany		East Germany	
Commodity	Quantity	Retail Price (DM)	Hours/ Minutes to Earn	Retail Price (Ostmarks)	Hours/ Minutes to earn

Durable Consumer Goods, continued

Refrigerator, 140-liter, compressor, with deep-freeze compartment | 1 | 300.00 | 56/17 | 1,350.00 | 355/16
Washing machine, drum system, 4 kg. dry washing | 1 | 680.00 | 127/35 | 1,200.00 | 315/47
Television, table set, 59 cm. tube | 1 | 563.00 | 105/38 | 2,110.00 | 555/16
Motorcar, passenger 40-45 h.p. | 1 | 4,625.00 | 876/44 | 17,750.00 | 4,671/03

Tariffs, Services, Household Necessities

Railway weekly ticket, 2d class, 15 km. | | 9.00 | 1/41 | 2.50 | 0/39
Electricity, domestic tariff | 10 kWh | 0.80 | 0/09 | 0.80 | 0/13
Gas, domestic tariff | 10 cubic meters | 1.80 | 0/20 | 1.60 | 0/25
Radio and Television, charge per set | per month | 7.00 | 1/19 | 7.00 | 1/50
Man's haircut, half long | per cut | 3.29 | 0/37 | 0.90 | 0/14
Lady's cold permanent wave | per treatment | 19.78 | 3/43 | 9.60 | 2/32

		West Germany		East Germany	
		Retail Price (DM)	Hours/Minutes to Earn	Retail Price (Ostmarks)	Hours/Minutes to Earn
Commodity	Quantity				

Tariffs, Services, Household Necessities, continued

Man's shoe repairs, (leather soles)	per pair	8.50	1/36	5.77	1/31
Brown coal briquettes	50 kg.	6.03	1/08	3.69	0/58
Dry cleaning and pressing, man's suit		7.84	1/28	3.70	0/58
Washing powder	150 gr.	0.80	0/09	1.25	0/20
Toilet soap, perfumed, 80 percent fat content	100 gr.	1.36	0/14	0/70	0/11

Note: Data for the Federal Republic are based on an official gross hourly wage of DM 5.33 for industrial workers, including those employed in underground and surface mining engineering. Data for East Germany are based on average gross hourly wage in 1969 of 3.80 Ostmarks for fully employed production workers in publicly owned industry and building. Price reductions for consumer goods in East Germany at September 1, 1969, are taken into account.

Source: Deutschland Archiv, Vergleich des deutschen Lebensstandards (May, 1970).

services, is maintained at a low level to favor low-income consumers. The use of subsidies to maintain low prices for certain foodstuffs, transportation, and services is common. The prices charged by the state to consumers bear little relation to the different production costs or the procurement prices paid to farms. The retail prices are naturally more uniform, and their main purposes are to preserve equilibrium in the market and, at the same time, a reasonable stability in the cost of living. Many consumer goods are priced below costs, but, on the other hand, prices for such luxury items as coffee and fruit are maintained at high levels. Thus, consumption patterns are controlled by the East German state. When consumption of basic foodstuffs is used as a measure of comparison, the average East German family is as well off as its West German counterpart; however, when income is devoted to the consumption of luxury goods, the contrast in the cost of living in East and West Germany is accentuated.

A comparison can also be made of the expenditures for various types of goods and services for a family of four persons. Table 15.8 presents a division of expenditures for consumer goods and services expressed in percentages for similar families in the FRG and GDR. The East German family spends a larger percentage of its income for goods, clothing, and other consumer durable and nondurable goods; the West German family spends a much larger percentage of its income on services. The difference in expenditures on housing is particularly pronounced, with the West German family spending almost four times as much in terms of a percentage of total expenditures as the East German family. It is necessary to point out, however, that rent is subsidized in the GDR. Over time the state has been unwilling for political reasons to raise rent. Expenditures on utilities also consume a greater percentage of family income in the FRG than in the GDR. In transportation and recreation the amount spent is also less on a percentage basis for the East German family. Entering into the comparison is the intangible effect of subsidies. Many services are subsidized, particularly in East Germany. Who ultimately pays the cost of subsidies? The answer more than likely is the consumer.

Per capita consumption patterns vary in East and West Germany, however. The average East German eats more starchy food and has a less varied diet. In 1969 per capita consumption of potatoes was 150 kilograms in East Germany, compared to 112 kilograms in West Germany. Per capita consumption of bread amounted to 92 kilograms in East Germany, compared to 64 kilograms in West Germany. Per capita consumption of meat, milk, and fruit is greater in West Germany; per capita consumption of vegetables is slightly higher in East Germany. In the consumption of other food types, which are generally considered as sumptuary items, West German per capita consumption is greater than East German consumption. A West German drinks more beer

TABLE 15.8

Structure of Expenditures in Four-Person
Household, East and West Germany, 1968
(percent)

Consumer Durable and Nondurable Goods	West	East
Food	37.6	47.7
Basic foodstuffs	31.8	36.7
Luxuries	5.8	11.0
Industrial goods	31.9	37.0
Shoes and other footwear	2.1	2.5
Clothing	9.6	13.8
Furniture	3.8	4.0
Electrical equipment (radios and TVs)	1.5	3.3
Other goods	14.9	13.4
Services	30.5	15.3
Rent	15.2	3.9
Utilities	4.9	1.9
Transportation	3.5	2.3
Culture and recreation	3.8	2.9
Other services	3.1	4.3

Source: Bundesministerium für Innerdeutsche Beziehungen, Bericht der Bundesregierung und Materialien zur Lage der Nation 1971 (Bonn), p. 141.

than his East German counterpart—178 liters to 92 liters. Per capita cigarette consumption is twice as high in West Germany as in East Germany. The per capita consumption of coffee in West Germany was 4.2 kilograms in 1969, compared to 2.2 kilograms for East Germany.

A major difference exists between East and West Germany with respect to the quantity and quality of consumer durable goods. Automobiles can be used as one example. They are more expensive and are in far less quantities in East Germany. In West Germany an Opel Kadett in 1969 cost DM 5,838; an East German Wartburg of comparable make cost 17,750 Ostmarks.* In terms of quality

---

*In 1969 only 12 East German families in 100 owned a car, compared with 50 percent of the families in the Federal Republic.

comparisons the West German car was superior. There is also a waiting period for the East German car. For other expensive consumer durables the West Germans also enjoy advantages in terms of both quantity and quality. A washing machine of comparable make cost DM 680 in West Germany and 1,200 Ostmarks in East Germany. Moreover, in terms of time needed to pay for the washing machine, the East German worker had to work three times as long as his West German counterpart. A refrigerator of comparable make cost DM 300 in the FRG and 1,350 Ostmarks in the GDR. These differences also carry over into consumer nondurables, with the quality of shoes and clothing being inferior in the GDR and the cost higher.

Despite the higher cost of consumer durable goods household ownership of certain goods shows little difference between the two countries. In 1969, for example, 91.5 percent of all households in the GDR owned radios, compared to 82.7 percent in the FRG; 66.3 percent of GDR households owned television sets, compared to 72.7 percent in the FRG.[18] This ownership in the GDR, however, is almost exclusively limited to black-and-white sets, for a color TV costs between 2,950 and 3,500 Ostmarks. In the possession of refrigerators and washing machines greater variations in ownership exist between the two countries. In 1969 48.3 percent of all East German households owned refrigerators, compared to 83.6 percent of all West German households; 47.7 percent owned washing machines, compared to 60.9 percent for West German households.[19]

Differences also exist in East and West Germany in the important area of housing. After the war acute housing shortages existed in both countries. In East Germany the construction of new housing was neglected until fairly recently in favor of resource allocation to a program of planned industrialization. In West Germany housing construction has received priority in terms of resource allocation. Rents for housing are lower in East Germany, but the quality of housing is better in West Germany. Retirement of old housing has been higher in West Germany, running at a rate of about 0.3 percent of total housing stock per year as against 0.15 to 0.25 percent for West Germany. Housing is also much more likely to have been constructed after World War II in West Germany. As of 1962 34 percent of housing in West Germany was built after the war, compared to 10.5 percent for East

---

The West German Volkswagen 1200 model cost DM 4,625 (868 hours of work). Its nearest equivalent in East Germany, the Wartburg 991 c.c., cost 17,750 Ostmarks (4,671 hours of work). A cheaper East German car, the Trabant, cost 10,000 Ostmarks but the waiting period as of 1969 was five to six years.

Germany. In 1969 alone 499,900 housing units were constructed in West Germany, compared to 70,300 housing units in East Germany.[20]

In 1968 living density in the GDR was 2.8 persons per apartment, compared to 3.1 persons in the FRG.[21] Living area per person, however, amounted to 23 square meters in the FRG, compared to 19 square meters per person in the GDR. Of apartments existing in 1968, half had been constructed in the FRG since the end of World War II, compared to 20 percent in the GDR. In apartments built since 1945 91 percent had indoor toilets in the FRG, compared to 70 percent in the GDR, and 79 percent had baths in the FRG, compared to 66 percent in the GDR. In 1961 and 1962 37 percent of the apartments in the FRG had central heating, compared to 20 percent of the apartments in the GDR. During the period 1962-66 75 percent of the apartments constructed in the FRG had central heating, compared to 46 percent for the GDR. In 1967 64 percent of all East German housing units were without central heating, a bath, and an inside toilet, compared to 20 percent for West Germany. Only 3 percent of all housing units in the GDR had a toilet, bath, electricity, central heating, and other conveniences, compared to 20 percent in the FRG.

Although the West German family may get more housing in terms of size and quality than the East German family, the rent is also more and constitutes a much larger proportion of total expenditures. In 1968 the rent payments of an average household in the GDR was only one-third that of a comparable household in the FRG. The difference, however, is less when the size of the housing unit is taken into consideration. The average living space per household in the GDR was 53 square meters, compared to an average of 71 square meters per household in the FRG. The rent burden per square meter in the GDR increases to 40 percent of the burden in the FRG.

TAXES AND TRANSFER PAYMENTS AND THEIR IMPACT ON INCOME DISTRIBUTION

To some extent a comparison of income distribution before the impact of taxes and transfer payments are taken into consideration is almost superfluous. Obviously, both taxes and transfer payments can alter the distribution of income significantly. Transfer payments can redistribute income in favor of one group as opposed to another. Subsidies can be used to support the living standards of consumers. But the question arises as to how these transfers and subsidies are financed. Often it turns out that transfers and subsidies are financed by the very groups that are supposed to benefit by them. On an a priori basis this appears to be particularly true where countries derive the bulk of their revenues to finance transfers and other expenditures through indirect taxes.

The extensive and one-sided use of indirect taxes is a basic characteristic of the fiscal systems of East Germany and other socialist countries—a characteristic that is surprising in view of the regressivity of indirect taxes. Indirect taxes, however, have certain advantages for the planned economies. First, they are cheaper to administer and more difficult for the population to evade. They are usually collected at the enterprise level. Second, they have less of an impact on worker incentives than income taxes. Indirect taxes give the impression that net wages are higher than they would be if income taxes were used. This money illusion makes workers much less aware of the impact of indirect taxes on changes in income than they would be aware of were they direct taxes.

Comparison of Taxes and Tax Burdens

In both East and West Germany the tax system is based on a legal framework that was established before World War II. Although postwar reforms modified the basic tax laws, the rubric of the tax system remains fairly intact. In West Germany the historical development of federal-state relations has meant a division of the taxing power, which has been maintained to the present. On the expenditure side there has also been an historical dichotomy of responsibilities on the part of the federal and state governments, which currently continues to exist. In East Germany, although there is a centralization of tax authority, county and local governments continue to possess some authority over taxes and expenditures. Certain taxes, such as the turnover tax (Umsatzsteur) represent a carry-over from the pre-World War II period.

The most important taxes in West Germany are the value-added and income taxes. The value-added tax is an indirect tax levied by the federal government and is the most important source of tax revenue in the FRG. Income taxes are levied by the states and are shared with the federal government. In addition, there are a myriad of other taxes that are under the jurisdiction of one level of government or another. In East Germany the two most important revenue sources are deductions from enterprise profits and the turnover tax. When profits are made by an enterprise, they are utilized in two ways—one part is remitted to the state budget and the other part is retained by the enterprise. That part returned to the budget can be viewed as a transfer of revenue rather than a direct tax. In addition to the two major state revenue sources the GDR also uses income taxation. One major difference between the FRG and GDR is that local governmental units in the GDR possess far less autonomy with respect to tax and expenditure policies.

Comparisons of tax burdens in East and West Germany have to be somewhat subjective. It can be said with respect to the East German tax system that there is heavy reliance on indirect taxation. Although deductions from profits are a revenue transfer, they are a part of total profits over and above costs of production and are incorporated in the final selling price. In this respect deductions from profits can be considered to have the same effect as sales taxes, since each can be shifted forward to consumers. In its basic features, the turnover tax resembles an excise tax. It is levied primarily on consumer goods, although some producer goods are also subject. So, in the final analysis much of the cost of supporting education, social welfare, national defense, investment, and other components of the economic system is borne by the East German consumer because deductions from profits and the turnover tax are included in the retail price of consumer goods.

In West Germany there is more of a balance between direct and indirect taxes. In 1968, for example, direct taxes, including social security contributions, accounted for 59.1 percent of total tax revenues, compared to 40.9 percent for indirect taxes.[22] The value-added tax and excise taxes constitute the basic consumption taxes. Excise taxes are levied on numerous products, which are either produced in West Germany or imported from abroad. The manufacturer, producer, or importer of taxable products is liable for payment of the excise tax but is expected to shift the tax to the buyer by including it in the price of the product. The value-added tax is also included in the price of a product and can be considered as a general tax on consumption. As in the case of other cost items, the question of whether an enterprise can shift the tax fully or in part to its customers depends on such economic factors as prices and competition.

The system of direct taxes, which includes income taxation and social security contributions, performs different functions in East and West Germany. In West Germany direct taxes are a primary means for the redistribution of income as well as being a very important source of government revenue. In East Germany the state itself regulates the distribution of income by setting wages and salaries. Direct taxes can be regarded as more of a control device rather than as a device for redistributing income. This control extends over individuals and enterprises.

Income tax rates on individuals in the GDR follow a three-tiered approach.[23] First, there is the income tax (levied on white and blue collar workers and on most other workers) whose progression ends at 20 percent. For professionals, i.e., authors, musicians, and actors, the tax progression ends at 30 percent, but for small businessmen and others whose incomes are earned from private enterprise, the rate of progression of the income tax extends to 95 percent. In the Federal Republic the rate of the income tax extends progressively from a minimum of 19 percent to a maximum of 53 percent on all income earners. It can be said that, in comparing the personal income tax systems of the GDR and FRG, tax rates are higher for the lower income groups in the GDR and lower for the higher income groups, while the opposite holds true. For example, the tax rate in East Germany on monthly incomes of between 400 to 500 Ostmarks, assuming a family with one child, is 20 percent compared to no tax in West Germany. On incomes of 800 to 900 Ostmarks, the rates are 22.5 percent and 19 percent, respectively.[24] On monthly incomes of 3,000 to 4,000 Ostmarks, however, the East German rate is 20 percent, compared to the West German rate of 33.4 percent.

It is to be emphasized that in East Germany the income tax rate is applied to normal wages and salaries. Certain income tied to performance is not subject to the personal income tax. For example, bonuses awarded for performance above a standard work norm are not subject to taxation.[25] The same holds true for awards, prizes, and other forms of special compensation. The end result is that the average East German worker pays less in income taxation than his West German counterpart.

Social security contributions are lower in the GDR than in the FRG. In East Germany the entire social security system is financed by employer and employee contributions of 10 percent of payrolls and earnings up to 600 Ostmarks a month per employee. These rates, as of 1970, have not been changed for a period of 20 years. Self-employed persons and members of collective farms pay different rates. The end result of social security financing is that expenses have outrun contributions. In 1969, for example, the share of state funds necessary to finance the difference between contributions and expenses was estimated to be about 50 percent. In West Germany social security contributions are based on the type of benefit received and have been increased several times during the 1960s.

It is possible to gain some idea of the burden of direct taxes in the FRG and GDR by comparing average family incomes, income taxes, and social security contributions, as in Table 15.9. Three time periods are used—1960, 1964, and 1967. Average family income as well as income taxes and social security contributions have risen more rapidly in West Germany.

Transfer Payments

It is also important to determine the amount of social welfare benefits the East and West German people receive for their

INCOME DISTRIBUTION AND LIVING STANDARDS 417

TABLE 15.9

Comparison of Average Family Income,
Income Taxes, and Social Security Contributions,
East and West Germany, 1960, 1964, and 1967

	1960		1964		1967	
	West	East	West	East	West	East
Item	(DM)	(Ostmarks)	(DM)	(Ostmarks)	(DM)	(Ostmarks)
Gross income	1,019	843	1,260	932	1,473	1,001
Income taxes	83	52	128	62	144	70
Social security contributions	57	46	71	50	84	53
Net income	879	745	1,081	820	1,245	878

Source: Deutscher Bundestag, Materialien zum Bericht zur Lage der Nation 1971, Drucksache VI/1690 (Bonn-Bad Godesberg: Dr. Hans Heger Verlag, 1971), p. 96.

contributions to social security. Regarding old-age pensions the East German pensioner receives on the average about one-third the amount of his West German counterpart. For example, the average old-age pension in 1968 in East Germany was 178 Ostmarks a month compared to DM 528 for the West German pensioner.[26] Moreover, the West German average has shifted over time to compensate for increases in the cost of living. In 1965 The east and West German averages were 164 Ostmarks and DM 474, respectively. It can be said that in East Germany the tax-transfer system is not designed to favor the older people.

In March 1971 some changes with respect to financing old-age pensions were made in the East German social security system.[27] Anyone earning above 600 Ostmarks a month, which is the cutoff point for the tax, could take out additional insurance for an amount up to 1,200 Ostmarks a month. Both the employee and employer would pay a tax of 10 percent on this extra amount of 600 Ostmarks. There are two points that can be made. First, the additional insurance is optional with the worker. Second, 55 percent of the work force earned less than the original 600 Ostmarks monthly maximum, so they would be ineligible for the additional benefits. In 1971 the minimum and maximum old-age pensions based on obligatory social security contributions were set at 160 Ostmarks and 366 Ostmarks.[28] The maximum is based on an average payment of contributions based on 600 Ostmarks during the last 20 calendar years.

A comparison can also be made of family allowances.[29] The family allowance, which involves a cash payment based on the number of children in a family, is considered a direct supplement to regular income from work. The West German family allowance system excludes the first child from the cash payment; the East German system provides a cash supplement of 20 Ostmarks for the first child. In West Germany a monthly allowance of DM 25 is paid for the second child, compared to an allowance of 20 Ostmarks in East Germany. The West German allowance for the third and fourth child is DM 60 a month and DM 70 for the fifth and subsequent children. The East German allowance is 50 Ostmarks a month for the third child, 60 Ostmarks for the fourth, and 70 Ostmarks for the fifth and subsequent children. As a device for redistributing income, the East German family allowance system can be considered the superior of the two systems, mainly for the reason that the first child in a family is not excluded from benefits. The family allowance as a supplemental source of income is more important in the GDR than in the FRG, mainly for the reason that the first child brings an allowance. Families in West Germany with a gross income of DM 13,200 or more are excluded from the allowance for the second child.

Sickness insurance benefits can also be compared for the two countries.[30] In West Germany cash benefits, including a contribution from the employer, equal to 100 percent of the base wage or salary are paid to a worker for the first six weeks of illness. From the seventh to the seventy-eighth week of confinement, an amount equal to 75 percent of the base wage or salary is payable, plus a supplementary benefit of 4 percent of the base for a worker's first dependent and 3 percent of the base for subsequent dependents. Maternity benefits equal to 100 percent of the base wage are payable for six weeks before birth and eight weeks after birth. In addition there is a maternity grant of DM 100 per birth. Nonworking wives are also eligible for maternity grants.

In East Germany sickness benefits equal to 50 percent of average weekly income for the calendar year are paid for the first six weeks of confinement. This base continues for 39 weeks. After the six-week period is over, supplemental benefits are also payable. Workers with two children receive 65 percent of average earnings; workers with three children receive 75 percent; workers with four children receive 80 percent; and workers with five or more children receive 90 percent. Maternity benefits are also available. Working mothers receive 100 percent of average weekly earning for six weeks before birth and eight weeks after birth. In addition there are maternity grants of 500 Ostmarks for the first child, 600 Ostmarks for the second, 700 Ostmarks for the third, 850 Ostmarks for the fourth, 850 Ostmarks for the fourth, and 1,000 Ostmarks for the fifth and subsequent children.

INCOME DISTRIBUTION AND LIVING STANDARDS

Medical benefits are somewhat similar in both countries. In West Germany persons who are covered by sickness insurance are entitled to compensation for the cost of hospital care and drugs and the fees of doctors and dentists in an amount usually equal to the full cost. There are some exceptions. For example, patients may be required to pay a maximum of DM 2.5 for medicine. In East Germany persons covered by insurance are also entitled to compensation for the cost of hospital care and the professional services of doctors and dentists. Normally there is no charge for the cost of drugs, except in special situations.

On balance it appears that there is little difference in the standard of benefits provided for sickness and maternity in each country. Compensation for loss of employment is higher in the FRG and the duration of the benefit is longer. On the other hand, the provision of special maternity grants tends to make birth a more lucrative phenomenon in the GDR. In both situations some observations are in order. In the event that an illness extends beyond the cut-off point of 39 weeks, the East German worker continues to draw special benefits from disability insurance. The birth grants, although generous in comparison with West German benefits, apparently have little, if any, effect on the East German birth rate, which is one of the lowest for industrial nations.

Compensation for injury from industrial accidents can be compared for the FRG and GDR.[31] In West Germany insured workers are covered for medical expenses resulting from job accidents. There are also disability pensions, which amount to two-thirds of a worker's weekly wage or salary provided that the disability is permanent. The minimum pension is DM 100 a month and the maximum is DM 2,100 a month. In addition a supplement of 10 percent of the pension is paid for each dependent under 18. Temporary disability benefits are similar to sickness benefits in that 65 percent of weekly wages or salaries is payable for a period usually of six weeks.

In East Germany payments for work accidents follow a similar pattern. Benefits are paid for both temporary and permanent disability. Temporary benefits are similar to sickness benefits. All medical expenses incurred as a result of work injury are covered. Permanent disability pensions equal to two-thirds of average monthly earnings are payable, plus supplements of 10 percent for each dependent child. For partial disability, pensions are pro rated on the basis of loss of work. Insistence on the prevention of industrial accidents has resulted in a low rate of injuries relative to the size of the labor force and the number of hours worked.

Unemployment compensation represents a fourth area of comparison. To some extent the comparison is irrelevant for the reason that a socialist economy is not supposed to have unemployment.

Although this is not actually the case, as witnessed by the rate of unemployment in Yugoslavia,* it is probably true in East Germany, with its static population and high level of economic activity. Unemployment has also been very low in West Germany. Benefits in West Germany ranging from 40 percent to 90 percent of earnings are payable for a period of 13 to 52 weeks. Cash supplements of DM 9 a week for the spouse and first child and DM 3 a week for the second and subsequent children are also payable. In East Germany unemployment benefits equal to 10 percent of earnings are payable after a seven-day waiting period for up to 26 weeks. Supplements are also available for dependents.

Other forms of social welfare benefits are available in both East and West Germany. In West Germany rent subsidies are paid to low-income families; in East Germany rent is controlled by the state and set at artificially low levels. In West Germany there is social assistance that covers such things as aid to the blind, medical care for the insane, educational grants to youths, and financial support for tubercular persons. Also included under social welfare benefits is financial assistance related to war and its aftereffects. Veteran's pensions and assistance to expellees and refugees are examples of this type of assistance. In East Germany there are welfare and charitable expenditures available to persons who are not eligible for benefits under the social security program. There are also a variety of benefits available to war victims and their dependents. Financial assistance is also provided to persons who wish to pursue an education.

It is possible to get a general idea of how much each country spends on social security and other social welfare measures. In West Germany social security expenditures in 1970 amounted to DM 85.6 billion and total expenditures for all forms of social assistance amounted to DM 123.6 billion.[32] A total of DM 85.5 billion, or one-third of all government expenditures, went for cash transfer payments of all types.[33] When transfer payments are expressed as a percentage of national income or personal income, the ratio for West Germany is one of the highest for the capitalist countries. In 1970 transfer payments amounted to 18.6 percent of personal income, compared to 12.7 percent for Sweden and 5.2 percent for the United States.[34] In 1965 social welfare expenditures amounted to 18.1 percent of the West German GNP, compared to 5.2 percent for Japan, 10.2 percent for the Soviet Union, 6.2 percent for the United States, 4.3 percent for Poland,

---

*The unemployment rate in Yugoslavia was as high as 8 percent during the 1960s and would have been higher were it not for the fact that part of the labor force has been exported to other countries.

INCOME DISTRIBUTION AND LIVING STANDARDS

9.5 percent for Hungary, 17.3 percent for France, and 16.9 percent for Czechoslovakia.[35] It is necessary to point out, however, that social welfare expenditures include war pensions and reparations—a category that contributes more to the social welfare total in West Germany than in most of the other countries.

In comparing East and West German social welfare expenditures education expenditures are not included. The concept of social welfare includes social security and insurance, aid to mothers, veteran's pensions, and other such transfer payments. In East Germany social security expenditures and other welfare measures are included under the category of social and cultural measures in the state budget. In 1970 nearly 40 percent of all expenditures in the state budget fell into this category. Social security expenditures amounted to 14.7 billion Ostmarks, the largest single expenditure in the state budget of total expenditures of 75.7 billion Ostmarks.[36] Receipts and disbursements are carried in the social insurance budget, which is a part of the state budget. Subsidies of various types are carried under the general category of miscellaneous expenditures and in 1970 amounted to 8.6 billion Ostmarks.[37] It can be said that about one-third of state budget expenditures in 1970 took the form of transfer payments and subsidies under the general category of social welfare.

Comparisons can be made of the extent of coverage and the financing of social security in East and West Germany. In the GDR it is estimated that 97 to 99 percent of the population is covered by one form of social security or another. Vitually all persons are covered by health insurance.[38] In the FRG 86.8 percent of the population was covered by health insurance in 1968.[39] It was estimated that 96 percent of all employees were covered by accident insurance. In the FRG persons not insured under social security usually have private insurance that covers them against social risks. In the GDR the social security system is centralized in control. Moreover, it is one component of the national economic plan. Benefits are integrated into the plan, as it involves household incomes. In the FRG the social security system is fragmented in administration and control, with separate insurance systems existing for farmers, government workers, miners, and other groups. In comparison to the strong integration of the social security system of the GDR into the state financial system, social security in the FRG is separate for the most part from the federal budget.

In both countries contributions of social security come from three sources—levies on employees, levies on employers, and subsidies from the national government. Outlays have tended to outrun contributions in each country, with the difference made up by increased contributions and government subsidies in the FRG. In the GDR, however, contributions have been held constant over time, with increasing support coming from the state budget. In West Germany contributions and their base differ for white and blue collar workers, miners, farmers, and other groups, with periodic adjustments occurring in each to compensate for cost-of-living increases. In the GDR contributions of 10 percent on payrolls and earnings up to 600 Ostmarks a month have remained unchanged for a period of 20 years. Self-employed persons pay a rate of 14 percent of the base of 600 Ostmarks, and members of the LPGs contribute 9 percent. In both East and West Germany family allowances are financed out of general state revenues.

In Table 15.10 a comparison of East and West German social welfare expenditures is presented for 1969. Included are pensions for blue and white collar workers, government employees, and farmers; medical care, maternity grants, and sickness benefits; family allowances of all types; unemployment compensation; payments and reparations associated with the war; social help; and other forms of social assistance. The table presents only direct cash outlays or transfer payments to individuals. Payments for various types of costs and payments in kind are not included, so the amounts are less than the actual totals spent on social welfare in each country. One interesting point is the tremendous difference in the two countries with respect to expenditures on war-related measures. There is also a marked difference in the amounts spent on pensions—the ratio of 7 to 1 in favor of the FRG reflecting the higher benefits paid to pensioners.

Transfer payments and subsidies unquestionably have an impact on the redistribution of income in both East and West Germany. Some general observations are in order. Family allowances benefit the child-rearing population in each country at the expense of families with no children and single persons. The allowance results in lateral income redistribution between families in the same income group. Since allowances are not taxed in either country, a family with four children would have a higher disposable income than a family with no children. In both countries family allowances are financed out of general budget revenues. Each country, but particularly the GDR, relies heavily on indirect taxation. The use of this revenue source negates the possibility that there is any vertical distribution from high- to low-income groups as far as the family allowance is concerned.

There appears in the aggregate little relationship between what the East German citizen pays directly in taxes to support the social security system and what he receives from the same system in the form of cash benefits that augment his personal income. The tax picture needs to be examined. The relationship between the contributions of individuals to the support of the social security system and the cash benefits that individuals receive from the system affords an interesting picture. Individuals in the aggregate pay far less in the

INCOME DISTRIBUTION AND LIVING STANDARDS

TABLE 15.10

Comparison of Cash Outlays for Social Welfare
Measures, East and West Germany, 1969

Types of Transfers	West Germany (million DM)	East Germany (million Ostmarks)
Pensions	58,527	8,661
Sickness and accident benefits and maternity grants	5,860	1,435
Assistance to families, including children's allowances	4,345	1,424
War-related measures	7,360	140
Unemployment compensation	1,480	—
Social help	1,200	81
Other measures	1,171	165
Total	79,943	11,906

Sources: Bundesminister für Arbeit und Sozialordnung, Sozialbericht 1970 (Bonn, 1970), p. 170; Staatliche Zentralverwaltung für Statistik, Statistisches Jahrbuch der Deutschen Demokratischen Republik, 1970 (East Berlin: Staatsverlag der DDR, 1970), p. 330.

way of taxes to support the system that what they draw from the system in the way of benefits. In 1969 individuals paid only one-fourth of total contributions to social security, while the state contributed one-half of total financial support. Given the indirect nature of the East German tax system, there is a diffusion of the real costs of the social system throughout the economy. Under such conditions there may be a considerable unplanned transfer of real income between social groups. Money income is reduced indirectly through the use of consumption taxes.

In Table 15.11 a breakdown of average household income in the GDR is presented for 1968. The purpose of the table is to present all sources of income to the average household in the GDR. This income comes from wages or salaries, transfer payments, interest, and other sources. From average gross income direct taxes are deducted to arrive at average disposable income. Excluded from the table are indirect taxes, which are properly viewed as a levy on consumption. Total consumption, which is excluded from the table, averaged 1,070 Ostmarks, of which 738 Ostmarks were spent on consumer durable and nondurable goods and 332 Ostmarks were spent on services.

TABLE 15.11

Breakdown of Average Monthly
Household Income, East Germany, 1968
(Ostmarks)

Income	Amount
Average gross work income*	989
Income from other sources	329
Social funds	136
Sick pay	20
Pensions	32
Childrens allowances	29
Education and culture	108
Housing	16
Interest, insurance, and lotteries	23
Other income	46
Gross income from all sources	1,318
Less	
Personal income tax	67
Social security contribution	71
Net income from all sources	1,180
Less	
Nonconsumable income	110
Other direct taxes	56
Savings	54
Disposable income	1,070

*Includes premiums and bonuses.

Source: Staatliche Zentralverwaltung für Statistik, Statistisches Jahrbuch der Deutschen Demokratischen Republik, 1970, (East Berlin: Staatsverlag der DDR, 1970), p. 363.

In 1969 West German wage and salary earners received DM 261.1 billion in the form of contributions. Total cash social security benefits paid out in 1969 amounted to DM 51.6 billion and medical services and other benefits amounted to an additional DM 23.1 billion.[40] Although a certain amount of the direct cash benefits of DM 51.6 billion went to other groups, it can be assumed that the bulk of the benefits went to wage and salary earners. In general, it can be said that wage and salary earners paid out 10.5 percent of their gross income in the form of social security contributions and received back transfer payments that amounted to around 18 percent of personal income. The contribution of employers to social security is ignored in the comparison. Realism requires that this tax be treated as a part of an employer's total labor costs, which are sooner or later reflected in the final value of goods and services sold.

The above comparisons do not take into consideration the fact that those persons who pay the social security tax are usually not the ones who derive the greatest benefits. Old-age pensions are a case in point. That there is often no quid pro quo relationship between taxes paid out and benefits received can be illustrated through the comparison of three different types of households for 1969. The first household consisted of two persons who received the bulk of their income

TABLE 15.12

Comparison of Income, Transfers, and Taxes for
Selected Households, West Germany, 1970
(DM)

	Household Type		
Income Source	1	2	3
Gross income from work	0.69	1,204.33	2,201.27
Income from savings and property	23.42	53.40	70.83
Other income (transfers)	485.36	82.27	115.60
State transfers	467.96	25.65	9.16
Gross income	509.47	1,340.00	2,387.70
Less			
Income and property taxes	0.07	95.97	273.17
Contributions to social security	6.22	132.49	67.26
Net income	503.18	1,111.54	2,047.27
Plus			
Other income, including bonuses	7.00	30.71	89.81
Disposable income	510.18	1,142.25	2,137.08

Source: Statistisches Bundesamt, Statistisches Jahrbuch für die Bundesrepublik Deutschland, 1971 (Wiesbaden: W. Kohlhammer Verlag, 1971), p. 477.

in the form of old-age pensions and other transfers; the second household consisted of four persons headed by a wage earner who made an average income; and the third household also consisted of four persons, headed, however, by a white collar worker or government employee with an above-average income. The comparisons are presented in Table 15.12. Average monthly incomes are used.

SUMMARY

The purpose of this chapter has been to compare income distribution in East and West Germany before and after taxes and transfer payments are taken into consideration. Income in West Germany comes from the ownership of labor or property or both; income in East Germany comes primarily from the ownership of labor. This income is augmented by transfer payments, but altered by taxes. On a gross income basis, regardless of the criterion used, income differentials widened between East and West Germany during the decade of the 1960s. When net income is used as a standard of comparison, the differentials between the two countries were narrowed somewhat. This is attributable to the higher rate of direct taxation in the FRG. There is less income inequality in East Germany than in West Germany, however. In fitting a Lorenz curve to income data in each country, there is a more even concentration of income by income groups in the FRG.

The impact of taxes and transfer payments on income redistribution is somewhat difficult to measure because of the reliance in both countries on indirect taxation. It can be said, however, that these taxes are regressive with respect to income and counterbalance the use of direct taxes. When stated income tax rates are compared, the rate for the FRG is generally lower than in the GDR. It is only in the higher income brackets that the progressivity of the West German income tax creates a higher tax burden. In both countries, however, the actual tax burden is different from the rates shown in the tax tables. Taxable income is reduced by allowances for deductions and exemptions of various types. Tax deductions for children are higher in the FRG than in the GDR. Certain types of income, such as special bonuses, are exempted from taxation in the GDR.

The East German standard of living, although higher than other socialist countries, is lower than West German living standards. Although living standards in the two Germanies were comparable before World War II, East Germany has lagged behind West Germany since the end of the war. In East Germany shortages of consumer goods developed in the 1960s but were alleviated to some extent when the reforms of the New Economic System provided added incentives to make production more responsive to demand. Although consumption of foodstuffs does not necessarily show a marked advantage in favor of the East or West German consumer, West Germans enjoy a far greater advantage in the quality and quantity of consumer durable goods, particularly automobiles and refrigerators. Automobiles are less available and more expensive in East Germany than in West Germany. In other areas that also comprise living standards East Germany lags behind West Germany. The quality of housing in East Germany is generally inferior to the quality of housing in West Germany. Until recent years investment in housing in the GDR has taken a back seat to industrial priorities.

NOTES

CHAPTER 1
1. Albert Speer, Inside the Third Reich (New York: Macmillan, 1970), pp. 560-61.
2. Ibid., p. 560.
3. Bruno Gleitze, Ostdeutsche Wirtschaft (West Berlin: Duncker & Humblot, 1956), pp. 191-93.
4. Walter Eucken, Grundzatze der Wirtschaftspolitik (Tubingen: Paul Siebeck, 1952).
5. Ludwig Erhard, The Economics of Success (Princeton, N.J.: Van Nostrand Co., 1963), pp. 7-10.
6. Ibid.
7. Henry Wallich, Mainsprings of the German Revival (New Haven, Conn.: Yale University Press, 1955).
8. Erhard, The Economics of Success, p. 97.
9. Ibid.
10. Statistisches Bundesamt, Statistisches Jahrbuch für die Bundesrepublik Deutschland, 1954 (Wiesbaden: W. Kohlhammer Verlag), p. 27.
11. Erhard, The Economics of Success, p. 99.
12. Statistisches Jahrbuch, 1962, p. 27.
13. Ibid., p. 27.
14. Gleitze, Ostdeutsche Wirtschaft, p. 170.
15. Ibid.
16. For a description of Soviet dismantling policies, see Heinz Kohler, Economic Integration into the Soviet Bloc (New York: Frederick A. Praeger, 1965), pp. 14-15.
17. Edwin M. Snell and Marilyn Harper, "Postwar Economic Growth in East Germany: A Comparison with West Germany," in U.S., Congress, Joint Economic Committee, Subcommittee on Foreign Economic Policy, Economic Development in Countries of Eastern Europe, 91st Cong., 2d sess., 1970, p. 565.
18. Staatliche Zentralverwaltung für Statistik, Statistisches Jahrbuch der Deutsche Demokratischen Republik, 1968, (East Berlin: Staatsverlag der DDR, 1968), p. 37.
19. Ibid.
20. Ibid., pp. 26, 257.
21. Ibid.
22. Ibid.
23. Ibid.

24. Snell and Harper, "Postwar Economic Growth," p. 561.
25. Ibid.

CHAPTER 2

1. Statistisches Bundesamt, Statistisches Jahrbuch für die Bundesrepublik Deutschland, 1970 (Wiesbaden: W. Kohlhammer Verlag, 1970), p. 25.
2. Presse und Informationsamt der Bundesregierung, Tatsachen uber Deutschland (Wiesbaden: Steiner Verlag, 1970), p. 85.
3. Deutsche Bundesbank, Monatsberichte der Deutschen Bundesbank (Frankfurt am Main, October 1971), p. 17.
4. Bundesministerium der Finanzen, Finanzbericht 1971 (Bonn, September 1970), p. 333.
5. Ibid., p. 335.
6. Ibid., p. 336.
7. Ibid., p. 337.
8. Ibid., p. 339.
9. Ibid., p. 340.
10. Presse und Informationsamt, Deutschland Heute (Wiesbaden: Steiner Verlag, 1966), p. 434.
11. Deutscher Bundestag, Jahresgutachten 1969 des Sachverständigenrates zur Begutachtung der gesamtwirtschaftlichen Entwicklung, Drucksache VI/100, (Bonn, December 1969), p. 188; (Bonn, 1970), p. 58.
12. Ibid., p. 127.
13. Ibid., p. 129.
14. Deutscher Bundestag, Materialien zum Bericht zur Lage der Nation 1971, Drucksache VI/1690 (Bonn-Bad Godesberg: Dr. Hans Heger Verlag, 1971), p. 272.
15. Statistisches Jahrbuch, pp. 264, 275.
16. Ibid., p. 264.
17. Statistisches Bundesamt, Agrarstatistische Arbeitsunterlagen, 1968/1969 (Wiesbaden, 1969), p. 42.
18. Ibid., p. 85.
19. Ibid., p. 32.
20. Statistisches Jahrbuch, p. 500.
21. Ibid., p. 275.
22. Ibid., pp. 281-82.
23. Ibid.
24. Ibid., p. 278.
25. Staatliche Zentralverwaltung für Statistik, Statistisches Jahrbuch der Deutschen Demokratischen Republik (East Berlin: Staatsverlag der DDR, 1970), pp. 296-97.

26. Bundesministerium der Finanzen, Drei Jahre Neuer Finanzpolitik (Bonn, 1969), pp. 10-11.
27. Bundesministerium der Finanzen, Die Finanzplanung des Bundes, 1968-1972 (Bonn, 1969), p. 18.
28. Ibid., p. 19.
29. Bundesministerium der Finanzen, Die Finanzplanung des Bundes, 1969-1973 (Bonn, 1970), p. 19.
30. Ibid., p. 20.

CHAPTER 3

1. For a review of occupation policies toward the coal, steel, and chemical industries, see U.S., Congress, Subcommittee on War Mobilization, A Program for German Economic and Industrial Disarmament, 1945.
2. Statistisches Bundesamt, Statistisches Jahrbuch für die Bundesrepublik Deutschland, 1970 (Wiesbaden: W. Kohlhammer Verlag, 1970), p. 191.
3. Ibid. The accompanying data is also on page 191.
4. Ibid., p. 494.
5. Fortune Magazine, September 15, 1968, pp. 132-38.
6. Fortune Magazine, August 1, 1971, pp. 150-54.
7. Statistisches Jahrbuch, p. 192.
8. Deutsche Bundesbank, Monatsberichte der Deutschen Bundesbank (Frankfurt am Main, October 1971), p. 17.
9. Bundesministerium der Finanzen, Bundeshaushaltsplan für das Haushaltsjahr 1971 (Bonn: Bundesdruckerei, March 1971), p. 31.
10. National Bureau of Economic Research, Foreign Tax Policies and Economic Growth (New York: Columbia University Press, 1966), pp. 114-22.
11. August Leth, Steuerlehre (Bad Homburg vor der Höhe: Dr. Max Gehlem Verlag, 1970), p. 72.
12. Ibid.
13. Based on personal estimates taken from Bundesministerium der Finanzen, Beteiligungen des Bundes 1969 (Bonn-Bad Godesberg: Dr. Hans Heger Verlag, 1971).
14. Estimates taken from ibid.
15. Bundeshaushaltsplan, p. 897.
16. Ibid., p. 898.
17. Ibid., p. 899.
18. "Die 100 grössten Industrie—Unternehmen der Bundesrepublik," Süddeutsche Zeitung (Munich, August 11, 1971).
19. Beteiligungen des Bundes, p. 56.
20. Ibid., p. 241. Other holdings are found on pp. 240-77.

NOTES

21. "Die 100 grössten Industrie," Süddeutsche Zeitung.
22. Beteiligungen des Bundes, p. 66.
23. Ibid., p. 68.
24. "Die 100 grössten Industrie," Süddeutsche Zeitung.
25. Beteiligungen des Bundes, p. 265.
26. Ibid., p. 97.
27. Ibid., p. 10.
28. Ibid., p. 104.
29. "Die 100 grössten Industrie," Süddeutsche Zeitung.
30. Beteiligungen des Bundes, p. 246.
31. "Die 100 grössten Industrie," Süddeutsche Zeitung.
32. Beteiligungen des Bundes, pp. 248, 250.
33. Leth, Steuerlchre, p. 72.
34. Ibid., p. 73.
35. Fortune Magazine, September 15, 1968, p. 132.
36. Fortune Magazine, August 1, 1971, p. 154.
37. Bundeshaushaltsplan, p. 898.
38. Ibid.
39. Ibid., p. 37.
40. Statistisches Bundesamt, Agrarstatistisches Arbeitsunterlagen, 1968/1969 (Wiesbaden, 1969), pp. 17-19.
41. Ibid., p. 18.
42. Ibid., p. 22.
43. Ibid., p. 21.
44. Bundeshaushaltsplan, pp. 35-37.

CHAPTER 4

1. Franz Klein, Die Grosse Finanzreform in der Bundesrepublik Deutschland (Bonn: Österreichische Zeitschrift für öffentliches Recht, 1970), pp. 127-48.
2. Bundesministerium der Finanzen, Finanzpolitische Mitteilungen (Bonn, February 1971).
3. Hans Kuntze, Einführung in die Mehrwertsteuer (Cologne: Informationsdienst der Sparkassen und Girozentralen, June 1967).
4. H. Mesenberg, Mehrwertsteuer und Aussenhandel (Bonn: Institut Finanzen und Steuern, October 1964), pp. 17-21.
5. August Leth, Steuerlehre (Bad Homburg vor der Höhe: Verlag Dr. Max Gehlen, 1970), pp. 108-10.
6. Ibid., pp. 111-12.
7. Bundesministerium der Finanzen, Untersuchungen zum Einkommensteuerrecht (Bonn: Wilhelm Dolfuss Verlag, 1970), pp. 353-55.
8. Ibid., p. 354.
9. Leth, Steuerlehre, pp. 70-72.
10. Ibid., p. 73.

11. Ibid., p. 96.

12. Statistisches Bundesamt, Statistisches Jahrbuch für die Bundesrepublik Deutschland, 1970 (Wiesbaden: W. Kohlhammer Verlag, 1970), p. 382.

13. Finanzpolitische Mitteilungen, p. 4.

14. Bundesministerium der Finanzen, Bundeshaushaltsplan für das Haushaltsjahr 1971 (Bonn: Bundesdruckerei, March 1971), p. 3209.

15. Leth, Steuerlehre, pp. 129-31.

16. Klein, Grosse Finanzreform, p. 137.

17. Hans Pagenholf, Wirtschaft und Politik, Heft 93 (Bonn: Institut Finanzen und Steuern, 1969), pp. 21-27.

18. Bundeshaushaltsplan, p. 31.

19. Ibid., p. 33. All listed social welfare expenditures are on pp. 33 and 34.

20. Ibid., p. 32.

21. Ibid., p. 36.

22. Ibid., p. 34.

23. Ibid., p. 31.

24. Ibid., p. 35.

25. Statistisches Jahrbuch, p. 373.

26. Ibid.

27. Leth, Steuerlehre, pp. 87, 88.

28. Finanzpolitische Mitteilungen, p. 5.

29. Ibid.

30. Bundeshaushaltsplan, p. 299.

31. Gesetz zur Förderung der Stabilität und des Wachstums der Wirtschaft, June 8, 1967.

32. Ibid., secs. 5-18.

33. Deutscher Bundestag, Drucksache V/3630 (Bonn, December 9, 1968), p. 12.

34. Ibid., p. 10.

35. Ibid., pp. 20, 21.

36. Ibid., p. 26.

37. Ibid., p. 39.

38. Institut Finanzen und Steuern, Der Bundeshaushalt (Bonn, 1970), p. 30.

39. Gesetz zur Förderung, sec. 8.

40. Martin Schnitzer, "The Swedish Investment Reserve: An Experience with 'Push Button' Fiscal Policy," The British Tax Review, March-April, 1968, pp. 98-108.

41. Deutscher Bundestag, Jahresgutachten 1969, Drucksache VI/100 (Bonn, December 1969), p. 19.

42. Bundesministerium der Finanzen, Finanzbericht, 1971 (Bonn, September 1970), p. 21.

43. Ibid., p. 10.

NOTES

CHAPTER 5
1. Bundesminister für Arbeit und Sozialordnung, Sozialbericht 1970 (Bonn, 1970), p. 172.
2. Ibid.
3. Ibid.
4. Bundesministerium der Finanzen, Bundeshaushaltplan für das Haushaltsjahr 1971 (Bonn: Bundesdruckerei, March 1971), p. 33.
5. Sozialbericht 1970, p. 172.
6. Bundeshaushaltplan, p. 32.
7. Sozialbericht 1970, p. 172.
8. Deutsche Bundesbank, Monatsberichte der Deutschen Bundesbank (Frankfurt am Main, October 1971), Appendix, p. 63.
9. Bundeshaushaltplan, p. 34.
10. French data is obtainable from Ministerie de L'Economie et des Finances, Le budget social de la nation pour 1970.
11. Bundeshaushaltplan, p. 35.
12. Sozialbericht 1970, p. 173.
13. Ibid., p. 172.
14. Social security and social welfare expenditures are found in Sozialbericht 1970, p. 172. GNP and national income data are found in Deutsche Bundesbank, Geschäftsbericht der Deutschen Bundesbank, 1970 (Frankfurt am Main, October, 1971) p. 7.
15. Bundesminister für Arbeit und Sozialordnung, Die Einkommens und Vermögensverteilung in der Bundesrepublik Deutschland (Bonn, 1971), p. 13.
16. Bundesminister für Arbeit und Sozialordnung, Übersicht über die Soziale Sicherung (Bonn, 1970), p. 26.
17. Ibid., p. 27.
18. Organization for Economic Cooperation and Development, National Accounts Statistics, 1953-69 (Paris, 1971), p. 176.
19. Ibid. Subsequent data is also found on the same page.
20. Statistisches Bundesamt, Statistisches Jahrbuch für die Bundesrepublik Deutschland, 1970 (Wiesbaden: W. Kohlhammer Verlag, 1970), p. 496.
21. Bundesministerium der Finanzen, Finanzbericht 1971 (Bonn, 1971), p. 16.
22. Ibid.
23. Tax data is in Finanzbericht 1971, p. 16. National income data is in Deutsche Bundesbank, Geschäftsbericht der Deutschen Bundesbank 1970 (Frankfurt am Main, April 1971) p. 7.
24. Swedish Taxpayers Association, The Role of Taxation in the Redistribution of Income in Sweden (Stockholm, 1962), p. 6.
25. August Leth, Steuerlehre (Bad Homburg vor der Hohe: Verlag Dr. Max Gehlen, 1970), pp. 23-69. All subsequent data on income taxation may be found on these pages.

26. Einkommens und Vermögensverteilung, p. 13.
27. Finanzbericht 1971, p. 49; and Einkommens und Vermögensverteilung, p. 13.
28. Josef Korner, "Struktur und personelle Verteilung von Lohn und Lohnsteuer in der Bundesrepublik Deutschland seit 1950," Studien zur Finanzpolitik, Heft 14 (Munich: Ifo-Institut für Wirtschaftsforschung, 1970), pp. 22-24.
29. Deutscher Bundestag, Materialien zum Bericht zur Lage der Nation, Drucksache VI/1690 (Bonn, 1971), p. 335, Table 95.
30. Deutscher Bundestag, Jahresgutachten 1969 des Sachverständigenrates zur Begutachtung der gesamtwirtschaftlichen Entwicklung, Drucksache VI/100 (Bonn, December 1969), p. 29.

CHAPTER 6

1. For a lucid description of the West German banking system, see the booklet published by the Bundesverband Deutscher Banken of Cologne, "The Banking System of the Federal Republic of Germany."
2. These functions are outlined in the annual report of the Deutsche Bundesbank, the latest of which is Geschäftsbericht der Deutschen Bundesbank fur das Jahr 1970 (Frankfurt am Main, April 1971).
3. Deutsche Bundesbank, Monatsberichte der Deutschen Bundesbank (Frankfurt am Main, October 1971), p. 28, Appendix, Table 10.
4. German International, July 1970, pp. 28-30.
5. Fortune Magazine, August 1971, p. 157.
6. German International, March 1971, pp. 26-28.
7. Fortune Magazine, August 1971, p. 157.
8. Ibid.
9. German International, August 1971, p. 12.
10. Geschäftsbericht der Deutschen Bundesbank, p. 135.
11. Monatsberichte der Deutschen Bundesbank, Tables 10 and 21(b).
12. Ibid., Table 21(b).
13. Ibid., Table 10.
14. Bundesministerium der Finanzen, Beteiligungen des Bundes 1969 (Bonn-Bad Godesberg: Dr. Hans Heger Verlag, 1971), p. 199.
15. Ibid. All data on the Reconstruction Loan Corporation is found on pp. 198-199.
16. Ibid., p. 195. Other data on the specialized banks can be found on pp. 194-206.
17. Monatsberichte der Deutschen Bundesbank, Table 10.
18. See the report by Deutscher Bundestag, Bericht über das Ergebnis einer Untersuchung der Konzentration in der Wirtschaft, Drucksache IV/2320 (Bonn, 1964). This report provides information concerning the extent of bank control over industry.

19. Most of the data concerning the links between the banks and West German industry can be found in the Commerzbank publication, Wer Gehort zu wem, 8th ed., 1969. The book reflects the strong trend toward industrial mergers in the West German economy. The edition gives tabulated information on the existing shareholdings of about 6,500 companies. Bank holdings are also included.
20. Monatsberichte der Deutschen Bundesbank, p. 13.
21. Deutsche Bundesbank, Geschäftsbericht der Deutschen Bundesbank für das Jahr 1967 (Frankfurt am Main), pp. 7-11.
22. Deutsche Bundesbank, Geschäftsbericht der Deutschen Bundesbank für das Jahr 1968 (Frankfurt am Main), pp. 5-7.
23. Deutsche Bundesbank, Geschäftsbericht der Deutschen Bundesbank für das Jahr 1969 (Frankfurt am Main), pp. 3-4. All 1969 data is taken from this annual report.
24. Deutsche Bundesbank, Geschäftsbericht der Deutschen Bundesbank für das Jahr 1970 (Frankfurt am Main), pp. 3-14. All 1970 data is taken from this annual report.
25. Deutsche Bundesbank, Monatsberichte der Deutschen Bundesbank (Frankfurt am Main, April 1971), p. 3.
26. Deutsche Bundesbank, Monatsberichte der Deutschen Bundesbank (Frankfurt am Main, November 1971), Appendix, p. 44.
27. Süddeutsche Zeitung (Munich), December 13, 1971, p. 14.
28. Monatsberichte der Deutschen Bundesbank (October 1971), p. 7.
29. Ibid., p. 5.
30. Süddeutsche Zeitung (Munich), December 13, 1971, p. 14.
31. Monatsberichte der Deutschen Bundesbank (October, 1971), p. 85.

CHAPTER 7
1. Helga Grebing, The History of the Trade Union Movement (London: Oswald Wolff, 1969), pp. 33-41.
2. Ibid., p. 54.
3. Ibid., p. 126.
4. Franz Lepinski, "The German Trade Union Movement," International Labor Review, 1964, p. 12.
5. Data provided by the Deutsche Gewerkschaftsbund.
6. Hans Limmer, Die Deutsche Gewerkschaftsbewegung (Munich: Gunter Olzog Verlag, 1970), p. 76.
7. Ibid., p. 78.
8. Limmer, Gewerkschaftsbewegung, p. 78.
9. Ibid., p. 113.
10. "Die Bundesvereinigung der Deutschen Arbeitgeberverbande, eine kleine Einfuhrung," published by the Confederation of German Employers' Associations.

11. Ibid.
12. Data provided by the Deutsche Gewerkschaftsbund.
13. Deutsche Bundesbank, Monatsberichte der Deutschen Bundesbank (Frankfurt am Main, October 1971), Appendix, p. 63.
14. Deutsches Institut für Wirtschaftsforschung, Wochenbericht (West Berlin, October 8, 1970), p. 296.
15. Wochenbericht (West Berlin, January 7, 1972), p. 2.
16. Deutscher Gewerkschaftsbund, Codetermination Rights of the Workers in Germany (Düsseldorf, June 1967), p. 30.
17. For a discussion of the role of trade unions during the Third Reich period, see Grebing, Movement, pp. 138-50; and Limmer, Gewerkschaftsbewegung, pp. 62-72.
18. For a discussion of worker participation in the management of Yugoslav enterprises, see Jiri Kolaja, Workers' Councils: The Yugoslav Experience (New York: Frederick A. Praeger, 1967.)
19. Codetermination Rights of the Workers in Germany, p. 30.
20. Ibid., p. 37.
21. Ibid., p. 38.
22. Ibid.
23. Federal Ministry of Labor and the Social Structure, Collective Bargaining and the Law Governing Collective Agreements (Essen: Druckhaus Sachsenstrasse, 1963), p. 10.
24. Federal Ministry of Labor and the Social Structure, The Labor Courts (Essen: Druckhaus Sachsenstrasse, 1963), pp. 7-12.
25. Ibid., p. 12.
26. Federal Ministry of Labor and the Social Structure, Conciliation and Arbitration and the Law as Applied to Labor Disputes (Essen: Druckhaus Sachsenstrasse, 1963), pp. 6-15.

CHAPTER 8

1. Staatliche Zentralverwaltung für Statistik, Statistisches Jahrbuch der Deutschen Demokratischen Republik (East Berlin: Staatsverlag der DDR, 1970), p. 3.
2. Ibid.
3. Ibid., p. 4.
4. Ibid., p. 3.
5. Ibid.
6. Verfassung der Deutschen Demokratischen Republik (East Berlin: Staatsverlag der DDR, 1968), pp. 39-61.
7. Ibid., pp. 39-44.
8. Ibid., pp. 45-49.
9. Ibid., pp. 49-50.
10. Eckart Fortsch, Die SED (Stuttgart: W. Kohlhammer Verlag, 1969), pp. 8-11.
11. Neues Deutschland, June 17, 1971, p. 1.

12. Fortsch, SED, pp. 105-23.
13. Staatliche Zentralverwaltung für Statistik, Statistisches Taschenbuch 1971 (East Berlin: Staatsverlag der DDR, 1971), p. 26.
14. Ibid.
15. Ibid., p. 28.
16. Ibid., p. 84.
17. Statistisches Jahrbuch, p. 294.
18. Ibid., pp. 296-97.
19. Deutsches Institut für Wirtschaftsforschung, DDR-Wirtschaft—eine Bestandsaufnahme (Frankfurt am Main: Fischer Bucherei Verlag, June 1971), pp. 217-19.
20. Statistisches Jahrbuch, p. 308.
21. Ibid., p. 309.
22. Bundesministerium für Gesamtdeutsche Fragen, Fünfter Tätigkeitsbericht, 1965-1969 (Bonn, 1969).
23. Ökonomisches Forschungsinstituts der Staatlichen Plankommission, Planung der Volkswirtschaft in der DDR (East Berlin: Verlag die Wirtschaftschaft, 1970), pp. 148-53.
24. Ibid., p. 149.
25. Ibid., p. 152.
26. Ibid., p. 153.
27. Gesetzblatt der Deutschen Demokratischen Republik, Teil II, No. 1 (East Berlin: Staatsverlag der DDR, January 6, 1971), pp. 13-15.
28. Zur Gestaltung des Ökonomisches Systems, pp. 153-58.
29. Neues Deutschland, May 5, 1971, p. 1.
30. Ibid., pp. 11-19. All industry data is on these pages.
31. Ibid., pp. 19-22. All agricultural data is on these pages.
32. Ibid., pp. 23-25. All housing and construction data is on these pages.
33. Ibid., p. 26.
34. Ibid., pp. 26-31. Education and housing data is on these pages.
35. Ibid., pp. 31-39. District planning data is on these pages.

CHAPTER 9

1. Deutsches Institut für Wirtschaftsforschung, Vierteljahrshefte zur Wirtschaftsforschung (West Berlin, 1969), pp. 227-29.
2. Ibid., p. 232.
3. Bundesministerium für Gesamtdeutsche Fragen, Fünfter Tätigkeitsbericht, 1965-1969 (Bonn, 1969), p. 99.
4. Ibid.
5. Ibid.
6. Ibid., p. 100.
7. Ibid.

8. Vierteljahrshefte zur Wirtschaftsforschung, p. 231.
9. Deutsches Institut für Wirtschaftsforschung, Wochenbericht (West Berlin, January 1971), pp. 25-31.
10. Deutsches Institut für Wirtschaftsforschung, Wochenbericht (West Berlin, January 28, 1969), pp. 25-31.
11. Staatliche Zentralverwaltung für Statistik, Statistisches Jahrbuch der Deutschen Demokratischen Republik, 1970 (East Berlin: Staatsverlag der DDR), p. 108.
12. Ibid., p. 39.
13. Ibid.
14. Staatliche Zentralverwaltung für Statistik, Statistisches Taschenbuch 1971 (East Berlin: Staatsverlag der DDR), p. 27.
15. Statistisches Jahrbuch der DDR, p. 108.
16. Ibid.
17. Ibid., p. 109.
18. Ibid., p. 58.
19. Manfred Melzer, "Der Entscheidungsspielraum des VVB in der DDR Betriebliche Kompetenzen durch Reformen erweitert?" Deutschland Archiv (Cologne: Wissenschaft und Politik Verlag, October 1970), pp. 27-29.
20. Gesetzblatt der Deutschen Demokratischen Republik, II, 20 (East Berlin: Staatsverlag der DDR, March 20, 1969), p. 137.
21. Gesetzblatt der Deutschen Demokratischen Republik, II, 41, "Anordnung über die Ermittlung der Kosten und Preise für Warme und Elektroenergie" (East Berlin: Staatsverlag der DDR, April 29, 1968), p. 241.
22. Ibid., p. 243.
23. Statistisches Jahrbuch der DDR, p. 110.
24. Ibid., p. 111.
25. Ibid., p. 109.
26. Ibid.
27. Ibid., p. 108.
28. Ibid., p. 54.
29. Statistisches Taschenbuch, p. 27.
30. H. Jorg Thieme, Die Sozialistische Agrarverfassung, (Stuttgart: Gustav Fischer Verlag, 1969), p. 54.
31. Statistisches Taschenbuch, p. 80.
32. Ibid.
33. Ibid., p. 81.
34. Ibid.
35. Ibid.
36. Gunther Mittag, Politische Ökonomie des Sozialismus (East Berlin: Dietz Verlag, 1969), pp. 874-77.
37. Ibid., p. 871.

38. Hans Schlenk, Der Binnenhandel der DDR (Cologne: Wissenschaft und Politik Verlag, 1970), pp. 45-49.
39. Ibid., pp. 51-53.
40. Ibid., p. 59.
41. Die Wirtschaft, January 16, 1969, p. 14.
42. Deutsches Institut für Wirtschaft, DDR-Wirtschaft (Frankfurt am Main: Fischer Handbucher, 1971), p. 214.
43. Ibid., p. 216.

CHAPTER 10

1. Staatliche Zentralverwaltung für Statistik, Statistisches Jahrbuch der Deutschen Demokratischen Republik, 1970 (East Berlin: Staatsverlag der DDR, 1970), pp. 17, 43.
2. Frederic L. Pryor, Public Expenditures in Communist and Capitalist Nations (Homewood, Ill.: Richard D. Irwin, 1968), p. 341.
3. Neues Deutschland (East Berlin), December 16, 1970, p. 3.
4. Deutsches Institut für Wirtschaftsforschung, Wochenbericht (East Berlin, January 28, 1971), p. 31.
5. Gesetzblatt der Deutschen Demokratischen Republik, II, 15 (East Berlin: Staatsverlag der DDR, December 19, 1969), pp. 264-68.
6. Ibid., p. 265.
7. Neues Deutschland, p. 2.
8. Ibid.
9. Wochenbericht, p. 32.
10. Ibid.
11. Ibid., pp. 32, 33.
12. Ibid., pp. 33, 34.
13. Ibid., p. 34.
14. Ibid.
15. Peter Mitzscherling, Soziale Sicherung in der DDR (East Berlin: Deutsches Institut für Wirtschaftsforschung, 1968), pp. 1-10.
16. Ibid., p. 9.
17. Wochenbericht, p. 33.
18. Ibid.
19. Ibid.
20. Ibid.
21. Neues Deutschland (East Berlin), January 22, 1968, p. 10.
22. Gesetzblatt der Deutschen Demokratischen Republik, II, 4 (East Berlin: Staatsverlag der DDR), January 14, 1971, pp. 33-34.
23. Gesetzblatt der Deutschen Demokratischen Republik, Umsatzsteuergesetz, Sonderdruck Nr. 673 (East Berlin: Staatsverlag der DDR, November 2, 1970), p. 2.

24. Ibid., p. 3.
25. Ibid., p. 4.
26. Gesetzblatt der Deutschen Demokratischen Republik, Einkommensteuergesetz, Sonderdruck Nr. 670 (East Berlin, Staatsverlag der DDR, November 2, 1970), p. 4.
27. Ibid., p. 5.
28. Ibid., p. 12.
29. Gesetzblatt der Deutschen Demokratischen Republik, I, 23 (East Berlin: Staatsverlag der DDR, December 15, 1970, p. 368.
30. Gesetzblatt der Deutschen Demokratischen Republik, Einkommensteuergesetz, p. 12.
31. Deutscher Bundestag Materialien zum Bericht zur Lage der Nation 1971, Drucksache VI/1690 (Bonn-Bad Godesberg: Dr. Hans Heger Verlag, 1971), p. 338.
32. Ibid., p. 122-31.
33. Gesetzblatt der Deutschen Demokratischen Republik, Korperschaftsteuergesetz, Sonderdruck Nr. 671 (East Berlin, Staatsverlag der DDR, November 2, 1970), pp. 4-6.
34. Gesetzblatt der Deutschen Demokratischen Republik, Gewerbesteuergesetz, Sonderdruck Nr. 672 (East Berlin, Staatsverlag der DDR, November 2, 1970), p. 3.
35. Gesetzblatt der Deutschen Demokratischen Republik, Vermogensteuergesetz, Sonderdruck Nr. 675 (East Berlin, Staatsverlag der DDR, November 2, 1970), p. 2.
36. Ibid., p. 3.
37. Gesetzblatt der Deutschen Demokratischen Republik, Grundsteuergesetz, Sonderdruck Nr. 676 (East Berlin, Staatsverlag der DDR, November 2, 1970), p. 2.
38. Gesetzblatt der Deutschen Demokratischen Republik, Grunderwerbsteuergesetz, Sonderdruck Nr. 677 (East Berlin, November 2, 1970), p. 3.

CHAPTER 11
1. Gesetzbuch der Arbeit der Deutschen Demokratischen Republik (East Berlin: Staatsverlag der DDR, 1969), pp. 37-39.
2. Verfassung der Deutschen Demokratischen Republik (Berlin: Staatsverlag der DDR, 1968), p. 17.
3. Löhne, Preise, Gewerkschaftsrechte, Vergleiche Zwischen Beiden Deutschen Staaten (Bonn: Neue Gesellschaft Verlag, 1971), p. 14.
4. Ibid., pp. 14-15.
5. Ibid., p. 15.
6. Deutscher Bundestag, Materialien zum Bericht zur Lage der Nation 1971, Drucksache VI/1690 (Bonn-Bad Godesberg: Dr. Hans Heger Verlag, 1971), p. 89.

NOTES

7. Löhne, Preise, Gewerkschaftsrechte, p. 16.
8. Ibid., p. 27.
9. Ibid., p. 28.
10. Ibid., pp. 17-19.
11. H. Jorg Thieme, Die Sozialistische Agrarverfassung (Stuttgart: Gustav Fischer Verlag, 1969), p. 62.
12. Ibid.
13. Ibid., p. 63
14. Ibid., p. 64.
15. Löhne, Preise, Gewerkschaftsrechte, p. 22.
16. Ibid., p. 23.
17. Dorothy Miller, "The Upper Ten Thousand in the GDR," Radio Free Europe (Munich, October 1969), p. 1. (Unpublished paper.)
18. Ibid., p. 2.
19. Ibid.
20. East Germany, Staatliche Zentralverwaltung für Statistik, Statistisches Jahrbuch der DDR 1970 (East Berlin: Staatsverlag der DDR, 1970), p. 58; West Germany, Statistisches Bundesamt, Statistisches Jahrbuch fur die BRD, 1970 (Wiesbaden: W. Kohlhammer Verlag, 1970), p. 16.
21. Staatliche Zentralverwaltung für Statistik, Statistisches Taschenbuch 1971 (East Berlin: Staatsverlag der DDR, 1971), p. 157.
22. Egbert Steinke, "Vergleich des deutschen Lebensstandards, FRG und GDR" (Handelsblatt, Dusseldorf, February 3, 1971), p. 24.
23. Materialien zum Bericht zur Lage der Nation, p. 332.
24. Ibid., p. 141.
25. Bundesministerium für Gesamtdeutsche Fragen, Zahlenspiegel, Ein Vergleich, BRD-GDR (Bonn, 1970), pp. 39-41.
26. Steinke, "Vergleich des deutschen Lebensstandards," p. 24.
27. Staatliche Zentralverwaltung für Statistik, Statistisches Taschenbuch 1971 (East Berlin: Staatsverlag der DDR, 1971), p. 131.
28. Ibid., pp. 131 and 137.

CHAPTER 12

1. Das Finanzsystem der DDR (East Berlin: Die Wirtschaft Verlag), 1962, pp. 7-19.
2. Gesetz über die Staatsbank der Deutschen Demokratischen Republik (East Berlin: Staatsverlag der DRR, December 1967), pp. 1-14.
3. Sibylle May Lang and Maria Elizabeth Rodan, "Veränderungen im Bankensystem der DDR," Sonderdruck aus Vierteljahrshefte zur Wirtschaftsforschung, 1968, Heft 3 (West Berlin: Deutsches Institut für Wirtschaftsforschung), pp. 402-10.

4. Gesetz über die Staatsbank, pp. 2-6.
5. Ibid., p. 6.
6. Gesetzblatt der Deutschen Demokratischen Republik, "Verordnung über die Bildung der Industrie und Handelsbank der Deutschen Demokratischen Republik," II, 2 (East Berlin: Staatsverlag der DRR, January 4, 1968), pp. 9-16.
7. Gesetzblatt der Deutschen Demokratischen Republik, "Verordnung über das Statut der Landwirtschaftsbank der Deutschen Demokratischen Republik," II, 55 (East Berlin: Staatsverlag der DRR, May 28, 1966), pp. 329-34.
8. Gesetzblatt der Deutschen Demokratischen Republik, "Verordnung über Landwirtschaftliche Investitions Kredite," II, 112 (East Berlin: Staatsverlag der DRR, November 6, 1968), pp. 883-85.
9. Satzung-Deutsche Aussenhandelsbank, 1969, pp. 2-4.
10. Statut-Genossenschaftsbank für Handwerk und Gewerbe, 1968, pp. 1-5.
11. Statut der Sparkassen der Deutschen Demokratischen Republik, 1968, pp. 1-6.
12. Gesetzblatt der Deutschen Demokratischen Republik, II, 13 (East Berlin, Staatsverlag der DDR, February 15, 1971), pp. 87-90.
13. Ibid., p. 88.
14. Ibid., p. 89.
15. Ibid.
16. Ibid., p. 90.
17. Gesetzblatt der Deutschen Demokratischen Republik, II, 112 (East Berlin: Staatsverlag der DRR, November 6, 1968), pp. 883-85.
18. Ibid., p. 884.
19. Ibid., p. 885.
20. Ibid.

CHAPTER 13

1. Verfassung der Deutschen Demokratischen Republik (East Berlin: Staatsverlag der DRR, 1968), p. 14.
2. Klaus Adam, "Der Freie Deutsche Gewerkschaftsbund in der sowjetisch besetzten Zone Deutschlands," Gewerkschaftliche Rundschau, January 1963, p. 16.
3. Gesetzbuch der Arbeit der Deutschen Demokratischen Republik, (Berlin: Staatsverlag der Deutschen Demokratischen Republik, 1969), p. 14.
4. Ibid., p. 53.
5. Satzung des Freien Deutschen Gewerkschaftsbundes, 1968, p. 32.

NOTES

6. Gesetzbuch der Arbeit, pp. 10-13.
7. Ibid., p. 23.
8. Satzung des Freien Deutschen Gewerkschaftsbundes, p. 18.
9. Ibid.
10. Ibid., p. 19.
11. Ibid., p. 31.
12. Ibid., p. 21.
13. Ibid., p. 23.
14. Ibid., p. 24.
15. Ibid., pp. 26-27.
16. Gesetzbuch der Arbeit, pp. 24, 25.
17. Ibid., pp. 71-74.
18. Ibid., pp. 37-39.

CHAPTER 14

1. For a prewar and postwar comparison of East and West German industrial development, see the following sources: Osteuropa Institut, Veränderungen in der Branchen und Regionalstruktur der Deutschen Industrie zwischen 1936 und 1962 (West Berlin, 1965); and Bruno Gleitze, Ostdeutsche Wirtschaft (West Berlin: Duncker and Humblot, 1956).
2. Staatliche Zentralverwaltung für Statistik, Statistisches Jahrbuch der Deutschen Demokratischen Republik, 1970 (East Berlin: Staatsverlag der DDR, 1970), pp. 35-38.
3. Staatliche Zentralverwaltung für Statistik, Statistisches Taschenbuch 1971 (East Berlin: Staatsverlag der DDR, 1971), p. 34.
4. Deutscher Bundestag, Materialien zum Bericht zur Lage der Nation 1971, Drucksache VI/1690 (Bonn-Bad Godesberg, January 15, 1971). This report, prepared by Peter Ludz and others at the request of the Brandt Government, provides a thorough and comprehensive comparison of the East and West German economy. The bulk of the data in this chapter is obtained from this source.
5. Deutsches Institut für Wirtschaftsforschung, Wochenbericht, VII, 6 (West Berlin, May 7, 1970), 51-56.
6. Ibid., p. 54.
7. Deutscher Bundestag, Materialband zum Agrarbericht 1971 der Bundesregierung, Drucksache VI/1800 (Bonn-Bad Godesberg, February 1971), p. 10. Subsequent data is found on pp. 10-28.
8. The 1970 data is found in Statistisches Taschenbuch 1971, pp. 78-84.
9. Edward F. Denison, Why Growth Rates Differ (Washington, D.C.: The Brookings Institution, 1967), p. 17.
10. Ibid., p. 308.
11. Statistisches Bundesamt, Statistisches Jahrbuch 1970 (Wiesbaden: W. Kohlhammer Verlag, 1970), p. 490.

12. Ibid., p. 500.
13. Ibid. All 1969 data is also found on the same page.
14. Deutsche Bundesbank, Geschäftsbericht der Deutschen Bundesbank für das Jahr 1970 (Frankfurt am Main, April 1971), p. 51.
15. Wochenbericht, I, 2 (West Berlin, January 7, 1972), pp. 2, 4. All comparative data is on these two pages.
16. Deutsche Bundesbank, Monatsberichte der Deutschen Bundesbank (Frankfurt am Main, January 1972), Appendix, p. 65.
17. Ibid., Appendix, pp. 53-67.
18. Wochenbericht (January 7, 1972), p. 2, and Monatsberichte der Deutschen Bundesbank (December 1971) Appendix, p. 67. All wage data is taken from these sources.
19. Wochenbericht (January 7, 1972), p. 12.
20. Ibid., p. 18.
21. Ibid.
22. Ibid. All income forecasts are found on this page.
23. Statistisches Taschenbuch 1971, p. 11.
24. Ibid., p. 34. Comparative data are found on this page.
25. Wochenbericht, (West Berlin, January 28, 1971), pp. 25-31.
26. Ibid., p. 27. Subsequent 1970 data is found on pp. 27-31.
27. Reported in Neues Deutschland, November 18, 1971, p. 1.
28. Statistisches Taschenbuch 1971, p. 27.
29. Wochenbericht (January 28, 1971), pp. 26-27.
30. Wochenbericht (January 27, 1972), p. 46.
31. Ibid. All subsequent 1971 data is found in this report, titled, "Die Wirtschaft der DDR am Beginn des Jahres 1972."
32. Plan data is found in ibid., pp. 46, 53, 54.
33. State budget figures are found in ibid., pp. 53, 54.

CHAPTER 15

1. U.S., Bureau of the Census, The Soviet Financial System, Structure, Operations, and Statistics, International Population Statistics Reports, Series P-90, No. 23 (Washington, D.C.: Government Printing Office, 1968), p. 134.
2. Jürgen Siebke, "Die Vermögensbildung der privaten Haushalte in der Bundesrepublik Deutschland," Forschungsauftrag des Bundesministeriums für Arbeit und Sozialordnung (Bonn, May 1971), p. 43. (Unpublished paper.)
3. Ibid., p. 61.
4. Friedrich-Ebert-Stiftung, Löhne, Preise, Gewerkschaftsrechte, Vergleiche zwischen beiden Deutschen Staaten (Bonn: Neue Gesellschaft Verlag, 1971), p. 16.
5. Statistisches Bundesamt, Statistisches Jahrbuch für die Bundesrepublik Deutschland 1971 (Wiesbaden: W. Kohlhammer Verlag, 1971), p. 466.

NOTES

6. Ibid., pp. 466-67.
7. Ibid., p. 473.
8. Lohne, Preise, Gewerkschaftsrechte, pp. 17-18.
9. Staatliche Zentralverwaltung für Statistik, Statistisches Jahrbuch der Deutschen Demokratischen Republik, 1970 (East Berlin: Staatsverlag der DDR, 1971), p. 127.
10. Gesetzblatt der DDR, "Verordnung über die Planung, Bildung und Verwendung des Prämienfonds und des Kultur und Sozialfonds für Volkseigene Betriebe im Jahre 1972," II, 5 (East Berlin: Staatsverlag der DDR, 1972) pp. 49-50.
11. Deutscher Bundestag, Materialien zum Bericht zur Lage der Nation, Drucksache VI/1690 (Bonn-Bad Godesberg, 1971), p. 88.
12. The East German average is found in Staatliche Zentralverwaltung für Statistik, Statistisches Taschenbuch 1971 (East Berlin: Staatsverlag der DDR, 1971), p. 131.
13. Source on West Germany is Bundesministerium für Arbeit und Sozialordnung, "Arbeits und Sozialstatistische Mitteilungen," Nos. 1-2, 1970, p. 17; source on East Germany is Statistisches Jahrbuch der DDR, 1970, pp. 22, 73, 124, 144.
14. Materialien zum Bericht zur Lage der Nation, p. 90.
15. Ibid., p. 96.
16. Staatliche Zentralverwaltung für Statistik, Statistisches Taschenbuch 1970 (Berlin: Staatsverlag der Deutschen Demokratischen Republik, 1970), pp. 45, 129.
17. Bundesministerium für Gesamtdeutsche Fragen, "Zahlenspiegel, Ein Vergleich—BRD-GDR," (Bonn, 1970), pp. 39-41.
18. Statistisches Jahrbuch der DDR, 1970, pp. 350-55 and Statistisches Jahrbuch, pp. 467-71.
19. Statistisches Jahrbuch der DDR, 1970, p. 463; and Statistisches Jahrbuch, p. 354.
20. Statistisches Jahrbuch der DDR, 1970, p. 158; and Statistisches Jahrbuch, p. 245.
21. Materialien zum Bericht zur Lage der Nation, p. 161.
22. National Accounts Statistics, 1953-1969 (Paris: Organization for Economic Cooperation and Development, 1971), p. 186. Social security contributions, although listed separately, are included under the category of direct taxes.
23. Gesetzblatt der Deutschen Demokratischen Republik, "Einkommensteuergesetz," Sonderdruck Nr. 670 (East Berlin: Staatsverlag der DDR, 1970), p. 5.
24. Ibid., pp. 7-11; and August Leth, Steuerlehre (Bad Homburg vor der Höhe: Dr. Max Gehlen Verlag), pp. 168-175.
25. "Einkommensteuergesetz," pp. 2-4.
26. "Zahlenspiegel," p. 40.

27. Neues Deutschland, March 12, 1971, p. 1.
28. Ibid.
29. Materialien zum Bericht zur Lage der Nation, p. 136.
30. Ibid., p. 126.
31. Ibid., p. 127.
32. Bundesminister für Arbeit und Sozialordnung, Sozialbericht 1970 (Bonn), p. 281.
33. Deutsche Bundesbank, Monatsberichte der Deutschen Bundesbank (Frankfurt am Main, October 1971), p. 7.
34. West Germany, Statistisches Jahrbuch 1971, p. 510; Sweden, Statistiska Centralbyran, Statistisk Arbol 1971 (Stockholm, 1972), p. 14; United States, Economic Report of the President 1971 (Washington, D.C.: U.S. Government Printing Office, 1972), p. 281.
35. Bundesminister für Arbeit und Sozialordnung, Übersicht über die Soziale Sicherung (Bonn), 1970, p. 32.
36. Deutsches Institut für Wirtschaftsforschung, Wochenbericht (Berlin, January 28, 1971), p. 31.
37. Ibid.
38. Materialien zum Bericht zur Lage der Nation, pp. 124-27.
39. Ibid.
40. Data taken from Bundesminister für Arbeit und Sozialordnung, Sozialbericht 1970, p. 170, and Sozialbericht 1971, pp. 228-32.

ABOUT THE AUTHOR

MARTIN SCHNITZER is Professor of Finance in the College of Business Administration at the Virginia Polytechnic Institute. He serves as a consultant to the Joint Economic Committee and the House Ways and Means Committee of the United States Congress and has served as a member of a Presidential task force on welfare problems.

Professor Schnitzer is a past editor of the *Virginia Social Science Journal* and has published a number of articles and books, including two Praeger Special Series titles; *Regional Unemployment and the Relocation of Workers* and *The Economy of Sweden*.

Dr. Schnitzer earned his Ph.D. in Economics at the University of Florida, has done advanced work in summer institutes at the Harvard Business School and the University of Virginia, and has been the beneficiary of grants for research work abroad.